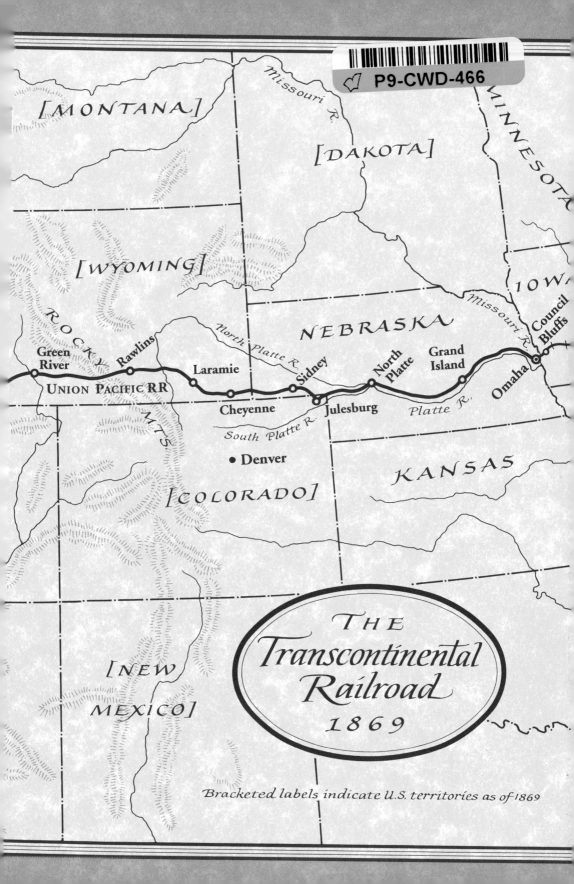

[MONTANA]

Missouri R.

[DAKOTA]

MINNESOTA

[WYOMING]

IOWA

ROCKY

Missouri R.

Council
Bluffs

Green
River

Rawlins

NEBRASKA

North Platte R.

North
Platte

Grand
Island

Omaha

Laramie

Sidney

UNION PACIFIC RR

Cheyenne

Julesburg

Platte R.

MTS

South Platte R.

● Denver

[COLORADO]

KANSAS

[NEW

MEXICO]

THE
Transcontinental
Railroad
1869

Bracketed labels indicate U.S. territories as of 1869

ALSO BY STEPHEN E. AMBROSE

Comrades: Brothers, Fathers, Heroes, Sons, Pals

The Victors: Eisenhower and His Boys: The Men of World War II

Americans at War

Citizen Soldiers: The U.S. Army from the Normandy Beaches to the Bulge to the
    Surrender of Germany, June 7, 1944–May 7, 1945

Undaunted Courage: Meriwether Lewis, Thomas Jefferson, and the Opening of the
    American West

D-Day: June 6, 1944: The Climactic Battle of World War II

Band of Brothers: E Company, 506th Regiment, 101st Airborne from Normandy
    to Hitler's Eagle's Nest

Nixon: Ruin and Recovery, 1973–1990

Eisenhower: Soldier and President

Nixon: The Triumph of a Politician, 1962–1972

Nixon: The Education of a Politician, 1913–1962

Pegasus Bridge: June 6, 1944

Eisenhower: The President

Eisenhower: Soldier, General of the Army, President-Elect, 1890–1952

The Supreme Commander: The War Years of General Dwight D. Eisenhower

Duty, Honor, Country: A History of West Point

Eisenhower and Berlin, 1945

Crazy Horse and Custer: The Parallel Lives of Two American Warriors

Rise to Globalism: American Foreign Policy, 1938–1992

Ike's Spies: Eisenhower and the Espionage Establishment

Halleck: Lincoln's Chief of Staff

Upton and the Army

S TEPHEN

The Men Who Built the

Transcontinental Railroad

1863–1869

S IMON & S CHUSTER   N EW   Y ORK

E. AMBROSE

Nothing Like It in the World

LONDON   TORONTO   SYDNEY   SINGAPORE

SIMON & SCHUSTER
Rockefeller Center
1230 Avenue of the Americas
New York, NY 10020
Copyright © 2000 by Ambrose-Tubbs, Inc.
Maps copyright © 2000 by Anita Karl and Jim Kemp
All rights reserved,
including the right of reproduction
in whole or in part in any form.
SIMON & SCHUSTER and colophon are registered trademarks
of Simon & Schuster, Inc.
Designed by Karolina Harris
Manufactured in the United States of America
1   3   5   7   9   10   8   6   4   2

Library of Congress Cataloging-in-Publication Data
Ambrose, Stephen E.
Nothing like it in the world: the men who built the transcontinental railroad,
1863–1869 / Stephen E. Ambrose.
p. cm.
Includes bibliographical references and index.
1. Railroads—United States—History—19th century. 2. Central Pacific
Railroad Company—History. 3. Union Pacific Railroad Company—History.
4. Railroad construction workers—United States—History—19th century. I. Title.
TF23 .A48 2000
385'.0973—dc21   00-041005
ISBN 0-684-84609-8

Acknowledgments

SOME years ago, when I handed the manuscript of my latest book in to my editor at Simon & Schuster, Alice Mayhew, she said she wanted me to do the building of the first transcontinental railroad for my next book. Even though I had been trained as a nineteenth-century American historian, I hesitated. First of all, I had been taught to regard the railroad builders as the models for Daddy Warbucks. The investors and builders had made obscene profits which they used to dominate state and national politics to a degree unprecedented before or since. John Robinson's book *The Octopus: A History of Construction, Conspiracies, Extortion*, about the way the Big Four ruined California, expressed what I thought and felt. What made the record of the big shots so much worse was that it was the people's money they stole, in the form of government bonds and land. In my view, opposition to the Union Pacific and the Central Pacific (later the Southern Pacific) had led to the Populist Party and then the Progressive Party, political organizations that I regarded as the saviors of America. I wanted nothing to do with those railroad thieves.

I told Alice to give me six months to read the major items in the literature, so I could see if there was a reason for a new or another book on the subject. So I read. In the process I changed my mind about many aspects of building the railroads and the men who got rich from investing in them. And I was delighted by the works in the basic literature. Most of them I quote from, and they can be found in the bibliography.

7

ACKNOWLEDGMENTS

I do need to make a specific mention of Maury Klein, whose magnificent two-volume history of the Union Pacific is a superb work for the general reader and the specialist or the writer. It is an absorbing story, beautifully told. Klein is a model for scholarship, for writing, and for thinking his subject through before making a statement. George Kraus, *High Road to Promontory: Building the Central Pacific Across the High Sierra*, is the basic source on the subject. There are many fine researchers and writers who have published books on the Union Pacific and Central Pacific roads. The two who have my gratitude and respect ahead of all others are Maury Klein and George Kraus.

After the reading, I decided that there was a lot of good literature already in existence on the railroads and that I could use it for stories, incidents, sources, and quotes, but none of the books were done in the way I was looking for. If I really wanted to know at least a part of the answer to Alice's question, How did they build that railroad?—rather than How did they profit from it? or How did they use their power for political goals?— I was going to have to write my own book to find out. So I did.

I have first of all to acknowledge that this book is Alice's idea. She didn't do the writing, to be sure, or try to guide my research or to suggest ideas for me to investigate or incorporate. She didn't hurry me, even though I had a bad fall in the middle of doing this book that put me out of action for a few months. She read chapters as I sent them in, and gave me encouragement, which was a great help, since I write for her. If she likes what comes out of my writing, I'm pleased. If she doesn't, I try again. But above all, she let me figure out the answer to her question.

My research assistants are all part of my family. First my wife, Moira, who always participated, making suggestions, offering ideas, listening and commenting, being there. Then my research assistant and son, Hugh Alexander Ambrose. Hugh is a trained historian, with his Master's degree in American history from the University of Montana. He did the basic research at the Library of Congress for me, and at the Bancroft Library on the University of California campus, and at Huntington Library, at the Archives at the Library of the Church of Latter-Day Saints in Salt Lake City, and on the World Wide Web. He mastered the literature, and he was my first reader on all the chapters. His many suggestions have been absorbed in the text. Without him there would be no book.

My son Barry Ambrose, my daughter-in-law Celeste, my older daughter, Stephenie, my niece Edie Ambrose (a Ph.D. in American history from Tulane), and another daughter-in-law, Anne Ambrose, all participated in the newspaper and magazine research. Edie read early chapters and gave me solid suggestions on everything from word choices to interpretations. I had decided at the beginning that this book was like doing Lewis and Clark, but unlike D-Day or my books on Cold War politics. Different in this way: there was no one around who had been there and could say, I saw this with my own eyes. I couldn't do any interviewing.

Next best thing, I thought, were the newspaper reporters. I knew that many big-city papers sent their own correspondents out west to report on how the railroad was being built. Reporters are always looking for what is new, what is fresh, asking questions, trying to anticipate questions. So Celeste, Barry, Edie, Anne, and Stephenie started reading 130-year-old newspapers on dusty microfilm readers. They found a lot of information and stories that I used throughout the book. They are diligent, imaginative, creative in going through the newspapers, and, like all researchers, they learn a lot in the process. I hasten to add that they get paid for their time and effort, but I must confess that I am defeated in any attempt to thank them enough.

I need to thank the librarians at the University of Montana, the Missoula City Library, the Helena Public Library, Bonnie Hardwick at the Bancroft Library at the University of California in Berkeley, Susi Krasnoo, Dan Lewis, and the staff at the Huntington Library in Pasadena, Jeffrey Spencer at the historic General Dodge House in Council Bluffs, Iowa, Lee Mortensen of the Nevada Historical Society in Reno, the staff of the California State Railroad Museum Library in Sacramento, Richard Sharp at the Library of Congress, Bill Slaughter at the Archives, Church of Latter Day Saints Library, the Hancock County Library in Bay St. Louis, Mississippi, and the staffs of many county historical or city historical museums that Hugh and I visited in 1997–98.

Ana DeBevoise, on Alice Mayhew's staff, has been a continual source of support, good thinking, and cheerfulness. The people at Simon & Schuster, from Carolyn Reidy and David Rosenthal on down, have done their usual and as always quite superb and professional job, which I have come to expect but which always makes me feel so lucky. Thanks to all of them.

A heartfelt thanks to the men and women who run the railroad museums in Sacramento (one of the best) and Ogden (also among the best) and Omaha (ditto). Hugh and I spent days examining the exhibits, learning, asking questions.

ACKNOWLEDGMENTS

Many railroad buffs were kind enough to send along information. Among them, Nathan Mazer, Bruce Cooper, and Ray Haycox, Jr. A special thanks to Brad Joseph, who built two wonderful models for me, one of the Golden Spike scene at Promontory, Utah, and the other of the drive of the Central Pacific over the Sierra Nevada mountains. Others who helped in various ways are Helen Wayland of the Colfax Historical Society and Joel Skornika of the Center for Railroad Photography and Art, Madison, Wisconsin.

Hugh and I are grateful to Chairman Richard Davidson, Ike Evans, Dennis Duffy, Carl Bradley, Brenda Mainwaring and Dave Bowler of the Union Pacific, and Philip Anschutz of the Anschutz Corporation, for making it possible for us to ride the rails. I wanted to see the track and grade from up front on a train on the original line. Thanks to Davidson and the UP people, as well as my dear friend Ken Rendell, we rode in the engine on a Union Pacific diesel locomotive from Sacramento to Sparks, Nevada (right next to Reno). Together Ken, Hugh, and I were in the cab (with engineers Larry Mireles and Mike Metzger), going around California's Cape Horn, climbing and descending the Sierra Nevada, having experiences of sight, sound, and touch that will never be forgotten.

At one point Mr. Mike Furtney of the railroad company, who was with us, said to me, "You know, Steve, there are thousands of men in this country who would pay us anything we might choose to ask to be up here on this ride." I said I knew that, although at the time I was not aware of just how many train enthusiasts there are in the country. Mike said, "You take the controls for a while." I said I wouldn't dare. He said the engineer would be right behind me, and insisted. So I got to drive a train up the Sierra Nevada, tooting on the whistle before every crossing. Somehow they didn't allow me to stay at the controls for the trip down the mountain.

On the return trip, led by Dave Bowler, we got off and walked through the tunnel at the summit—No. 6, as it was called in 1867. We picked up some spikes and a fishplate. For anyone who has been there and is aware of how men armed only with drills, sledgehammers, and black powder drove a tunnel through that mountain, it is a source of awe and astonishment.

Mr. Davidson gave me and Moira permission to ride in a special train going from Omaha to Sacramento for a steam-engine display. The locomotive would be No. 844, with the legendary Stephen Lee as engineer.

ACKNOWLEDGMENTS

The fireman was Lynn Nystrom. This was the last steam engine bought by the UP—in 1943—and it was used until the late 1950s, then neglected, then restored to become the pride of the railroad today.

We rode from Omaha to Sparks in such splendor as we had never imagined. Ken Rendell was with us for the first half of the trip, Richard Lamm for the second. Bob Kreiger was the engineer for the second cab, also steam, called No. 3985.

For the most part we rode in the cab, pulling into sidings for the night. It was extraordinary. I counted more than thirty-seven handles and knobs on the cab's panel in front of me, none with an explanation of how they worked or why they were there. But throughout the trip Steve Lee would adjust them without looking at them.

The engine is sacred for many reasons. It is in the cab of a locomotive that a mere man can control all that power, it is from there and there only that a man riding on a train can see ahead. It is the eyes, ears, brains, motor power, and central nervous system for the long string of cars it is pulling along.

To be in the locomotive of a steam-driven train, riding from Omaha to Reno, was for me, Moira, Ken, and Dick a memorable experience. First of all, Steve Lee and Lynn Nystrom are big guys, 250 or more pounds each, who put every ounce of themselves into their job, which they love more than nearly anyone I've ever met. They are impressive because of their size, their skill, and their personalities. Nearly all the towns we went through in Nebraska, Wyoming, Utah, and Nevada are railroad towns, and so far as we could tell every adult living there knew Steve, Bob, and Lynn. The engineers would whistle, the spectators would wave.

What impressed me the most, however, was the size of the crowds. The local newspaper or the radio station had a small item the day before the UP's 844 came through, announcing the trip. From what we could tell, every resident was beside the tracks, or up on a ridge we passed under, or out on a bluff that offered a view. Thousands of spectators. Tens of thousands. Among them were all ages and people from both sexes, every one of them with a camera.

I've led a life that makes me accustomed to people pointing cameras at me because of the man I'm with, whether a movie star or director or a top politician. I've never known anything like this. The size of the crowds, their curiosity, their involvement in the scene were stunning. Much of the time we were paralleling Interstate 80. When that happened, we caused a traffic jam. People went just as fast as the train—at sixty-one miles per hour—and gaped. At one point the automobiles were lined up seven full miles behind us. At rest stops, we would see semi-truck drivers on top of their vans, taking pictures with their little cameras. I asked Steve Lee if he had ever stopped to take a picture of a semi-truck. He said no. He added that the semi-truck drivers never stopped to take a picture of a diesel locomotive.

It was then I learned how America has lost her heart to steam-driven locomotives.

One day on the trip we left the 844 for an afternoon in Cheyenne to go by automobile to the Ames Monument and then on to the site of the Dale Creek Bridge. We walked through the cuts that led to the bridge, where we gathered up some spikes and other items. The gorge itself is more than formidable. I can't imagine any twenty-first-century engineer deciding to put a bridge across it. I'm sure there are some who might, but I don't know them.

The most memorable feature of the trip was the presence of Don Snoddy, the historian of the Union Pacific, and Lynn Farrar, who held the same post for decades at the Southern Pacific. They ate meals with us, were with us in the observation car, sat with us at various sidings, and talked. They are wonderful sources. They know damn near everything about the railroads. As one example, riding north of Laramie, they began pointing out grading that had been abandoned. Every town on the line had a story to go with it. Don and Lynn pointed out what happened here, there, all over. They talked about how this was built, and that, or what this or that slang word meant. And anything else. It was a thrill for us to be with them for a week. Then they read the script and saved me from many, many errors. Don was also the driving force behind the trip from Omaha to Ogden.

My thanks to the Union Pacific for making it possible for me and Moira to take the trip that will always sparkle above all others for us.

For Alice Mayhew

Contents

Contents

16

Introduction

NEXT to winning the Civil War and abolishing slavery, building the first transcontinental railroad, from Omaha, Nebraska, to Sacramento, California, was the greatest achievement of the American people in the nineteenth century. Not until the completion of the Panama Canal in the early twentieth century was it rivaled as an engineering feat.

The railroad took brains, muscle, and sweat in quantities and scope never before put into a single project. It could not have been done without a representative, democratic political system; without skilled and ambitious engineers, most of whom had learned their craft in American colleges and honed it in the war; without bosses and foremen who had learned how to organize and lead men as officers in the Civil War; without free labor; without hardworking laborers who had learned how to take orders in the war; without those who came over to America in the thousands from China, seeking a fortune; without laborers speaking many languages and coming to America from every inhabited continent; without the trees and iron available in America; without capitalists willing to take high risks for great profit; without men willing to challenge all, at every level, in order to win all. Most of all, it could not have been done without teamwork.

The United States was less than one hundred years old when the Civil War was won, slavery abolished, and the first transcontinental railroad built. Not until nearly twenty years later did the Canadian Pacific span the Dominion, and that was after using countless American engineers and laborers. It was a quarter of a century after the completion of the American road that the Russians got started on the Trans-Siberian Railway, and the Russians used more than two hundred thousand Chinese to do it, as compared with the American employment of ten thousand or so Chinese. In addition, the Russians had hundreds of thousands of convicts working on the line as slave laborers. Even at that it was not until thirty-two years after the American achievement that the Russians finished, and they did it as a government enterprise at a much higher cost with a road that was in nearly every way inferior. Still, the Trans-Siberian, at 5,338 miles, was the longest continuous railway on earth, and the Canadian Pacific, at 2,097 miles, was a bit longer than the Union Pacific and Central Pacific combined.

But the Americans did it first. And they did it even though the United States was the youngest of countries. It had proclaimed its independence in 1776, won it in 1783, bought the Louisiana Purchase (through which much of the Union Pacific ran) in 1803, added California and Nevada and Utah (through which the Central Pacific ran) to the Union in 1848, and completed the linking of the continent in 1869, thus ensuring an empire of liberty running from sea to shining sea.

H O W it was done is my subject. *Why* plays a role, of course, along with financing and the political argument, but *how* is the theme.

The cast of characters is immense. The workforce—primarily Chinese on the Central Pacific and Irish on the Union Pacific, but with people from everywhere on both lines—at its peak approached the size of the Civil War armies, with as many as fifteen thousand on each line.

Their leaders were the big men of the century. First of all Abraham Lincoln, who was the driving force. Then Ulysses S. Grant and William T. Sherman. These were the men who not only held the Union together north and south but who acted decisively at critical moments to bind the Union together east and west. One of these men was president, a second was soon to be president, the third turned down the presidency.

Supporting them were Grenville Dodge, a Union general who was the chief engineer of the Union Pacific and could be called America's greatest railroad-builder; Jack and Dan Casement, who were also generals during the war and then the heads of construction for the line; and many engineers and foremen, all veterans, who made it happen. Dodge and nearly everyone else involved in building the road later commented that it could not have been done without the Civil War veterans and their experience. It was the war that taught them how to think big, how to organize grand projects, how to persevere.

The financiers could move money around faster than anyone could imagine. The Union Pacific was one of the two biggest corporations of its time (the other was the Central Pacific). It took imagination, brains, guts, and hard work, plus a willingness to experiment with new methods to organize and run it properly. Many participated, mainly under the leadership of Thomas "Doc" Durant, Oakes Ames, Oliver Ames, and others. For the Central Pacific, the leaders were California's "Big Four"— Leland Stanford, Collis Huntington, Charles Crocker, and Mark Hopkins—plus Lewis Clement and his fellow engineers, James Harvey Strobridge as head of construction, and others. Critical to both lines was the Mormon leader, Brigham Young.

The "others" were led by the surveyors, the men who picked the route. They were latter-day Lewis and Clark types, out in the wilderness, attacked by Indians, living off buffalo, deer, elk, antelope, and ducks, leading a life we can only imagine today.

The surveyor who, above all the rest, earned everyone's gratitude was Theodore Judah. To start with, the Central Pacific was his idea. In his extensive explorations of the Sierra Nevada, he found the mountain pass. Together with his wife, Anna, he persuaded the politicians—first in California, then in Washington—that it could be done, and demanded their support. Though there were many men involved, it was Judah above all others who saw that the line could be built but only with government aid, since only the government had the resources to pay for it.

Government aid, which began with Lincoln, took many forms. Without it, the line could not have been built, quite possibly would not have been started. With it, there were tremendous struggles, of which the key elements were these questions: Could more money be made by building it fast, or building it right? Was the profit in the construction, or in the running of the railroad? This led to great tension.

The problems the companies faced were similar. Nearly everything each line needed, including locomotives, rails, spikes, and much more, had to be shipped from the East Coast. For the Central Pacific, that meant transporting the material through Panama or around South America. For the Union Pacific, it meant across the Eastern United States, then over the Missouri River, with no bridges, then out to the construction site. For much of the route, even water had to be shipped, along with lumber. Whether the destination was Sacramento and beyond or Omaha and beyond, the costs were heart-stopping.

Except for Salt Lake City, there were no white settlements through which the lines were built. No white men lived in Nebraska west of Omaha, or in Wyoming, Utah, or Nevada. There was no market awaiting the coming of the train—or any product to haul back east—except the Mormon city, which was a long way away until the lines met. There were problems with Indians for the Union Pacific, Indians who had not been asked or consented or paid for the use of what they regarded as their lands. For the Central Pacific, there was the problem of digging tunnels through mountains made of granite. That these tunnels were attempted, then dug, was a mark of the American audacity and hubris.

The men who built the line had learned how to manage and direct in the Civil War, and there were many similarities, but one major difference. Unlike a battle, there was but one single decisive spot. The builders could not outflank an enemy, or attack in an unexpected place, or encircle. The end of track, the place where the rails gave out, was the only spot that mattered. Only there could the line advance, only there could the battle be joined. The workforce on both lines got so good at moving the end of track forward that they eventually could do so at almost the pace of a walking man. And doing so involved building a grade, laying ties, laying rails, spiking in rails, filling in ballast. Nothing like it had ever before been seen.

Urgency was the dominant emotion, because the government set it up as a race. The company that built more would get more. This was typically American and democratic. Had there been a referendum around the question "Do you want it built fast, or built well?" over 90 percent of the American people would have voted to build it fast.

Time, along with work, is a major theme in the building of the railroad. Before the locomotive, time hardly mattered. With the coming of the railroad, time became so important that popular phrases included "Time was," or "Time is wasting," or "Time's up," or "The train is leaving the station." What is called "standard time" came about because of the railroads. Before that, localities set their own time. Because the railroads published schedules, the country was divided into four time zones. And it was the railroads that served as the symbol of the nineteenth-century revolution in technology. The locomotive was the greatest thing of the age. With it man conquered space and time.

*I*T could not have been done without the workers. Whether they came from Ireland or China or Germany or England or Central America or Africa or elsewhere, they were all Americans. Their chief characteristic was how hard they worked. Work in the mid–nineteenth century was different from work at the beginning of the twenty-first century. Nearly everything was done by muscle power. The transcontinental railroad was the last great building project to be done mostly by hand. The dirt excavated for cuts through ridges was removed one handheld cart at a time. The dirt for filling a dip or a gorge in the ground was brought in by handcart. Some of the fills were enormous, hundreds of feet high and a quarter mile or more in length. Black powder was used to blast for tunnels, but only after handheld drills and sledgehammers had made an indentation deep enough to pack the powder. Making the grade, laying the ties, laying the rails, spiking in the rails, and everything else involved in building the road was backbreaking.

Yet it was done, generally without complaint, by free men who wanted to be there. That included the thousands of Chinese working for the Central Pacific. Contrary to myth, they were not brought over by the boatload to work for the railroad. Most of them were already in California. They were glad to get the work. Although they were physically small, their teamwork was so exemplary that they were able to accomplish feats we just stand astonished at today.

The Irish and the others who built the Union Pacific were also there by choice. They were mainly young ex-soldiers from both the Union and the Confederate armies, unmarried men who had no compelling reason to return home after Appomattox (especially the Confederates). They were men who had caught the wanderlust during the war, that most typical of all American desires, and who eagerly seized the opportunity to participate in the stupendous task of building a railroad across a wilderness.

It is difficult to get information on individuals in the workforce. The workers didn't write many letters home, and few of those that were produced have been saved. They didn't keep diaries. Still, their collective portrait is clear and compelling, including who they were, how they worked, where they slept, what and how much they ate and drank, their dancing, gambling, and other diversions.

They could not have done it alone, but it could not have been done without them. And along with winning the Civil War and abolishing slavery, what they did made modern America.

Chapter One

PICKING THE ROUTE

1830–1860

AUGUST 13, 1859, was a hot day in Council Bluffs, Iowa. The settlement was on the western boundary of the state, just across the Missouri River from the Nebraska village of Omaha. A politician from the neighboring state of Illinois, Abraham Lincoln, went to Concert Hall to make a speech. It attracted a big crowd because of Lincoln's prominence after the previous year's Lincoln-Douglas debates and the keen interest in the following year's presidential election. Lincoln was a full-time politician and a candidate for the Republican nomination for president. The local editor called Lincoln's speech—never recorded—one that "set forth the true principles of the Republican party."

In the audience was Grenville Mellen Dodge, a twenty-eight-year-old railroad engineer. The next day he joined a group of citizens who had gathered on the big porch of the Pacific House, a hotel, to hear Lincoln answer questions. When Lincoln had finished and the crowd dispersed, W.H.M. Pusey, with whom the speaker was staying, recognized young Dodge. He pointed out Dodge to Lincoln and said that the young engineer knew more about railroads than any "two men in the country."

That snapped Lincoln's head around. He studied Dodge intently for a moment and then said, "Let's go meet." He and Pusey strolled across the porch to a bench where Dodge was sitting. Pusey introduced them. Lincoln sat down beside Dodge, crossed his long legs, swung his foot for a moment, put his big hand on Dodge's forearm, and went straight to the point: "Dodge, what's the best route for a Pacific railroad to the West?"

Dodge instantly replied, "From this town out the Platte Valley."

Lincoln thought that over for a moment or two, then asked, "Why do you think so?"

Dodge replied that the route of the forty-second parallel was the "most practical and economic" for building the railroad, which made Council Bluffs the "logical point of beginning."

Why? Lincoln wanted to know.

"Because of the railroads building from Chicago to this point," Dodge answered, and because of the uniform grade along the Platte Valley all the way to the Rocky Mountains.

Lincoln went on with his questions, until he had gathered from Dodge all the information Dodge had reaped privately doing surveys for the Rock Island Railroad Company on the best route to the West. Or, as Dodge later put it, "He shelled my woods completely and got all the information I'd collected."[1]

*T*HE transcontinental railroad had been talked about, promoted, encouraged, desired for three decades. This was true even though the railroads in their first decades of existence were rickety, ran on poorly laid tracks that gave a bone-crushing bump-bump-bump to the cars as they chugged along, and could only be stopped by a series of brakemen, one on top of each car. They had to turn a wheel connected to a device that put pressure on the wheels to slow and finally to stop. The cars were too hot in the summer, much too cold in the winter (unless one was at the end nearest the stove, which meant one was too hot). The seats were wooden benches set at ninety-degree angles that pained the back, the buttocks, and the knees. There was no food until the train stopped at a station, when one had fifteen or fewer minutes to buy something from a vendor. The boiler in the engine was fired by wood, which led to sparks, which sometimes—often—flew back into a car and set the whole thing on fire. Bridges could catch fire and burn. Accidents were common; sometimes they killed or wounded virtually all passengers. The locomotives put forth so much smoke that the downwind side of the tracks on the cars was less desirable and it generally was on the poorer side of town, thus the phrase "the wrong side of the tracks."[2]

Nevertheless, people wanted a transcontinental railroad. This was because it was absolutely necessary to bind the country together. Further, it was possible, because train technology was improving daily. The locomotives were getting faster, safer, more powerful, as the cars became more comfortable. More than the steamboat, more than anything else, the railroads were the harbinger of the future, and the future was the Industrial Revolution.

*I*N 1889, Thomas Curtis Clarke opened his essay on "The Building of a Railway" with these words: "The world of to-day differs from that of Napoleon more than his world differed from that of Julius Caesar; and this change has chiefly been made by railways."

That was true, and it had happened because of the American engineers, one of whom said, "Where a mule can go, I can make a locomotive go."[3] The poetry of engineering, which required both imagination to conceive and skill to execute, was nowhere more in evidence than in America, where it was the most needed. In England and Europe, after George Stephenson launched the first locomotive in 1829, little of significance in design change took place for the next thirty years. In America nearly everything did, because of the contempt for authority among American engineers, who invented new ways to deal with old problems regardless of precedent.

America was riper than anywhere else for the railroad. It gave Americans "the confidence to expand and take in land far in excess of what any European nation or ancient civilization had been able successfully to control," as historian Sarah Gordon points out. The railroad promised Americans "that towns, cities, and industries could be put down anywhere as long as they were tied to the rest of the Union by rail."[4]

Between 1830 and 1850, American engineers invented the swiveling truck. With it placed under the front end of a locomotive, the engine could run around curves of almost any radius. It was in use in 1831 on the Mohawk and Hudson Railroad. There was nothing like it in England. So too equalizing beams or levers, by means of which the weight of the engine was borne by three of the four driving-wheels, which kept the train on rough tracks. Or the four-wheeled swiveling trucks, one under each end of a car, which let the freight or passenger cars follow the locomotives around the sharpest curves. Another American invention was the switchback, making it possible for the locomotives to chug their way up steep inclines.

Something else distinguished the American railway from its English parent. In America it was common practice to get the road open for traffic in the cheapest manner possible, and in the least possible time. The attitude was, It can be fixed up and improved later, and paid for with the earnings.

The wooden bridge and wooden trestle were invented by Leonardo da Vinci in the sixteenth century and put to use for railways by American engineers beginning in 1840. The Howe truss, invented by an American, used bolts, washers, nuts, and rods so that the shrinkage of new timber could be taken up. It had its parts connected in such a way that they were able to bear the heavy, concentrated weight of locomotives without crushing. Had the Howe truss bridges not tended to decay or burn up, they would still be in use today.

The railways made America. Everyone knew that. But there was much left to do. Henry V. Poor, editor of the *American Railroad Journal*, wrote a year before the Lincoln-Dodge meeting, "In a railroad to the Pacific we have a great national work, transcending, in its magnitude, and in its results, anything yet attempted by man. By its execution, we are to accomplish our appropriate mission, and a greater one than any yet fulfilled by any nation." The mission was, he summed up, to establish "our empire on the Pacific, where our civilization can take possession of the New Continent and confront the Old."[5]

OBVIOUSLY Dodge wasn't the only engineer who did surveying on the west side of the Missouri River. But he envisioned and convinced Lincoln that the transcontinental railroad should be on a road running almost straight out the forty-second parallel from Omaha, alongside the Platte Valley until it reached the Rocky Mountains and then over the mountains to meet the railroad coming east from California. With help from many others, Dodge and Lincoln inaugurated the greatest building project of the nineteenth century.

LINCOLN'S first query to Dodge—the best route for a Pacific railroad—was, next to slavery, the foremost question in his mind. He was one of the great railroad lawyers in the West. Born on February 12, 1809, to frontier parents, Lincoln had grown up poor. He educated himself and became a lawyer—a "self-made man," in the words of his political hero, Senator Henry Clay of Kentucky. At age twenty-three, he had entered politics as a candidate for the Illinois state legislature over an issue that would remain with him for the rest of his life, railroads. There was a plan in the legislature to build a railroad from the Illinois River to Springfield. In a campaign speech Lincoln declared that "no other improvement . . . can equal in utility the rail road." It was a "never failing source of communication" that was not interrupted by freezing weather, or high or low water. He admitted that there was a "heart-stopping cost" to building a railroad, however.[6]

Lincoln lost the election, running eighth in a field of thirteen candidates. But his campaign speech was remarkable. The *Rocket,* built in Britain by George Stephenson, had undergone its first successful trial at Rainhill in 1829, only two years earlier. The first American train, *The Best Friend of Charleston,* made its initial run in 1830, the second, *The Mohawk & Hudson,* in 1831. But that year the twenty-two-year-old Lincoln, with less than a year of formal education, was contemplating a railroad in Illinois and was right on the mark about the advantages and disadvantages it would bring, even though, like most Americans and all those living west of the Appalachian Mountains, he had never seen one. He had read about trains in the Eastern newspapers, but his travels had been limited to horseback or buggy, raft or boat.

The American future was hitched to this new thing, to conquer the distance across the continent which was so vast. There were bountiful farm lands that were waiting for immigrants to turn the soil. But without railroads or rivers there was no way to move products of any size from the territories in the West to markets on the East Coast or in Europe. As early as 1830, William Redfield (eighteen years later elected the first president of the American Association for the Advancement of Science), who maintained a lifelong interest in railroads, published a pamphlet in New York City proposing a railroad to cross the country to the Mississippi, with extensions going on to the Pacific.[7]

In 1832, the *Ann Arbor Emigrant* in Michigan called for a railroad from New York City to the Great Lakes, then over the Mississippi River and on to the Missouri River, then up the Platte, over the mountains, and on to Oregon. Lincoln and nearly every person in the United States wanted it done. The agitation grew over the nearly three decades between 1830 and Lincoln's meeting with Dodge in Council Bluffs. The 1830 population was 12.8 million. By 1840, it was up to seventeen million. By 1850, it had grown to twenty-three million, putting the United States ahead of Great Britain. Then it jumped up to thirty-one million by 1860.[8]

Lincoln was a gifted pilot on Western rivers and eager to build canals—in 1836, when he was in the legislature, he cast the deciding vote for a bill to authorize the state to loan $500,000 to support the bonds of the Illinois and Michigan Canal. But even more, he wanted those railroads, which had so many advantages over canals, and he wanted the federal government to let the state use the sale of public lands to raise the money to promote railroads.

Lincoln was ahead of but still in touch with his fellow citizens. By 1835, "railroad fever" had swept America. It was inevitable in a country that was so big, with so many immigrants coming in, creating a desperate need for transportation. Despite the limitations of the first trains—their cost, their unproved capabilities, their dangers—everyone wanted one. Railroads were planned, financed, laid throughout the East and over the mountains. Even though the Panic of 1837 slowed building considerably, by 1840 nearly three thousand miles of track had been laid in the United States, already more than in all of Europe.

So many people and so much land. And the locomotive was improving year by year, along with the track and passenger and freight cars—trains were getting faster, safer, easier to build. By 1850, the lantern, cowcatcher, T-rail, brakes, skill of the engineers, and more improvements made a transcontinental railroad feasible. Pennsylvania, with enormous deposits of both coal and iron, had more rail manufactures than all of England.

A s one observer noted, "The key to the evolution of the American railway is the contempt for authority displayed by our engineers."[9] The engineers were there to build a transcontinental railroad, as they had built so many tracks, curves, and bridges by the beginning of 1850. The country owned so much land that paying for a railroad was no problem—just create a corporation and give it so much land for every mile of track it laid. Lincoln was a strong proponent; in 1847, just before beginning his only term in Congress, he wrote a letter to the *IL Journal* that supported the Alton and Sangamon Railroad and called it "a link in a great chain of rail road communication which shall unite Boston and New York with the Mississippi." He also strongly urged the United States to give 2,595,000 acres of land adjacent to the proposed road to Illinois, to enable the state to grant that land to the IC.[10]

In a complicated case for the Alton and Sangamon, Lincoln won a decision before the Illinois Supreme Court that was later cited as precedent in twenty-five other cases throughout the United States.[11] With seven hundred miles north and south through the state, with a branch to Chicago, the IC was the longest line in the world. The following year, 1852, he defended the yet-unfinished Illinois Central in a case involving the right of the state legislature to exempt the railroad company from county taxes. Not until January 1856 (the year the IC was completed) did the Illinois Supreme Court deliver a decision that accepted Lincoln's argument that the railroad was exempt. Lincoln handed the IC a bill for $2,000. The railroad rejected it, claiming, "This is as much as Daniel Webster himself would have charged." Lincoln submitted a revised bill for $5,000. When the corporation refused to pay, he brought suit and won.[12]

Lincoln was at the forefront of the burst of energy created by the combination of free lands, European immigration, capitalists ready to risk all, and the growth of railroads. As a lawyer who had to ride the circuit on horseback or in a buggy, he knew how great was the demand for passenger trains. This was true everywhere, as the nation created railroads east of the Mississippi River at a tremendous pace, with Illinois one of the leaders. In the 1850s, Illinois constructed 2,867 miles of track, more than any other state except Ohio. This transformed the state's economic and social order and presented new challenges for the Illinois legal system.

Lincoln was a leader in the fray over how to establish the first state railroad regulations: What was the responsibility of a railroad to occupants of lands adjoining the track? What was a railroad's relationship with passengers and shippers? Who should regulate the affairs between stockholders and directors? These and many other questions kept Lincoln involved as he became what an eminent scholar has called "one of the foremost railroad lawyers in the West."[13] He was the main lawyer for the IC in tax cases, in what has been characterized as "Lincoln's greatest legal achievement, . . . the most important of Lincoln's legal services." His cases have been pronounced by scholar Charles Leroy Brown "of extreme delicacy," which Lincoln worked on "quietly, following a program of strategy, maneuver and conciliation," saving the IC millions of dollars in taxes.[14]

In 1857, he was thus the natural choice to argue one of the most important cases about railroads. The Rock Island Bridge Company had built the first bridge across the Mississippi River for the Chicago, Rock Island and Pacific Railroad. This was an innovation of immeasurable proportions, for it meant the country would be able to cross its north-south rivers with railroad tracks, the essential step to building the first transcontinental railroad. But when a steamboat ran into one of the Rock Island's piers, the boat was set on fire and burned up. The owner sued the bridge company. The city of St. Louis and other river interests supported the principle of free navigation for boats, whereas Chicago and the railroad interests stood by the right of railway users to build a bridge.

Lincoln represented the Rock Island Bridge Company in the landmark case. He went to the river and examined the rebuilt bridge, measured the currents in the river, and interviewed river men, all based on his experience as a pilot. At the trial he argued that the steamboat had crashed into the bridge because of pilot error, but he also put the case into a broader context, nothing less than national economic development. He pointed out that there was a need for "travel from East to West, whose demands are not less important than that of the river." He said the east-west railroad connection was responsible for "the astonishing growth of Illinois," which had developed within his lifetime to a population of a million and a half, along with Iowa and the other "young and rising communities of the Northwest."

The jury deadlocked, and the court dismissed the case. It was thus a victory for the railroad.[15] When an Iowa court later found against the builders and ordered the bridge removed, the Supreme Court overruled and declared that railroads could bridge rivers. Had Lincoln never done another thing for the railroads, he had earned their gratitude on this one.

When Lincoln met Dodge in Council Bluffs in 1859, the IC was the largest rail system in the world. The Hannibal and St. Joseph Railroad was running trains to the Missouri River and laying tracks on the other side. In January 1860, it ran a small engine on tracks spiked to telegraph poles and laid on the ice over the Missouri. Thus the train came to Kansas and the Great Plains. This was not unexpected. With the improvement of train technology plus the discovery of gold in California, and because of the extreme difficulty of getting to California, there was an overwhelming demand for a transcontinental railroad.

Picking the Route

. . .

IN 1853, Congress had called for a survey of possible routes. Secretary of War Jefferson Davis, of Mississippi, sent out four teams of surveyors to explore alternatives from the north, near the Canadian border, to the south, near the Mexican, from the forty-ninth parallel on the north to the thirty-second on the south. They did path-breaking work, and eventually a railroad would be built over each route. Their work was published in eleven large volumes by the government, with stunning drawings and maps. They did not explore the forty-second parallel.[16]

The Pacific railroad surveys did the opposite of what Congress said it wanted. They presented a much more favorable picture of Western climate and resources than had previously been assumed. What was thought of as "The Great American Desert," they reported, turned out to be ready for settlement, or at least much of it, with fine agricultural lands and a wealth of minerals. Further, the surveys showed that not one but several practical routes for railroads existed.[17]

The explorers could not settle the question of where to build. Slavery made it impossible. Davis wanted the thirty-second-parallel line. He maintained that a route from New Orleans through southern Texas, across the southern parts of the New Mexico and Arizona Territories, and on to San Diego was the obvious one, because it would cross the fewest mountains and encounter the least snow. That was true. But no free-state politician was ready to provide a charter or funds for a railroad that would help extend slavery. The Free-Soilers wanted Chicago or St. Louis or Minneapolis as the eastern terminus, but no slave-state politician was willing to give it to them.

That is why Lincoln's question to Dodge was inevitably an integral part of the question of slavery's future in the American Republic, an economic question that was also the burning political and overwhelmingly moral question of the day. Lincoln, meanwhile, was about to accept seventeen lots in Council Bluffs as collateral for a loan he was considering making to fellow attorney Norman Judd. So he was in Iowa, among other reasons, to see for himself if the lots were worthwhile as collateral. The answer to that question was the railroad potential of the Great Plains.

THE day he met Lincoln, Grenville Dodge was twenty-eight years old. Born April 12, 1831, in Massachusetts, the son of a common laborer, he had worked on his first railroad at age fourteen, as a surveyor for Frederick Lander, who became one of the ablest surveyors in the exploration of the West. Lander was impressed by Dodge and told him to go to Norwich University in Vermont to become an engineer. He also gave Dodge his first vision of a Pacific railroad.

In 1848, Dodge entered Norwich, where the enthusiasm for railroad expansion was at a fever pitch. He found a faculty in Norwich who were, in his words, "filled with enthusiasm for expansion of railroads from the Atlantic to the Pacific." Like them, Dodge was also strong for steam power. In his diary in the fall of 1850, he wrote: "Forty-three years ago today, on October 12, 1807, Fulton made his first steamboat trip up the Hudson River. How wonderful has been the effect of his discovery. In the short space of forty-three years steam power has revolutionized the world."[18] Two months later, Dodge moved to Illinois, where the Rock Island was just getting ready to grade for the track. He worked for the Rock Island and other railroads. All travel to the West was still over the Indian trails and the plank roads and down the canal. There was much to do.

In January 1852, Dodge went to work for the IC. The railroad drove up the price of lands per acre from $1.25 to $6 in 1853, and to $25 by 1856, the year it was completed. But the twenty-one-year-old Dodge was more interested in the Rock Island's construction to the west than in the IC headed south. He quit the IC in 1853 and went back to work with the Rock Island, writing his father, "It is the true Pacific road and will be built to Council Bluffs and then on to San Francisco—this being the shortest and most feasible route."[19]

He was right about part of this. The Chicago, Rock Island was the first railroad to cross Illinois from Chicago to the Mississippi River. Henry Farnam, who had railroad experience in Connecticut, and Chicago resident Joseph Sheffield had done a survey westward from Rock Island. In 1852, they made another survey across Iowa, this time for the Mississippi and Missouri Railroad, organized by the Rock Island with Peter A. Dey as engineer.

In the autumn of 1852, Dodge made an application to Dey. Dey later said that he took Dodge on that fall and "very soon I discovered that there was a good deal in him. I discovered a wonderful energy. If I told him to do anything he did [it] under any and all circumstances. That feature was particularly marked. He so enhanced my opinion of him that in May, 1853, when I came out to Iowa City to make surveys from Davenport west, I took him with me."[20] Since Dey was one of the best railroad engineers in the country, if not the best, that was gratifying. Dodge called Dey "the most eminent engineer of the country, [a man] of great ability, [known for] his uprightness and the square deal he gave everyone."[21] Dey put the youngster to work on a construction party, then as a surveyor across Iowa for the M&M.

Iowa was a natural link between the roads being pushed west from Chicago and any road crossing the Missouri River. When Chicago became a railroad center, Iowa became the necessary bridge between the Midwest and the Far West. The M&M had made a bargain with the Davenport and Iowa City Railroad by promising to complete the main line from Davenport to Iowa City in two years. Two weeks after this agreement, Dey went to work, with Dodge helping. Then Dodge went surveying on his own, west of Iowa City, with the Missouri River as his destination.

*I*T was 1853. Dodge led a party of fourteen men, including a cook and a hunter. He hoped to make the Missouri before the snow fell. His expenses ran to $1,000 per month. He was pleased by the opportunity and overjoyed at the wilderness he was entering. He wrote his father, "Oh, that you could come out and overtake me on the prairies of Iowa, look at the country and see how we live." He was also ready to seize the main chance: he told his father, "We shall make an examination of the great Platte as far into Nebraska as we think fit."[22]

Dodge loved the flaming sumac, the gold tinge of the willows, the turning leaves on the cottonwood beside the rivers, and on the elms, black oak, and hard maple, the silvered wild grass, the variety and numbers of animals. All were fascinating to the young engineer from New England. He saw his first Western Indians, a group of Otoes, who fled. On a late afternoon in November, Dodge, on a solitary horseback reconnaissance in advance of his party, drew up at the edge of a great crescent of cliffs and beheld the river that thereafter always held him in thrall.

The Missouri was sprawled out on the floodplain that twisted and turned, gnawing at the sandbars in its sweep between the villages of Omaha and Council Bluffs. The Mormons had arrived at the latter in their wanderings in 1846 and left in 1852, en route to Salt Lake City. This reduced the population of Council Bluffs from six thousand to fewer than twenty-five hundred (Omaha had about five hundred residents).

But Dodge knew, at his first glance, that here was the site for the eastern terminus for the first transcontinental. On November 22, 1853, his party caught up with him, the first surveying party to traverse Iowa from east to west. There would be others, and a race was on, but it would be fourteen years before a train crept into Council Bluffs, even as the Union Pacific reached out from Omaha into the mountains.

Dodge crossed the Missouri on a flatboat. On the western side, he had the party continue to scout while he went on ahead to examine the country to the Platte Valley, some twenty-five miles farther west. Dodge went up the Platte, looked around and studied its bank, and liked what he saw.

Dodge asked every immigrant he ran into, plus the voyagers and Indians, for all the information they could furnish on the country farther west.[23] On the way home he took out a claim on the Elkhorn River. It was the first major tributary of the Platte, only twenty or so miles west of Omaha.

Having completed the location of the M&M, Dodge took a leave and went back to Illinois to marry Anne Brown on May 28, 1854. The couple then returned to his claim on the Elkhorn, where he built a cabin and took out claims for his father and his brother, who joined him in March 1855. Together they plowed the virgin prairie and began to farm. Emigrants crossing Nebraska in 1855 never saw a white man's house between the Dodge cabin on the Elkhorn and Denver.

I N July 1855, two exhausted and seriously ill men rode up to Dodge's cabin on spent horses. Dodge was amazed; one of them was Frederick Lander, the man who had influenced him to go to Norwich University. He welcomed Lander and his companion, helped them off their horses and into the cabin, nursed them, and got their story. Lander said he had been surveying for the government from Puget Sound, in the Washington Territory, to the Missouri River, that he had started with six men but only he and the man with him had survived. Still, he had completed his survey.

That evening, Dodge and Lander sat on the banks of the Elkhorn, watching the fireflies and talking railroads. "Dodge," Lander said, "the Pacific railroad is bound to be built through this valley and if it doesn't run through your claim, I'll be badly mistaken."

"I've already figured that it will," Dodge replied. "How else could it go from the Missouri River if built this far north?"

Lander reported that Jefferson Davis, the secretary of war, didn't want the railroad to be so far north. "He wants the Pacific railroad to be to the south. I'm going to oppose his views as soon as I get to Washington."

And he did. Davis had reports that stressed the thirty-second parallel as quicker, cheaper, and more dependable than any of the others. Lander, in his report, made a frank comparison of the route from the thirty-second and the one from the forty-second (which would make Omaha or its vicinity the eastern terminus). "The northern route is longer than the southern," he confessed, "but of central position, it can be more readily defended in time of war; it can be more cheaply constructed; and, when built, will command and unite important and conflicting public and private interests." He also pointed to a further and enormous advantage— the railroad would stay on flat ground, near water, by following the valley of the Platte.[24]

Dodge agreed. He sought the route using the private funds of Farnam and railroad promoter Dr. Thomas Durant, who had interests in the Rock Island. In 1856, Dodge had made a private survey up the Platte Valley to and beyond the Rocky Mountains, and reported to his financiers. Farnam and Durant set out to induce Eastern capital to help complete the road across Iowa, then across the Missouri River into Nebraska and farther west. On the basis of Dodge's reports, they selected Council Bluffs as the place for the Rock Island to end and the Pacific railroad, when the government decided to build it, to begin. This was an adroit and far-seeing move in 1857, and it induced Dodge to make a claim across the Missouri River and near the town of Council Bluffs. Railroad activity was down, however, because of the Panic of 1857.

But this economic downturn must be kept in perspective. In the 1850s, an average of 2,160 miles of new track was laid every year. More miles of track were laid in the United States, mainly in the north, than in all the rest of the world, and by 1859 just under half of the world's railroad tracks would be in the various states of the Union. The brand-new rail network would carry some 60 percent of all domestic freight.[25]

The growth of railroads in the United States had been astonishing. The tracks more than doubled in each decade. In 1834, there were but 762 miles. In 1844, it was up to 4,311 miles. By 1854, the trackage numbered 15,675 miles. On January 1, 1864, the amount of completed railway had grown to 33,860 miles, with sixteen thousand more miles under construction, most of it in the Northern states.[26]

In 1858, Farnam and Durant—who had a medical degree but never practiced and instead operated on Wall Street, where he was called

"Doc"—asked Dodge to visit them in New York City, at the office of the Rock Island Railroad, located over the Corn Exchange Bank. Dodge thus was present at a meeting of the board of directors, where a secretary read his report on the Platte route. "Before he was half through," Dodge reported, "nearly every person had left the room, and when he had finished only Mr. Farnam, Doc Durant, the reader and myself were present." Dodge had heard one of the directors say "he did not see why they should be asked to hear such nonsense." But Dodge told the two remaining directors: "I believe your road will draw the bulk of emigration crossing the Missouri. From Council Bluffs it will then go up the north side of the Platte River along the Mormon trail. The Pacific railroad is bound to be built along this trail."[27]

Farnam and Durant believed him. And they acted on that belief, saying they felt "that if they could stimulate interest in the Pacific road it would enable them to raise funds to complete their line across the State." Dodge went to work making a grade* east from Council Bluffs.[28]

BY no means was anything, much less everything, settled, even though in 1856 both political parties had advocated the transcontinental railroad in resolutions. But whether there would be a Pacific railroad as long as the United States remained half slave, half free, was a long way from being decided. "Can we, as a nation, continue together *permanently—forever*—half slave, and half free?" Lincoln had written to a Kentucky correspondent in 1855.[29] If the country did not change, no one could tell where or if the Pacific railroad would run.

But if the railroad was to be built beside the Platte River, it was the buffalo and the Indians who first picked it out. Then it was used by the mountain men and the fur traders, then by the travelers on the Oregon Trail, then it became the route for the Mormon emigrant trains and their handcarts. It was called the Great Platte Valley Route. Lander and Dodge had seen immediately that this was the route for the Pacific railroad. Dodge once remarked that any engineer who overlooked the Platte Valley route as a natural highway to the mountains was not fit to follow the profession.[30]

Peter Dey almost agreed. "Dodge and I read up everything on this sub-

---

* The bed of a railroad track.

ject," he declared. "We read all the government reports of everything that had been discovered regarding the routes across the continent. Dodge was deeply interested in them and I was to a considerable extent. . . . He made his claim on the Elkhorn river . . . [because] it was his belief that the Platte valley would be the line."[31] But Dey wasn't ready to go as far as Dodge. He said that Dodge had "taken a great fancy to the Missouri River" and that the sprawling, muddy stream held a fascination for him: "He always felt at home along its shores."

Dodge, meanwhile, was collecting oral and written information about the country west of his farm and studying the routes from the Missouri River to the Pacific Coast. He drew up his own map of the country, "giving the fords and where water and wood could be found, etc." He called it "the first map of the country giving such information."[32]

The old M&M had new directors in 1856.* They got started by telling the citizens of Pottawattamie County (where Council Bluffs is located) that if the citizens would vote for a $300,000 bond issue for the railroad, they would begin to grade for track eastward across Iowa. Then they crossed the river to Omaha to tell the citizens that, for a $200,000 bond issue from them for the M&M, work would start in Council Bluffs during the year. The Council Bluffs bonds were voted June 13, 1857, but in October the road went into the hands of receivers because the Panic of 1857 caused everything to fall through. Western Iowa and eastern Nebraska saw land that had boomed to $7 an acre fall to $1.

In 1858, Dodge decided to move across the river and make his permanent home in Council Bluffs, where he went into banking, milling, merchandising, contracting, freighting, and real estate—a good indication of how varied were the interests of businessmen in the Missouri River towns in the late fifties. He bought lots in the "Riddle Tract," down on the Missouri River floodplain, the same location as the lots Lincoln was willing to assume in 1859 as collateral.

The *Council Bluffs Bugle* was very suspicious. "It has been rumored that G. M. Dodge, in consequence of being so largely interested in the Riddle Tract, was bound to make his surveys in such manner as would insure his own investments."[33] Dodge was buying for the M&M, which wanted to

---

* John A. Dix, president; Henry Farnam, the road's builder; and Doc Durant, who was an investor and became one of America's greatest and most successful manipulators and is generally regarded as one of the shrewdest railroad financiers.

retain a portion of the land for the road's shops and yards and to subdivide the remainder and place them on the market. Norman Judd, attorney for the M&M and a legal and political associate of Lincoln, borrowed
the money from Lincoln to buy seventeen lots for $3,500, using the lots
as collateral.

*I*N the spring of 1859, Dodge went up the valley of the Platte on a third
survey for Henry Farnam of the Rock Island. He got back to Council
Bluffs on August 11, the day before Lincoln arrived in town. Lincoln had
been making some political speeches in Iowa and Nebraska. When he
reached St. Joseph, Missouri, he could have taken the only line of railroad across the state to return to Illinois, but instead he had gone aboard
a stern-wheel steamboat that toiled up the Missouri River for nearly two
hundred miles to Council Bluffs. Lincoln wanted to check out what the
situation was with regard to the Pacific railroad, because of—as J. R.
Perkins, Dodge's first biographer, noted—"his far-seeing plans to identify
himself with the building of the great transcontinental railroad."[34]

The Republican paper in town, the *Nonpareil*, gave Lincoln a warm welcome, saying that "the distinguished 'Sucker' [Iowa slang for someone from
Illinois] has yielded to the solicitations of our citizens and will speak on the
political issues of the day at Concert Hall. The celebrity of the speaker will
most certainly insure him a full house. Go and hear old Abe."[35]

The next morning, Lincoln, his friends the Puseys, and other citizens
of the town strolled up a ravine to the top of the bluff, to view the landscape. From the point where he stood, now marked with a stone shaft and
a placard, the vast floodplain of the Missouri stretched for twenty miles
north and south and for four miles to the west, to Omaha. What he saw
was similar to what Lewis and Clark had seen fifty-five years earlier, in
1804, when they stood on the same bluff. (Their visit is also marked by a
statue and a placard.) In 1859 as in 1804, there were no railroad tracks
crossing each other, no houses, only unbroken fields of wild grass and
sunflowers, but there were a few streets in the rapidly growing village of
Omaha running up and down the river hills.

It is unknown whether Lincoln knew Lewis and Clark had been there.
Certainly he knew that they were the first Americans to cross the continent, east to west, and that they had reported there was no all-water
route.

To his friend Pusey, Lincoln said, "Not one, but many railroads will center here."[36] The next day, in answer to his question, he learned from Dodge how right he had been. He thus began an association with Dodge that would make the two of them the great figures of the Union Pacific Railroad.

*I*N 1859, one of the most prominent newspaper editors in America, Horace Greeley—founder and editor of the *New York Tribune*—made a famous trip west to California. He published his account of the trip in his 1860 book *An Overland Journey from New York to San Francisco in the Summer of 1859*. "Let us resolve to have a railroad to the Pacific—to have it soon," he wrote. "It will add more to the strength and wealth of our country than would the acquisition of a dozen Cubas." He said he had made the long, fatiguing journey in order to "do something toward the early construction of the Pacific Rail road; and I trust that it has not been made wholly in vain." But he also said that part of the route he covered, the part over the Humboldt Valley in Nevada and in the desert beyond, was unfit for human life. "I thought I had seen barrenness before," he wrote, but in that territory "famine sits enthroned, and waves his scepter over a dominion expressly made for him."[37]

*D*ODGE returned to Council Bluffs, but not to his businesses. He wanted to build the railroad to the Pacific; he loved doing surveys through virgin country; he loved the life of the camp. He continued to roam up the Platte. Lincoln went into the race for the Republican nomination for president. Norman Judd, who was working for him, wrote to Dodge in May 1860, "I want you to come to the Republican convention at Chicago and do what you can to help nominate Lincoln."[38] Dodge did, along with a strong group of Iowa delegates who were connected with the Rock Island line, including H. M. Hoxie of Des Moines, who later received the contract to construct the first one hundred miles of the Union Pacific; John Kasson of Des Moines, attorney for the railroad and a prominent Republican; J. B. Grinnell, who founded the town and college of Grinnell along the route of the M&M; and others.

In Chicago, Dodge and most of the Iowa delegates joined with other railroad men who considered Lincoln's nomination and election as vital to their plans to build the Pacific road west from Council Bluffs along the forty-second parallel. They included John Dix, president of the Rock Island, Durant, Farnam, Judd, and others. Together, they were able to get John Kasson to write the railroad plank for the Republican platform, calling for the government to support a transcontinental railroad.* Along with all the railroad men from Illinois, they worked where and how they could for Lincoln—who was appreciative, of course, but who had bigger things on his mind than even the transcontinental railroad, starting with slavery. Dodge, Judd, and the others used every opportunity to let the Iowa and Illinois delegates know that with Lincoln the nation would have a president whose program was bound to include the building of the Pacific railroad along the line of the forty-second parallel.

On issues that had nothing directly to do with the transcontinental railroad, Lincoln was elected. In all the excitement that followed, the railroad men stayed at work. Peter Reed, a friend of Dodge from Moline, went to Springfield, Illinois, and on December 14, 1860, wrote to Dodge. He said he had had a private audience with Lincoln and "I called his attention to the needs of the people of Nebraska and the western slope of Iowa. I said to him that our interest had been badly neglected. I told him that I expected to see some men from Council Bluffs in regard to this matter and that you were one of them. He said that his sympathies were with the border people, as he was a border man himself. I think that we are all right with Mr. Lincoln, especially as we have N. B. Judd with us."[39]

Dodge wanted to add his own weight. In early March 1861, just before Lincoln's inauguration, he joined Farnam and Durant to go to Washington. He wrote his wife, "I came here with Farnam, Durant [and some others] and we are busy before the railroad committees. Compromise measures have passed the House but will be killed in the Senate."[40]

Dodge's group was in the capital on the eve of civil war, contending for a single route for the Pacific railroad, to run from Council Bluffs straight west. Judd was there and helping, although his mind was more on getting the ambassadorship to Germany (which he did). Taking into account all that was going on around Lincoln's inaugural, it seems near impossible that Dodge and the others were there arguing for their own version of the

---

* "A Railroad to the Pacific Ocean is imperatively demanded by the interests of the whole country; the Federal Government ought to render immediate and efficient aid in its construction."

railroad—but it was happening. Lincoln, on the train from Springfield as he headed east, had taken a turn at driving the locomotive.

Dodge went to the inaugural and told his wife, "Old Abe delivered the greatest speech of the age. It is backbone all over." Then he got to the point: "It looks as though we can get all our measures through and then I'll make tracks for home."[41]

Two weeks after Lincoln's inauguration, Dodge and two office-seekers called on Lincoln to press the railroad. Dodge wrote his wife, "Politically the skies are dark. Lincoln has a hard task before him, but he says that he thinks he can bring the country out all right. . . . I have carried all my points except one."[42]

Dodge went off to New York, where he agreed to drop his personal business in Council Bluffs and identify himself with the Rock Island railroad. Almost a month later, on April 12, 1861, the Confederates fired on Fort Sumter and the Civil War was under way. Dodge put the railroad aside and joined the army. Holding the country together north and south was more important to him than linking it together east and west. But the latter aim never left his mind, or Lincoln's.

Chapter Two

GETTING TO CALIFORNIA
1848–1859

Oh, California—that's the land for me!
I'm going to Sacramento with my washbowl on my knee!

LEWIS AND CLARK had led the way to the Pacific. They did so by foot, pole, paddle, sail, or on horseback, whatever worked and whatever they had available. No progress had been made in transportation since ancient Greece or Rome, and none when they got back to civilization, in 1806. Steam power was first applied to boats the following year, and two decades later to the development of the steam-driven locomotive. George Washington could travel no faster than Julius Caesar, but Andrew Jackson could go upstream at a fair pace, and James K. Polk could travel at twenty miles an hour or more overland. The harnessing of steam power brought greater change in how men lived and moved than had ever before been experienced, and thus changed almost everything, but it meant nothing outside the seaboard or away from a major river, or until a track had been laid connecting one point with another.

In 1846, the young republic had completed the process of stretching the boundaries of the nation to the Pacific, in the north through a treaty with Great Britain that extended the existing continental line along the forty-ninth parallel; in the south, in 1848, by taking California and other Southwestern territory from Mexico. In Oregon the good land and bountiful rainfall had attracted Americans, but they could only get there via the Platte River Valley and then up the wagon route through the mountains.

Throughout the Pacific Coast, the territories from California north to

Washington were like overseas colonies: immensely valuable, but so far away. They could be reached by sea—but the United States had nothing like a two-ocean navy—or overland via carts drawn by horses and oxen. But it took seemingly forever. Americans knew how difficult or impossible it was to defend overseas colonies—even for Great Britain, with the mightiest fleet of all. The French could not hold on to Haiti, or Canada, or Louisiana, just as the British could not hold their North American colonies.

A land communication between the mother country and the colonies was critical—but until the coming of the railroad, the distances separating the United States east of the Missouri from its Western colonies precluded any significant connection save by sea. That meant going around the continent of South America or making a hazardous trip over the Isthmus at Panama. If the United States was to be what Jefferson had dreamed of, an empire of liberty stretching from sea to shining sea, it was imperative that a transcontinental railroad be built as soon as possible.

But where? As noted, up until Lincoln's inauguration, the slave states blocked the free states and vice versa. This was so even though, after 1848 and the discovery of gold on a branch of the American River about forty miles west of present-day Sacramento, everyone agreed on the need. Indeed, it sometimes seemed as if everyone were going to California. Adventurers came from all parts of the United States and all over the world, from China and Australia, from Europe, from everywhere. By the end of 1849, the population of California was swelling, with more coming. How they got there, with no railroad, is a long story.

*C*HARLES Crocker said later, "I built the Central Pacific."[1] Collis Huntington, Leland Stanford, Theodore Judah, and Mark Hopkins could say the same or something near it. For sure, Crocker had lots of help, and people to point the way—but he was the one who could claim without blushing that he built it.

Born in Troy, New York, on September 16, 1822, Crocker commenced selling apples and oranges at nine years of age, then carrying newspapers. "I was always apt at trade, when a boy I would swap knives and could always get ahead. I was a natural leader in everything." He moved to Vermont to make a living, but "I was too fast for that country. Everything there was quiet and staid. You didn't dare laugh all day Sunday until sundown came." He struggled with poverty, working sixteen hours a day for $11 a month. He never went to any school beyond eighth grade. In his twenties, he was certain he could do whatever was required at any job or trade. He was about five feet ten or eleven inches tall, with smooth clear skin, blue eyes, a high forehead, and a tremendous appetite. He was, in many ways, a typical American.[2]

In 1849, he got gold fever and gathered together his two brothers and four other young men. He purchased four horses and two wagons and his party made its way to South Bend, Indiana, where the members spent the winter working to make some money. In the spring they took off for St. Louis. At Quincy, Illinois, on the bank of the Mississippi, Crocker learned that the Missouri River was still frozen up, so he used the en-forced wait to lay in a supply of corn, which he had the young men shell. Then he took the corn down to St. Louis, with instructions for the others to make their way overland with the horses and wagons through Iowa to the Missouri River. In St. Louis he purchased more goods, and set off on the first steamer that ascended the river that spring.

Near Council Bluffs, Crocker reunited with his men. They were all ap-palled at the price of supplies and food—flour was $25 a barrel and scarce at that. They were offered $3 a bushel for their shelled corn but turned it down. Crocker insisted on staying on the east bank for ten days, to let the horses fatten up on the grass and to wait for the grass on the west bank to grow high enough to pasture the horses. Finally, on May 14, they rafted the river and "the next day started on our trip leaving civilization behind us."[3]

Crocker's foresight was rewarded. Thanks to the shelled corn in one of the wagons, the party could travel faster than those who depended on grass alone. When they got to the Platte River, the road was lined with teams, so much so that they were always in view. Crocker's party made about thirty miles a day, in part thanks to his leadership. "They would all gather around me and want to know what to do," he later said.[4] Once, when one of his horses strayed away, he went looking and found the horse. The men who were supposed to be looking after the animal were sitting on the banks of the river playing cards. Crocker brought them to the camp, called for all the cards, burned them, and gave a blistering lec-ture: "We are going across the plains. We don't know where we are going. We don't know what is before us. If we don't reserve all our power we might not get to California. It won't do to play cards. We must have our wits about us, watch our horses, and keep everything in ship-shape."[5]

The Crocker party was going up the Platte River on its northern bank. The Platte, as everyone who traveled it then or now knows, runs a mile wide and an inch deep, with innumerable sandbars and willow stands, and a constant shifting of channels. It was and is immensely picturesque and tremendously irritating to those who had to cross it. Crocker did not. He was on the Great Plains of North America, which stretched out forever under an infinity of bright-blue sky, except when a storm hit, cutting the vision down to nothing. The Plains were flat or gently rolling.

Robert Louis Stevenson described Nebraska: "We were at sea—there is no other adequate expression—on the Plains. . . . I spied in vain for something new. It was a world almost without a feature, an empty sky, an empty earth, front and back. . . . The green plain ran till it touched the skirts of heaven. . . . Innumerable wild sunflowers bloomed in a continuous flower-bed [and] grazing beasts were seen upon the prairie at all degrees of distance and diminution . . . in this spacious vacancy, this greatness of the air, this discovery of the whole arch of heaven, this straight, unbroken, prison-line of the horizon."[6]

On May 25, Crocker's party were camping beside the Platte River, eating supper in a tent. A powerful wind came up, blew down the tent, and scattered the meal. The men's hats followed along with their plates and pots, all gone. A typical day on the Great Plains. On June 2, the party passed Fort Laramie in Nebraska Territory, on the North Platte branch of the river, where they had someone shoe their horses (they were entering rocky ground) at 25 cents per shoe. There too they met the legendary mountain man and guide Kit Carson, who had brought on a drove of mules from Taos, New Mexico, to sell to California-bound parties.

On June 9, the party crossed the North Platte on the Mormon Ferry, paying $4 for each wagon and 25 cents for horses. The ferrymen told Crocker that twenty-five hundred teams had already crossed.[7] Following them, Crocker drove across a barren, sandy, alkali country twenty-eight miles without water to the Sweetwater River, flowing east out of South Pass in the Wind River Range of the Rockies.

On June 15, Crocker stood on the summit of the Rockies at South Pass, seven thousand feet above the sea. Although he was on the Continental Divide, it was "on a plane so level we could not tell by the eye which way it sloped." The party found and drank at Pacific Spring, the first water they had encountered that flowed west. By June 18, they had covered another seventy-five miles across inhospitable land to make it to Green River. There the men camped to wait their turn for the ferry, paying $7 for each wagon. Because no grass grew around there—it was all grazed away—they drove the horses two miles down the river, to a meadow, for the night. By this time Crocker had in his company about twenty horses and ten men. He would put two men out on guard duty with the horses. On this night it was Crocker's and C. B. DeLamater's turn. Since they were the first party there, they selected the choicest spot and picketed the horses.

Another party, with about fifty horses and mules and half a dozen men, came up and grumbled about Crocker's taking the best ground. Toward sunset, Crocker and DeLamater drove their horses down to the river to drink; on returning, they found the new party had staked their horses and mules in the choice spot.

"That ground is ours," said Crocker. He drove their animals off and staked out his horses. The newcomers were very abusive and threatened to pull Crocker's stakes.

"You do, if you dare," Crocker said, as he pulled a pistol and proclaimed his right to the good spot. After some shouting and threats, the newcomers backed down. This was but one of a number of instances when Crocker had to use his pistol to uphold his rights, something he was proud of: he later told an interviewer that "a man who is well assured of his own position and shows bold front, need not fear anybody."[8] And DeLamater said of him, "Charley would look at another man's pistol and break out in one of his hearty laughs. . . . He was always cool and self-possessed in the presence of difficulties—courageous in maintaining his own rights, never intentionally encroaching upon the rights of others."[9]

Many adventures ensued as these young men crossed one of the most demanding, arduous, and exhausting landforms in the world. Crocker and his men would make frequent excursions to examine the picturesque features. DeLamater kept a diary: June 28, "Heavy hail storm. Hail as large as musket balls." July 4, "Camp in Thousand Spring Valley—were awakened this morning by our guard firing a Salute in honor of the day. They burst one gun trying to make a big noise."

On July 6, the party came to the Humboldt River, in the process passing the grave of a man killed less than a week earlier by an Indian. DeLamater wrote that, whereas "our hardships had been comparatively light this far," as soon as they struck the Humboldt the hardships were "thick and fast." The river—called the "Humbug" by the travelers—was over-flowing because of melting mountain snow, so Crocker took them up to the bluffs and across sagebrush and alkali flats to get some grass, camping during the day and traveling at night, all the way to the "sink of the Humboldt." There "the river spreads out in meadows and sinks into the earth," DeLamater wrote, but "we fared better than thousands of others. I never saw so much suffering in all my life. We gave medicine here, a little food there, but had to pass on with the crowd, striving to reach the goal, or our fate might be as theirs—sickness—a lonely death—and a shallow nameless grave."[10]

At the sink of the river there were splendid meadows and grass in abundance, so Crocker paused for a few days to recuperate. Then, leaving behind everything superfluous, including one of the two wagons and ten of the twenty horses, with all but one of the men walking, the party set out. They had waited until sunset to cross the thirty miles or so of alkali flats to reach the Carson River. "A dreary tedious journey," DeLamater called it. Four hours after sunrise, the party reached "the sweet cool water of the Carson and its brooks and grassy meadows. It was like Paradise." The hardships everyone had suffered since leaving the Missouri were instantly forgotten. "The future was before us with its golden crown."

Traders from California had crossed the Sierra Nevada to bring flour, bacon, and other provisions for the Easterners—at $1.50 per pound. "But each days travel brought us nearer to California and provisions were cheaper." In a few days the party crossed the summit of the Sierra Nevada. On August 7, they were in Placerville, California.[11]

It had taken Crocker and his team—young men, all in good condition, with some money and supplies plus horses and wagons—almost half a year to cross the plains and mountains. They had pushed themselves as hard as they ever had, getting more out of themselves than they had thought possible, and seen more dead, dying, and ill men than they had ever laid eyes on before. Thousands of others had gone before, or at about the same time, or shortly after Crocker, all headed for the gold in the hills. Virtually every one of them swore, "Never again."

COLLIS Huntington was born on October 21, 1821, in Litchfield Hills, Connecticut, fifteen miles west of Hartford, the sixth of nine children. He did manual labor and attended school for about four months each winter. He did well in arithmetic, history, and geography, but was defeated by grammar and spelling.[12] At age fourteen he was an apprentice on a farm for a year at $7 a month and keep. Then he got a job with a storekeeper, whom he impressed by memorizing both the wholesale and retail cost of every item in the cluttered stock and then calculating, without pencil or paper, the profit that could be expected from each piece. At age sixteen he went to New York City, where he bought a stock of clocks, watch parts, silverware, costume jewelry, and other items, then set off to Indiana as a Yankee peddler. When he was twenty-one, he drifted to Oneonta, in central New York. There he went to work for his older brother Solon, who had built a store. He did so well that when he was twenty-three years old he went into a partnership with Solon, contributing in cash the considerable sum of $1,318. That was on September 4, 1844; two weeks later, Collis went to Cornwall, Connecticut, to marry Elizabeth Stoddard, whom he had been courting.[13]

For the next four years, he went to New York City to make purchases for the Oneonta store. As in the past, he did well. In the 1890s, Huntington told an interviewer, "From the time I was a child until the present I can hardly remember a time when I was not doing something."[14] There were other young men, in New York State and elsewhere in America, getting ahead in the 1840s, a great age for just-beginning businessmen. But few did as well or moved as fast as Huntington, who seized the main chance before others even knew it was there. His looks, his self-assurance, and his bulk all helped; he weighed two hundred pounds and had a great round head and penetrating eyes. Strong as an ox, he claimed he never got sick.* He made it a habit to take charge of any enterprise in which he was involved.

Doing well in Oneonta with his brother, however, was not enough. Late in 1848, Huntington embraced the rumors of gold for the taking in California. He persuaded five other young men in town to come with him on a trip by sea to California. They joined many others. In the month of January 1849, eight thousand gold seekers sailed for California in ninety ships, to go around South America's Cape Horn and then north along the coast.

Huntington, however, decided to take his chances on the shortcut

---

* He did once, in 1849 in California, when amoebic dysentery dropped his weight from 200 to 125 pounds. With self-medication, he recovered.

across Panama. This was a bold, risky decision. After his steamer made its way from New York City to the Colombia shore, his plan was that he and his party would hire natives with canoes to take them up the Chagres River to its headwaters, then travel by mule down to Panama City to await a boat going to San Francisco. The drawbacks were the expense, the possibility of missing boats going north, and, more serious, the danger of contracting tropical fever.

Huntington was twenty-seven (a little older than Crocker), and he was leaving with no illusions about striking it rich on a gold-bearing stream. His companions and thousands of others headed toward California were looking for an easy fortune, but Huntington headed west in his already developed capacity as a trader. He brought with him to New York and had loaded on his steamer a stock of merchandise, including a number of casks of whiskey, which he intended to sell to the argonauts. He had no interest in the "mining and trading companies" forming at the New York docks. His interest was in starting a store, with his brother Solon sending on the goods from New York.[15]

On March 14, 1849, Huntington and his mates bought steerage tickets for $80 each on the *Crescent City*. It left the next day—about the same time that Crocker started west—with around 350 argonauts on board. Twenty-four-year-old Jessie Benton Frémont—daughter of Senator Thomas Hart Benton of Missouri, who was a leading advocate of the Pacific railroad—was on the ship, on her way to California to meet her explorer husband, John Charles Frémont. He had just completed his fourth expedition through the Western reaches of the continent, this one in search of a usable railroad route to the Pacific.

Huntington was a long way from California and from building a railroad. On the first days out of New York, his concern was with the health of his mates and fellow passengers. Except for him, they were all seasick, vomiting nearly every morning and night and always full of queasiness. They had gone around the tip of Florida and past Cuba before the sea settled down. On March 23, after eight days at sea, the *Crescent City* hove to a mile or so off the mouth of the Chagres River. Huntington went ashore in a native canoe, along with some others, to discover that Chagres was a miserable place. He managed to hire natives to get 260 people to Panama City. It took three days to get the passengers and baggage to Gorgona, the headwaters of the river—a miserable trip. The passengers had to sleep for a few hours each night on a mud bank or slumped in the canoes. The natives had only poles to push the canoes along, and they had to be on the way at dawn in order to utilize every moment of daylight.

At Gorgona the Americans faced a twenty-mile trail over the low mountains, a trail full of potholes and fallen trees. By the end of March, the rainy season had begun and mud was everywhere. It took two days to cover the twenty miles. At the end of the trip, all were appalled by Panama City. It rained continually. Mud, mildew, and fungus oozed everywhere. Sanitation in the tent city was lacking or completely absent. Unwashed raw fruit caused epidemics of dysentery. Malaria and cholera were common, as were threats of smallpox. Vice, depravity, and selfishness thrived.[16]

Huntington and his companions had hoped to catch the *Oregon* as it steamed north on its maiden voyage, but they missed it and had to wait for another ship. The argonauts settled down to wait, meanwhile fighting with each other. Not Huntington. He went into business, selling his medicines (badly needed) and getting other stuff to sell. On his way from Gorgona, he had noticed ranches with food and other provisions—such as primitive cloth, rush mats, and the like—for sale. The business thrived. His buying and selling required frequent trips through the fever-laden jungle. Huntington estimated that he made the crossing at least twenty times. "It was only twenty-four miles," he recalled. "I walked it." What was for other men sheer agony was for Collis Huntington a challenge.

Once he varied his routine. There was a decrepit schooner on a little river. "I went down and bought her," he recalled, "and filled her up with jerked beef, potatoes, rice, sugar and syrup in great bags and brought everything up to Panama and sold them." Stuck on the beach at Panama City for nearly two months, Huntington managed to make $3,000.[17]

May 18, Huntington and his companions escaped via the Dutch bark *Alexander von Humboldt*, with 365 passengers plus crew. Once away from the coast, the *Humboldt* was becalmed. Day after day the bored passengers went through beans, weevily biscuits, tough beef, and vile-tasting water. After a week, all provisions had to be rationed. Finally, on June 26, five weeks since setting off, wind finally stirred the sails. Still, not until August 30, after 104 days at sea, did the *Humboldt* enter San Francisco Bay. Huntington gazed at one of the world's most magnificent harbors, but what he most noticed was the deserted ships. On inquiry, he discovered that, when ships tied up at the wharves, all the crew—from wherever—immediately deserted and headed for the gold.

He had made it, and in the process he earned more money in Panama than he had had with him when he started. And he had avoided tropical fever. But it had been a trip of nearly half a year, dangerous and arduous beyond description, something he never wanted to do again.

ONLY those who were young, physically fit, and full of ambition would dare try to cross Panama, or go overland, from the eastern United States to the Pacific. There was a third way, by boat around Cape Horn, but that took at least six months and was eighteen thousand miles long, not to mention dangerous and expensive.

Lieutenant William T. Sherman went via that route in the first year of the Mexican War, 1846. A West Point graduate in 1840, he had been on recruiting duty in Zanesville, Ohio, when the war began. For Sherman it was "intolerable" that he was missing the hostilities. He left his sergeant in charge and made his way east, traveling by stagecoach (there were no trains west of the mountains). At Pittsburgh he found orders relieving him from recruiting and putting him in Company F, Third Artillery, which was gathering at Governors Island to take a naval transport to California. He took trains from Pittsburgh to Baltimore, then Philadelphia, and finally New York, "in a great hurry" for fear he might miss the boat. He made it, along with 113 enlisted men and four other officers from the company, plus Lieutenant Henry W. Halleck of the Engineers.

The *Lexington* was at Brooklyn, at the Naval Yard, making preparation, which meant taking on the stores sufficient for so many men for such a long voyage. The War Department authorized the officers to draw six months' pay in advance, so they could invest in surplus clothing and other necessaries. When the ship was ready, on July 14, 1846, a steam tug towed her to sea.

Off the *Lexington* sailed, for the tip of the continent. On fair days the officers drilled the men in the manual of arms, or put them to work on the cleanliness of their dress and bunks, with some success. They played games, never gambling, "and chiefly engaged in eating our meals regularly," according to Sherman. "At last," he added, "after sixty days of absolute monotony, the island of Raza, off Rio Janeiro, was descried." After a week in port, taking on supplies, the ship was off again. In October, the *Lexington* approached Cape Horn. "Here we experienced very rough weather, buffeting about under storm stay-sails, and spending nearly a month before the wind favored our passage and enabled the course of the ship to be changed for Valparaiso." At last the swelling sea at Cape Horn was left behind, and two months after leaving Rio, the *Lexington* reached Valparaiso.

There the officers replenished their supplies and the voyage was resumed. Now they were in luck: for the next forty days, they had uninterrupted favorable trade winds. Once they had settled down to sailor habits, time passed quickly. Sherman had brought along all the books he could find in New York about California, and he the other officers read them over and over. About the middle of January, the ship approached the California coast, but when land was made, there "occurred one of those accidents so provoking after a long and tedious voyage." The navigator misread the position of the North Star, and the ship was far north of its destination, Monterey, the capital of Upper California. The captain put about, but a southeast storm came on and buffeted the ship for several days. Eventually it got into the harbor.[18]

It was January 26, 1847. The *Lexington* had left New York 202 days earlier. She was a United States Navy vessel, with a crew of fifty. Her passengers were all young men, fit and eager. The ship of no nation tried to stop her or impede her progress. Yet it took her over half a year to get from New York to Monterey. Her route was the only way to get any goods too large to be handled by horses and a stagecoach from the East Coast to the West Coast.

Besides Sherman's Company F, Third Artillery, there were other American military units, navy and army, either in or making their way via land or sea to California, which the United States was taking over by right of conquest. Sherman traveled up and down the coast, finding the country very lightly populated. San Francisco, then called Yerba Buena, had some four hundred people, most of them Kanakas (natives of the Sandwich Islands). There was a war on; gold had not yet been discovered.[19] But the conclusion of the war, the taking of full legal possession by the United States, and the discovery of gold, all in the next year, led to the rush to California.

The problem of getting there remained. Crossing the Great Plains on one of the emigrant roads meant more than half a year and included crossing the Rocky Mountains, then the Great American Desert, then the Sierra Nevada range. Taking a ship to Panama meant the extreme dangers of catching a mortal fever while crossing the Isthmus and hoping to catch another ship headed north at Panama City. Going all the way around South America by ship was expensive, boring much of the time, and often dangerous. California became a magnet for the argonauts from around the world, especially from the United States, but it must be doubted that ever before had such a desirable place been so isolated.

STILL they came on. One was Mark Hopkins, born on the eastern shore of Lake Ontario on September 3, 1814, who worked as a store-keeper and then a bookkeeper in New York City. About five feet eleven inches tall and weighing 160 pounds, with a straight nose and a neatly cropped beard and dark hair, he cut a handsome figure, and by age thirty-five was making a good salary. He could have been thought of as a man settled in his ways, but it wasn't so. When news of the discovery of gold reached him, he joined with twenty-five others to form a mining company, the New England Trading and Mining Company. The partners invested $500 each. With the money they bought supplies and mining equipment that none of them knew how to use.

In January 1849, they set sail for Cape Horn. It was the beginning of a 196-day trip plagued by storms, bad food, not enough drinking water, and a tyrannical captain. They finally arrived in San Francisco on August 5, 1849. The partners quarreled and soon broke up.[20] After some fruitless wandering around San Francisco and up in the mountains, looking for a spot to start a store, Hopkins in February 1850 went to Sacramento to set up shopkeeping. It was, as it happened, at 52 K Street, next door to a store Huntington had opened. Both men lost their investments in the terrible fire of 1852. Both immediately rebuilt. Out of shared interests and mutual troubles, they developed an abiding affection for each other, different though they were in ages and personalities. They became partners and switched from general-store merchants to dealing in heavy hardware for farms and mines.[21]

CROCKER, Huntington, Sherman, and Hopkins were part of a wave of immigration into California. The forty-niners, who came before statistics keepers from the government appeared to count them, were followed by more fortune seekers some years, less in others. In 1850, a record 55,000 emigrants, nearly all male, headed west from the Missouri bound for California. About 5,000 died from a cholera epidemic, so the next year the emigration count was down to 10,000. But by 1852, it was back up to 50,000. By 1860, more than 300,000 argonauts had made the overland journey.

They came whatever the cost and danger, the boredom or the time lost, the misery of the journey. In 1850, the year the territory became a state, there were in California, according to the U.S. Census, 93,000 white residents and 1,000 Negroes. Some 86,000 of the white population were males, 7,000 females. They were young, more than half under age twenty-four. A decade later, by 1860, the population had jumped more than four times, to 380,000 whites. It included 53,000 "other races," mainly Chinese, but those under twenty-four years of age still predominated. As Lieutenant Sherman put it, "During our time, California was, as now, full of a bold, enterprising, and speculative set of men, who were engaged in every sort of game to make money."[22]

Although they came from different ports and different continents and by different routes, the bulk of the Californians were young Americans who had families back east. They were accustomed to a civilized life— cities, towns, newspapers, roads and wagons, mail, industries. A bit of this was available in California, but there were no industries to serve the population's needs. There was no foundry to make iron products, especially railroad tracks, no plant to make carriages, either horse-drawn or for a train, or one to make a locomotive, or a gun, or powder. It took months to receive a letter, more months to deliver a reply.

At the beginning of the twenty-first century, California led the world in technology and transportation. America and the remainder of the world followed the trend set in California. But in the middle of the nineteenth century, California had made no progress at all. Whatever folks wanted, they had to import, which was terribly expensive and took what seemed like forever.

Most of the young Americans in California were there to pan for or, later, to mine gold, or to make money, wherever and however. "Not only did soldiers and sailors desert," William Sherman noted, "but captains and masters of ships actually abandoned their vessels and cargoes to try their luck at the mines. Preachers and professors forgot their creeds and took to trade, and even to keeping gambling-houses."[23]

There were exceptions. Crocker, Huntington, and Hopkins were storekeepers. Sherman was in the army. But what the state needed was men to plow, to harvest, to sail ships, to engage in manufacturing, to build houses, roads, bridges, and railroads.

There were few among the argonauts who had such skills. In November 1849, Sherman was ordered to instruct Lieutenants Warner and Williamson of the Engineers to survey the Sierra Nevada, to look for a way for a railroad to pass through that range, "a subject that then elicited universal interest." But Lieutenant Warner was killed by Indians, and that cast a pall over the whole enterprise.[24] In any event, there were no rails or spikes or locomotives of any kind in California.

Nor any railroad, come to that, but one was wanted. In 1852, a group of optimistic Californians formulated plans for a railroad to run north and east from Sacramento to tap the rich placer-mining regions of the lower Sierra slopes. Captain William T. Sherman was one of the group. The name of the line was "Sacramento Valley Railroad," and stock was sold at 10 percent down. The next year, after a trip east, Sherman resigned from the army and became a banker in San Francisco and vice-president of the Sacramento Valley Railroad. But the need for an experienced railroad engineer became obvious, and in late 1853 the president of the corporation sailed to New York to find such a man. He conferred with Governor Horatio Seymour of New York State (elected 1852) and his brother Colonel Silas Seymour, who knew and recommended a twenty-eight-year-old engineer, Theodore D. Judah.

Ted Judah was born on March 4, 1826, in Bridgeport, Connecticut. His father, an Episcopal clergyman, moved to Troy, New York, while Ted was still a boy. Ted passed up a naval career to go to the Rensselaer Polytechnic Institute in Troy, where he graduated with an engineering degree. It was an age and a place of great railroad-building. Young Judah threw himself into it with gusto, imagination, and energy. From 1844 on, he was continuously engaged in planning and construction, mainly of railroads. He worked on the Troy and Schenectady Railroad; the New Haven, Hartford and Springfield Railroad; the Connecticut River Railway; the Erie Canal; and several other projects.

At age twenty-one, he married Miss Anna Ferona Pierce, daughter of a Greenfield, Massachusetts, merchant. She was an artist, a lively writer, a splendid personality, and the perfect choice as someone to help his career. She moved with her husband twenty times in a half-dozen years. They went to Niagara Falls, where he planned and built the Niagara Gorge Railroad, one of the great feats of engineering of the 1840s. In an 1889 letter, Anna Judah wrote, "Our cottage on the banks of the river, between the falls and the suspension bridge, is still there, with the beautiful view of both falls and whirlpool rapids below the bridge. He selected the site, built the cottage, there had his railroad office and did his work for that wonderful piece of engineering."[25] Obviously he was a man of many talents, most of all for the America of his day, where everything was booming, and where engineers who knew what they were doing were in great demand.

In 1854, Judah was in Buffalo, building part of what would later become the Erie Railroad system. An urgent telegram from the Seymour brothers summoned him to New York City. He went, had a meeting, and three days later sent Anna a telegram: "Be home tonight; we sail for California April second."

He got back to Buffalo that evening. "You can imagine my consternation on his arrival," Anna wrote. He burst through the door and blurted out, "Anna, I am going to California to be the *pioneer railroad engineer* of the Pacific coast. It is my opportunity, although I have so much here."

She was not about to stand in his way. He had read and studied for years the problem of building a continental railway, and talked about it. "It will be built," he used to say, "and I am going to have something to do with it."[26]

Big talk for a young man still in his twenties. But he was a quick study, hard worker, inventive, sure of himself, not much on humor, and supremely competent—which is why nearly every railroad then being built in the East wanted Judah to be its engineer. Besides being fully employed, Judah had reason to be suspicious of California—everything had to be imported, and his brother Charles, already there, had told him in correspondence something of the harshness of life there. He went anyway, not so much to build the little Sacramento Valley Railroad as to find the route, and the money, and the construction gangs, to build the first transcontinental railroad.[27]

He could hardly wait to get going. In April 1854, three weeks after meeting with the Seymours and the president of the Sacramento Valley Railroad, he had swept up Anna, returned to New York, and was off by steamer for Nicaragua. The ship was crowded, mainly men searching for wealth. But Judah found a number of men returning to California, and he sat at the dining table with them, soaking up all he could about the new land. At Nicaragua he and Anna proceeded by the Nicaragua River and Lake for the Pacific Ocean, where they boarded a crowded Pacific Mail steamer bound for San Francisco. In the middle of May, they arrived in San Francisco. Judah proceeded at once to Sacramento, where he immediately got to work for the Sacramento Valley Railroad.

Until that time, no train whistle had ever been heard west of the Missouri River. Nevertheless, the Californians wanted, needed, had to have a railroad connection with the East. The state legislature passed resolutions demanding that the federal government make it possible. This wasn't calling for the impossible, for by 1854 train technology had advanced far enough to make a transcontinental railroad feasible.

The track structure of a railroad is a thing on which everything else depends. By 1850, Robert L. Stevens's development of all-iron rails in place of wooden rails with a strap-iron surface had been adopted everywhere—and in form and proportion it is still in use today. Stevens also developed the hook-headed spike for fastening the rail to the wooden ties, and connected the rails together at the ends by a rail chair, a device in the rough shape of a "u" that was spiked to the joint tie. Another development: wooden ties surrounded by ballast had replaced the stone blocks (which gave a too-rigid support). Locomotives, developed mainly in the United States, had by 1850 increased in weight and power (by 1860, they were up to forty to fifty tons, with four lead wheels and four driving wheels, thus designated a 4-4-0). New devices were constantly being added, including the reversing gear, the cab for engine driver and fireman, the steam whistle, the headlight, the bell, the equalizing levers and springs, engine brakes, and more, even the cowcatcher on the front of the locomotive. New passenger and freight cars had evolved. Bridges were built to carry trains across rivers and gorges.

It had been thought originally that human beings could not travel at sixty miles per hour, that trains could not climb an incline or go around a curve. But soon engineers discovered that they could climb a grade of 2 percent, or 106 feet per mile, and that a train could manage a curve of ten degrees (radius 574 feet). And sixty miles per hour did not harm the passengers.[28]

O<small>N</small> May 30, 1854, Judah reported to the owners of the Sacramento Valley Railroad that the line from Sacramento to Folsom, on the western edge of the Sierra, was more favorable than any he had ever known. There were no deep cuts to make, no high embankments to be built, and the grade was nearly as regular and uniform as an inclined plane. A railroad could be built at a cost of $33,000 per mile, including everything. He had counted the potential freight-and-passenger traffic on the route and calculated probable earnings for the corporation. They would be huge. "With such a Road and such a business," he concluded, "it is difficult to conceive of a more profitable undertaking."[29] He was too low on his cost estimate and too high on the earning potential, but not by much.

In June, the *Sacramento Union,* one of the leading newspapers in the state and one where Judah had friends, reported, "Mr. Judah is pushing the survey and location with as much rapidity and energy as is consistent with correctness."[30] By June 20, his surveys had reached Folsom. On November 30, the Sacramento Valley Railroad, financed by stock on which investors had put 10 percent down, signed a contract with a well-known firm of Eastern contractors, Robinson, Seymour & Company, for a total of $1.8 million, of which $800,000 was paid in capital stock at par and $700,000 in 10 percent twenty-year bonds ($45,000 per mile).

On February 12, 1855, actual grading commenced with a one-hundred-man workforce. Robinson, Seymour started sending rails and rolling stock on the clipper ship *Winged Racer.* It arrived in June. On August 9, the first rail west of the Missouri, and the first in California, was laid. Two days later, Judah, assisted by three officials of the company, carried a handcar to the tracks and took the first ever railroad ride in California, for a distance of four hundred feet.

Shortly thereafter, the locomotive *Sacramento* landed on the levee, and on August 17 a trial trip to Seventeenth Street delighted the delegation from San Francisco, hundreds strong, who made the journey. By January 1, 1856, the road was bringing in $200 a day. By Washington's Birthday, it had been completed to Folsom and held a grand opening excursion and a ball.[31] A railroad had come to the Pacific Coast.

Over the following months, Judah worked on various railroad surveys and projects; the Sacramento Valley Railroad had a difficult time staying in business, because receipts from the placer mines west of the Sierra fell off and the population of the canyon towns diminished. He was with the California Central Railroad and the Benicia and Sacramento Valley Railroad Company, and then became chief engineer of a yet-to-be-built line called the Sacramento Valley Central Railroad.

Meanwhile, in 1856, he and Anna made three sea voyages back east, to go to Washington to promote a transcontinental railroad, on the correct assumption that only the federal government could afford—by selling the public lands it held—to finance it. By then the railroad across the country had become an obsession with the young engineer. He was ambitious, accustomed to thinking big and getting done what he set out to do, and eager to seize the opportunity. Anna later wrote, "Everything he did from the time he went to California to the day of his death was for the great continental Pacific railway. Time, money, brains, strength, body and soul were absorbed. It was the burden of his thought day and night, largely of his conversation, till it used to be said 'Judah's Pacific Railroad crazy,' and I would say, 'Theodore, those people don't care,' . . . and he'd laugh and say, 'But we must keep the ball rolling.'"[32]

JEFFERSON Davis's report on a Pacific railroad route came out in twelve volumes. The reports were almost as valuable as those of Lewis and Clark. They contained descriptions of every possible feature of the physical and natural history of the country, with numerous plates beautifully colored, barometric reconnaissances, studies of weather, and more. But, according to Judah's biographer Carl Wheat, "It is doubtful if an equal amount of energy was ever spent with so small a crop of positive results."[33] Newly elected Representative John C. Burch of California later wrote, "The Government had expended hundreds of thousands of dollars in explorations, and elaborate reports thereof had been made . . . yet all this did not demonstrate the practicability of a route, nor show the surveys, elevations, profiles, grades or estimates of the cost of constructing the road."[34]

As everyone expected, Davis recommended the Southern route, New Orleans to Los Angeles. To make it happen, Davis had ordered the importing of a corps of camels to provide animal power in the desert. The United States had paid $10 million to Mexico for the Gadsden Purchase (named for James Gadsden of South Carolina, who negotiated the treaty). The Purchase included the southern part of present-day Arizona and New Mexico, which Davis considered the preferred route to the Pacific. No free-state politician would accept such a route. Nor would Judah.

IN 1856, Ted and Anna Judah arrived in Washington on their second trip. There he wrote a pamphlet (published January 1, 1857) that he distributed to every member of Congress and the heads of administrative departments, entitled *A Practical Plan for Building the Pacific Railroad*. He called the railroad "the most magnificent project ever conceived," but added that, though it had been "in agitation for over fifteen years," nothing had been done, except for Davis's useless explorations. Not a single usable survey had even been made. Cutting to the heart of the failure, he wrote, "No one doubts that a liberal appropriation of money or public lands by the General Government ought to insure construction of this railroad, but the proposition carries the elements of its destruction with it; it is the house divided against itself; it [the Pacific railroad] cannot be done until the route is defined; and if defined, the opposing interest is powerful enough to defeat it."

What was needed was facts. Facts based on solid foundations—that is, a genuine survey, one on which capitalists could base accurate cost calculations. The capitalists didn't care how many different varieties and species of plants and herbs, or grass, were located where; they wanted to know the length of the road, the alignment and grades of the proposed railroad, how many cubic yards of dirt to be moved. Any tunnels? How much masonry, and where can it be obtained? How many bridges, river crossings, culverts? What about timber and fuel? Water? What is an engineer's estimate of the cost per mile? What will be its effect on travel and trade?

With such information the capitalist might invest. But the facts were not there, because "Government has spent *so much* money and time upon *so many routes* that we have no proper survey of any one of them."

Judah discussed other factors, such as snow, hostile Indians, probable operating conditions, the development of locomotives, rates and tariffs, and the like. The U.S. Army would benefit.* Then his conclusion: "It is hoped and believed . . . that Congress will, at this session, pass a bill donating alternate sections of land to aid in the construction of this enterprise."[35]

Judah's pamphlet was a splendid idea and an eloquent presentation. The land grant solved at a stroke the problem of financing. But although practical and sensible, it said nothing about whether the eastern terminus of the railroad should be in a free state or a slave state. Congress talked about Judah's proposal, at length, but nothing came of it. A number of bills were submitted, but sectional jealousies defeated every one of them.

---

* It cost $30 million a year to supply the Western troops, by horse or ox team.

Judah wrote to the *Sacramento Union* in January 1859 from Washington that "there is no chance this session of Congress to do anything toward developing the Central Route. The President [James Buchanan] is in favor of the extreme Southern Route for the Pacific Railroad, and, it is understood, will veto any bill for a road over any other to the Pacific."[36] By the spring of 1859, it was clear that if California, Oregon, and the other Western territories (especially Washington and Arizona Territories) wanted a transcontinental railroad they must move of their own accord.

On April 5, 1859, the legislature of California, acting apparently under Judah's urging, passed a resolution calling for a convention to consider the Pacific railroad. Judah returned from the East to attend as representative from Sacramento. The convention opened in Assembly Hall in San Francisco on September 20, 1859, with over one hundred in attendance. Debate centered on the route to be adopted and the western terminus. Judah said such decisions should be left to the corporation picked to build the road, but the convention adopted a resolution recording its "decided preference" for a central route to Sacramento. Having lost there, Judah won on his motion to keep the government from becoming an interested party by keeping it out as a stockholder; such action, he said, "shuts the door to fraud, corruption, or political dishonesty. It affords no hobby to ride, and presents no stepping stone to power, advancement or distinction."[37]

Judah was on the mark, here and in most other resolutions he sponsored and supported. On October 11, the convention's executive committee appointed him as its accredited agent to convey its memorial to Congress, a selection that was universally applauded. The *San Francisco Daily Alta California* newspaper, for example, wrote, "In saying that no better selection could have been made for this responsible duty, we but reiterate what is well known to all who are acquainted with Mr. Judah. Few persons in California have a more thorough acquaintance with the question of the construction of the Pacific railroad than has Mr. Judah, and his services in this capacity will be invaluable."[38]

ON October 20, 1859, Judah and Anna sailed for Panama on the steamer *Sonora* on their third trip east. He was thirty-three years old. He had shown himself to be a practical engineer capable of building railroads and bridges wherever, whenever. He had built the only railroad then running in California. He had great imagination and a most persuasive way of putting his ideas. He had a gracious wife. Only nincompoops called him "Crazy Judah." Those who knew what they were about, such as the delegates to the convention or the newspaper editors, called him inspired. While Crocker, Huntington, and Hopkins were running their stores, and newcomer Leland Stanford was dabbling in politics, and William Sherman had sold out or lost everything in California and was currently a schoolmaster in Louisiana, Theodore D. Judah was preparing the way for the greatest engineering achievement of the nineteenth century.

Chapter Three

THE BIRTH OF
THE CENTRAL PACIFIC
1860–1862

*T*HE railroad Judah wanted, dreamed about, lusted for, was determined to build, had the support, if not the financial backing, of nearly all Americans. The swift growth of California and the West Coast, the obvious fact that as soon as the railroad was built farms and towns would spring up and land values would increase along much of the line across America, the slowness and costs of mail, Indian troubles on the Great Plains and in the Northwest, the so-called Mormon War that sent columns of troops into Utah during 1857–58, the opening of Japan and new commercial treaties with China, among other things, made the desirability of a Pacific railroad obvious to all.

They could not agree on where. It was not just the Southerners who blocked the Northerners; within California, where slavery was never an important issue, the delegates to the 1859 convention from southern California and Arizona objected strongly to a San Francisco or Sacramento terminus. They wanted Los Angeles or San Diego, and argued that, since the Sierra Nevada were almost entirely in California, the railroad would have to be built to the south, where the mountains were not so awesome.

Building the railroad would be, according to William T. Sherman in a letter to his brother John, a congressman from Ohio, "a work of giants. And Uncle Sam is the only giant I know who can grapple the subject."[1]

Sherman was right. No railroad anywhere crossed a continent. To build it would take real men, dedicated men, adventurous men, men of muscle and brain power, men without equal. They must be giants to build it without steam shovels, pile drivers, or power saws, without pipes with water running through them, without portable houses and hospitals, with no internal-combustion-engine trucks and jeeps to move materials, or much of anything else commonplace in the twentieth century to build a railroad. The line had nearly two thousand miles to cross, with great stretches of desert where there was no water, plus vast areas without trees for ties or bridges, stones for footings, or game for food. Then there were three major mountain ranges, the Rockies, the Wasatch, and the Sierra Nevada. There the wind howled and the snow came down in great quantities, the creeks and rivers ran through one-thousand-foot and deeper gorges, the summits were granite, and neither man nor animal lived.

Over most of the route there were no cities except Salt Lake City, no settlements, no farms, no roundhouses, no water pumps, and, except for the mines on the flanks of the Sierra Nevada, there was nothing to carry in, nothing to carry out. The only way to get tracks forward to the end of line was to carry them across tracks already laid. The road would be of a size unprecedented anywhere in the world, and it would go in advance of settlement through an area whose remoteness and climate discouraged or completely precluded rapid migration.

In historian Oliver Jensen's words, to travel the route of the first transcontinental railroad at the beginning of the twenty-first century "is to wonder whether we are today the equals of men who with their bare hands laid those long ribbons of metal over a century ago."[2]

What it would take was the backing of the government, because only the government had the resources—money and land—to finance the project. No corporation, no bank was big enough. In a democracy, it was mandatory to turn to the elected representative body to get the thing done.

*J*UDAH had no doubt that it could be done. On October 20, 1859, he and Anna had set out from San Francisco on the *Sonora* headed for Panama and then it would be on to New York, where he intended to ride a train to Washington to seek money and land from the Congress and the President. Even before the couple left San Francisco Bay, Judah had met California Representative John C. Burch. "Our introduction was immediately followed by a statement to me in detail of the objects and purposes of his mission," Burch later wrote.[3] It was the only thing on Judah's mind, the sole thing he would talk about. As Burch told a meeting of the Territorial Pioneers of California on April 13, 1875, "Never have I seen a more unselfish laborer for a public work, never knew a more self sacrificing spirit than his."[4]

On the trip Judah worked on a bill incorporating the wishes of the Sacramento Convention, including a terminus at Sacramento. Burch, who accompanied them, went over the bill. He and Judah had become, in Burch's words, "immediate and intimate friends. No day passed on the voyage that we did not discuss the subject, lay plans for its success, and indulge pleasant anticipations of those wonderful benefits so certain to follow that success." Burch naturally wanted to know more than just an outline. Judah knew what information was wanted and was ready to answer any and all questions. "On the various provisions of a proper bill to invite the introduction of capital into the work," said Burch later, "and, in short, on every conceivable point he was armed with arguments, facts and figures, and so thoroughly that all questions of political economy involved were of easy solution to his mind."[5]

BURCH was so impressed with what Judah had to say and the way he said it that he agreed to sponsor Judah's bill in the House. Anna helped. Senator Joseph Lane of Oregon was also on the *Sonora* and was naturally in on the Pacific-railroad discussion. One night, at dinner with Burch and Lane, Anna asked, "Would there be any advantage in establishing a Pacific Railway Exhibit on Capitol Hill?" She explained that she had packed the charts her husband had used at the convention, as well as samples of ore, minerals, and fossils she and he had picked up on their Sierra expeditions. Further, she had her sketchbook and a few of her paintings of the mountains. Her husband nodded yes. Burch said it was a splendid idea. Lane agreed.[6]

On his arrival in Washington, Judah sought out California's senators, who read and supported the bill. On December 6, 1859, he got an appointment with President James Buchanan. Together with Burch and Senator William Gwin, he went to the White House to see Buchanan, who had problems of his own but allowed Judah to present the proceedings of the convention in Sacramento. "He received us graciously," Judah wrote, and "expressed himself generally in favor of the Pacific Railroad."[7] In so doing, Buchanan was reversing his own earlier position, but his Democratic Party—like the Republicans—had in 1856 adopted a resolution favoring a Pacific railroad.[8]

Congress had recessed, so Judah and Anna headed west by rail, to promote his railroad bill and to collect "some reliable information with regard to the operating of engines on heavy grades, which becomes highly important in view of solving the question of crossing the Sierra Nevada mountains, as it established the fact that grades as high as one hundred and fifty feet per mile can be overcome and operated with perfect safety." He found out that such was actually the case with the Baltimore and Ohio, which in crossing the Appalachian Mountains provided an example of what could and should be done. On his way west, he also spoke to investors, and at meetings in New York, Albany, Syracuse, Buffalo, Cleveland, Columbus, Chicago, and Cincinnati, in order, as he said, "to awaken as much interest as possible in our efforts."[9]

O N returning to Washington, with Burch's support, Judah was given a room in the Capitol to promote his railroad. Judah was a born genius at publicity, at pushing projects, and at persuasiveness. At Anna's suggestion, he made the room into the Pacific Railroad Museum, displaying maps, diagrams, surveys, reports, and other data, as well as her collection and paintings. He had it completed by January 14, 1860, and from then until he left for California a half-year later he was, in his words, "constantly engaged in endeavoring to further the passage of a Pacific Railroad Bill." Scores of members of both houses, officials of the departments and bureaus, plain citizens, reporters, and editors came to call. "His knowledge of his subject was so thorough," Representative Burch said, "his manners so gentle and insinuating, his conversation on the subject so entertaining that few resisted his appeals."[10]

More than a few, it turned out. Judah was not convincing enough. There were practical problems—how to get over mountains, across rivers, through deserts—and the location, ever the location. Southerners would not support any railroad north of the Mason-Dixon Line. Judah was in the galleries when Representative Samuel Curtis of Iowa, chairman of the House Select Committee on the Pacific Railroad, introduced a bill to build a transcontinental road from Iowa to Sacramento. Curtis had a number of inducements to investors in his bill, including giving land along the route to the corporation that built the road, but his bill differed from the one Judah and Burch were working on in that Curtis proposed a generous government loan of $60 million (thought to be about half of the projected costs). This loan was to be in the form of 5 percent thirty-year bonds which the newly formed corporation could sell on the open market. The debt would be repaid when the bonds matured.

Southerners tacked onto the measure a provision calling for a parallel route through the Southwest. Missouri and Iowa were fighting over the eastern terminus. Curtis's bill was sent back to committee for further consideration. That was almost surely a death warrant, but Curtis and his supporters got the bill entered on the calendar for the coming session. It would not be debated until December 1860.

*T*HERE was good news for Judah that spring of 1860. In May, in Chicago, Abraham Lincoln was nominated for president by the Republicans on a platform that called for full government support of the Pacific railway. In June, Congress passed an act granting federal aid to an overland telegraph from Missouri to San Francisco. That act cut through the quibbling over whether or not the federal government could support an internal improvement in states as well as in the territories. (The telegraph line was completed in 1861.)

There was bad news too. Visitors came to Judah's Pacific Railroad Museum to gawk, to talk, to be impressed, and to ask questions—chiefly, How do you propose to get across the Sierra Nevada mountains? It was one thing for the Baltimore and Ohio to cross the Appalachians, another altogether to attempt the Sierra.

"He made up his mind," according to Anna, that he would never go to Washington again till he had been on the Sierra Nevada and made a survey, so that when he returned it would be "with his maps, profiles, estimates etc. etc. for a railroad across the same."[11] He was sure it could be done, but he had to convince the politicians, so that "what I believe without the surveys I can intelligently show to senators, members of congress, etc. With facts and figures they cannot gainsay my honest convictions, as now."

In the summer of 1860, Judah and Anna set sail for California. Judah wrote a report to the executive committee of the convention, which had sent him to Washington. He covered in considerable detail his own activities and what had happened to his bill, and Curtis's bill, but had to confess that "the debate on the slavery question, and other matters of little moment [sic], left us no time for the consideration of the Pacific Railroad Bill." Then he made up his expense account. He said the whole trip cost him $2,500, but he was charging the convention only $40, to cover his printing expenses.[12]

Never before, one would guess, and never again, one would be certain, has anyone turned in such a low expense account. Never before or since has anyone wanted a railroad so badly. Anna later wrote, "Oh, how we used to talk it all over on the steamer enroute to California in July, 1860."[13] Judah was now determined that, rather than ask Congress again to support some hypothetical company which would pick its own route, they should first organize the company itself and then present to the Congress accurate and definite surveys of its particular route.

To make that possible, immediately on arrival in Sacramento, Judah set off for the Sierra. He may have been on the payroll of the Sacramento Valley Railroad, whose owners wanted him to hunt for a wagon road from Dutch Flat over the mountains past Donner Lake to the mines in Nevada. Or maybe not—it isn't certain. In any event, he was doing what he loved best, sleeping in the open, camping out in wilderness mountain country, cooking over a fire, eating with his back to a tree, watching out for mountain lions, taking barometric readings to establish altitude, mapping out a route, noting the flora and fauna, looking everywhere, enjoying life as few people ever have.

Anna wrote that he went over the different passes, including Henness, Beckworth, and Donner. "No one knew what he was doing! The 'engineer' was in the mountains. I remained in Sacramento among friends."[14] Sometimes she joined him on his excursions, painting while he measured.

Judah was working his way up the ridge line between the North Fork of the American River and the Bear River in California, going from Auburn through Clipper Gap to Illinoistown (soon renamed Colfax), past Cape Horn, on to Dutch Flat, and then, possibly, to Emigrant Gap and Donner Pass. This was rugged mountainous country, extremely picturesque, but it seemed there was no chance for a railroad beyond Dutch Flat. At Cape Horn, for example, two miles above Illinoistown, the drops beneath the old unused wagon road Judah was following were as much as fifteen hundred feet. It seemed to everyone who had been there that it was impossible to build a rail line around Cape Horn.

Everyone, that is, except Judah. The man who had built the suspension bridge at Niagara Falls knew that it mattered not if grade for the track was built above a fifteen-hundred-foot drop or over a fifteen-foot drop. What interested him most were the widely spaced saddles in the ridge line. By weaving in and out of them, the railroad could ascend toward the ultimate crest of the mountains on an even grade not in excess of the capability of the locomotives, or a maximum of a hundred feet per mile.[15]

BY this time, early October 1860, most of America was discussing the presidential election, with the South threatening to secede if Lincoln and the Republicans won. But out in California, Judah was preparing his maps and reports on the Sierra. A letter arrived, from a Dutch Flat druggist, Daniel W. Strong, called "Doc" by his customers. Doc had heard about Judah's exploring and wanted to show him the old emigrant road from Donner Lake, which had been abandoned after the Donner tragedy in 1846–47. Doc was sure it was the best place to build a railroad, because there the east-west ridge reached the summit of the chain on what amounted to a plateau. Everywhere else the Sierra crested twice, parallel ridges with a deep valley between them. Here there was only one crest, so a railroad climbing up from Dutch Flat would have to surmount only it. The chief engineering problem would be to find a way down a thousand-foot rocky wall past Donner Lake and along Donner Creek to the canyon leading to Utah formed by the Truckee River.

The day Doc Strong's letter arrived, Judah set out to see him at Dutch Flat. Anna wrote about what happened when they met. The two men became fast friends immediately. Strong, "truly a mountaineer," led Judah on horseback up the ridge to Donner Pass. "No one knew what they were doing!" according to Anna. She adds, "Dr. Strong used to tell a thrilling story of their last night in the mountains [when they] came near being snowed in and were obliged to get up in the middle of the night from their camp and started out in the darkness to find the trail and none too soon were they." Her husband "could not sleep or rest after they got into Dutch Flat and Strong's store, till he had stretched his paper on the counter and made his figures thereon.

"Then, turning to Dr. Strong, he said for the first time, 'Dr. I shall make my survey over this, the Donner Pass or the Dutch Flat route, above every other.'"[16]

"The next morning," Strong wrote, Judah "said to me, 'Give me some writing materials'—I produced some and he sat down and drew up what he called 'articles of association' [for the Central Pacific Railroad] and he shoved them across the table to me and said, 'sign for what you want'" in the way of stock.[17]

*I*T was mid-October. Judah wanted to create the corporation immediately. Under California laws, it was required that a railroad corporation have subscriptions to capital stock in the amount of $1,000 for each mile of road projected, 10 percent of which was to be paid in cash to the company treasury before incorporation. Judah estimated the mileage from Sacramento to the Nevada state line to be 115 miles, meaning he and Strong needed subscriptions of $115,000. While Judah went to work on a pamphlet designed to entice big investors in San Francisco, Strong worked on the mining communities of Dutch Flat, Illinoistown, Grass Valley, and Nevada City and brought in $46,500. Judah set out to get the nearly $70,000 remaining.

He wrote a pamphlet, published November 1, 1860, entitled *Central Pacific Railroad Company of California*.* He opened with the statement that he and Strong had "some newly discovered facts with reference to the route of the Pacific Railroad through the State of California." He claimed incorrectly that the line was short, only eighty miles from the foothills to Truckee Lake. "No serious engineering difficulties present themselves."[18]

Five days later, Abraham Lincoln was elected president. The next day, the South Carolina legislature called by unanimous vote for a convention to meet on December 20 to consider secession. The only thing that mattered to Judah at the moment was that, with the Republicans in control of Congress and the distinct possibility that the Southern representatives would walk out, the chances for passing the Curtis Bill or something like it were greatly enhanced. All of which gave him added incentive to get the Central Pacific incorporated.

* This was the first public use of the name Central Pacific.

Anna wrote that "night and day he talked and labored with the capitalists in San Francisco." On November 14, 1860, he wrote Strong, "I have struck a lucky streak, and shall fill up the list without further trouble. I have got one of the richest concerns in California into it."[19] The next evening, he left Anna at the San Francisco Russ House "firm in the faith that the gentlemen he was to meet that evening in the office of a leading law firm would give him the aid he required to make his survey the following spring; in other words—would be his backers, for the Pacific R.R. Co. He left me in high hopes."

Judah was shattered by the reaction. His potential backers scoffed at his idea. For example, how did he know he could build a line across the Sierra Nevada for $70,000 per mile? Judah had not made a proper survey and needed money to do so. And what about the snow? Judah had not a shred of information about how to keep the road free of snow. Besides, there was no guarantee the Congress would pass the Curtis or any other bill aiding the railroad, and even if it did, building the thing would take twelve to twenty years. Judah shook his head—he asserted he could do it in seven years. They said they could make more money quicker in other investments.

Judah went back to his wife and told her, "Pack your bag, for I am going up to Sacramento on the boat to-morrow. Remember what I say to you to-night so you can tell me sometime. Not two years will go over the head of these gentlemen I have left to-night, but they would give all they have to have what they put away to-night; I shall never talk or labor any more with them—I am going to Sacramento to see what I can do with the wealthy business men of that city."[20]

S TARTING the day after he arrived, Judah held several meetings at the St. Charles Hotel in Sacramento, on J Street. At some as many as thirty men were present, at others fewer than a dozen. Dr. Strong was there, along with merchant Lucius Booth, James Bailey (a Sacramento jeweler), Cornelius Cole (later congressman and senator from California), B. F. Leete (one of Judah's surveyors), and some others.

One of those present was Charles Crocker—now weighing 250 pounds—who was running a dry-goods store in town, had been present for the organization of the Republican Party in California (1856), and had just been elected to the state legislature. Collis Huntington was also there, with his partner in their general store, Mark Hopkins. So was Le-land Stanford, also a storekeeper but intensely involved in politics as a Republican candidate for state treasurer and later for governor.

"We none of us knew anything about railroad building," Crocker later said, "but at the same time were enterprising men, and anxious to have a road built, and have it come to Sacramento."[21]

Judah presented his case. He had decided to forget about a transcon-tinental railroad and concentrate instead on getting up to the Califor-nia mountains, perhaps crossing them to the Nevada line. According to Anna, what he told the assembled potential investors, nearly all of them Sacramento store owners, was: "You are tradesmen here in Sacra-mento city, your property and your business is here—help me make the survey, I'll make you the Central Pacific railroad company and with the [congressional] bill passed, you have the control of business which will make your fortune in trades, etc. etc. If nothing more, why, you can own a wagon road [from Dutch Flat over the mountains] if not a rail-road."[22]

Ears turned up and attention concentrated on Judah. Here was what the merchants wanted to hear. They could sell more of their goods, ex-pand their business, and stifle competition. Their property would become more valuable. They could control the traffic from their city to the Nevada mines and thus control that market. Judah told them that he had crossed the crest of the Sierra on twenty-three separate occasions, that he was convinced the Donner Pass route beyond Dutch Flat was the best, and that he had to have financial backing for the purpose of making a careful instrumental survey of the proposed line.

"I think every one present," Cornelius Cole later wrote, "agreed to take stock in the concern. Several subscribed for fifty shares each, but no one for more than that. I took fifteen shares . . . and subsequently ac-quired ten more."[23] The initial money was to pay for a survey beginning on the levee on Front Street and then heading up the American River.

Judah had his start. He told Anna the next morning, "If you want to see the first work done on the Pacific railroad look out of your bed room window. I am going to work there this morning and I am going to have these men pay for it."

She replied, "I am glad, for it's about time somebody else helped."[24] Looking out the window later that morning, she saw her husband and a few helpers run their lines down the muddy streets with chains and stakes and heavy brass instruments.

ONE man, in fact, had refused to subscribe at the meeting. He was Collis Huntington, who later admitted: "I did not give anything. When the meeting was about to break up, one or two said to me, 'Huntington, you are the man to give to this enterprise.' I gave two or three hundred for a road. . . . I did not want any of the stock. This railroad was a thing so big there was not much use starting out expecting to do much towards building it. I told Mr. Judah as I left—'if you want to come to my office some evening I will talk with you about this railroad.'"

Judah was there the next evening. He talked and talked, and convinced Huntington to put up $35,000 to do a thorough instrumental survey. "I said all right I will pay that, but I will not agree to do anything after that," Huntington stated about the single best deal he ever made. "I may go on," he added, "but don't promise to do anything now but make a survey." He, his partner Hopkins, Stanford, James Bailey, Crocker, and Lucius Booth were all Sacramento merchants with goods to sell to Nevada miners, who were almost as numerous and as much in need of goods as those in California had been a decade before.[25]

"We organized a corps of engineers in the spring [of 1861]," Crocker later said, "and sent them with Mr. Judah at the head to run a line along the mountains to the Big Bend of the Truckee River [today's Wadsworth, Nevada]. It was merely a trial line; what we called a base line—but from that we found that the grades which Judah had said could be obtained were actually practicable, and were obtained."[26]

JUDAH, accompanied by Strong and others, made his way to Dutch Flat that spring, then waited for the snows to melt before going on. Strong said that it took "pretty much all summer to make the survey to the State Line."[27] At various times Huntington, Crocker, and Stanford joined Judah in the Sierra for a personal look. At one point Huntington, Judah, and a hired Chinese employed to carry blankets and provisions spent a week in the canyon of the Feather River and decided it was wholly impractical for a railroad.

ON June 28, 1861, with the Civil War already under way, the Central Pacific Railroad of California came into formal existence. It was incorporated with Stanford as president, Huntington vice-president, Hopkins treasurer, James Bailey secretary, Judah chief engineer, and with Stanford, Crocker, Bailey, Judah, Huntington, Hopkins, Strong, and Charles Marsh as directors. Their combined wealth, according to Huntington, was $159,000. Neither Congress, the state of California, nor any syndicates of capitalists had put a single penny into the corporation. California's first and greatest historian, Hubert Howe Bancroft, commented that for so "stupendous and hazardous an enterprise it appears an act of madness or of inspiration. . . . Many said that those Sacramento merchants who had ventured upon it would sink their personal fortunes in the canyons of the Sierra."[28]

Stanford had become the Republican candidate for governor, which was still the chief political concern in California, despite the beginning of the Civil War back east. Judah wrote Strong, "Election and politics so monopolize everything here now that our people have very little time to talk railroad matters. . . . I am trying to put my little road upon its legs, and it looks rather favorable, but like everything else, can do nothing with it until after the election."[29]

On August 7, 1861, Judah was quoted in the *Union* as saying, "The problem as to crossing the Sierra Nevada has been solved."[30] It had indeed. William Hood, for many years chief engineer of the Central Pacific, declared in 1925, "Were there now no railroad over the Sierra, the Donner Lake Route would still be selected over all others as the best possible route."[31]

On September 4, Stanford won election as governor. Three weeks later, Judah placed before the partners his written report on the results of his months of careful work.

It was a masterpiece. Judah opened by listing the most objectionable features of locating the railroad in the Sierra Nevada: first, the great elevation to be overcome; second, the impracticability of river crossings on account of the deep gorges cut by the rivers; third, that the Sierra possessed two distinct summit ranges to be crossed. But the line he had found ran up the ridge, with maximum grades of but 105 feet to a mile, and with no major canyons or rivers to cross. As for the double summit, he had found a route that entirely avoided the second range. His line ran up the divide between the rivers "from gap to gap" in order to secure the best possible gradients—and was in fact the line followed by the Central Pacific.

He discussed the snow problem and was unduly optimistic—"a Railroad Line, upon this route, can be kept open during the entire year," even though the snow would constitute a not inconsiderable problem. He thought that eighteen tunnels, mainly through the mountains towering above Donner Lake, would be driven with relative ease, even the longest, at 1,370 feet. The route contained extensive forests of pitch and sugar pine, fir, and abundant quantities of cedar and tamarack, which would make excellent supports for bridge trusses and crossties and provide lumber for buildings. He concluded the report with a list of the maps and profiles attached to the original copy.[32]

If Huntington, Crocker, Hopkins, Stanford, and the others needed any convincing that Judah knew more about the Sierra Nevada and about railroads than anyone else, his report did it. Judah, meanwhile, spent September mapping his surveys, making profiles, and gathering information for use with the Congress. He was confident he could go to Washington on a ship to get at least some aid. On September 2, he had written Strong, "I think the next Congress will be a favorable one to procure lands from the Government, and perhaps it may be money; but of the latter I do not feel by any means so certain; but the lands [i.e., alternate sections granted by Congress to the railroad for every mile built] do not create any debt, and the feeling towards California ought to be a good one."[33] That last phrase was very much on the mark, for California's gold and silver—and Nevada's—were helping pay for the war just started, and there was a fear in Washington, sparked by some loose talk in California, that the state might follow the South and leave the Union.

The directors—one of whom had just been elected governor on a Republican ticket—would have none of secession. Instead, on October 9, well pleased with Judah's report, they adopted a resolution: "That Mr. T. D. Judah . . . proceed to Washington, on the steamer of the 11th Oct. inst., as the accredited agent of the Central Pacific Railroad Company of California, for the purpose of procuring appropriations of land and U.S. Bonds from Government, to aid in the construction of this Road."[34]

Judah was off. He had with him everything to convince the congressmen, including charming sketches of Donner Pass done by Anna to hang in his railroad museum in the Capitol, not to mention his own intimate and unique knowledge of railroads and the mountains. Best of all, the

Deep South congressmen represented states that had left the Union, meaning they had left Congress, which meant that the votes to block any route north for slavery were no longer there. Let them go, Judah must have thought, and good riddance to such bad seeds. A prominent historian of the railroad, Robert Russell of Western Michigan University, puts it as his opinion that because the Southerners were gone "Congress was enabled to enact Pacific railway legislation several years earlier than it otherwise could have done."[35]

To add to Judah's already overflowing pleasure and confidence, a fellow passenger was newly elected Representative Aaron A. Sargent of California. Thus, as Judah explained it, "a good opportunity was afforded for explaining many features of our project not easily understood . . . which explanations were of great service to us in future operations." As indeed they were. Judah spent the days during the long voyage showing Sargent his maps, the evenings extolling the benefits of a transcontinental railroad.[36] Sargent was convinced and promised his help.

On arrival at New York, Judah worked up a report on the Sierra surveys of which he published a thousand copies. He distributed it, as he said, "among railroad men, where likely to do us most good, sending copies to President Lincoln, the heads of Departments and to our Senators and Representatives in Congress." And he saw to it that the report was published in the *American Railroad Journal*.[37]

Even before Judah arrived in Panama, there was an event of grand importance to the scientific and industrial revolution and for the building of railroads: the first transcontinental telegraph line was opened. By the time Judah reached New York, the glamorous year-and-a-half life of the Pony Express was over.[38]

BACK on the Pacific Coast, the principals of the Central Pacific—Stanford, Crocker, Huntington, and Hopkins—moved on their own, apparently without Judah's knowledge, by drawing up on November 27, 1861, articles of association for the Dutch Flat and Donner Lake Wagon Road Company. Four hundred shares of stock at $1,000 each were issued, with Crocker as president and Hopkins as secretary and treasurer. The owners' explanation was that the wagon road ran along Judah's line into Nevada and was to help the Central Pacific cross the mountains. It would be used to transport supplies such as rails in ox- and mule-drawn wagons to construction forces working in advance of the railroad as far away as the eastern slope of the Sierra. But the real object may have been to collect tolls on the road from Nevada miners and California merchants. Three toll gates were established—at Dutch Flat, Polley's Station, and Donner Lake. Whatever Judah (who had thought of the road first) was able to get out of Washington, these guys were going to get their investment back—and make some money—off the wagon road.[39]

In Washington, Judah had much to work with, including the fact that he had been in the capital three times already, was well known to the congressmen, had been lobbying for land grants and money, and had convinced most of the non-Southerners. And this time, December 1861, he had with him a detailed engineering plan and supporting data and a bona fide corporation ready to start. And he had the active support of Congress. And the president of the corporation was the incoming Republican governor of California. A few days before the session began, Senator James A. McDougall of California helped Judah draft a bill that followed, in general, the Curtis Bill. Sargent took active charge of it in the House, where it was introduced.

Huntington came to the capital right after Christmas to find Judah discouraged. Although he had his survey maps and Anna's Sierra paintings on display in his railroad museum, and had shown them and talked to many members of Congress, nothing concrete had happened. The House Select Committee on the Pacific Railroad had not even met.[40]

INDEED, it was almost impossible, in those first months of the war, to get Congress to concern itself with anything other than raising and equipping the Northern army. The North had lost Fort Sumter on April 12–13, 1861. Lincoln had called for militia to suppress the Rebellion and proclaimed the blockade of Southern ports. On July 21, the North had lost the First Battle of Bull Run. On July 24, Lincoln had replaced General Irvin McDowell with General George B. McClellan. In December, Dakota Territory was formed from parts of Minnesota and Nebraska Territories, along with Nevada Territory from part of Utah Territory.

Despite these events, on January 21, 1862, Sargent—encouraged by Judah and Huntington—took a bold step when, in the midst of debate on another subject, he got the floor and spoke at length on Judah's work, accomplishments, and estimates, and pointed to the Pacific railroad as a military necessity to the nation. He made all the familiar arguments: the government would save millions of dollars in transporting troops, munitions, and mail; the Western Indians would be quelled; emigration to the coast would speed up; the Great Plains would be developed; trade with Japan and China would jump; California's loyalty to the Union would be assured; no foreign army would dare attack California.

Judah complained that Sargent spoke before an empty hall, but the speech had its effect. Within a week, the House appointed a special subcommittee of the Pacific Railroad Committee to work on Judah's bill.[41]

Judah was an excellent lobbyist. He got an appointment as secretary of the Senate Pacific Railroad Committee (with Senator McDougall as chairman) and as clerk of the subcommittee on the Pacific railroad in the House, where Sargent was a member. The appointments gave Judah what amount to a semiofficial standing before Congress. He had charge of all the committee papers and documents, and, even more surprising and momentous, the privilege of the floor of both Senate and House. Any lobbyist at any time would give his right arm for the privileges Judah had. He held the key position and he used it well.

The debate over the bill in the House was ferocious. At one point in the spring of 1862, Judah had to step in to deal with the grave danger that consideration would be extended until the next session, which probably meant the end of the bill. Much of the debate centered on the amounts of money or land to go to the corporations building the road, or on how to ensure the construction of the middle part of the line by companies that were to start at either end. Judah would give a little here, take a little there, while keeping focused on getting the bill as a whole passed.[42] He accepted—knowing vaguely what it would cost—an amendment by Representative Thaddeus Stevens. Stevens, who owned a foundry in Pennsylvania, insisted on a requirement that all rails and other ironwork be of American manufacture. Stevens declared he was for passing the law not because of the iron rails he could sell but because someday the Southerners would return to Congress "with the same arrogant, insolent dictation which we have cringed to for twenty years, forbidding the construction of any road that does not run along our southern border."[43] There were other quibbles—the gauge of the track (to be decided by the President), the grade (no higher than 116 feet to the mile), the curves (none over ten degrees, which eliminated the use of switchbacks and forced the companies to resort to far more expensive tunnels), and more.

*F*ORTUNATELY for Judah, for the Central Pacific, and for the line running west from the Missouri River, whatever it was to be named, the President took as active an interest as his time allowed. Lincoln made it clear to the congressmen that despite the war he advocated the bill's passage and the construction of the road, and he wanted it started right away. Grenville Dodge, then serving as a general in the Union Army, said that Lincoln told him and others that the road had to be built "not only as a military necessity, but as a means of holding the Pacific Coast to the Union."[44]

On May 6, 1862, one month after General Ulysses Grant won the first victory for the Union at Shiloh—but at a tremendous cost in lives—and after the Union *Monitor* fought for five hours against the Confederate *Merrimac* in the first battle ever between ironclad gunboats, and while General George B. McClellan and his army were stuck in the Peninsula of Virginia, the House passed the Pacific Railroad Bill by a vote of 79 to 49.

Two days later, on May 8, Judah called for a meeting of the Senate Pacific Railroad Committee. Once again there were troubles and delays. Representative Justin Morrill of Vermont, who could be farseeing on some matters,* commented sourly that those who were putting up the capital were not interested in building a railroad west from the Missouri River, or in the Central Pacific, if it went farther east than the Nevada silver mines, through uninhabited territories. The railroad, he charged, was interested in grabbing off subsidies at either end. Besides, Morrill grumbled, the nation could hardly afford both guns and railroads. Why not wait until after the war?[45]

Judah stayed with it. When the war was over—surely not too long now—there would be lots of ex-soldiers looking for work, lots of money from investors seeking profitable ventures, lots of need for the railroad. Robert Russell argues that, because the war had accustomed Congress to appropriations of vast proportions, the bill went through; he adds that it was a matter of pride with many congressmen "to demonstrate that the Union was strong enough to crush rebellion and take measures to insure its future prosperity at the same time."[46]

---

* He was the sponsor of the Morrill Act, which granted to each loyal state thirty thousand acres for each senator and representative for the purpose of endowing at least one state agriculture college. The "Morrill Land Grant" act made possible the great state universities. It passed on July 2, 1862.

On May 23, 1862, Judah wrote to the editors of the *Sacramento Union*, "The Pacific Railroad is a fixed fact and you can govern yourselves accordingly." He added that the bill would come up for a vote "in about 10 days when, should our armies have met with no serious reverses, we may reasonably expect the passage of the Pacific Railroad Bill through the Senate."[47] That same day, Confederate General Stonewall Jackson led eighteen thousand men on an attack at Front Royal in the Valley of Virginia to force the Union forces to retreat to Winchester, where he again struck and routed them on May 25. Jackson then marched north, and suddenly the capital was under threat.

But Jackson was stopped—he had to march toward Richmond because of McClellan's threat to that city—and the Senate passed the bill on June 20, by a vote of 35 to 5. The House concurred in the Senate amendments a few days later and sent the completed bill forward to the President. Lincoln signed it on July 1, even as Malvern Hill, the last battle of the Seven Days' Battles in the Peninsula, was being fought, costing McClellan's army a thousand dead and three thousand wounded and greatly depressing the nation.

*T*HE Pacific Railroad Bill was complicated to an almost incomprehensible degree. It had to be substantially changed two years later, and still was the basis for innumerable lawsuits over the next two decades and eventually the creation of the Populist and the Progressive parties. But its basic outline was what Judah wanted. It called for the creation of a corporation, the Union Pacific (the name being a nice touch in 1862), that would build west from the Missouri River, while the Central Pacific would build east from Sacramento. Capital stock of the UP was to be a hundred thousand shares at $1,000 each, or $100 million. Both roads would have a right of way of two hundred feet on both sides of the road over public lands and would be given five alternate sections (square miles) on each side per mile, or sixty-four hundred acres per mile.*

The railroad corporations would receive financial aid in the form of government bonds at $16,000 per mile for flat land, $32,000 for foothills,

---

* Far from costing the government anything, the granting of land meant that the alternate sections retained by the government would increase enormously in value as the railroads progressed and finally joined.

and $48,000 per mile for mountainous terrain after they had built forty miles approved by government commissioners. They would also get land for stations, machine shops, sidings, and other necessary structures, as well as whatever they needed in the way of earth, stone, timber, and other available materials for construction.

The corporations could get advance money in the form of 6 percent government bonds. This was a loan, not a gift; the bonds were to constitute a first mortgage on the railroads. The government was loaning its credit, in other words, not its money—the railroads would have to sell the bonds. And pay for them. The contract was that the government should pay the 6 percent interest on the bonds in semiannual payments, but that the whole amount of the loan, principal and interest, should be repaid in thirty years, minus the sum of the value of the services performed for the government during that time in carrying mails, transporting troops, government stores, and so forth.

The Central Pacific was required to complete fifty miles within two years and fifty miles each year thereafter, and the entire road was to be completed by July 1, 1876, under pain of forfeiture.[48]

That was by no means all of it, but it was enough for Judah to flash the first word to his Sacramento colleagues by the newly established telegraph: "We have drawn the elephant. Now let us see if we can harness him."

*H*OW well he had done his work can hardly be imagined today. At the time, forty-four members of the House, seventeen senators, and the secretary of the Senate tried to sum it up. They gave Judah a signed written testimonial of appreciation:

> Learning of your anticipated speedy departure for California on Pacific Railroad business, we cannot let this opportunity pass without tendering to you our warmest thanks for your valuable assistance in aiding the passage of the Pacific Railroad bill through Congress.
>
> Your explorations and surveys in the Sierra Nevada Mountains have settled the question of practicability of the line, and enable many members to vote confidently on the great measure, while your indefatigable exertions and intelligent explanations of the practical features of the enterprise have gone very far to aid in its inauguration.[49]

If any one man made the transcontinental railroad happen, what Horace Greeley called "the grandest and noblest enterprise of our age," it was Theodore D. Judah.

Henry V. Poor, at the time the editor of the *American Railway Journal*, said that the North, upon the outbreak of the Civil War, "inferring its powers from its necessities, instinctively and instantly made a bold and masterly stroke for empire as well as for freedom."[50]

Chapter Four

THE BIRTH OF
THE UNION PACIFIC
1862–1864

*T*HE men who founded the Union Pacific were like Lincoln's generals, some of them good, many of them bad, most of them indifferent. No American president had ever before had to fight a civil war involving hundreds of thousands of troops. No one had founded anything like the Union Pacific, which, like the Central Pacific, had in front of it the most formidable task imaginable.* The wonder isn't how many things they screwed up, but how much they did right.

*T*HE 1862 Pacific Railroad Act authorized the creation of the Union Pacific Railroad.† The bill mandated the 163 men appointed in the act to serve as a board of commissioners who were to work out a provisional organization of the company. They held their first meeting in Chicago.

---

* As Representative William Holman of Indiana said during the debate over the original Pacific Railroad Bill, "This road could never be constructed on terms applicable to ordinary roads. . . . It is to be constructed through almost impassable mountains, deep ravines, canyons, gorges, and over arid and sandy plains. The Government must come forward with a liberal hand, or the enterprise must be abandoned forever."

† Which made it the first corporation chartered by the national government since the Second Bank of the United States (created in 1816, it lost its charter in 1836).

They were prominent railroad men, bankers, and politicians, with five commissioners appointed by the President. When the three-day meeting opened on September 2, 1862, only sixty-seven of the directors bothered to attend and, like those who were absent, they had deep doubts about how this railroad was going to be built. They selected Samuel R. Curtis as temporary chairman; Curtis at this time was a major general in the Union Army. Mayor William B. Ogden of Chicago was made president, and Henry V. Poor of New York, editor of the *American Railway Journal*, secretary. Everyone present agreed with Samuel Curtis's belief that, "notwithstanding the grant is liberal, it may still be insufficient."[1]

The directors also agreed that their biggest problem was the first-mortgage nature of the government bonds, which would make it near impossible for the company to sell its own bonds. But there were many other difficulties needing attention. Most of all the project needed promoters who were tough and practical. Men who could lobby Congress for a new, more generous bill as well as convince their fellow citizens to buy stocks and bonds in the company. Men who would organize the vastest enterprise ever seen in North America, except for the Union and Confederate armies, and push the railroad across the continent in the face of every obstacle.

GENERAL Dodge, meanwhile, was cutting a swath for himself in the Union Army. He was wounded at the Battle of Pea Ridge, Arkansas (March 6–8, 1862), and it was while he was recovering in the hospital in St. Louis that men interested in the Pacific railroad had visited him and urged him to leave the army. "I have enlisted for the period of the war," was Dodge's reply.[2]

Two months later, he had got another plea to quit the army and go to work for the Pacific railroad. This time it came from Peter Reed of Moline, Illinois, a politician and promoter of the Rock Island line. With the Pacific Railroad Bill on the verge of passing, he reminded Dodge, "You once told me that if we could get the Pacific railroad through you would quit the army and identify yourself with it. In the first place, Dodge, you cannot possibly last where the labor and excitement are so great. . . . The Pacific railroad is a big lick in your affairs and mine, and you can hardly keep out."[3] Dodge again refused.

In June 1862, out of the hospital, Dodge wrote his wife, "I am at my old job again—railroading." The Union Army had to build its own lines to move troops and supplies in the South, and Dodge was building a road sixty-four miles long, to Corinth, Mississippi. He stayed with building new roads or repairing old ones. In his memoirs, Grant said of Dodge, "Besides being a most capable soldier, he was an experienced railroad builder. He had no tools to work with except those of the pioneer—axes, picks and spades." He had men making the tools, others working on bridges, others making the grade, still others laying the track. "Thus every branch of railroad building," Grant wrote, "was all going on at once. . . . General Dodge had the work finished in forty days after receiving his order."

Grant was destined to play a major role in the building of the American railroad system. Like Lincoln, he was enamored with the trains. He had first seen one while on his way to West Point in 1839. It ran from Harrisburg to Philadelphia. When he got on it, "I thought the perfection of rapid transit had been reached. We traveled at least eighteen miles an hour when at full speed, and made the whole distance averaging as much as twelve miles an hour. This seemed like annihilating space."[4] That last sentence summed up exactly the sentiments of the thinking men of the age.

After Dodge had completed laying the track to Corinth, Grant put him to repairing lines torn up by the enemy. "The number of bridges to rebuild was 18, many of them over deep and wide chasms; the length of the road repaired was 182 miles."[5] As Dodge's biographer J. R. Perkins says, with only a bit of exaggeration, "Railroading was new; much of the machinery was defective, and the art of road building was all but in its infancy."[6]

Nevertheless, Dodge did magnificently, impressing Grant and his other superiors and railroad men. For example, he put in crib piers for the Mobile and Ohio Railroad. When officials of the company, after the war, ordered them taken out and truss bridges put in, one of them examined the wartime work and remarked, "General Dodge must have thought the war was going to last forever."[7]

His wife wrote him that she wanted him to resign and take up the $5,000-per-year salary the railroad was offering if he would become the chief engineer for the UP. Dodge wrote back, "My heart is in the war; every day tells me that I am right, and you will see it in the future."[8]

●　●　●

*B*EFORE adjourning on September 5, 1862, the first meeting of the appointed directors of the Union Pacific arranged to open stock-subscription books in thirty-four cities and advertise the sale in numerous newspapers. With the glittering promise of a transcontinental railroad that looked to make tons of money, and with all the loose cash floating around from wartime profits and inflation, the directors were certain—or at least hopeful—that the Northerners would flock to do their patriotic duty and sign up. Alas. In the first four months of sales, a grand total of forty-five shares were sold to eleven brave men.

Brigham Young, leader of the Mormons, was easily the biggest buyer, and the only one to pay in full, for his five shares, which made him the UP's first—and for a long time only—stockholder "in good standing."[9] Doc Durant, the Wall Street speculator who had apparently put up the money for some of the other purchasers, bought twenty shares (at 10 percent down) for himself and made the rounds of his friends, looking for them to subscribe. George Francis Train, an erratic promoter and self-styled "Champion Crank," who had earned a fortune in shipping and had been involved with Durant in a speculation on contraband cotton, took twenty shares.

*D*ODGE was a man who had no fear of taking risks. In the spring of 1863, he had in his camp nearly one thousand former slaves who had walked off their plantations to gather around Union troops. Dodge put them to work. Then he said to reporter Charles A. Dana, "I believe that the negroes should be freed. They are the mainstay of the South, raising its crops and doing its work while its able-bodied men are fighting the government." Dana published the statement. Dodge went further in his actions than in his words. He began arming former slaves, saying as he did so that "there is nothing that so weakens the south as to take its negroes."[10]

From the perspective of the twenty-first century, Dodge was exactly right. But among the men of the 1860s era, he created great consternation. They were not at all sure they wanted the slaves to be free, and for sure they did not want the African Americans bearing arms for the Union. Thus Dodge was surprised and worried when, in the spring of 1863, he received a dispatch from General Grant ordering him to proceed to Washington to report to President Lincoln. There was no explanation, and Dodge confessed, "I was somewhat alarmed, thinking possibly I was to be called to account." But on arriving in Washington, he discovered that Lincoln wanted to talk railroads, even though Robert E. Lee and the Army of Northern Virginia were just then preparing to march into Pennsylvania.

The President had been charged by the act of 1862 with fixing the eastern terminus of the UP. He recalled his 1859 talk with Dodge and wished to consult with him. Nearly every village on the Missouri River wanted the transcontinental to start at its site. Lincoln showed Dodge pleas from towns on both sides of the Missouri, from fifty miles above and below Council Bluffs. "I found Mr. Lincoln well posted in all the controlling reasons covering such a selection," Dodge wrote, "and we went into the matter at length and discussed the arguments presented by the different competing localities."

Dodge reiterated his belief in the Platte Valley route, with Omaha as the best terminus. He pointed out that, from a commercial and engineering point of view, there was no other choice. The great Platte Valley extended from the base of the Rocky Mountains in one continuous reach for six hundred miles east to the Missouri River. And, Dodge added, he had surveyed the valley the whole way and then crossed the mountains, and told Lincoln that the divide of the continent at the head of the river ran through an open country not exceeding eight thousand feet in elevation, while to the north and south the Rocky Mountains towered from ten to thirteen thousand feet high.

In his blunt manner, Dodge also told Lincoln that the act of 1862 had many deficiencies in it, which he enumerated, adding that they made it difficult to raise capital. Lincoln agreed and said he would see what could be done. He was very anxious that the road should be built and wanted to do his part. And he agreed with Dodge about the terminus.

Dodge told him it would be difficult at best for private enterprise to build it. He said he thought it should be taken up and built by the government. Lincoln interjected that the government would give the project all possible aid and support, but could not build the road. As Dodge remembered his words, Lincoln said that the government "had all it could possibly handle in the conflict now going on, [but it] would make any change in the law or give any reasonable aid to insure the building of the road by private enterprise."[11] This was unprecedented, beyond anything imagined by either Alexander Hamilton or Henry Clay, the first secretary of the Treasury and the later senator, who had started the promotion of government aid to internal improvements.

*E*LATED by the President's reaction, Dodge took the train to New York, where he met Durant ("then practically at the head of the Union Pacific interests," in Dodge's words) and told him of Lincoln's views. Durant "took new courage" at the news, as Dodge recalled.

Durant also asked Dodge once again to resign from the army and go to work for the UP. Dodge once again refused. He had just said publicly, "Nothing but the utter defeat of the rebel armies will ever bring peace. . . . I have buried some of my best friends in the South, and I intend to remain there until we can visit their graves under the peaceful protection of that flag that every loyal citizen loves to honor and every soldier fights to save." That was a splendid speech, straight from the heart.[12] It speaks volumes about Dodge's patriotism and dedication.

But if he could make a little money out of the war, and out of the railroad, he was willing. He wrote Durant of his desire "to identify myself with the project in some active capacity. But I probably can do you more good in my present position while matters are being settled by Congress and others." Once Lincoln had announced the terminus, Dodge added, Durant should "telegraph my Brother at Council Bluffs, so that he can invest a little money for me. . . . *Bear this in mind.*"[13]

*E*VEN with Durant and Train out there selling for all they were worth, and even though the Union won a major victory at Gettysburg on July 1–3, 1863, and another when Vicksburg surrendered to Grant on July 4, it was not until September, a whole year after the shares went on sale, that two thousand shares were subscribed at $1,000 each—the minimum 10 percent that had to be put down for a $10,000 share. With the down payment, there was a total of $2 million for a road that was going to cost anywhere from $100 million to $200 million or perhaps more.

It was too risky a proposition for most American capitalists. No one knew if a train could be run over the Rockies in winter, or what the road over the mountains and through the desert would cost to build. With a war on, there were too many, too fat, profits to be made in shorter-term, less risky investments. People could not imagine how big this project was going to be, or the potential returns.

But with the 10 percent in hand, the UP was able, on September 25, 1863, to call for a meeting of the stockholders for October 29, 1863. On that day, the original commissioners were discharged and a board of thirty directors elected. The next day, the board elected General John A. Dix, who had been associated with the M&M Railroad, as president. Dignified, polite, but at sixty-five years of age an old man by mid–nineteenth century standards, Dix was known to everyone of note in New York and most of those in Washington. But he was a titular chief only.

The real leader of the corporation was Doc Durant, who took the title of vice-president, with Henry Poor as secretary. Durant had in his hands reports of the earlier surveys by Peter Dey and his then assistant Grenville Dodge. Durant told the board that two months earlier he had sent Dey west again, with four parties of engineers and a geologist, to survey the entire route, all paid for by his own money.[14]

So the Union Pacific was born, more than a year after Congress passed the Pacific Railroad Bill and Lincoln signed it.

VICE-PRESIDENT Durant went right to work. "Want preliminary surveys at once to make location of starting point," he telegraphed Peter Dey in Omaha. "Delay is ruinous. Everything depends on you." On November 5, 1863, Dey hurried to New York. Over the next two weeks, Durant pressed Lincoln to make his decision on the starting point. He finally did so on November 17, a day when the President was distracted: in two days, he was to make some remarks at the dedication of the Union cemetery at Gettysburg. Nevertheless, Lincoln managed to scratch off an executive order defining the terminus as "so much of the western boundary of the State of Iowa as lies between the north and south boundaries of . . . the city of Omaha."

Lincoln put more thought into what he would say in Gettysburg, and it came out much better. Still, Durant was satisfied. Despite the lack of a railroad running to Council Bluffs, not to mention a bridge there over the Missouri River, the Union Pacific would make Omaha the starting point.[15]

DURANT wanted to get started yesterday. The Central Pacific had already had its groundbreaking ceremony, eleven months earlier. Doc decided the UP must have a ceremony of its own in Omaha, if only to get some publicity. He ordered Dey to rush preparations and be ready on December 1, 1863. On November 30, he sent a telegram to his chief engineer: "You are behind time for so important an enterprise. Break ground on Wednesday."[16]

Dey did so, and the ceremony was grand. Citizens of Omaha flocked to the bottomland near the ferry landing at Seventh and Davenport Streets. The governor of Nebraska Territory turned the first shovel of dirt. There were bands, whistles, cannon, flags, and fireworks. George Francis Train was the orator, wearing the only white suit west of the Mississippi. He was described as "visionary to the verge of insanity." His speech put to shame any previous hyperbole. "America possesses the biggest head and the finest quantity of brain in the phrenology of nations," was one of his opening stretchers. He was said to be "a man who might have built the pyramids." He read congratulations from Lincoln and other dignitaries. Secretary of State William Seward, a longtime promoter of the Pacific railroad, had written: "When this shall have been done disunion will be rendered forever after impossible. There will be no fulcrum for the lever of treason to rest upon."[17]

Later, the mayor hosted a banquet and ball at the Herndon House. Train wired Durant: "Five (5) o'clock the child is born." The Doctor was not impressed. "May as well have had no celebration as to have sent such meager accounts. Send full particulars."[18]

The groundbreaking had brought the speculators into Omaha in droves, and the local residents tried to accommodate them. Train bought five hundred acres, some of it for as much as $175 per acre.[19] Dodge's brother Nathan wrote him, "Every man, woman and child who owned enough ground to bury themselves upon was a millionaire, prospectively."

But then it turned out that Omaha might not be the terminus after all. Durant was exploring a line north of the city, through Florence, and another south of Omaha, at Bellevue; indeed, on the same day as the groundbreaking he had chosen the Florence line.

A week after the groundbreaking ceremony in Omaha, Lincoln, in his Annual Message to Congress, praised the Central Pacific and the Union Pacific, with what most railroad men would regard as little cause, when he referred to "the actual commencement of work upon the Pacific Railroad, under auspices so favorable to rapid progress and completion."[20]

• • •

The Birth of the Union Pacific

DURANT was into this thing to make money, not to build a railroad. He was as flamboyant as the most freewheeling man on Wall Street could be. He would bet a fortune on almost anything. He moved too fast for other fast-money boys to keep up with him. In this case, he had bought land north and south of Omaha and wanted to play the three contenders against each other. In January 1864, Durant ordered Dey to survey yet another line, this one from De Soto (more than twenty miles north of Omaha) west. Dey was furious. He wrote Dodge that Durant was "managing it as he has everything else that is in his hands. A good deal spread and a good deal do nothing. He considers it a big thing, the Big Thing of the age, and himself the father of it."

Instead of deciding on a line, Durant bombarded Dey with new possibilities. "If the geography was a little larger," Dey wrote Dodge, "I think he [Durant] would order a survey round by the moon and a few of the fixed stars, to see if he could not get some more depot grounds."

It was Dodge's turn to grow furious. "Let me advise you to drop the De Soto idea," he wrote Durant. "It is one of the worst." Logic, nature, and President Lincoln dictated that the route run from Omaha to the Platte River and then west along the Platte Valley.[21]

Still the Doctor persisted in his bewildering variety of schemes. He was negotiating with the businessmen of Omaha, Bellevue, Florence, and De Soto all at once, demanding they give the railroad land for depots, rails, water storage, and more, and he had them in competition against each other.

On January 1, 1864, President Dix signed a document formally appointing Peter Dey the chief engineer of the UP. He named Colonel Silas Seymour the consulting engineer, also at Durant's suggestion. Seymour was a crusty, overweight, eccentric, domineering dandy with little railroad experience and was later referred to as the "interfering engineer." But his brother Horatio was governor of New York and a leading Democratic candidate for president, and Durant thought it wise to have friends in both parties.[22]

Engineer Dey wanted to get going on his surveys. He had hired two fine engineers, Samuel B. Reed and James A. Evans, to run a line from the Black Hills* to Salt Lake—that is, across the southern part of today's

* The easternmost thrust of the Rocky Mountains, in eastern Wyoming, not to be confused with today's Black Hills of South Dakota.

Wyoming and northeastern Utah. They needed to start at once if they were going to finish by the autumn of 1864. But Durant would not approve their expenditures—or Dey's salary, for that matter.

On April 4, 1864, Dey wrote Dodge, "Durant is vacillating and changeable and to my mind utterly unfit to head such an enterprise. . . . It is like dancing with a whirlwind to have anything to do with him. Today matters run smoothly and tomorrow they don't." If the men in charge back in New York would only give him the money to run the operation and otherwise leave him alone, Dey said, "I could build the work for less money and more rapidly than can be done the way they propose to do it." But of course that couldn't be done.

As Maury Klein, author of a two-volume history of the Union Pacific and easily its finest historian, comments, "Thus was the Union Pacific charged with mismanagement before it had laid a single rail."[23]

*T*HIS was hardly a surprise, because conservative capitalists (the majority) would not risk their fortunes or reputations on the road. They regarded its stocks and bonds as a reckless gamble for high stakes at long odds. Who was there among them willing to wager on long shots?

George Francis Train was one. He knew that construction would require an enormous amount of capital, that it would be years before the road could return any dividends, and that therefore some way had to be found to raise money and provide short-term profits. He further knew that a construction company would attract investment, because it could make money through the government loans plus the company's sale of the land grant and of its own stocks and bonds. A separate construction company would also limit the liability of investors to the stock they held. Moreover, as stockholders in both the construction and the railroad company, the investors could make a contract with themselves. "I determined," Train said later, "upon introducing this new style of finance into the country."[24]

Sounds simple, and it was. Although he had failed to sell the UP, Train said, "an idea occurred to me that cleared the sky." He mentioned it to the Doctor, who gave him $50,000 to put it into action. In March 1864, Train and Durant bought control of an obscure Pennsylvania corporation called the Pennsylvania Fiscal Agency that had been chartered five years earlier to do damn near anything it wished. The company had not even organized until May 1863, and then it had transacted no business until March 3, 1864, when Durant and Train were made directors. In May the board of directors was expanded to bring in more men from the UP. Train renamed it the Crédit Mobilier of America and made it into a construction company. The two principals, Durant and Train, were able to sell lots of stock in a company that couldn't miss. Ben Holladay, founder and owner of the stagecoach line, bought $100,000; so did many others. Train took $150,000, Durant more than double that. Train later claimed that he had created "the first so-called 'Trust' organized in this country."[25] Crédit Mobilier was on its way.

Greatly simplified, the process worked this way: The Union Pacific awarded construction contracts to dummy individuals, who in turn assigned them to the Crédit Mobilier. The UP paid the Crédit Mobilier by check, with which the Crédit Mobilier purchased from the UP stocks and bonds—at par, the trick to the whole thing—and then sold them on the open market for whatever they would fetch, or used them as security for loans. The construction contracts brought huge profits to the Crédit Mobilier, which in turn was owned by the directors and principal stockholders of the UP. In short, it didn't matter if the UP ever got up and running and made a profit, because the Crédit Mobilier would make a big profit on building it. Profit that it would pay out to its stockholders in immense amounts.

As historian Thomas Cochran comments, "The procedure was a general one in the building of western railroads, and often resulted badly for the original small investors who had bought the railroad bonds or stocks at or near par." But for the insiders it meant excessive profits. "In addition, it necessarily tended to vest control of the railroad in the hands of the chief stockholders of the construction company."[26]

CHARLES Francis Adams, Jr., grandson of two presidents and one of America's leading intellectuals and columnists, became a principal critic of the Crédit Mobilier, which became the greatest financial scandal of America in the nineteenth century. But when he became president of the Union Pacific in the 1880s, he would see things in a different light. He told Halsey Merriman, a scathing critic of the original board of directors of the railroad, "It is very easy to speak of these men as thieves and speculators. But there was no human being, when the Union Pacific railroad was proposed, who regarded it as other than a wild-cat venture. The government did not dare to take hold of it. Those men went into the enterprise because the country wanted a transcontinental railroad, and was willing to give almost any sum to those who would build it. The general public refused to put a dollar into the enterprise. Those men took their financial lives in their hands, and went forward with splendid energy and built the road the country called for. They played a great game, and they played for either a complete failure or a brilliant prize."[27]

A LMOST everyone in Congress knew that the 1862 act would have to be revised, modified, changed. Representative James G. Blaine of Maine, a future perpetual candidate for president, later observed, "Such was the anxiety in the public mind to promote the connection with the Pacific that an enlarged and most generous provision was made for the completion of the road." The struggle with the South, he added, meant "that no pains should be spared and no expenditures stinted to insure the connection with . . . the interests of the Atlantic and Pacific Coasts."[28]

One congressman noted, "Mr. Lincoln said to us that his experience in the West was that every railroad that had been undertaken there had broken down before it was half completed. . . . He had but one advice to us and that was to ask sufficient aid. . . . He said further that he would hurry it up so that when he retired from the presidency he could take a trip over it, it would be the proudest thing of his life that he had signed the bill in aid of its construction."[29]

In May 1864, a bill to provide sufficient aid was introduced into the House; a similar bill was introduced into the Senate by Senator John Sherman, General William Sherman's brother. They and most others believed that there had to be more inducement for capitalists to invest. Representative Hiram Price of Iowa put it this way: "I do not believe that there is one man in five hundred who will invest his money, and engage in the building of this road, as the law now stands."[30] But some politicians still held back. Representative E. B. Washburne of Illinois called the revised bill "the most monstrous and flagrant attempt to overreach the government and the people that can be found in all the legislative annals of the country." He charged that the bill had fallen into the hands of "Wall Street stock jobbers who are using this great engine for their own private means."[31]

Washburne was right about that last. Durant was in Washington handing out money and stocks of the UP. Huntington of the CP was also there, working for the new bill. When it finally passed in late June, Washburne noted a "tempest of wildest disorder" in the packed galleries and corridors in which "lobbyists, male and female," crowded and jostled each other.[32]

On July 2, 1864, Lincoln, always the railroads' first and finest friend, signed the bill into law. It was everything Durant and his fellow directors, and Huntington and his, could have wanted.

The Pacific Railroad Act of 1864 allowed the directors of the UP and the CP to issue their own first-mortgage bonds in an amount equal to the government bonds, thus putting the government bonds in the status of a second mortgage. The government bonds (actually, the loan to the railroads) would be handed over by Washington upon the completion of twenty miles of track rather than forty. In mountainous regions the companies could collect two-thirds of their subsidy once the roadbed of a twenty-mile section was prepared—that is, graded. Also, the companies were given rights previously denied, to coal and iron and other minerals in their land grants, which were meanwhile doubled to provide ten alternate sections on each side of every mile, or about 12,800 acres per mile. To attract investors, the par value of UP stock was reduced from $1,000 to $100, and the limit on the amount held by any one person was removed.

The act allowed the Central Pacific to build up to 150 miles east of the California-Nevada border and limited the UP to building no more than three hundred miles west of Salt Lake City, but no meeting point was designated. Maury Klein has pronounced his judgment: the act included these and other provisions that were "monuments to ambiguity." But as he also points out, "The object was to induce private parties to build the road that everyone agreed must be built."[33]

Lincoln did two other things for the UP. First, on November 4, 1864, he approved the first hundred miles of the permanent location of the tracks, as requested by Durant—from Omaha to the west. Second, as directed by the bill, he set the gauge at four feet eight and a half inches, the so-called "standard gauge" urged on him by Eastern railroaders.

*H*OW much Durant and Huntington spent to make the 1864 act pass no one has ever found out. A lobbyist hired by Durant, Joseph P. Stewart, distributed $250,000 in UP bonds, with $20,000 of them going to

Charles T. Sherman, eldest brother of the senator and the general, for "professional services." Doc also gave to congressmen's campaign funds, including one for S. S. "Sunset" Cox. Others got their shares, including a young New York lawyer named Clark Bell who got $20,000 for drawing up the act.

Durant was a genial paymaster. An associate called him "the most extravagant man I ever knew in my life." Another called Durant "a fast man. He started fast, and I tried to hold him back awhile, but he got me to going pretty fast before we got through. He was a man who when he undertook to help to build a railroad didn't stop at trifles in accomplishing his end." So too with George Francis Train. As soon as the bill passed, he went off to Omaha ("the seat of Empire," as he called it) for the first of three trips that year. He charged the UP $4,000 for "expenses and services."[34]

On July 2, 1864, the day Lincoln signed the act, Confederate General Jubal Early, commanding a part of Robert E. Lee's army, crossed the Potomac River to invade Maryland, and by July 11 he was within five miles of Washington. On July 13, Early was driven back. Grant then gave command of the Army of the Shenandoah to General Philip Sheridan, who in the late summer and fall turned defeat into victory. Grant meanwhile was fighting the terribly costly but ultimately successful battles around Petersburg, Virginia, while Sherman was marching with a hundred thousand men through Georgia. On September 1, 1864, Sherman would march into Atlanta and later burn it to the ground.

Dodge served Sherman in two ways, first as commander of the left wing of the Sixteenth Army Corps, second as Sherman's personal director of a pioneer corps of fifteen hundred men rebuilding railroads and bridges destroyed by the Confederates as they retreated. Sherman later said that the greatest single piece of bridge construction he ever saw was at Roswell, Georgia, where Dodge's men built a bridge fourteen hundred feet long. Sherman wrote Dodge, "I know you have a big job, but that is nothing new for you. . . . The bridge at Roswell is important and you may destroy all Georgia to make it strong."[35]

Just before Sherman occupied Atlanta, Dodge went to the front to look over the field before attacking. It was mid-afternoon when he reached the entrenchments. "The boys cautioned me about exposing myself," he later wrote, "and one of them said that if I wanted to see the enemy I could look through a peep-hole they had made under a log. I put my eye to this peep-hole, and the moment I did so, I was shot in the head. I went down immediately."[36]

It was a bad wound. He was unconscious for two days, and word went out that he was dead. But Sherman reached him at the end of the second day, just as he was regaining consciousness. "Doctor," Sherman said, "Dodge isn't going to die. See, he's coming to."[37]

DODGE went to the hospital, first in Chattanooga, then in Nashville, finally at Council Bluffs, where the whole town turned out to hear him. "I trust that I can return to Sherman's army in a few days," was all he said.[38] He had been in town for but a week when he received a telegram from Durant, urging him as soon as he could travel to come to New York to meet with UP officials. In the first week in October, Dodge did so. Doc wanted him to resign from the army and take the position of chief engineer with the railroad. Dodge said no. Instead he took a boat down to City Point, Virginia, where Grant had his headquarters.

He stayed a week. Grant had him inspect the various divisions and corps in his army, then asked Dodge if he would take command of one of them. No, Dodge answered—he preferred to serve in the West. Grant did not think he was up to serving with Sherman again, but humored him, and suggested that he go west by way of Washington and call on President Lincoln. Grant gave no special reason.

Dodge went to Washington on Grant's own boat. In the capital he went to the White House, where Lincoln greeted him cordially. After pleasantries, Dodge got up to leave. Lincoln reached out with that long arm of his, put his hand once again on Dodge's forearm, and told him to wait until the two of them were alone. By and by they were, and Lincoln locked the door. After reading aloud something by humorist Artemus Ward, which always gave him a laugh, Lincoln turned to the Army of the Potomac. Did Dodge think Grant could defeat Lee? Could he take Richmond? Dodge said yes. Lincoln placed his hand on Dodge's and said with great emotion, "You don't know how glad I am to hear you say that."[39]

Shortly thereafter, Grant and Lincoln sent Dodge farther west than he had bargained for, all the way to St. Louis, where he became commander of the Department of the Missouri. Lincoln wanted him there because

Missouri, although still in the Union, was a slave state with markedly mixed motives. Grant wanted him there because of the problems confronting the government from the Indian situation on the Great Plains, because of the tides of emigration just moving out onto the Plains, and to protect the UP when it began building.

Dodge's record in the Civil War could not have been better. What counted most was his skill with railroads. But what mattered for his future was more than what he had learned about the construction of railroads; it was the friendships he had earned. Grant, Sherman, and Sheridan had started a relationship with Dodge that grew over time. They trusted him, as he did them. They would do anything in their power for him, and he for them. Union General O. O. Howard observed that "Dodge could talk to Sherman as no other officer dared to do."[40]

On December 6, 1864, the newly re-elected Lincoln, who had Sherman's capture of Atlanta and Grant's triumphs in northern Virginia behind him, delivered his Annual Message to Congress. The war was his principal topic, but he gave a paragraph to the transcontinental railroad, calling it "this great enterprise." He said it "has been entered upon with a vigor that gives assurance of success, notwithstanding the embarrassments arising from the prevailing high prices of materials and labor. The route of the main line of the road has been definitely located for one hundred miles westward from the initial point at Omaha City, Nebraska, and a preliminary location of the Pacific Railroad of California has been made from Sacramento, eastward, to the great bend of the Truckee River, in Nevada."[41]

By that December, engineer Dey had graded and spent $100,000 on twenty-three miles of line from Omaha west to the Platte Valley. And he exploded when Silas Seymour, the consulting engineer, demanded that it be abandoned. Seymour—and his backer, Durant—favored a route up Mud Creek, a detour to the south in the shape of an oxbow, which added nine miles. It would bring in an extra $144,000 in government and company bonds, plus 115,200 acres of federal land grants, and more profits for the Crédit Mobilier.

There was another dispute. Dey had estimated $30,000 per mile as the cost out of Omaha and up the Platte Valley. But in the fall of 1864, the UP had accepted a proposal from Herbert "Hub" Hoxie, an Iowa politician selected by Durant as a front man—meaning most of all that he was willing to carry out Doc's intentions. Hoxie said he would build the road for $50,000 to $60,000 per mile for the first 247 miles. On September 23, the contract was signed, and almost immediately turned over to Crédit Mobilier. Durant then instructed Dey to resubmit his own proposal and make it $60,000 per mile. Dey brooded over Durant's order for five weeks before writing Durant that he believed that amount "would so cripple the road that it would be impossible to ever build [it]."

Dey thought about it some more, and on December 7, one day after Lincoln's triumphal speech to Congress, he wrote President Dix to tender his resignation. "My reasons," he said, "are, simply, that I do not approve of the contract made with Mr. Hoxie . . . and I do not care to have my name so connected with the railroad that I shall appear to endorse this contract." He wanted no part of the whole thing, and so, reluctantly, he "resigned the best position in my profession this country has ever offered to any man."[42]

When Dey left Omaha on the last day of 1864, the Union Pacific had yet to lay a single rail. The corporation had graded just over twenty miles of roadbed and put down not one tie, much less rail.

*F*OR all its problems and travail in getting started, the UP and its western mate the CP were about to become the biggest businesses in America. The Erie, the New York Central, the Pennsylvania, the Baltimore and Ohio, the Illinois Central, the Michigan Central, and the Michigan Southern, all railroads built before the war, were then the largest business enterprises in the nation. Running them required wholly new methods, just as financing and building the UP and the CP did, and the last two were destined to be much larger than their predecessors.

The general superintendent of the Erie, Daniel C. McCallum, described his problems and practices in dealing with the new methods of management brought on by the sheer size of the railroads:

A Superintendent of a road fifty miles in length can give its business his personal attention and may be constantly on the line engaged in the direction of its details; each person is personally known to him, and all questions in relation to its business are at once presented and acted upon. . . .

In the government of a road five hundred miles in length a very different state exists. Any system which might be applicable to the business and extent of a short road would be found entirely inadequate to the wants of a long one.[43]

The UP and the CP and the other, lesser railroads were about to bring a revolution to America. As historian Alfred D. Chandler says, "As the first private enterprises in the United States with modern administrative structures, the railroads provided industrialists with useful precedents for organization building. . . . More than this, the building of the railroads, more than any other single factor, made possible this growth of the great industrial enterprise. By speedily enlarging the market for American manufacturing, mining, and marketing firms, the railroads permitted and, in fact, often required that these enterprises expand and subdivide their activities."[44]

Alexander Hamilton and Henry Clay had wanted American manufacturing to grow, but they could imagine nothing like what happened after the Civil War. Nor could Lewis and Clark, who had led the way west. Nor Thomas Jefferson. And none could foresee the way in which the UP and the CP created a precedent for government aid to business, or how the government could create a new class of capitalists. Men of great fortune, already tied to the Republican Party. Men ready to take great risks and to accept great profits.

Chapter Five
JUDAH AND THE ELEPHANT
1862 – 1864

*I*MMEDIATELY after the Pacific Railroad Act of 1862 had passed the Congress and been signed by the President, Judah had gone to New York to purchase materials and supplies for the Central Pacific. Three weeks later, on July 21, he had left matters in the hands of an agent and, together with Anna, set sail for California. His intention had been to make certain that the merchants from Sacramento who owned or controlled most of the bonds and stock of the Central Pacific Railroad Company—Crocker, Huntington, Stanford, and Hopkins (the Big Four, as they were beginning to be called) could indeed harness the elephant.

They couldn't do it without Judah. As he had told them in his report, "The principles which produced this result were control and *harmony*." On June 30, 1862, he had already filed with the secretary of the interior a map of the route he had picked, because the bill provided that, upon such filing, the federally owned lands for fifteen miles on either side of the projected route would be withdrawn from pre-emption, meaning that a citizen could not buy or make a claim on them. This was a first step in clinching the bargain between the CP and the federal government.[1] Judah had gotten started.

There were many people depending on him. Word of the passage of the Pacific Railroad Bill had spread through Sacramento, causing great excitement. On July 12, the *Sacramento Union* reported that "the firemen's parade last evening in honor of the passage of the bill was the most

brilliant affair of its kind that has ever taken place in this city. The procession was a mile long and the route was one blaze of torches and fireworks . . . and there were 100 mottoes carried in the line, all of them
appropriate and pithy." One read, "Little Indian Boy, Step Out of the
Way for the Big Engine." Another said, "The Pacific Railroad—Uncle
Sam's Waistband." And a third: "Fresh No. 4 Mackerel, Six Days from
Belfast."[2]

On his way to California, Judah had written a report on his activities
in New York after the bill passed. He said he had found that prices had
advanced rapidly with the coming of war. Iron rails, for example, that
went for $55 a ton in 1860 now cost $115 a ton and were going up. Common spikes had climbed from 2.5 cents per pound to 6.5. Blasting powder
had risen from $2.50 to $15 a keg. Shipping was costing much more: each
ton of rails fetched $17.50 in shipping charges to San Francisco. Insur-
ance premiums had also soared. Huntington had gone to New York to
handle purchases "upon the best terms he could get, before further advances [in prices] took place."[3]

Judah hoped to lay the first fifty miles of track by the fall of 1863, more
than a year away. His agent had managed to get a contract for eight locomotives, deliverable in January 1863, to be paid for entirely in government bonds—when these were issued. Also a contract for five thousand
tons of rail, and for eight passenger, four baggage, and sixty freight cars.
Huntington had paid for all this with pledges from himself and the others, relying on his and the other members of the Big Four's reputations for
never walking away from a debt. But although he had fistfuls of stocks
and bonds, he had no buyers. Besides, the federal law making paper
money ("greenbacks") legal tender almost killed the bonds: the value of
the paper money sank with each Union Army reverse, sometimes to as
low as 35 cents on the dollar, and in California, by legislative fiat, only
silver or gold could be used in contracts, to pay workers, or to buy goods.

Huntington was described by an acquaintance as a man who was
"something tigerish and irrational in his ravenous pursuit. He was always
on the scene, incapable of fatigue, delighting in his strength and the use
of it, and full of love of combat. . . . If the Great Wall of China were put
in his path, he would attack it with his nails."[4] But he still couldn't get
anyone in the East to buy his railroad bonds.

In 1862, Huntington worked New York, Washington, and Boston,
spending three days in New York, two in Boston, and two in the capital,

where he "borrowed, hocked and huckstered." In Boston, he walked into the office of Oliver Ames, older brother of Representative Oakes Ames and fellow owner of the Ames shovel factory, the biggest and best in the country, from whom Huntington, Crocker, and Hopkins had bought thousands of shovels for California's gold miners. The Ames shovel was declared to be "legal tender in every part of the Mississippi Valley" and was known even in South Africa. At the beginning of the Civil War, the business was valued at $4 million, and the war enormously increased its prosperity.

Huntington didn't try to sell Ames any bonds. Instead he offered a fistful of them as security for a loan of $200,000, promising that he and his partners would guarantee the interest payments on the bonds if the CP failed to meet its semiannual obligations. Huntington had with him "a paper testifying to our responsibility and our honor, as men and merchants, that whatever we agreed to we would faithfully adhere to."

Ames told Huntington to come back tomorrow. Meanwhile, he checked on the record and found not a single instance of an overdue bill. The next morning he made the loan and gave Huntington a letter of introduction. On a similar promise, Huntington managed to purchase $721,000 worth of rolling stock.[5]

*I*N mid-August 1862, Judah arrived at Sacramento. McClellan was pulling the Union troops out of the Virginia Peninsula, and the Second Battle of Bull Run was less than two weeks away. Still, two pieces of good news greeted Judah. First, the secretary of the interior had telegraphed the government's acceptance of his location map and withdrawn from sale, pre-emption, or private entry the federal land and the promised land-grant acreage along the route. Second, the city of Sacramento had given to the CP thirty acres along its levee (thirteen hundred feet of riverfront) for the company's headquarters, depots, shops, and roundhouse.

That gift brought on the first dispute between the Big Four and their chief engineer. Judah insisted that the company build a handsome office building in Sacramento, and he personally designed an impressive brick edifice that he claimed could be built for $12,000. He was peremptorily voted down at a board meeting. Instead, at Huntington's telegraphed orders, an unpainted shack was raised in one working day at a cost of $150.

CP business was as always conducted in an office over Stanford's grocery store on K Street.[6]

At the same time Judah was disagreeing with Huntington and Stanford, the Central Pacific was being criticized by men who had a monopolistic interest in this or that aspect of the railroad. For example, the company that brought ice from Alaska to the San Francisco market feared that the CP might replace it with ice from the Sierra Nevada. Those who ran freight lines within the state, most especially the Sacramento Valley Railroad, jumped on various aspects of the CP. A major criticism, repeated by the state's most prestigious newspaper, the *Daily Alta California*, charged that all the CP intended to do was build its line to Dutch Flat, where it would end, and from which everyone would have to use the wagon road owned by the Big Four to get to the sprawling markets in Nevada. On August 22, 1862, just after arriving, Judah took out an advertisement in the *Sacramento Union* asking anyone who knew of a better route over the mountains to step forward with the facts. No one did.[7]

JUDAH spent the early fall working on his annual report. Meanwhile, the Battle of Antietam had been won by the Union, but the Confederate Army of Northern Virginia had escaped. And on September 22, 1862, Lincoln had issued the Emancipation Proclamation.

Judah issued his report on October 22, 1862. It was primarily a puff piece designed to sell shares and bonds. He claimed, for example, that the government's use of the road would be so great as to repay the company's own bonds, along with other stretchers. He badly underestimated the cost of driving tunnels through mountains ($50 a foot, he said; $1,000 per foot was closer to the reality). He said that the CP had been given the privilege from Congress of building its line easterly from the California-Nevada line until it met the UP's line coming from Omaha, which wasn't true but allowed him to write, "I am positive in the opinion, that it will be found advisable to undertake the construction of about 300 miles easterly"—that is, halfway to Salt Lake City. He also noted that the CP would make a fortune from the business within California and from the Nevada trade. "The conditions which produce these results are extraordinary," he admitted, "unlike those which govern the business conditions of any other railroad ever built."[8]

Judah believed what he said. He wanted more stock. So did others. In November, he and his friends James Bailey, who had accompanied him to Washington, and grocer Lucius Booth purchased more stock (Judah was being paid as chief engineer in small amounts of stock), although not nearly so much as Charles Crocker, who, along with Huntington, Stanford, and Hopkins, "resolved [in Crocker's words] that we would go in and subscribe enough stock to organize the company and control it."[9] Each bought an additional 345 shares. Crocker eventually ended up with a hundred thousand shares.

*J*UDAH spoke of the Central Pacific as "my railroad," but it wasn't, any more than the railroads back east he had built, or the Sacramento Valley Railroad, were his. He had thought of it, dreamed of it, laid out the line for it, gone to Washington to convince the Congress and the President to get behind it. He had invited in the men who financed it. But it wasn't his.

With the onset of winter in 1862–63, the men whose railroad it was went to work. The Big Four wanted to make big money, just like Doc Durant, George Francis Train, and their cohorts. Big money meant the same as with the UP, milking the construction. So Charlie Crocker drew up a contract awarding the Charles Crocker Contract and Finance Company and several minor companies the right to build the first stretch of the road. That would be Sections 1 to 18, from Sacramento to today's Roseville. This was later amended, but its essence remained.

It was an almost identical device to the Crédit Mobilier. The Big Four awarded to Charles Crocker & Company the contract for building the road as well as for supplying all materials, equipment, rolling stock, and buildings. Even better than the Crédit Mobilier, according to railroad historian Robert E. Riegel, was the ability of Crocker & Company "to get its accounts into such shape that no one has ever been quite able to disentangle them."[10]

All the Big Four were involved in Crocker's company, but not Judah. Huntington was in New York, which became his permanent home as he raised money and bought needed equipment and supplies, leaving Hopkins with his power of attorney. Judah and Bailey protested, and Judah said at a board meeting of the CP that he openly doubted Crocker's ability to do the work. But two days after Christmas, the board awarded

Crocker & Company the contract. Two days after that, Crocker resigned from the CP board (keeping his stock) to avoid charges of conflict of interest.* His contract named him the general superintendent and called for paying him $400,000 for the first eighteen miles of track, with $250,000 in cash, $100,000 in CP bonds, and $50,000 in stock.

This was almost too much for Judah. He felt "his" railroad was being stolen from him. He suspected, correctly, that all the Big Four were owners of the construction company. He feared they might bankrupt the CP to profit from its building. He wondered why the CP's treasury was either low or bare while there was always plenty of money for the wagon road out of Dutch Flat, in which he had no interest.[11]

Judah had a right to complain and he used it often, but, then, the Big Four were also putting in their time and reputation, plus their money. In an interview years later, Crocker pointed out, "We actually spent our own money building that road up to Newcastle [beyond Roseville] and it left every one of us in debt."[12] (Crocker sold his store for the money.) Stanford was trying to get funds from cities—Sacramento and San Francisco especially—and counties and the legislature. Huntington was selling stocks and bonds in the East. But except for loans from the Ames brothers and a few others, the Big Four were operating on their own.

But operate they did. On January 8, 1863, the company had its groundbreaking event. Governor Stanford was there, and Crocker—but Huntington was in New York, Hopkins declined, and Judah was in the Sierra Nevada. Though it rained and was otherwise miserable, there was a large crowd representing every section of the state, high officials, preachers to bless the work, and many ladies. The *Sacramento Union* called attention to the stands, with the national flag adorning each end, a brass band playing "Wait for the Wagon," and a large banner bearing a representation of hands clasped across the continent from the Atlantic to the Pacific, with "the prayer of every loyal heart, 'May the Bond Be Eternal,'" printed on it.

Crocker introduced Stanford. The governor gave a long and dull speech, including this pledge: "There will be no delay, no backing, no uncertainty in the continued progress." After he was done and a prayer

---

* His place on the board was taken by Hopkins's brother E. B. Hopkins, who had just been named interim chief justice of California by Governor Stanford, who was also president of the CP.

made, Stanford took up a shovel and turned the first earth for the road. Then Crocker turned a spadeful and made a short speech. He promised, "All that I have—all of my own strength, intellect and energy—are devoted to the building [of this road]."

The rhythmic "thud, thud," of the CP's steam pile driver—its only modern technology—could be heard working on the banks of the American River. The little ten-horsepower driver was lifting a nineteen-hundred-pound hammer three times a minute and placing thirty-foot pilings into the riverbed at the rate of seven a day. Crocker picked up on the sound and told the audience, "The work is going right on, gentlemen, I assure you."[13]

After four decades of agitation, promotion, boosters, politics, demands, concerns, embarrassments, alarm, consternation, delays, and more, the first transcontinental railroad was under way. As the *Sacramento Union* put it, "Everybody felt happy because, after so many years of dreaming, scheming, talking and toiling, they saw with their own eyes the actual commencement of a Pacific Railroad."

N OT until February did the ground dry out sufficiently for Crocker to get to work making a grade for the road. The only other work actually under way was the construction of the bridge over the American River at Sacramento. Getting laborers was devilishly difficult. "Most of the men working on the road were merely working for a stake," Stanford recalled. "When they got that, they would go off to the mines, and we could not hold them, except in rare instances, more than a very little while." Small wonder in California, where their base pay was less than $3 a day. The *Union* announced that there were two hundred men at work on the grading, but the work they did was widely separated, and as the diggings went upriver and thus got closer to the gold and silver deposits more men walked off the job.

Crocker decided to take charge himself. He would learn railroad construction by doing it. He later said, "If it becomes necessary to jump off the dock in the service of the company, instead of saying, 'Go, boys!' you must pull off your coat and say, 'Come on, boys!' and then let them follow."[14] He put all of his 250 pounds into it, bringing energy and dynamism to the job. And he so loved doing it he even gained weight over the next few years.

He shortly had redwood pilings up to thirty feet long stacked on the Sacramento levee, waiting to support the future railroad bridge over the American River, along with timbers for trestles, and imported ties as well. Soon the materials were coming in at the rate of a schooner-load a day. Judah, meanwhile, in New York, had ordered forty-two freight cars, six locomotives, six first-class passenger coaches, along with switches, turntables, and other track equipment for the first fifty miles of the CP—leaving Huntington to find some way of paying for them, which he did, despite having to bid against the federal armies.[15]

*T*HE Pacific Railroad Bill specified that the Sierra Nevada would commence where Lincoln said they commenced. This was a matter of great importance to the men paying the bulk of the cost of building the line. They decided to work on Lincoln, the man responsible, first of all through officials in California. Governor Stanford asked the state's official geologist, Josiah D. Whitney (after whom California's highest mountain is named), where was the point at which the mountains began.

Whitney set off in a buggy with Charles Crocker as his guide. Whitney felt that of course the Sacramento River was the ultimate base of the region's tilt, and thus the place where the mountains began, but the land to the east was as flat as it could be. Crocker took him to Arcade Creek, about seven miles to the east, and there showed Whitney a fan of reddish earth that came out from the foothills. Whitney said that seemed to him as fair a place to begin as any, and put that opinion down on official paper.

If the CP could get Lincoln to accept that opinion, it would move the Sierra Nevada fifteen miles west, thus bringing the railroad an extra $240,000 in government bonds.

Aaron Sargent, Judah's old friend, was no longer in the Congress but still in Washington, and he took the information to the President. He showed Whitney's report to Lincoln and argued for Arcade Creek as the beginning point for the Sierra. Lincoln said that seemed about right to him. As Sargent commented, "Here you see, my pertinacity and Abraham's faith moved mountains." (Another report has Lincoln saying, "Here is a case in which Abraham's Faith has moved mountains.")[16]

Judah was opposed. There was no way the mountains began at Arcade Creek. He refused to sign an affidavit, telling Strong he could not because "the foothills do not begin here."[17] But his protest went unheeded. The Big Four were glad to get the extra subsidy. Judah complained to Anna, "I cannot make these men appreciate the 'Elephant' they have on their shoulders, they won't do what I want and must do." He went on, "We shall just as sure have trouble in Congress as the sun rises in the east if they go on in this way. They will not see it as it is. Something must be done." But as to what, he couldn't figure. He certainly couldn't come up with the money to pay for that something. Nevertheless, he told Anna, "I have brought them a franchise and laid it at their door. Rightly used it gives them unlimited credit throughout the world, and they would beggar it!"[18]

DESPITE Judah's misgivings, there was more money coming in. In April 1863, as Lee's army prepared to swing into Chancellorsville to fight General Joe Hooker's army, Governor Stanford managed to prod the California legislature into donating to the CP millions of dollars in state bonds, to be issued at the rate of $10,000 per mile after the completion of specified amounts of track. In return, the railroad agreed to transport, without charge to the state, convicts for prison, inmates for insane institutions, materials for the state agricultural fair and indeed for all state buildings, and state militia. Stanford also got the legislators to authorize Sacramento and Placer Counties to vote on the issuing of bonds for the purchase of stock from the railroad, as well as the city of San Francisco. In the event, Sacramento voted for $300,000 and thirty acres of city land for the CP's use. Placer gave $250,000, and San Francisco voted for $600,000.

Many were jealous of the CP and more than a few were determined to wreck it. A typical slander: "The whole matter resolves itself simply into this: Leland Stanford & Co. have . . . bamboozled the people out of a stupendously magnificent franchise, worth hundreds of millions. . . . It is to them, and to them alone, that all the benefits, all the profits inure." To which the editor of the *Sacramento Union* quite rightly replied, "If it is worth so many millions, why should not the county of Placer become a subscriber, and thus obtain an interest in those millions?"[19] Nevertheless, the sums voted for were not immediately available. They were held up by various court actions. It took more than a year and a half to get San Francisco to pay up.

WORK on the railroad proceeded, slowly. Judah was out in front of the graders, laying out the exact line through Dutch Flat and over the summit. In the mountains he was always happy. In this case, even happier, because he had hired two young engineers who were proving to be godsends. One was the thirty-three-year-old Samuel Skerry Montague, lured by Judah away from the Sacramento Valley Railroad. Montague was a rangy, slim, black-bearded New Hampshire man. He had failed at gold mining in California but taught himself location engineering. He had an undoubted skill as a surveyor and railroad man, especially with such a master as Judah to teach him. The other was Lewis M. Clement, a Canadian canal engineer hired by Judah because, like Montague, he had an ability to learn.

One day Judah sent Clement off by himself to do some surveying, to see how he would do. When Clement returned much earlier than anticipated, Judah said sternly, "I did not expect to see you back until you had finished, young man."

"I *have* finished," Clement replied, as he handed to Judah a complete report. Together that summer Montague and Clement helped Judah and the crews solve many of the engineering problems in building a railroad in one of the world's toughest mountain ranges.[20]

Down in the American River Valley, progress was painfully slow. Still, Crocker was learning. The labor problems were excruciating. Only the bridge over the river went as planned. For the rest, Crocker had to wait until fall for the first rails to arrive, which meant that some of the original grading washed out in heavy rains and had to be redone. That meant more shoveling for the graders, more loading of dirt and debris onto handcarts, more dumping, more cash to be paid out by the CP.

In the war, meanwhile, at the beginning of May 1863, the Army of Northern Virginia defeated the Union forces at Chancellorsville, and General Robert E. Lee began his preparations to invade Pennsylvania. In the Western theater, Grant began the siege of Vicksburg, Mississippi. In California, despite the Union's heavy losses in battle and the perilous state of the war, work on binding the Republic together east to west continued.

I N early May 1863, Judah came down from the mountains to attend a directors' meeting in Sacramento. There the Big Four announced that they were tired of bearing all the costs themselves and wanted every director to be equally responsible for the money required to build the road.

Judah was unwilling and unhappy. On May 13, he wrote his friend and Dutch Flat resident Doctor Strong, "I had a blowout about two weeks ago and freed my mind, so much so that I looked for instant decapitation. I called things by their right name and invited war; but counsels of peace prevailed and my head is still on." Only barely. Meanwhile, "my hands are tied." Judah reported, "We have no meetings of the board nowadays, except the regular monthly meeting, which, however, was not had this month, but there have been any quantity of private conferences to which I have not been invited." Thinking it over, Judah added, "I try to think it is all for the best, and devote myself with additional energy to my legitimate portion of the enterprise."[21] He and his assistant Lewis Clement were working at the railroad offices regularly until past midnight, making estimates of the costs of eventual repair shops and other buildings.

In early summer, Judah had his next report printed and distributed. He used it to reply to a severe criticism raised by L. L. Robinson, who was one of the owners of the Sacramento Valley Railroad and one of the leading figures charging that the CP intended only to build the railroad to Dutch Flat and thereafter make money off the wagon road. Robinson also charged that Judah had made his original surveys over the Donner Pass while he was working for the Sacramento Valley line. Further, he wanted to know why the CP had not used the older line from Sacramento to Auburn and thus saved money. Because, Judah said, first of all the Sacramento line was eight miles longer than his location from K Street in Sacramento to Auburn. Second, the congressional appropriations in the Pacific Railroad Bill of 1862 did not apply to any already constructed road. Third, the bill required American iron rails, whereas the older line was constructed with English rails. Fourth, the Sacramento Valley line was heavily mortgaged, and the federal aid in the bill was to constitute a first lien on the road. Fifth, because the old road needed a great deal of repair and rehabilitation work. There were other reasons, but this was enough.[22]

Judah's report saved the CP, and thus its principal owners, the Big Four. Nevertheless, trouble persisted, and got worse. Judah did not approve of Crocker's construction methods and was suspicious—rightly— that the other three in the Big Four were sharing the stock of the CP that Crocker & Company were receiving. That July, Huntington returned from New York for a short but squalid visit. The Union had won a three-day battle at Gettysburg and thus turned back the Confederate offensive.

On the next day, July 4, Grant had forced Vicksburg to surrender. Still, there was trouble in California.

Judah wrote Strong, "Huntington has returned and has . . . more than his usual influence. . . . The wagon road seems to be a tie which unites them [the Big Four] and its influence seems to be paramount to everything else. . . . They do not hesitate to talk boldly, openly before me, but not to me, about it. They talk as though there was nobody in the world but themselves who could build a wagon road."[23]

Huntington walked along the riverbank to observe Crocker's grading and was furious. "I had given orders that the railroad was to go up I Street to Fifth and thence to B Street and out to the levee," he later said. But Judah had his own ideas and was running over the slough beyond I Street to Sixth and E Streets, and then out to the new levee, where the line diverged to the north and crossed the American River. According to Huntington, at the slough "water overflowed every year," and Judah's route would require more of the riprap-stone ballasting to protect the embankment. Work had been going on for several days when Huntington saw it. He admonished Judah, who told him that the other directors had approved his route. "I replied," said Huntington, "it will cost $200,000 more at least to put the road here, and I then ordered him to move the road."[24]

Huntington was pigheaded, but Judah was also stubborn. He refused to carry out Huntington's order, and the road is today on his line.

Huntington and Judah argued about everything. Judah felt that he was being pushed to a back seat as a hired hand on "his" railroad. Huntington was almost contemptuous of Judah. Some five years later, he said in a letter to E. B. Crocker, "There never were two peas more alike than Gen'l Dodge and T. D. Judah." He was one of the very few men who knew them both, and the only one to compare them to two peas. "If you should see Dodge you would swear that it was Judah," he went on, "and if you had anything to do with him you would be more than satisfied. The same low cunning that he [Judah] had. Then a large amount of that kind of cheap dignity that Judah had."[25]

In Huntington's view, Judah had nothing to complain about. The CP had picked him up when no one else would. The directors had raised his salary from an initial $100 a month to almost $500 per month and given him a stock-option plan that let him purchase five hundred shares of $100 stock at half-price. And he still demanded deference. To hell with that.

At a stockholders' meeting in mid-July 1863, the crisis came to a head.

Huntington proposed adding to the board, while Judah and Strong, along with their friends Bailey and Booth, resisted. By the end of the meeting, the board's two new members were Asa Philip Stanford and Dr. John Morse, the former Leland Stanford's brother and the latter Huntington's friend.

Judah wanted to mortgage, at 2 percent interest per month, the equipment that Huntington had bought in the East. Huntington argued that such a course would create a crushing interest load for the CP and impair the credit standing he had relied upon with Ames and other eastern men who had loaned the company money. Better to assess the stockholders for additional money to pay up on their stocks more rapidly than originally intended. The directors agreed. Hopkins began demanding that the directors pay for their stock in full, something the others in the Big Four began to do, even as they bought out other shareholders at sharply discounted prices. Hopkins asked Judah to pay at least 10 percent on the stock he had been given in lieu of salary. Judah protested that this was a tax on money already paid him, but he managed—just barely—to do it. Then he returned to the mountains, determined to turn the tables on the "shopkeepers."[26]

Judah felt that the Big Four were outright cheating—especially in the matter of where the Sierra Nevada began, and on the Dutch Flat wagon road—and were guilty of misusing the public trust and public monies.

Huntington's next actions deepened his anger. The day after the shake-up of the board, Huntington later recorded, there was "a good deal of hubbub."[27] He overruled Judah on some engineering decisions and, when Judah objected, said bluntly, if Judah and other objectors didn't like it why not buy out the Big Four? This degenerated into a shouting match. Huntington said, in a snide manner, that Judah could have all the stock of all the members of the Big Four at $100,000 each if he could raise the money.

As Huntington well knew, Judah and Bailey did not have the money to take that option. But the two men were determined that the Big Four had to go. They went into San Francisco to see if banker Charles McLaughlin, who owned the Western Pacific Railroad, might be willing to buy out the Big Four. But although he was interested, when McLaughlin heard that Huntington was willing to sell he sent Bailey a telegram: "If old Huntington is going to sell out, I am not going in." Bailey, discouraged, sold out himself, which left Judah standing alone.[28]

There were some obvious lessons here. First, how hard it was going to be to raise money for a railroad that so far didn't run anywhere. Second, Huntington's reputation was as high on the West Coast as on the East. Third, neither Huntington nor any other member of the Big Four had the slightest intention of selling out unless he had to do so, and even then wouldn't unless someone had a gun at his head. But for Judah the only lesson was that he could not raise the needed funds in San Francisco and it was necessary to go to New York if he wished to persist.

Huntington insisted that, since Judah and his friends could not come up with the money to buy out the Big Four, they must sell.[29] Judah apparently did, at least to the extent of trading in his five hundred shares of the CP for $100,000 in the CP's railroad bonds. He also may have sold his share of the franchise of the Nevada Central Railroad to Charles Crocker for $10,000 cash. And Bailey, who did sell out, was replaced on the board by a friend of Mark Hopkins.[30]

Judah was still the chief engineer, drawing a salary that was now up to $10,000 a year, although not necessarily paid in cash. At this time he also received $25,000 from the board, though in stock, not bonds.

But Anna later wrote, "Oh, some of those days were terrible to us! He felt they [the Big Four] were ungrateful to their trust and to him."[31] Judah made contact with money men in the East, most of all Cornelius Vanderbilt, who may have told Judah he was ready to buy out the Big Four but before he did so he wanted more details about the railroad. Probably using the $10,000 he had received from Crocker for Nevada Central Railroad stock, Judah bought tickets for Anna and himself to New York.

DESPITE the victories at Gettysburg and Vicksburg, the summer of 1863 went badly for the Union. There was no follow-up in Virginia against Lee's army. Out west there was better news: on July 9, the Union forces captured Port Hudson, Louisiana, and thus opened the Mississippi River. But less than a week later, a four-day draft riot took place in New York City, marked by burning, looting, and other outrages. Irish immigrant laborers, lowest paid of all, attacked African Americans and lynched several of them. Regular-army troops were sent from Gettysburg to the city to put down the rioters. There were other antiblack riots in other Northern cities, notably Detroit. At the end of the summer, the Confederates won a major victory in the two-day Battle of Chickamauga,

Tennessee, and drove the Union forces back into Chattanooga, where a siege began. The Union had expected victory after Gettysburg. That did not happen. The war still had a long way to go, and many Northerners were beginning to wonder if victory was worth the price in men's lives.

Nevertheless, in California the fight going on was over who would own the Central Pacific Railroad. Determined to bring about a change, on October 3, 1863, Judah and Anna set off on the steamer *St. Louis.* Unknown to the couple, a few days later, while sailing south, they passed the *Herald of the Morning,* which was coming north after leaving New York months ago, carrying the CP's first hundred tons of rail, the first locomotive, and other assorted hardware. Three more of the CP's cargoes were not far behind, carrying three more locomotives. The first came onto the Sacramento levee four days later, with the others soon after. The four locomotives were named the *Governor Stanford,* the *Pacific,* the *C. P. Huntington,* and the *T. D. Judah,* weighing (respectively) twenty-five tons, thirty tons, nineteen tons, and nineteen tons. Judah knew none of this, but he had arranged to meet Vanderbilt in New York and was confident he could have his way.

Napoleon, asked what qualities he looked for in his generals, replied, "Luck. Give me generals who are lucky."

Judah, up to now, had been lucky enough to cross the Isthmus several times without suffering a single day of sickness. But on this trip, he was caught in a rainstorm and got soaked in helping the women and children on board the steamer. Anna wrote, "I feared for him and remonstrated, for I knew he was doing too much—but he replied, 'Why I must, even as I would have some one do for you—it is only humanity.' That night he had a terrible headache and from that time grew worse and worse."

He apparently had contracted yellow fever. Anna sat by his bed "night and day to care for him—but it was terrible."

One night he roused himself and said, "Anna, what cannot I do in New York now? I have always had to set my brains and will too much against other men's money—now, what I cannot do!" He also managed to write a letter, with a shaking hand, to Dr. Strong. He said he had a "feeling of relief in being away from the scenes of contention and strife which it has been my lot to experience for the past year, and to know that the responsibilities of events as regards the Pacific Railroad do not rest on my shoulders." But if he were successful in the East, "there will be a radical change in the management of the railroad and it will pass into the hands of men of experience and capital," unlike the corrupt and incompetent men then in charge. If he failed, he warned, the Big Four would "rue the day they ever embarked on the Pacific Railroad.

"If they treat me well," he went on, referring to the Big Four, "they may expect similar treatment at my hands. If not, I am able to play my hand." He expected to return from New York with Vanderbilt and others in his party.[32]

On October 26, 1863, the same day Charlie Crocker saw the first of the CP rails spiked to the ties, the Judahs arrived in New York. Anna managed to get her husband transported to a hotel on Wall Street. There the surgeon of the steamer left them alone. She kept Judah awake by dipping her finger in the brandy bottle and having him take it that way. A doctor at the hotel cared for him, but, as Anna wrote, "we will pass over that terrible week." The doctor said that Judah was an overworked man and that such men fell victim to the fever. In a week he was dead. Anna put up a monument for him that contains his name, dates—March 4, 1826–November 2, 1863—and the words "He rests from his labors."[33] She buried him in a quiet country cemetery outside Greenfield, Massachusetts.

Specifically what Judah had hoped to accomplish in New York is not clear. He wanted to persuade Vanderbilt and others to buy out the Big Four. Why he wanted them to do so is plain enough, but how he thought they could manage the building of the biggest railroad in the country from a continent away is not. He hoped to bring Vanderbilt, his baggage bulging with money, to California with him to buy out the Big Four while he became the chief of construction as well as the chief engineer. With Montague and Clement working for him, he had two of the finest engineering assistants in the country, and he was certain he could do it.

But there is no indication that Vanderbilt was prepared to plunge into a California-to-Nevada railroad, much less move to the West Coast.

Luck. Had Judah lived, the history of the country might have been different. Speculation can go in all directions. There might have been no Big Four, or any of their legacies. The railroad from Sacramento over the Sierra Nevada out to the Salt Lake would have been built, but by whom, when, where, and with what name is pure guesswork.

It is impossible to say what Judah might have become, what he might have done. What we do know is that he had a fierce determination; that he could dream the biggest dreams; that he was a superb engineer with the keenest eye for terrain; that he knew his profession as well as anyone; that he could pick able assistants (Montague and Clement stand out); that he had married exceedingly well; that he could be amazingly convincing with his wife, with businessmen like the Big Four, with politicians either in California or in Congress, with the President of the United States, with other engineers, and with the public; that he was honest and trustworthy; and more.

But we also know that, although he could convince the Big Four and others to put their money and talent into the building of the Pacific railroad, he could not manage them. With those four he could never achieve harmony. Judah knew how stresses and strains worked on bridges, curved tracks, anything mechanical, but not how they worked on human beings. The Big Four wanted to build the railroad fast, at the greatest possible profit to themselves. He wanted to build it well. They got it done their way and he was squeezed out.

O N October 26, 1863, Charlie Crocker's men spiked the first rails to their ties. There was no ceremony, because of Huntington's telegram: "If you want to jubilate over driving the first spike," he wrote, "go ahead and do it. I don't. Those mountains over there look too ugly. We may fail, and if we do, I want to have as few people know it as we can. . . . Anybody can drive the first spike, but there are many months of labor and unrest between the first and last spike."[34] Nevertheless, the *Sacramento Union* noted the occasion and commented, "Nothing looks to the public as much like making a railroad as the work of laying down the iron on the road bed."[35]

By November 10, the first CP locomotive to arrive in California, named the *Governor Stanford*, made the first run ever for the Central Pacific.[36] The engine cost $13,688. It was more than ten feet tall and fifty feet long, with four driving wheels of four and a half feet in diameter. The driving rods and pistons were of wrought iron. The bell, made of brass, was painted maroon, green, red, orange, and yellow. Gold initials, "C.P.R.R.," were on the red tender. Locomotive and tender, with a full load of wood and water, weighed forty-six tons, making the *Governor Stanford* the biggest man-made thing in California. A twelve-pound cannon fired to mark the occasion.

It wasn't much of an occasion. The crowd was there—hangers-on mainly—to participate by climbing aboard the freight cars or cheering the train, but it went only as far as Twenty-first Street, where the tracks ended.[37] At least the war was going better for the Union: on November 25, General Grant's army won the Battle of Chattanooga and drove the Confederates back into Georgia.

The CP's acting chief engineer, meanwhile, appointed by the directors, was Samuel S. Montague. His first job was to survey the route as far as the Big Bend of the Truckee River, more than forty miles east of the California-Nevada line. Montague and a small team of surveyors completed this job in December 1863. Despite this achievement, Montague remained "acting" until March 1868. (He then stayed with the CP as chief engineer until 1883.)[38]

ROLLING stock arrived in Sacramento on a haphazard basis. Ships that brought the cut lumber for the car bodies did not have the iron frames and wheels for the cars. Tools were not delivered. Platform cars, used to deliver rails and ties to the end of track, came in ahead of passenger cars. By February 1864, however, enough had arrived for Stanford and Hopkins to show off Crocker's achievement. They took a party of thirty prominent men, including politicians, to see what had been accomplished. The rails by then reached to Junction (today's Roseville), sixteen miles out from Sacramento. There the passengers took horse-drawn carriages to seven miles beyond Newcastle.

They saw the graders at work and were filled with admiration for men who could perform such a demanding task. Engineers might do the surveys while Crocker oversaw the whole and bossed it, but it was the men who did the work—bending, digging, shoveling, throwing the dirt up on the embankment, bringing in the ballast by the cartload, and dumping it—who impressed people. Back behind Newcastle, where the track was being laid, it was the men who picked up the ties from the horse-drawn wagons, dropped them on the grade, lined them up. Others dropped the rails and made certain they were the requisite spread apart (four feet eight and a half inches), spiked them in with their heavy sledgehammers—three blows to a spike—and connected the ends with a fishplate. This was work fit to break a man's back, and they did it for $3 or so per day, plus board.

Many of the men were Irish immigrants who had just arrived in America. Crocker signed them up through agents in New York and Boston and had them shipped west at a terrific expense, plus time. There was some drunkenness, strikes, and slowdowns. Crocker petitioned the War Department for five thousand Confederate prisoners of war, without luck. He tried for newly freed African Americans, again with no luck. He tried for immigrants from Mexico. Same result. Some nineteen hundred out of a two-thousand-man crew he hired that summer fled for the Nevada mines almost as soon as they arrived at the end of track and had been fed a warm meal. They drove Acting Chief Engineer Samuel Montague nearly mad.[39]

GRADING work, as Lynn Farrar, a Southern Pacific historian described it, uses pick-and-shovel work most efficiently when low cuts or fills—one and a half to two feet—are required. Fills are made by what is called "casting"—i.e., shoveling. If there are over three feet of material, it can be double-casted—that is, it requires two "throws" to get the material into place for the grade. In most cases earth was plowed by heavy steel plows drawn by up to twelve oxen (it is more efficient to use an earth scraper, but the CP never used one). For distances greater than five hundred feet it was economical to "waste and borrow"—that is, dispose of cut material by "wasting" it and then "borrow" material for an adjacent fill. The location surveyors always tried to find a line that would "balance" the grading between cuts and fills so that there would be a minimal amount of moving of material.[40]

For seven miles beyond Newcastle, the cuts and fills were said by the *Sacramento Union* to be as great as any found in the nation. In the thirty-one miles from Sacramento to Newcastle, the grade of the roadbed rose steadily until, after Rocklin, it reached 105 feet to the mile, then grew to nearly 116 feet per mile (the steepest allowed by the Congress, and steeper than any other ascent in the Sierra Nevada). As the *Union* put it, "The labor of ascending the mountains is fairly begun."[41]

Bloomer Cut, just beyond Newcastle, would take months to complete. It was a sixty-three-foot-deep cut that ran eight hundred feet long, composed of naturally cemented gravel that had to be moved out one wheelbarrow at a time. The workingmen used black powder to loosen up the gravel at Bloomer. As much as five hundred kegs of blasting power a day in early 1864—more than most major battles in the ongoing Civil War—

at a cost of $5 to $6 per keg.[42] Every foot of the way through this cut had to be blasted with gunpowder, with the rock so hard that it was sometimes impossible to drill into it for a sufficient depth for blasting purposes. Shot after shot would blow out as if fired from a cannon.

After the blast the men used picks and shovels to fill their wheelbarrows or one-horse carts and to move the gravel out. The wedge they cut had almost vertical walls. This was the first of the obstacles to be overcome by the CP's workforce before it would meet with the UP's rails coming west, wherever that might be. How many sore, blistered, bleeding hands the Bloomer Cut required was not recorded, or how many damaged backs or crushed knees.

The men's boss on the spot was James Harvey Strobridge. He was thirty-seven years old, out of Ireland, over six feet in height, agile, energetic. He could curse with the men and lose his temper at any moment. He had worked on railroads in the East, then come to California, where he had worked for Crocker before being promoted. Crocker later recalled, "I used to quarrel with Strobridge when I first went in. Said I, 'Don't talk so to the men. They are human creatures. Don't talk so roughly to them.' Said he, 'You have got to do it, and you will come to it. You cannot talk to them as though you were talking to gentlemen, because they are not gentlemen. They are about as near brutes as they can get.' I found out that it was true."[43] More bad news. Strobridge lost the sight of his right eye at Bloomer Cut, when black powder was delayed and ended up exploding in his face.[44]

The *Sacramento Union* didn't write about such things. It was always upbeat. This was because it wanted the railroad built. Furthermore, the Big Four had decided on a policy that would later be widely adopted by twentieth-century corporations, which was to do everything possible to attract favorable mention from the media. In this case little or no money changed hands. But the editor of the *Union* did accept $2,000 worth of CP stock in 1863 and another $1,600 worth in 1864. His reporter in Washington got another ten shares. These bribes, called "gifts," were charged to the CP's construction account. Given the CP's many enemies and the terrible things being said about it, the directors judged that the favorable publicity was worth it.

Excursions were a way to generate excitement. On March 19, 1864, the CP provided an excursion to the end of track—then twenty-two miles out—for nearly two-thirds of the California state legislature, plus their families and friends. Two brand-new passenger cars, painted yellow on the outside and quite plush within, plus seven platform cars (a freight car with seats nailed down crosswise, but without a roof or sides), provided the transportation. Governor Stanford led the way, along with a brass band. The weather was fine. The legislators voted a month later to guarantee the CP's bond interest.

DESPITE the forward-looking publicity, however, the CP was going broke. The state had not paid what it had pledged, and the bonds from the U.S. government could not be collected until forty miles of the road had been completed and approved. Charlie Crocker later said about this time, "We could not borrow a dollar of money. We [the Big Four] had to give our personal obligations for the money necessary to carry us from month to month. There was not a bank that would lend the company a cent." For seventeen consecutive days there was nothing in the treasury—yet California law required that the men be paid in gold. Crocker, Hopkins, Stanford, and Huntington had to give their personal obligations for money to pay workers and to buy rails and other materials, putting up the bonds of the company besides as security. Crocker was not paid for the first eighteen miles until he took company bonds at 50 cents on the dollar. Meanwhile, his labor force continued to disappear into the mines. "I had become thoroughly warmed up to the building of this road," he later told an interviewer for H. H. Bancroft. "My whole heart was in it. I was willing to do anything to push it forward and I took great risks in doing it."[45]

The state legislature finally had agreed to guarantee the interest on $1.5 million of CP 7 percent bonds, but Hopkins managed to sell only a few before a suit was brought against the bill on the grounds of unconstitutionality. Though the company eventually won the suit, its bond sales were blocked until January 1865.[46]

On March 25, 1864, the locomotive *Governor Stanford* pulled into Sacramento with a load of granite from a quarry twenty-two miles to the east. This was the Central Pacific's first freight train. Exactly one month later, the company began regular passenger service to Roseville, three trains per day in each direction. On inaugural day, the train made eighteen miles in a bit less than forty minutes. Later, it averaged twenty-two miles per hour. In its first week, the CP carried 298 passengers and earned

$354.25. A pittance, but a heartening reversal of constantly paying out money without ever taking any in.[47]

The lack of money was an embarrassment, but the Big Four managed to overcome at least some of it with their own money. One employee who was worth his salary and more was Alfred A. Hart, a photographer hired by Stanford in 1864 to make a record in film of the construction of the road. He did a superb job, beyond anything any of the Big Four could have imagined, at the very least the equal of what a modern photographer could do with modern cameras. He got started right, making several memorable photographs of the locomotive C. P. *Huntington* as it crossed the American River Bridge.[48]

By the end of the first week of June, Crocker's men had laid track to Newcastle. Passenger trains began the run from Sacramento to Newcastle. There horse- and ox-drawn stages met the train and carried customers to Auburn; Dutch Flat; Steamboat Springs, Colorado; Virginia City, Nevada; and intermediate towns.

Huntington came back to California in June, to straighten things out. He persuaded the others that each man could do a little more. "Huntington and Hopkins," he said, "can, out of their own means, pay five hundred men for a year. How many can each of you keep on the line?" They said 150 men each. The result was an agreement to keep eight hundred men working for a year.[49]

ON June 14, the Dutch Flat and Donner Lake Wagon Road opened. It belonged to the Big Four, who had paid $350,000 for it out of their own funds. It would soon be doing a million-dollar-a-year business. The owners of the Sacramento Valley Railroad, much put out, published a pamphlet entitled *The Great Dutch Flat Swindle!!* It claimed once again that the CP had no intention of going beyond Dutch Flat, that its only plan was to build to that point, stop, and make money through the wagon road. The pamphlet ignored the surveys by Montague beyond the California-Nevada border, but it did cause some consternation among the stockholders of the CP.

CHARGES from L. L. Robinson and others who owned the never-built San Francisco & Washoe railroad had to be met. They were accusing the

Big Four of personal corruption. So effective were their charges that the Placer County Board of Supervisors, which held some $250,000 in CP stock, appointed two of its members, A. B. Scott and D. W. Madden, to investigate the Central Pacific's books. They worked their way through the books and concluded that the charges against the company were "evidently a machination of the brain of some individual who has no regard for the true interests of Placer County."[50]

*I*N March 1864, Lincoln appointed Grant as commander-in-chief of all Union forces. At the beginning of May, Grant sent the Union Army of the Potomac into the Battle of the Wilderness, which was indecisive despite horrendous casualties. But he still continued the offensive in northern Virginia, fighting a five-day battle at Spotsylvania in which he lost about ten thousand men, and he still continued after Lee. On June 1–3, he fought the Battle of Cold Harbor, losing about seven thousand men in one hour. But he continued to attack, and by June 18 he was besieging Petersburg, south of Richmond. General Sherman, meanwhile, started from Chattanooga into Georgia and by July was besieging Atlanta. On September 1, he captured and later burned the city. This victory raised Northern morale, as did the Union Navy's capture of Mobile, Alabama, on August 23. So did the early-October victory over Confederate cavalry at Winchester, Virginia. On October 31, Nevada became the thirty-sixth state. And on November 8, Lincoln was re-elected. It now appeared certain that the Union would be saved, North and South. It was up to the railroads to bring it together East and West.

*T*HE CP may have been broke, but as Huntington liked to brag, at any one time it had an average of about $1 million worth of equipment in transit. At the beginning of July 1864, the Big Four got some rare good news. Huntington had returned east and he sent a telegram from Washington informing his partners that the Pacific Railroad Bill had been redrawn and they could begin collecting their government bonds for every twenty instead of forty miles of track laid and approved by the government inspectors. There were many other favorable provisions in the bill. They were not home free, but things were looking up. Collecting what was their due from the government, however, proved to be difficult.

In November, the company put out a report on the condition of the line. The CP had some earnings, about $110,000 from passengers, the mail, and freight. Stock sales, however, were a scrawny $723,800 (not counting the subscriptions from Placer and Sacramento Counties). There was no cash on hand. A month later, Sam Montague published his annual report. Bloomer Cut had been finished but not yet tracked. He said that the 396,800 acres of land grants due from the government (but not yet granted) would bring in far more than $1.25 per acre, because it was mainly superb agricultural land. Further good news: his own survey had revealed that he could cut back on Judah's original route and eliminate several tunnels, thus saving time and money.

The bad news was that the cost of building the first thirty-six miles in 1863 and 1864 was nearly $3 million, or what Judah had anticipated spending for the first fifty miles. And not a single tunnel had yet been started. But as for the gaps, Montague had decided to bridge them with trestling, which, if made properly of pine, would last from eight to ten years. They could then be replaced with embankments, transporting the material on the cars at much less expense. Montague went on to report that the CP now had five locomotives, six first-class passenger cars, two baggage cars, and fifty freight cars.[51]

CP stock was then selling, if it sold, for 19 cents on the dollar. Its bonds went for half of par. Crocker, who admitted that he was suffering from severe insomnia, later recalled of the last part of 1864, "I would have been glad, when we had 30 miles of road built, to have got a clean shirt and absolution from my debts; I would have been willing to give up everything I had in the world, in order to cancel my debts."[52] The day after Christmas 1864, he lamented, "If we only had the Gov. Bonds in hand, that would help our credit amazingly, and crush out our enemies." But it would be five months before the company got those bonds.[53]

The Big Four were now fully aware of the prophecy of Judah's remark to Anna: "I cannot make these men appreciate the 'elephant' they have on their shoulders."[54] What they would do about it remained to be seen.

Chapter Six

LAYING OUT THE
UNION PACIFIC LINE
1864–1865

*T*HE surveyors came first. It was fitting, since they enjoyed life in the open more than most men. They were like the early-nineteenth-century mountain men, adventurous, capable of taking care of themselves, ready for whatever the wilderness threw at them. They were out in front of civilization, enjoying the views, the air, the campfire, the game cooked over it, drinking pure water from the rivers, creeks, and lakes, exploring the country, mapping it. For the surveyors it was pure joy.

Nothing could be done until they had laid out and marked the line. On flat ground, with no trees, the work involved in surveying was relatively easy, but there is precious little terrain on earth that has no ridges, bumps, ravines, or watercourses. Because a nineteenth-century train could not run up or down an incline of much more than 2 percent or go around a sharp curve, the hills or ridges had to be cut through to keep the tracks close to or at the level. The ravines had to be filled for the same purpose, or else a bridge had to be strung across them. In foothills, not to mention mountainous country, the task was far more difficult.

The surveyors who went first—Dodge, Dey, or Judah—were spared the task of laying out the exact line for the graders to follow, but they had to pick a general course that would work. They had to find passes through the mountains that could be reached from the ridges that kept below a 2 percent grade. They wanted to avoid major lakes and rivers. At stream crossings, they were looking for places that could be bridged without un-

125

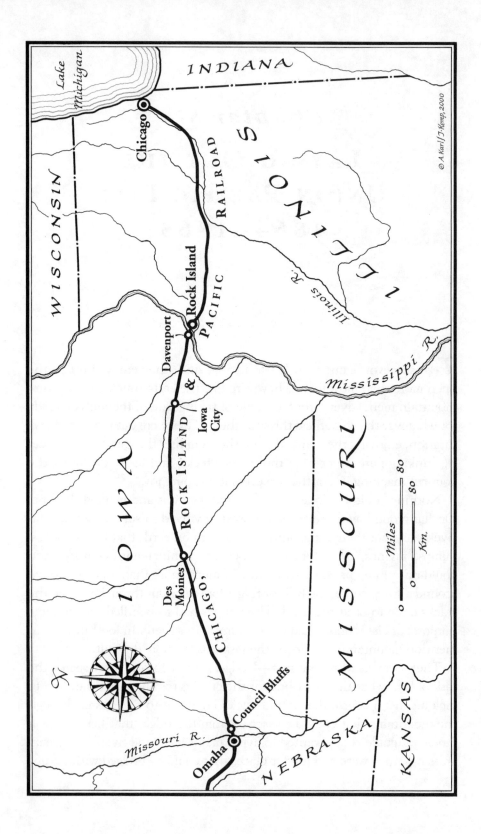

due difficulty. They hoped to hold the cuts and fills down to a minimum. They hoped to avoid major snowstorms that would fill the road and prevent train passage. In open, relatively flat country, they wanted to be next to or near streams, or at a place where water could be dug, since the steam engines required water to operate, as did the workers, men, and animals. Staying as far away as possible from Indians was another goal, but staying near buffalo and other animals was desirable. Most of all, the CP wanted to find a route that was as straight as possible to the east, while the UP wanted to go straight west.

The surveyors had nearly two thousand miles to cover, over every kind of terrain. They had no airplanes to provide them with a view from above. There were no helicopters, and no balloons. And for nearly the whole of the route, there were no maps. There was almost nothing to indicate settlements, for other than Salt Lake City, there were none of any size and only a few hamlets. Nor were there any topographical maps. They had nothing to indicate lakes or rivers, or the shape of the mountains over or around which the railroad would pass. Like Lewis and Clark and other explorers, they had only a vague idea of what lay ahead.

Despite their handicaps, the original surveyors and the ones who followed to mark out the line for the graders did a grand job. Nearly a full century later, in the 1950s and 1960s, when the surveyors flying in airplanes and helicopters and equipped with modern implements and maps laid out a line for Interstate 80, they followed almost exactly the route laid out by the original surveyors. Travelers in the twenty-first century driving on I-80 are nearly always in sight of the original tracks.

*T*HE story of Theodore Judah's initial examination for the Central Pacific and his report on crossing the Sierra Nevada has already been told. For the Union Pacific, Grenville Dodge was the first man—he recommended following the Platte River to the base of the Rocky Mountains—and Peter Dey was the second. On September 6, 1862, only four days after the initial meeting of the directors of the Union Pacific in Chicago, they instructed Dey to examine and report to them "the passes between the one hundredth and the one hundred and twelfth parallels of longitude."

Dey examined three routes west of Julesburg, Colorado. The first followed the valley of Lodgepole Creek coming out of the Black Hills, then went up and over the Black Hills through Cheyenne Pass and down to the Laramie Plains. The second followed the North Fork of the Platte River through western Nebraska, went over the Continental Divide via the relatively easy crossing called South Pass, then west to the Green River in western Wyoming. The third followed the South Platte River to Denver and then led up the Rockies to cross the Continental Divide at Berthoud Pass.

Dey concluded that the North Fork line would be much too long and dangerous, and going across Berthoud Pass would be beyond the capacity of nineteenth-century track builders and locomotives. Although the Denver newspapers, politicians, and businessmen wanted the tracks to come through the city, Dey was right. In fact, there was no railroad over Berthoud Pass until 1926. Dey picked the route over Cheyenne Pass (later called Lone Tree Pass, then Evans Pass, then Sherman Pass, ultimately changed to Sherman Summit and finally Sherman Hill). On November 4, 1864, Lincoln approved Dey's route.

Brigham Young also wanted the tracks to run through his city. And he was, with Durant's help, a member of the UP board of directors. On October 23, 1863, Young wrote to Durant saying that he had engineers ready to lay out a route through the Weber River Canyon down to Salt Lake City. In January 1864, he asked when Durant wanted him to begin work, promised workers to make the grade and lay the tracks, and reminded Durant that in the Weber Canyon there were "extensive coal beds." He concluded that he was "in readiness to aid in completing a work of such magnitude and usefulness as the Pacific Railroad."[1]

Young's eagerness and the potentially lucrative coal deposits notwithstanding, what was needed most of all, at least at first, was a line through the Wasatch Range into the Salt Lake Valley. Accordingly, Dey recruited two fine engineers, Samuel B. Reed and James A. Evans, to head separate parties to find a passage. On April 25, 1864, Dey wrote to Reed instructing him to run a line from Salt Lake City up to where the Weber River broke through the mountains, then east up the Weber Canyon to Echo Creek, and then on to Wyoming. Dey wanted Reed and Evans to examine other routes, but he thought the Weber-Echo would be best, although he admitted "that is rugged country and there is not enough known of that region to give you more than a general outline." Dey concluded, "As a general rule it will be safe to sacrifice distance and straight lines to cost of construction, the aim of the company being to secure a line they can afford to build."[2] That last admonition remained to be seen.

• • •

*R*EED headed west in April 1864, first by train to the end of track at Grinnell, Iowa, then by stagecoach to Omaha. It was an excruciating ride. In Omaha there was a rush of gold seekers trying to get to the latest discovery, in Montana. "Hundreds pass through here every day," Reed wrote, "old men, young men, the lame and the blind with women and children all going westward seeking the promised land." The stage ride to Salt Lake City consumed thirteen days, and he was more than glad to get there, for "I have never been in a town of this size in the United States where everything is kept in such perfect order. No hogs or cattle are allowed to run at large in the streets and every available nook of ground is made to bring forth fruit, vegetables or flowers for man's use."[3]

Reed met with Brigham Young, who gave him equipment and fifteen men. After training them, Reed headed north to where the Weber River emerged from the Wasatch Range onto the valley. He went up the canyon until he came to Devil's Gate, "the wildest place you can imagine." After further progress upstream, he came to Echo Creek and followed it across the mountains to Bear River, north of the Uinta Mountains and near present-day Evanston, Wyoming. From there it was almost straight east to Omaha.

The exploration took Reed four months. He never enjoyed work so much. The brilliance of the air, the warm days and cold nights, the beauty of the scene, and the idea that he was the advance agent in transforming this land from nature's wilderness to civilization, all transformed him.[4] From August to November, he did more surveying, looking for a route south of the Weber River, then for one leading west from Salt Lake City, and finding neither. He returned to Omaha by stage. It was a bone-rattling trip, twenty days and nights of blizzards that, he moaned, "almost froze the life blood out of me."[5] He could only hope that 1865 would be better. Another surveyor was Ogden Edwards. His assistant, Hezekiah Bissell, called him "the hardest drinker I ever saw. His regular drink was two pony glasses of straight whiskey." Yet Edwards was a highly regarded surveyor.[6]

*D*OC Durant was a man heartily disliked. He had few redeeming qualities to overcome his arrogance, bluster, quick and often wrong judgments, bossiness, show-business attributes, and lack of common sense. Yet he did well, sometimes, in picking out the men he wanted in charge of building the UP, especially the man at the top. All through the Civil War, he had kept asking Grenville Dodge to be his chief engineer. On that one he was exactly right. His problem was getting Dodge to accept.

There was no chance of it so long as the war went on. Nor so long as the Native Americans of the Plains were burning, looting, raping, and robbing the American settlers in their homesteads or villages. Grant had appointed Dodge to command the Department of the Missouri, comprising all the land between the Missouri River and the Rocky Mountains. On January 15, 1865, Lincoln sent Dodge a telegram ordering him to pay special attention to Missouri, whose citizens were badly divided between North and South; he was needed to keep the peace.

But both Dodge and Grant believed that Dodge's main task was to curb the Indians, who had done great damage. On January 7, 1865, Sioux, Cheyenne, and Arapaho rode into Julesburg, Colorado, killed fifteen soldiers and a number of civilians, and burned every building. Farms along the Platte River were also burned to the ground. Among those killed was Lieutenant Casper Collins, for whom Casper, Wyoming, is named. Dodge wrote that Collins was found "horribly mutilated; his hands and feet were cut off and his heart torn out. He was scalped and had over 100 arrows in him."[7] After witnessing one Native American meeting, the wandering British reporter Henry Morton Stanley put it succinctly: "The Indian chiefs were asking the impossible. The half of a continent [they wanted] could not be kept as a buffalo pasture and hunting ground."[8]

In 1865, Dodge moved his headquarters out of St. Louis to Fort Leavenworth, on the Missouri River in Kansas. It was cold. The thermometer dipped below zero almost nightly, and sometimes to as low as thirty below just before dawn. To meet the Indian threat, Dodge sent out a general order to all district commanders on the Great Plains: "Place every mounted man in your command on the South Platte route; repair telegraph lines, attack all bodies of hostile Indians large or small; stay with them and pound them until they move north of the Platte or south of the Arkansas [River]. I am coming with two regiments of cavalry to the Platte line and will open and protect it."[9] In so doing, Dodge was carrying out his specific injunction from Grant, "to remove all trespassers [Indians] on land of the Union Pacific Railroad."[10] He toured the country and had every soldier on the Platte in the saddle instead of by a fire in the stockades. Shortly, the general manager of the Overland Telegraph notified Washington that telegraphic communication had been resumed from the Missouri River to California.

Grant wired him a query: "Where is Dodge?"

The manager telegraphed back, "Nobody knows where he is but everybody knows where he has been."[11]

DODGE was not employed by the Union Pacific and he had not seen Dey's report to the directors recommending the route up Lodgepole Creek. His job was to look for Indians making depredations on white settlers, but he was also looking for a route over the Black Hills. If he was looking for himself, to make something for himself out of his exertions, then so be it. If he was looking for his country, so much the better. If he was looking for his superior—William T. Sherman, who in 1865 had been made commanding officer of the Military Division of the Mississippi, embracing the land lying between the Mississippi River and the Rocky Mountains—then he was doing exactly what his superior wanted.

As Sherman took up his new duties, he recorded in his *Memoirs*, "My thoughts and feelings at once reverted to the construction of the great Pacific Railway, which was then in progress. I put myself in communication with the parties engaged in the work, visiting them in person, and assured them that I would afford them all possible assistance and encouragement." Not that he had all that much faith. When he heard the politicians talk of throwing a railroad line across the Great Plains and Rocky Mountains, Sherman said, he was at first "disposed to treat it jocularly."[12]

DODGE'S campaigning, although critical to the UP, met with strong objections from Durant and his fellow directors. Durant wired Dodge reminding him that he had promised to become the railroad's chief engineer upon the expiration of the war. The directors offered him $10,000 a year and stock in the Crédit Mobilier to resign from the army and begin work at once. In his reply, Dodge pointed out the obvious: no railroad could be built across the Plains until the Indians had been subdued.

General Sherman, meanwhile, had come to realize the correlation of the Indian campaigns and the task of the chief engineer of the UP. He backed Dodge in everything he did and communicated his belief to the UP directors. No one in the United States was then ready to do battle with William T. Sherman. The directors therefore telegraphed word to Dodge that the position of the chief engineer would be held open for him until he had completed his campaign against the Indians.[13]

*A*SIDE from lines marked by surveyors and Dodge, what the UP needed most was money. President Lincoln was once again there to help out. On January 20, 1865, the President called Congressman Oakes Ames into his office. Lincoln called him "the broad shouldered Ames." Ames arrived immediately after dinner and stayed until well after midnight. The two men talked about the UP. "Ames, you take hold of this," Lincoln said. "If the subsidies provided are not enough to build the road, ask double, and you shall have it. The road must be built, and you are the man to do it. Take hold of it yourself. By building the Union Pacific, you will become the remembered man of your generation."[14] Ames, glad to have Lincoln appeal to him, began putting money and his political clout into the enterprise. He and his brother Oliver bought $1 million worth of Crédit Mobilier stock, and he loaned the UP $600,000.[15]

It certainly needed it. Durant ordered the railroad built with the oxbow south of Omaha as an integral part of it, which would bring in more government money and lands—when built.* Meanwhile, the fight over the oxbow had cost the UP almost $500,000 and even more in good will. The *Chicago Tribune* called the oxbow an "outrage" perpetrated by "a set of unprincipled swindlers" intent on "building the road at the largest possible expense to the Government and the least possible expense to themselves."[16]

Be that as it may, Durant had other problems. Engineer Samuel Reed reported that his surveys were "extremely difficult and dangerous" because of the "hostility of the Indians everywhere. Until they are exterminated, or so far reduced in numbers as to make their power contemptible, no safety will be found in that vast district extending from Fort Kearney to the mountains, and beyond."[17]

* As it was, but when E. H. Harriman took over the road—which was bankrupt at the time, 1901—he straightened it out, using Dey's original line.

In addition to laying out the route, Durant faced a logistical nightmare. To get building materials to Omaha required shipping them up the Missouri River from St. Joseph, Missouri, 175 winding miles on a river that was navigable by steamboat only for three or four months per year. The only wood available in the area for ties was cottonwood, which was so wet that it could last but two or three years, and the UP needed twenty-five hundred ties for each mile. Laborers were hard to get, so hard that Dodge offered captive Indians for the grading. Irishmen had been contracted in New York, and they worked hard, but they also played hard and were likely to strike when they were not paid.

*I*N April 1865, as the Civil War came to an end, Lincoln was shot and killed. The sadness of Lincoln's death was somewhat compensated for by the end of the war. Though the best and most powerful friend the transcontinental railroads ever had was gone, for Durant and the UP, the first thing that meant was thousands of unemployed young men from the Union and Confederate armies. For both the CP and the UP, it meant the unleashing of great quantities of money. With almost explosive force the industrial, financial, and transportation systems of the North were let loose. The United States began to take its place as a world power.

The Gilded Age was about to begin, but before America could industrialize, it needed a transportation system. On July 22, 1865, *Harper's Weekly* ran an article on "Railroads in Peace-Time" that summed up what had been accomplished and predicted what was to come. "From 1859 to 1864 the business of the roads had more than doubled," it opened. And in June 1865, "Traffic returns show an average increase over last year of 30 to 40 per cent—far in excess of those of the most active period of the war." The magazine said, "This is an astounding fact, one for which not one among the best-informed railroad men or Wall Street financiers was prepared." In fact, they had all predicted that the end of the war would mean a sharp downturn in railroad traffic. The article went on to state, "Our roads, at best, are only half built. They only cost, on the average, $40,000 a mile," whereas the British roads cost $170,000 per mile, the French roads $101,000.

For the United States, there was no limit that the magazine could see.[18] The future for the railroads looked especially bright to the west of the Missouri River and east of the Sierra Nevada, where the government owned nearly all of the land and would give much of it away to the railroads.

T HE surveyors were critical to making it happen. For the UP, although the general route north of the Platte River had been set, the exact line had not. Meanwhile, with all his worry about labor and ties and rails and locomotives and money and more, Durant and the UP managed to spike not one rail until July 1865.

Still, the corporation had surveyors working out in front. Among them was Arthur Ferguson, one of four sons of the first chief justice of the territorial Supreme Court of Nebraska and one of the early congressmen from the state. Arthur was reading law, preparatory to taking his bar exam (he graduated from the University of Iowa with the degree of LL.B. in 1870). Between 1865 and 1869, he worked spring, summer, fall, and on one occasion through the winter for the UP as rodman and assistant engineer. He kept a journal, sometimes missing a day or more, sometimes months, but often writing in rich detail. He is described as a long-faced, rather solemn-looking man, but he kept a fine journal.[19]

In the summer of 1865, the twenty-four-year-old Ferguson went to work as a surveyor for the civil engineers who were locating the track from the mouth of the Loup River, at the village of Columbus, Nebraska, along the north side of the Platte River for 150 miles west. Previous surveyors had already marked the line from Omaha to Columbus. Ferguson's party consisted of fifteen men, including assistants, teamsters, and cooks, carried by several covered wagons drawn by horses and mules. They slept on buffalo robes in five white duck wall tents. They got up early, traveled all day, and pitched their tents around a central campfire.

Immediately after a breakfast of meat, bread, potatoes, and strong coffee, the teams were hitched and "we were all rolling over the prairie westward." Very occasionally they saw a cabin or a few acres of sod-breaking by some hardy pioneer. By noon of the second day, they were at the banks of the Elkhorn River, "one of the most crooked and winding streams I ever saw." It would run nearly a mile to make a gain of only a few hundred feet. The banks were fringed with beautiful grasses and flowers. The river ran sixty feet below the banks. "Before us was spread a vast plain as far as the eye could reach." As they traveled farther west, they came to Raw Hide Creek, a small muddy stream that took its name from an 1849 event in which a man headed to California for the goldfields was caught by Indians, who proceeded to skin him alive and torture him to death.

On August 2, the party reached Columbus, where it camped for four days in order to provide supplies for the survey, primarily "stake timber" for the line. Thus did one of the principal problems of building a track across the Great Plains present itself: there was no timber for the next two hundred miles or so. The surveyors needed stakes to mark the line.

When the party got going, the wagons hauling the supplies went ahead to make camp along the Platte, while the surveyors with a wagon carrying their instruments, food, and stakes went to the line and started staking it. They worked until noon. After an indifferent lunch packed in their wagon, they started out again, and by nightfall had gone ten miles. By the third day of ten miles per day, the party camped "at the deserted homestead of some settler who had been run off by the savages. Quite a number of whites had been killed some time previous by roaming war parties of Sioux." But the Indians did not bother the surveyors, who were well armed. The surveyors were usually well north of the Platte River, while the remainder of the party went forward to set up camp. Since the surveyors often worked until dark, the others would make a large camp-fire to guide them in.

Each day, the surveyors followed the route laid down by Dodge, Dey, Reed, or Evans. They used the wooden spikes to leave a message for the graders—here is the exact line. Sometimes it was flat; sometimes it crossed ridges that would have to be cut; sometimes there were drainage ditches that must be filled, or occasional creeks that must be bridged. Sometimes the surveyors found a way to go around ditches or ridges, which saved time and money even though curves would have to be built to accommodate the track. Such devices of economy explain why today the old track bed seems to wander whereas the replacement laid out in the twentieth century runs in a straighter line.

DODGE was determined that the UP be built just as soon as he could bring peace to the Great Plains. In September 1865, while returning from the Powder River campaign in today's Wyoming, he set out to discover a pass over the Black Hills (today's Laramie Mountains). He wasn't hope-ful, because of the short slopes and great height of the hills on the eastern side, but he never overlooked anything. Striking Lodgepole Creek on the first day of fall, Dodge took six mounted men with him to explore up the creek (which eventually discharged itself into the South Platte River, near Julesburg). When he got to the summit of Cheyenne Pass, he headed south along the crest of the mountains to get a good view of the country. His other troops were meanwhile passing south down the east base of the Black Hills. He was on the divide of the hills (not the Continental Divide, which is to the west, near present-day Rawlins). It was a most beautiful spot, with meadows spreading out, covered with grass and flowers, buttes and outcroppings, ravines, no trees to speak of, with the Medicine Bow Mountains to the west and south and the Laramie Mountains to the north, and the Black Hills surrounding him.

About noon, Dodge and his party and a group of Cheyennes discovered each other.* He gained the high point, then began to signal to his troops at the base of the mountains, meanwhile dismounting and starting down the ridge between Crow Creek and Lodgepole Creek. He kept the Cheyennes at bay by firing at them occasionally. It was nearly night when his troops saw his smoke signal and came to his relief.

In going down the ridge separating the two creeks (Crow Creek flows into today's Cheyenne, Wyoming, and Lodgepole Creek flows to the city's north), Dodge wrote, "We followed this ridge out until I discovered it led down to the plains without a break." He said to his men, "I believe we have found the crossing of the Black Hills." He marked the place by a lone tree. Dodge's mentor Dey might have questioned his use of the verb "discovered" in his account, but never mind. Dodge, like Dey, had found the way to go.[20]

*B*EHIND the surveyors came the graders. There were a few hundred of them, mainly recruited in New York or other Eastern cities, some immigrants born in Ireland or elsewhere in Europe, some second-generation Americans. They were lured to the West by the promises of steady work

---

* Dodge was approximately at a spot on today's Interstate 80, about twenty-five miles west of the junction of I-15 and I-80, at eight thousand feet of altitude, or fifteen feet short of the highest point on the I-80 system. There is a sign there that points to, alas, geographical features of the countryside rather than Dodge's adventure.

and high wages—as much as $2 or even $3 a day, sometimes more. They were mostly young veterans of the Civil War, with little or nothing to go home to. In Nebraska they were organized into teams.

They were commanded by various bosses. The "boarding boss" was at the top—his tent went up first when camp was made. Then came the camp doctor, if there was one—often there was not—whose job was relatively easy, because when the water was good and the food untainted the health of the men was excellent. They lived in the open air, worked hard, ate and slept well. If there was no camp doctor, the boarding boss had a medicine chest filled with bandages and a few simple remedies.

There were various stable bosses who assigned the men to their jobs. Each boss might have one hundred horses and mules working his wagons, but he knew them all by name. The driver and the harness for a team were never changed, and each driver was responsible to the boss, who was expected to turn the outfit back to the contractor at the end of the season in as good shape as when he took it.

Then there were the walking bosses, who had their eyes constantly on the men. They used vigorous profanity and time checks to keep the men working. If a boss caught a man loafing, he cursed at him. The next time, he cursed in a louder voice. The third time, the walking boss called the timekeeper and gave the man his time, adding for the enlightenment of the others, "This is not a Salvation Army, but a grading outfit."

Occasionally the Irishmen went on strike—whenever Durant failed to forward their pay. When it did not arrive on time, they turned volatile and surly. "What a time we have been having here for the last four weeks," a weary contractor reported in the summer of 1865, "with Irishmen after their pay, I can assure you it is enough to make men crazy."[21]

The men worked with shovels (sold by Ames, of course), picks, wheelbarrows, teams, and scrapers. The younger men were usually the drivers, the older ones did the plowing and filling. The men in their late teenage years or early twenties were generally the shovelers. The job of all was to lay out a grade for the track, one that was level with only a bit of curve, two feet or more above the ground, so it would not be flooded out. Mainly that required digging dirt, filling a wheelbarrow with it, taking it to the grade, and dumping it. Sometimes two men used a dump wagon drawn by a horse.

They dumped the dirt onto the bare ground. First the grass and roots had to be removed and tossed aside—not turned over. The dumping boss was a man with a good eye and an unmistakably Irish accent. He stood on the grade and indicated with his shovel where he wanted the dirt dumped. He leveled the dirt with his shovel, and under his constant care the grade grew with just the proper pitch until the top was leveled off, ready for the crossties. The grade at the top was wide enough for one or two tracks, or twelve feet from "shoulder to shoulder."

Promptly at noon, the big watch of the walking boss snapped and he called out "Time!" Every man in the outfit heard him, as did the mules and horses. Everything stopped. The animals were unhitched and put to water. Then the men went to the boarding tent, where their appetites made even the coarsest fare taste good, if not delicious. At one o'clock, the shrill voice of the walking boss was heard and the men went back to work—although after the hearty meal it took a vast amount of profanity to get them stepping again.

The bosses, it was widely agreed, were not tyrants. The average grader had muscles like steel and could take care of himself in a rough-and-tumble fight, and anyway the bosses did not resort to pick handles. There were exceptions, but generally they ruled with comparative ease. And they got the grade done.

When the bosses couldn't level the grade, the scrapers, drawn by oxen or up to four horses, were called in to do the job. When solid rock was encountered in a ridge line, which was seldom in the Great Plains, the men used hand drills and stuffed the hole with black powder. When the rocks blew apart, the remainder of the cut was dug out and leveled. A cut was done entirely by hand. The men would form an endless chain of wheelbarrows. For fills, the dirt was dumped in. The land yielded nothing but some limestone for masonry work. There was no gravel for ballast, so mainly sand was used.

At night, after supper, the men would play cards or sing songs, such as "Poor Paddy he works on the railroad" or "The great Pacific railway for California hail, bring on the locomotive, lay down the iron rail." Others were "Pat Malloy," "Whoop Along Liza Jane," or "I'm a rambling rake of poverty, the son of a gamboleer." The low notes of the Jew's harps and harmonicas floated across the cool night air. The songs were sung almost regardless of harmony and in contempt of tune.

By mid-October 1865, the *Omaha Weekly Herald* reported that the graders were up to the Loup River (Columbus) and advance teams were rapidly making their way across the next hundred miles. Preparations were being made for putting in the foundations of the Loup Fork Bridge, which, at fifteen hundred feet in length, was "a great work in itself" and was scheduled to be erected in the spring of 1866.[22] The trestles were being made in Chicago in accordance with measurements and instructions laid out by the surveyors.

*B*EHIND the graders came the track layers. In 1865, they made only forty miles, just beyond the Elkhorn River, and their story is best saved for later. Meanwhile, the white population of the Great Plains was increasing. Each year about a hundred thousand persons traveled either part or all of the way across the Plains. Many of them became a part of the 10 percent of transfrontier population occupying what the Census Bureau called the "vacant spaces on the density map." Historian Oscar Winther comments: "They were the hunters, trappers, traders, miners, lumberjacks, soldiers, government agents, and cowmen; they were the vanguards of migrants en route from old to new locations; they were the packers, teamsters, stage and express men, sutlers, travelers, and floaters of all types." It was estimated that they numbered 250,000 by 1870.[23]

*D*URANT'S problem was money. He brought much of it on himself by his extravagance. He had hoped to raise money through a subscription to Crédit Mobilier, but it had fallen flat. Then, with great fanfare, the UP tried a public stock subscription, but Charles Sherman, the general's brother who was working for the UP, said that the offering failed so utterly that "not a dollar was subscribed."[24] Another director complained to Durant, "You do spend an *awful* pile of money." He borrowed money at 19 percent per annum. "We were deeply in debt," Oakes Ames recalled, "and very much embarrassed, and we were using our credit to the utmost extent in driving the work along."[25]

Much of it couldn't be helped. There was no timber, and only thin groves of cottonwood, so the immense amounts needed for ties, trestles, buildings, and other purposes had to be shipped up the Missouri River. The UP's first locomotive, called the *General Sherman*, had arrived via this route along with two flatcars, with two other locomotives and more flatcars to follow in 1865. The Burnettizer—a machine that treated the cottonwood through a vacuum device that drew out the water in the trees, putting a zinc solution in its place—was also at hand.* Cotton-wood made ties that were too soft and perishable, even when Burnet-tized, but the cost of importing hardwood was prohibitive.

Oakes Ames put in some more of his money and persuaded Cyrus H. McCormick, the inventor of the reaper, and others to buy stock in the Crédit Mobilier. Durant meanwhile drove the work as best he could, which meant primarily by telegraphic orders. He told the contractors to use cottonwood, which when treated would last for three years, long enough for train tracks coming from the east to reach Council Bluffs and thus reduce the cost of hardwood timber ties from Wisconsin. Other telegrams read, "How much track now laid how much do you lay per day?" "Increase your force on ties. Important the track should be laid faster, cant you lay one mile per day." "What is the matter that you cant lay track faster." "Run the Burnetizing machine night and day." "I insist on being fully advised."[26]

And so on. What Durant needed was to secure government loans on the track already laid, but the UP got nothing until it had completed acceptable track. Working at a furious pace, the crews managed in 1865 to finish forty miles of road with all the required sidings, station houses, and water stations before the weather laid them off.[27]

ONE young engineer working for the UP, James Maxwell, who had previously been employed by the Pennsylvania Railroad, was astonished by what he saw in the Platte River Valley: plenty of wild game, along with the excitement of exploring a new country and a little element of danger from hostile Indians to give zest to everything. In a memoir written in 1896, he said, "This was a grass country. On the river bottoms it grew to be over seven feet in height." Some surveyors said the grass was as much as ten feet high. Maxwell went on, "In riding a buggy a person would have to stand up to see over the top of the grass. In running a line

---

* The Burnettizer was a huge, one-hundred-by-five-foot cylinder, sent to Omaha by steamship. By 1866, the company had three of them. After the water was drained and the zinc solution put in, the ties were heated and dried. The ties cost 16 cents each to be processed. The UP saved money in building, but spent much more in replacing the cottonwood ties—but by then the railroad was completed. This was in accord with the general principle: Nail it down! Get the thing built! We can fix it up later.

through such grass, he was liable to be lost." That fall he thought it "very beautiful to see the fires at night, from the various camps, circling around the hills among the short grass, but when the grass in the bottom lands caught fire, it was a grand and appalling sight." A young surveyor named H. K. Nichols wrote in his diary, "The valley is one of the most fertile I suppose in the states."[28]

That fall of 1865, out on the Plains, the young surveyor Ferguson saw unusual sights. Near today's Grand Island, "for a distance of ten miles the prairie is one vast prairie-dog village. For miles and miles the ground is completely covered with their holes, and on most of them, as far as the eye can reach, you will see them sitting upright on their haunches." Some of the men shot and ate them, but not Ferguson.

At Fort Kearney, on the south bank of the Platte, there were some four hundred troops in quarters, both infantry and cavalry. At this point four men from the surveyors' party said they were damned if they would go on, for it was here that the Indian danger became acute and would remain so until the Rocky Mountains. Here too the party received its military escort, a sixty-man company of the Twelfth Missouri Cavalry, which Dodge had just sent to Fort Kearney. "The soldiers were very much dissatisfied at this action," Ferguson recorded, "and at times were on the point of rebelling against their officers. They said that they had enlisted for the war to fight rebels and not to go out into the western wilderness to fight Indians." But when the party set out again the following day, half the Twelfth Missouri stayed with the surveyors while the other half stayed with the main party on the river.

Ferguson described the soldiers' way of making camp. "It is a busy and lively sight," he wrote, "after the day's march to see the troopers busily engaged in rubbing down their animals, for whom they have quite an affection, calling them by pet names. Their campfires burn brightly after nightfall and the solemn tread of the sentinel, with bright gleaming carbine, assures us if, in the still hours of night we are attacked, the enemy will receive a warm reception."

West of Kearney, "the country becomes wilder and more desolate." The grass grew several feet in the spring and summer but by mid-September was dead. Vast prairie fires illuminated the country at night, vast volumes of black smoke rose up during the day. "The air is full of flying cinders and the smell of burning grass. We come across vast herds of wild game, mostly antelope." At night the party slept with loaded arms by their sides, additional ammunition cartridges in their hats beside their heads, along with their loaded revolvers.

The soldiers, who spent the day scouting to the north, often returned with antelope, deer, or part of an elk strapped behind their saddles. By October, the Platte was so low it could be forded everywhere, and at times the men would wade out to the small islands to gather in the grapes that grew in wild profusion.

On November 1, the party reached the hundredth meridian (near today's Cozad, Nebraska), which had been the objective point. The men expected to return to Omaha, the soldiers to Fort Kearney. They were all eager to do so, for the nights were getting much colder. But their leaders held them over to triangulate the Platte. Finally, at daylight on November 10, they received permission to start home. "At the call of the bugle, the soldiers as one man flung themselves into the saddle and commenced the march."

But in an hour, they saw two individuals approaching them, who turned out to be Jacob House and James A. Evans. House was a UP division engineer, and Evans a surveyor who had, at Dey's orders, among other things, run the original line along the north bank of the Platte. They announced that they had come to take charge of the party, which was to continue its survey to the south, down to the Republican River. The decision to go on straight west had not yet been reached; the railroad might well bend to the south, then west to Denver. This news came as "a surprise and a great disappointment to us," Ferguson recorded. Some of the party said they would not go on.

Evans dismounted and told those who refused to continue to step forward three paces. No one dared.

"All right, men," Evans proclaimed. "Turn about and march back to the old camp."

The troops joined the railroaders. The soldiers "complained a great deal. They said that in case of an attack they would leave us to ourselves and do nothing towards our defense."

The next morning was "very cold." Clouds laden with snow moved in. The men had to cross the Platte River, which was in places up to their armpits and terribly cold. The following day, "we passed the new-made graves of some twelve men who had recently been killed by the savages." Snow began, and by mid-afternoon "we were in the midst of a furious storm." The party pitched its tents in a cottonwood grove. "We all had a terrible night of it. The cold was severe and the ground was so damp and wet that it was next to impossible to sleep. The horses were fed with large quantities of cottonwood limbs."

After two more dismal nights, Ferguson and the men and troopers started for the Republican. "We are now in the midst of the worst Indian country in the entire West," he wrote. "It is the very stamping ground of the war parties of various tribes." No wonder. "This is the great buffalo country of the West," he noted, "and sometimes a black, surging mass can be seen extending in every direction as far as the eye can reach, the herd running up into thousands and thousands." The soldiers wasted their ammunition by shooting them in sport, "leaving them on the ground for the wolf and the raven."

Despite an abundance of animal life such as no modern man has ever seen, and only Lewis and Clark and their men and a few other white men had seen before, Ferguson was struck by the scene. "This is a terrible country," he wrote, "the stillness, wildness and desolation of which is awful. Not a tree to be seen. The stillness too was perfectly awful, not a sign of man to be seen, and it seemed as if the solitude had been eternal."[29]

Shortly thereafter, the party returned to Omaha, the soldiers to Fort Kearney. They would start again, from the hundredth meridian, when the weather became fair.

*T*HE 1864 Pacific Railroad Act required the UP to complete the first hundred miles of track by June 27, 1866. Durant had talked confidently of building that amount in 1865, but he didn't come close. In September 1865, he confessed that the UP would be lucky to complete sixty miles by the end of the year, but he didn't come close to that either. By December 31, the UP had laid forty miles of track. Because the 1864 bill had reduced the number of miles completed before the bonds would be given out from forty to twenty, that feat meant that, when the government commissioners accepted the UP's forty miles of track, the railroad would get $640,000 of government bonds ($320,000 per twenty miles, or $16,000 per mile).

In addition, Durant had gathered together in Omaha a set of superb workers who were just waiting for the warm winds of spring before starting out again, either to lay track or to grade or survey. They were tough, hardy, eager. And with the war over, there were thousands of young men, all veterans of either the Union or the Confederate Army, who were looking for work. The UP's first locomotive had arrived. Further, Durant had faced up to the need for reorganization, on which he expected to get started immediately.

Meanwhile, he was pushing his original surveyors as hard as he could. He had pulled Evans in, but Samuel Reed was still out there, working well beyond the valley of the Great Salt Lake into areas that were a long way away for the UP. Still, Durant wanted to know. In the fall, he had told Reed to find a route from Salt Lake to the Sierra Nevada.

Reed set out, intending to go via the valley of the Humboldt River to the valley of the Truckee, on the California-Nevada border. In November, he wrote to Durant. He was unhappy to report that he had not reached the Truckee, because of lack of water, but he had made a line from Salt Lake to the place where the Humboldt sank into the ground. After that the desert stopped him. Reed reported that he could run a line from the Salt Lake to the valley of the Humboldt "without a cut or fill exceeding 15 feet or grades exceeding 75 feet per mile."[30]

That was good news, even though it would be a considerable time before either the UP or the CP could take advantage of it. But the anticipation was running at a fever pitch. The Denver-based *Rocky Mountain News* spoke for nearly all of America when it stated, "There is one theme everywhere present. The one moral, the one remedy for every evil, social, political, financial and industrial, the one immediate vital need of the entire Republic, is the Pacific Railroad."[31]

The editors of the *Railroad Record,* however, were critical of the way Durant and company were laying the track. "We confess that we are not satisfied," they wrote. "Neither is the country, which has a right to expect more vigor in its construction." The sloth and poor-quality construction (for example, sand rather than gravel was being used for ballast), according to the *Record,* were "an insult to the generosity and magnanimity of the American public."[32]

Chapter Seven

THE CENTRAL PACIFIC
ATTACKS THE SIERRA NEVADA
1865

*I*n 1862, Clarence King graduated from Yale's distinguished Sheffield Scientific School. In 1863, he crossed the Great Basin and the Sierra Nevada by mule, got a job with the California Geological Survey, began to build his reputation, and, still well short of his thirtieth birthday, landed another job. It was to do the Fortieth Parallel Survey for the federal government along the lines of what would become the first transcontinental railroad.

With a team of scientists, King examined the southeastern corner of Wyoming (today's Cheyenne) through Utah and Nevada to the crest of the Sierra Nevada. His task on what became known as the "King Survey" was to describe the flora, fauna, minerals, and other natural features. He later became the first director of the U.S. Geological Survey.[1]

In his book *Mountaineering in the Sierra Nevada*, King wrote about those mountains based on his 1866 exploration: "For four hundred miles the Sierras are a definite ridge, broad and high, and having the form of a sea-wave." On the eastern face, "buttresses of somber-hued rock jut at intervals from a steep wall." On the western face, "long ridges of comparatively gentle outline" dominate. "But this sloping table is scored from summit to base by a system of parallel transverse canyons, distant from one another often less than twenty-five miles. They are ordinarily two or three thousand feet deep, falling at times in sheer, smooth-fronted cliffs, again in sweeping curves like the hull of a ship, with irregular, hilly flanks opening at last through gateways of low, rounded foot-hills out upon the horizontal plain of the San Joaquin and Sacramento. Every canyon carries a river, derived from constant melting of the perpetual snow."

This western slope faces a moisture-laden, aerial current from the Pacific. The wind strikes first on the Coast Range, which forces it up, and it there discharges, as fog and rain, a great sum of moisture. "But being ever reinforced, it flows over their crest, and, hurrying eastward, strikes the Sierras at about four thousand feet." Below, the foothills are habitually dry. Above, it is nearly always wet, for the wind condenses on the mountains' higher portion a great amount of water that "piles upon the summits in the form of snow, which is absorbed upon the upper plateau by an exuberant growth of forest."[2]

The Sierra Nevada that King described are the principal topographical feature of the American Far West. They are a massive granite block. On the eastern front they rise from four thousand feet or more in the north to seven thousand feet or more in the south. The western face is some fifty to sixty miles broad with a gradual rise of 2 to 6 percent. The summits, many enveloped in glaciers, run from six thousand feet in the north to ten thousand feet west of Lake Tahoe in the center. There are twelve peaks exceeding fourteen thousand feet in the south.

*I*F California was the land of superb natural bays, gold, silver, and other minerals for the picking, fertile agricultural lands, the best weather anywhere in the continent for humans, animals, and plants, and no warlike Indian tribes to resist the coming of the Americans, it was also a land that the Americans could scarcely get to or out of because of that granite block between them and the Eastern United States. It was as if those mountains had been designed to divide California permanently from the remainder of the country. They were too big, too snowy, too steep, too rugged, too extensive, too formidable ever to be crossed easily. The mountains challenged even humans on foot, as the fate of the Donner Party (1846–47) made clear.

The idea of driving a railroad over or through the Sierra Nevada was so audacious as to suck out the breath of those who heard it discussed. The audacity of Ted Judah in proposing it, even though he had found a place where there was just one summit to cross instead of two, and of the Big Four in taking him up on it, was monumental. Nothing like it had been done, anywhere. Not east of the Mississippi River over the Appalachians. Not in Europe. Not in Asia. Nowhere. Charles Crocker, who proposed to do it, later said, "People laughed at the time of building a railroad across those mountains."[3]

To get a locomotive through that granite would require tunnels. Without them, no locomotive could get over the summits, even at the passes or with switchbacks. Tunnels through granite had no precedent. To make it happen, a way had to be found. Early in 1865, the Central Pacific went to work on the apparently unsolvable problem.

First money had to be found. That seems hard to believe for a much-needed and much-anticipated railroad whose president was also governor of the state of California, a railroad with millions in bonds pledged to it from the federal government, a railroad that could sell its own stocks and bonds, a railroad that had Collis Huntington raising money in Boston and New York, but it was so. A railroad that was building in the land of milk and honey, gold and silver, needed money. Nevertheless, there was no money at the beginning of 1865, only horrendous expenses.

As soon as the UP and the CP went into the market for rail—they could use only iron made in the United States, by act of Congress as decreed in the Pacific Railroad Bills—the prices jumped 80 percent, from $41.75 to $76.87 per ton, and by 1865 had jumped again, to $91.70 per ton. Shipments via the Panama Isthmus cost $51.97 per ton, meaning that rail delivered at San Francisco cost $143.67 per ton. Then came the charges for transfer from ships at San Francisco to the lighter, then unloading at Sacramento, then for transportation up the Sacramento River.

Locomotives went up in price too. Two engines in 1865 cost the CP $79,752. The CP paid it, more or less gladly, because, as Assistant Chief Engineer Lewis Clement explained to Leland Stanford, "the power of those engines is absolutely necessary to supply materials needed for construction; without these engines there will be delay."

As the grading and then the tracks made their way up the Sierra Nevada, the expenses increased. As Clement explained, the ground was kept bare for the graders by having half of the men shoveling snow. After storms, the entire grading force was put to work removing snow. There were many other costs, especially as the tunnels began to be driven through the granite and as part of the CP's workforce moved east of the mountains. But there was no money, either to pay the laborers or for supplies. Until 1865, the CP operated, mainly, on the Big Four's money or on loans. In 1863 and 1864, not a penny in aid reached the railroad.

Still it operated, even though in the winter of 1864–65 it was down to about five hundred workmen. On January 7, 1865, Strobridge placed an advertisement in the *Sacramento Union:* "Wanted, 5,000 laborers for constant and permanent work, also experienced foremen. Apply to J. H. Strobridge, Superintendent. On the work, near Auburn."[4]

Many applied, few stayed. What the white men wanted was what they had come to California to get—riches. At around $3 per day, the CP was not offering them any riches, but they were broke. New silver strikes in Nevada promised riches. The prospective rich men needed a ride to get there and a stake to support them once there. A week's work on the CP would suffice. So, of the almost two thousand laborers who signed up to work for Strobridge, fewer than a hundred were there after a week.[5]

Clement recalled that, among the laborers, "mining was more to their liking than the discipline of railroad work. They were indifferent, independent, and their labor high priced. Labor sufficient for the rapid construction of the Central Pacific was not then on the coast and the labor as it existed could not be depended upon—the first mining excitement meant a complete stampede of every man and a consequent abandonment of all work."[6]

Crocker and Strobridge kept at it. By the spring of 1865, Bloomer Cut was graded and tracked.* On April 5, after two years of strife and litigation, the California Supreme Court handed down a favorable decision: it ordered the San Francisco Board of Supervisors to pay to the CP $400,000 in stock bonds as a gift, instead of the $600,000 stock subscription authorized by the citizens of the city in 1863. Thereby, the city avoided being a stockholder, which meant it could not be held liable for debts (but also could not participate in the profits). The CP had paid $100,000 to win the suit, so it realized $300,000. It was the contention of the CP, quite unprovable, that, had the full $400,000 been available in 1864, the CP could have built its track well into Wyoming.

On May 13, 1865, the same day the train began carrying passengers and

---

* The steep sides of this rocky cut stand today just as the builders left them. The cementlike rock that dulled drills and broke picks and resisted blasting powder shows no signs of disintegration. The line now runs through two tunnels to the north.

freight to Auburn, Huntington sent a telegram to Stanford: "I received yesterday twelve hundred and fifty-eight thousand dollars ($1,258,000) United States bonds for account of Central Pacific Railroad of California."[7] That represented the government's loan to the CP for work completed in 1864, from Sacramento to Newcastle. The company got bonds at $16,000 per mile for the first seven miles, where, according to geologist Whitney and President Lincoln, the Sierra Nevada began, and $48,000 per mile for the next twenty-four miles, to Newcastle. Unfortunately, the CP had already borrowed against the money. Still, it helped.

With the money and the progress, everything was looking up. That summer, Mark Hopkins wrote to Collis Huntington that business was constantly increasing (in the first ten months of 1865, the company would earn $313,404 from the mails, passengers, and freight, with an operating expense of $93,448). The workforce was up to twenty-five hundred and on the increase, despite the desertions for the mines. More iron, engines, and cars were needed as soon as possible. Hopkins thought the CP could build all the way to the Salt Lake and perhaps farther. Meanwhile, he expected it to get to Dutch Flat in 1866. And, he noted, "the public here, in Nevada and at the East begin to exhibit an impatient interest in the progress of the Pacific R.R., which we cannot afford to disregard."[8]

*T*HERE was small chance that the Big Four and their workers would disregard the sentiment. In fact, none. The CP was charging ahead. What it needed to keep up the momentum was workers. When the tracks reached Auburn, the railroad was entering the Sierra for real. By far the toughest terrain lay ahead, up to and then down from the summit. In the spring of 1865, the CP went at that problem. By June 10, the railhead was at Clipper Gap, a lumber settlement forty-three miles east of Sacramento and 1,751 feet above sea level. It was now into its assault on the Sierra Nevada. It began reaching toward Illinoistown.

*T*HE CP had gotten that far by using its wits and common sense. In February, a month after Strobridge's all-but-fruitless call for labor, Charlie Crocker had met with him and raised the question of hiring Chinese. He said some twenty of them had worked, and worked well, on the Dutch Flat and Donner Lake Wagon Road.

"Stro," as he was known to his friends, was opposed. He said all the whites currently working for him would take off, and anyway what did the Chinese know about railroad construction?[9] They couldn't possibly do the work. They averaged 120 pounds in weight, and only a few were taller than four feet ten inches. "I will not boss Chinese!" he declared.

"They built the Great Wall of China, didn't they," replied Crocker. Besides, "who said laborers have to be white to build railroads?"

Strobridge, still skeptical, agreed to hire fifty local (that is, living in Auburn) Chinese and try them out for a month under white supervisors.[10]

There were in California at that time some sixty thousand Chinese, nearly all adults and the great proportion of them males. They had come for the same reason as the whites, to make money, first of all in the gold-fields. But California law discriminated against them in every way possible, and the state did all it could to degrade them and deny them a decent livelihood. They were not allowed to work on the "Mother Lode." To work the "tailing," they had to pay a "miner's tax," a $4-per-head so-called permission tax, plus a $2 water tax. In addition, the Chinese had to pay a personal tax, a hospital tax, a $2 school tax, and a property tax. But they could not go to public school, they were denied citizenship, they could not vote, nor could they testify in court. Nevertheless, they paid more than $2 million in taxes. If Chinese dared to venture into a new mining area, the whites would set on them, beat them, rob them, sometimes kill them. Thus the saying, "Not a Chinaman's chance."

They were called "coolies," a Hindu term meaning unskilled labor. The British picked it up and then passed it on to the Americans, who applied it to Chinese. The politicians cursed them, vied with one another about who hated the Chinese the most, declared them to be dregs, said they worried about the terrible habits the Chinese brought with them. One of the leaders in this ranting and raving was Governor Stanford. While campaigning, he had called the Chinese the "dregs of Asia" and "that degraded race." In 1858, the California legislature banned any further importations. Still they came.

It got so bad that a young Californian appointed to collect the miner's tax wrote in his diary, "Had a China fight. Knocked down some and drawed out our pistols on the rest. . . . Had a great time. Chinamen's tails cut off. Down at the Little Yuba River shot a Chinaman. Had a hell of a time." That same tax collector later was appointed by President Ulysses S. Grant to be ambassador to Japan.[11]

In the Bancroft Library at the University of California, Berkeley, there are Chinese-English and English-Chinese phrase books from 1867. The English-speakers learned how to say in Chinese: "Can you get me a good boy? He wants $8.00 per month? He ought to be satisfied with $6.00. I think he is very stupid. Come at seven every morning. Go home at eight every night. Light the fire. Sweep the rooms. Wash the clothes. Wash the windows. Wash the floor. Sweep the stairs. Trim the lamps. I want to cut his wages." Two phrases that never appear in the English-Chinese book are, "How are you?" and "Thank you."

The Chinese could learn to say in English, to employers: "Yes, madam," "You must not strike me," and so forth. To authorities, "He does not intend to pay me my wages. He claimed my mine. He tries to extort money from me. He took it from me by violence. He assaulted me. The man struck the Chinese boy on the head. He came to his death by homicide. He was murdered by a thief. He was shot dead by his enemy. He was flogged publicly twice in the streets. He was frozen to death in the snow."[12]

White men despised the Chinese even as they used them. They constantly compared the Chinese to another subordinate group, white women. The Chinese were small, with delicate hands and hairless faces and long, braided hair. One editor called them "half-made men," which fit nicely with their two most common jobs, laundrymen and domestic servants. But the same editor referred to their "dreadful vitality."[13]

After 1858, many Chinese had come to America in response to pamphlets put out by the several companies of Chinese merchants residing in San Francisco, advertising the high price of labor. The merchant companies took their pay from a percentage of a man's earnings, plus a large bonus. They agreed to return a man to China free of charge; in the event of sickness he would be cared for; in case of death they would send the body home to be buried in the Celestial Empire. These contracts were faithfully fulfilled. Nonetheless, the ships rivaled the slave ships for gruesomeness.

In California the Chinese could find work as domestics: cooks, laundrymen, housekeepers, gardeners, errand boys, and so on. Like most previous immigrants, they sent back to China letters to their families, urging their wives, children, parents, brothers, and sisters to come. They landed in San Francisco, which had the largest number of Chinese and was known to them in their own language as "the big city—Tai Fau—first city." Next came Sacramento, the "Yi Fau," or the second city. Marysville was the third city.[14]

In 1868, *Lippincott's Magazine* ran an article on "The Chinese in California." "The purpose of every Chinaman in coming here is to amass such a sum—trifling in our eyes—in three or four years, as in China will give him support for life." The Chinese "toiled without ceasing." He never spent his money. No white man could ever surpass his industry. "He may have less muscle, but by his untiring persistence he accomplishes more work than the Caucasian." There were no clumsy men among the Chinese, who "quickly got the 'hang' of whatever you set them at, and soon display a remarkable adroitness." There was a "spirit of adventure" in them, which sent Chinese to Nevada, Idaho, and Montana for work. "Every Chinaman reads and writes, and in figures he is our superior." To some extent they adopted the American costume—pants, boots, soft hats. But never coats. The pigtail "is sacred. Never can a Chinaman be persuaded that he can survive the loss of that emblem of dignity." The article concluded with a plea for the federal government to do something to protect the Chinese—after all, it said, there was a Freedmen's Bureau to protect the newly freed slave.[15]

AFTER a month's labor, Strobridge admitted, albeit grudgingly, that the Chinese had performed superbly. They worked as teams, took almost no breaks, learned how to blast away rocks, stayed healthy and on the job. Engineer Montague praised them and declared in his 1865 report, "The experiment has proved eminently successful."[16]

The CP began to hire them locally, offering $28 a month, then $30, then $31. Those were big wages even when the men had to pay for their own food. Crocker turned to a labor contractor in San Francisco, Koopmanschap, and had him look across the state for two thousand more "coolies," and even to import them from China if necessary. Before the end of 1865, there were seven thousand Chinese at work on the line, with just under two thousand whites.[17]

Lee Chew was one of them. In 1903, he wrote an autobiographical sketch for *Independent* magazine. As a boy, he slept with the other boys in his village, thirty of them in one room. Girls had their own house, with a room that slept forty. Lee Chew worked on a ten-acre farm where his father grew potatoes, rice, beans, peas, yams, and fruits. He went to school to learn how "the great Emperors of China ruled with the wisdom of gods and gave to the whole world the light of high civilization and the culture of our literature, which is the admiration of all nations."

In 1860 or thereabouts, the sixteen-year-old Lee Chew went to Hong Kong with five other boys and they got steerage passage on a steamer, where they almost starved. But in San Francisco they went to the Chinese quarter and he got a job with an American family as houseboy at $3 a week. Then he got a job with the railroad that lasted three years and he saved enough money to open his own laundry.

Many years later, when Theodore Roosevelt was president, Lee Chew gave it as his opinion that the Chinese in America "were persecuted not for their vices but for their virtues. No one would hire an Irishman, German, Englishman or Italian when he could get a Chinese, because our countrymen are so much more honest, industrious, steady, sober and painstaking."[18] A Chinaman who came back to Lee Chew's village from the United States "took ground as large as four city blocks and made a paradise of it. He had gone away from our village as a poor boy. Now he returned with unlimited wealth, made in America."

CHARLIE Crocker claimed it was impossible to tell Chinese apart (they were just like Indians, he said). Thus, fearing paying double wages, he devised a scheme of employing, working, and paying them wholesale.[19]

The CP organized the Chinese into gangs of twelve to twenty men, one of whom was an elected headman, another the cook. Crocker hired Sam Thayer, who spoke a number of Chinese dialects, to teach the men something of the English language. The headman collected all the wages, giving some to the cook to purchase provisions from the Chinese merchants. Other amounts went for clothing and opium. (The Chinese laborers used the drug on Sunday, their day off, to relax.) At the end of the month, each worker got his remaining $20 or more. Each gang had a white, usually Irish, boss, and the whites usually monopolized the skilled work, such as trestling, masonry, and actual rail-laying. The Chinese did the grading, made cuts and fills, blasted, felled trees, and, most arduous of all, drilled the holes and put in and lit the black powder while driving tunnels.

In May, Mark Hopkins wrote to Huntington, "We find a difficulty in getting laborers on the RR work. Prospecting generally takes off our men." But sixteen hundred Chinese were then employed, and "without them it would be impossible to go on with the work."[20] Crocker's brother E.B. wrote that spring to Representative Cornelius Cole, "I can assure you the Chinese are moving the earth and rock rapidly. They prove nearly equal to white men in the amount of labor they perform, and are far more reliable. No danger of strikes among them . . . I tell you Cole we are in dead earnest about this R.R. and you take 6 or 8 men in real earnest, and if they have any brains and industry they will accomplish something."[21]

*I*T had been Judah's original plan to bridge the deeper ravines and gaps between Newcastle (below Auburn) and Illinoistown with timber structures, but with the Chinese there to fill and push the carts, wherever possible earthen embankments ("fills") were used. In a five-mile stretch from Auburn to Newcastle, the only wooden structures were the Newcastle trestle (86 feet high and 528 feet long), a trestle near Auburn at 30 feet high and 416 feet long, and a few others.

But even the Chinese didn't solve every problem. The embankments were often impractical. Soil covering the ridge was only a foot or so deep, so scraping up enough dirt to make heaps fifty to a hundred feet high and several hundred feet long was impossible. Therefore, the engineers decided, early in 1865, to build trestles. When the railroad was finished, earth could be hauled in by train and the trestles replaced by fills.

In historian Wesley Griswold's phrase, the trestles stood like "transfixed centipedes, straddling the gaps in the ridge with their massive multiple pairs of legs from immense pines, planted at 16-foot intervals, their feet braced in masonry."[22] The trestles, whose support timbers were called "bents" by the engineers, came originally from hundreds of thousands of feet of lumber cut in coastal forests of the Northwest, brought to the site by schooner and flatcar.

But after Newcastle was reached, CP lumbermen started hacking away at huge trees closer at hand, giant red firs and others. The bridges that were built out of sturdy timber and laced together and steadied by rows of horizontal beams looked like many-legged structures. Their spindly appearance scared hell out of the passengers, who gazed down as much as a hundred feet (at Deep Gulch, for example). Still the bridges managed to stand the weight of a locomotive and cars. "The boom of the powder blast is continually heard," the *Auburn Stars and Stripes* reported. "Frowning embankments rise as if by magic. High trestle bridges spring up in a week."[23]

HUNTINGTON had meanwhile filed a work-route map with the secretary of the interior covering the entire area from the California-Nevada border to the Great Salt Lake. He simply ignored the clause in the Pacific Railroad Bill that limited the CP to 150 miles east of the border. With that map, Huntington got the race between the UP and the CP started.[24]

On June 10, the rails reached Clipper Gap, about halfway between Auburn and Illinoistown. Toward the end of that summer, the railhead became Illinoistown, fifty-four miles from Sacramento. The elevation was 2,242 feet. From there to the summit was about fifty miles. The grade climbed almost forty-eight hundred feet, to 7,042. The grade went up the dividing ridge between the North Fork of the American River, which lay to the south, and Bear River, which was to the north.

This was the toughest. The hardest. The most expensive. The fifty miles that would be the most time-consuming. It took a full year to reach Dutch Flat from Illinoistown, sixty-seven miles from Sacramento. After that the difficulties increased, including more blasting, cutting, and filling, another precipitous gorge to be bridged, massive pinewood stands to be cleared, numerous tight curves to be plotted.

The engineers contemplated drilling fifteen tunnels through the granite—five on the west slope, one at the summit, and nine on the east. The longest, at 1,659 feet or 553 yards (or 113 yards beyond a quarter-mile), twenty-six feet wide and twenty feet high, would bore through the summit itself (No. 6). More than five hundred kegs of black powder would be consumed each day. Hundreds of gullies and ravines had to be filled, and at least eight long trestles built, with spans from thirty-eight to sixty feet high and from 350 to 500 feet long. Huntington had thirty vessels at sea simultaneously, bringing supplies and locomotives to California.

The task facing the CP was not only improbable, it was unique in engineering annals. The grading alone would exceed $100,000 per mile. Tens of thousands of tons of granite would have to be chipped and blasted from the mountains. Smaller chunks of it could be used for ballast on the track; big pieces could be sold to construction firms in California.

Strobridge divided his work crews into five parts. The largest, some five thousand men and six hundred teams of horses, were sent ahead of Illinoistown to work on Cape Horn. Another thousand men were detailed to clearing the right-of-way. Smaller teams of three to four hundred men each were put to work boring entrances for the first three tunnels.

One of the most feared stretches ran three miles along the precipitous gorge of the North Fork of the American River, nicknamed "Cape Horn." The slope was at an angle of seventy-five degrees, and the river was twelve hundred to twenty-two hundred feet below the line of the railroad. There were no trails, not even a goat path. The grade would not be bored through a tunnel but, rather, built on the side of the mountain, which required blasting and rock cuts on the sheer cliffs. The mountain needed to be sculpted, because the roadbed would be curved around the mountain. The curves that hugged the monolith were either up grade or, sometimes, down. Men had to be lowered in a bos'n's chair from above to place the black powder, fix and light the fuses, and yell to a man above to haul them up. With regard to Cape Horn and the tunnels, *Van Nostrand's Engineering Magazine* said in 1870, "Good engineers considered the undertaking preposterous."[25]

One day in the summer of 1865, a Chinese foreman went to Strobridge, nodded, and waited for permission to speak. When it was granted, he said that men of China were skilled at work like this. Their ancestors had built fortresses in the Yangtze gorges. Would he permit Chinese crews to work on Cape Horn? If so, could reeds be sent up from San Francisco to weave into baskets?

Strobridge would try anything. The reeds came on. At night the Chinese wove baskets similar to the ones their ancestors had used. The baskets were round, waist-high, four eyelets at the top, painted with symbols. Ropes ran from the eyelets to a central cable. The Chinese went to work—they needed little or no instruction in handling black powder, which was a Chinese invention—with a hauling crew at the precipice top.

Hundreds of barrels of black powder were ignited daily to form a ledge on which a roadbed could be laid. Some of the men were lost in accidents, but we don't know how many: the CP did not keep a record of Chinese casualties.[26]

The Chinese workingmen, hanging in their baskets, had to bore the holes with their small hand-drills, then tamp in the explosives, set and light the fuse, and holler to be pulled out of the way. They used a huge amount of powder that was shipped to them from Sacramento. Crocker had a "spark-proof" car built to transport it, with iron sides, a door lined with India rubber, and a tin roof which could not catch fire from sparks and could be blown off in the event of an explosion. The CP made it in the railroad's workshops at E and Sixth Streets in Sacramento. This car alone was allowed to haul explosives to the work sites, and it never had an accident.[27]

The Chinese made the roadbed and laid the track around Cape Horn. Though this took until the spring of 1866, it was not as time-consuming or difficult as had been feared. Still, it remains one of the best known of all the labors on the Central Pacific, mainly because, unlike the work in the tunnel, it makes for a spectacular diorama. As well it should. Hanging from those baskets, drilling holes in the cliff, placing the fuses, and getting hauled up was a spectacular piece of work. The white laborers couldn't do it. The Chinese could, if not as a matter of course, then quickly and—at least they made it look this way—easily. Young Lewis Clement did the surveying and then took charge of overseeing the railroad engineering at Cape Horn.

What Clement planned and the Chinese made became one of the grandest sights to be seen along the entire Central Pacific line. Trains would halt there so tourists could get out of their cars to gasp and gape at the gorge and the grade.[28]

DANGEROUS as the Cape Horn work was, clearing the roadbed was worse. The Chinese who did it had the task of making an avenue a hundred feet wide on either side of the roadbed, mainly to provide room for the graders and to prevent tall trees from crashing down on the track. At least twenty-five feet on each side of the grade had to be cleared and leveled. Not only trees and stumps, but rocks, other obstructions, and vegetation of all types had to be removed. Past Illinoistown, the growth included some of the world's largest trees, hundreds of feet high.

One three-hundred-man gang spent a full ten workdays clearing a single mile of right-of-way. The trees were shipped to sawmills to be fashioned into ties and trestling. Then the stumps had to be blasted from the soil. Ten barrels of black powder were needed to free each one. In any one week, the crews used as much explosives as did Generals Lee and McClellan at Antietam. Every time the powder charge was exploded, chunks of rock and tree flew through the air. They were like missiles fired by nature at the army invading it.[29] (In World War II, the GIs in their foxholes got wounded more often by splinters flying through the air during a German barrage than by the shrapnel itself.) When a congressional investigator expressed incredulity at the amount of black powder used for any one stump, Clement told him, "These are not *Yankee* forests, but forests with trees four, six, and eight feet in diameter." They were often 150 feet tall.[30]

*T*HE first two groups, other than CP workers, to get a glimpse of what was being accomplished were George Gray and his assistants, and Schuyler Colfax accompanied by three journalists and some others.

Gray went because he had been invited by the Big Four to make an inspection of the completed line and the grading beyond the end of track. He had a reputation as one of the best railroad engineers in the country, and had previously been the first chief engineer of the New York Central Railroad. A favorable review by him would have a big effect on the potential bond- and stockholders; an unfavorable one was too painful to contemplate.

Gray, with a wagon load of instruments and a team of assistants, set to his inspection in late June. He was impressed and more. He found the CP's line to be of "first quality throughout," from the seating of its bridges and the quality of its brickwork to the spacing of its ties and the construction of its depots, and had no reservations whatsoever. He sent his report to the President, the secretary of the interior, the CP headquarters, the *Railroad Record* and other publications.

The CP was so delighted that, in late July 1865, it published Gray's report as a pamphlet. Among other things, he wrote: "From the examination I have made, having traveled the distance on horseback or on foot, I feel confident that the railroad can be constructed over the Sierra Nevada . . . within two years. . . . It is quite a remarkable feature of your route that so elevated a mountain range can be surmounted with such comparatively light grades and curves." In short order, the CP made Gray its consulting engineer.[31]

The other party, led by Schuyler Colfax, the Speaker of the House of Representatives and a future vice-president of the United States, left Omaha in July for a tour to the Pacific. Colfax went to the end of track of the UP, which was less than halfway to the Elkhorn River, then took stages to Denver. His party included Samuel Bowles, editor of the *Springfield* (Massachusetts) *Republican*; William Bross, editor of the *Chicago Tribune* and lieutenant governor of Illinois; and Albert D. Richardson, one of the most distinguished correspondents of the Civil War, from the *New York Tribune*, Horace Greeley's newspaper. From Denver the party went on a posh new Concord coach loaned by its owner, Ben Holladay, himself. It reached California in late summer.

Stanford invited the Speaker and his party to travel with him to the CP's end of track, then at mile 50 (just short of Illinoistown). Off they went, with plenty of wines, brandies, and good food. Stops were made to inspect tracks, trestling, and culverts, and to view the Chinese workers. Stanford made a grand gesture when the train got to the end of track: he renamed Illinoistown as "Colfax."

The reporters were enthusiastic, especially Richardson. He wrote of the Chinese, "They were a great army laying siege to Nature in her strongest citadel. The rugged mountains looked like stupendous ant-hills. They swarmed with Celestials,* shoveling, wheeling, carting, drilling and blasting rocks and earth, while their dull, moony eyes stared out from under immense basket-hats, like umbrellas."[32]

From Colfax, the party moved up the line of the graders by horseback. They rounded the spectacular point of Cape Horn. At Gold Run, sixty-three miles east of Sacramento, the Speaker and reporters got into a six-horse coach and set out for the summit, still forty or so miles away. Richardson saw "an endless sweep of dense forest and grand mountains, among graceful tamaracks, gigantic pines and pyramidal firs." At the summit, reached shortly after sunset, "the wild, gloomy grandeur is far more impressive than by day. It is boundless mountain piled on mountain—unbroken granite, bare, verdure less, cold and gray."

After a night at Donner Lake, the travelers climbed up to the summit to talk with the surveyors. That night, they stayed together in a guest house. Richardson wrote about the company officials who were working

---

* The white men called the Chinese the "Celestials" because they came from the Celestial Kingdom.

on the details of the route over the summit: "The candles lighted up a curious picture. The carpet was covered with maps, profiles and diagrams, held down at the edges by candlesticks. On their knees were president, directors and surveyors, creeping from one map to another, and earnestly discussing the plans of their magnificent enterprise. Outside the night wind moaned and shrieked, as if the Mountain Spirit resented this invasion of his ancient domain."[33]

*T*HAt fall of 1865, the CP went to work on the tunnels. Six of the thirteen that it would have to blast out before getting to the east slope were clustered in a stretch of two miles at the top of the long climb to the summit. The biggest, No. 6, right at the summit and within a few hundred feet of Donner Pass, was, as noted, 1,659 feet long and as much as 124 feet beneath the surface. The facings—where the blasting began—were 150 feet from the summit.

Clement planned it. In mid-October, when the end of track and supply base were at Colfax, Chief Engineer Montague started the Chinese working in shifts—eight hours per day, three shifts through the twenty-four hours—at each end of the formidable summit. There was only room for gangs of three men. One would hold the rock drill against the granite, while the other two would swing eighteen-pound sledgehammers to hit the back end of the drill.

Of all the backbreaking labor that went into the building of the CP and the UP, of all the dangers inherent in the work, this was the worst. The drills lost their edge to the granite and had to be replaced frequently. The CP soon learned to order its drills in hundred-ton lots. The man holding the drill had to be steady or he would get hit by the sledgehammer. The man swinging the hammer had to have muscles like steel. When a hole was at last big enough for the black powder, the crew would fill it, set a fuse, yell as loud as they could while running out of the range of the blast, and hope. Sometimes the fuse worked, sometimes it didn't.

Often the workers had put in too much powder and most of it blew toward them—harmlessly as far as the granite was concerned, but at great danger to the Chinamen. Clement's assistant, Henry Root, explained that "more powder was used by the rock foreman than was economical," for the simple reason that the workers were told that time, not money, was of the essence. At Summit Tunnel alone, three hundred kegs of blasting powder a day went up, costing $53,000 to $67,000 per month.[34]

Progress was incredibly slow. With men working round the clock, between six and twelve inches per twenty-four hours was normal.[35] Crocker gave orders to establish permanent work camps on each side of the summit, to facilitate the round-the-clock drilling, blasting, scraping, shoveling, and hauling by the Chinese. He figured there was no night or day within a tunnel. The men worked in groups of twenty or so, because only a handful could work at any one time.[36]

BY the middle of the summer of 1865, cargoes of Chinese laborers signed up by Koopmanschap had begun arriving in San Francisco.* They were shipped forward by riverboat to Sacramento, then to the end of track by train, then by foot to work on the grading. Strobridge's workforce soon doubled and continued to grow. The CP had to learn how to put them to useful work, no difficult problem, and to house and feed them, which required some imagination, principally from the Chinese.

The CP used tents for housing as long as the weather remained warm. The Chinese men, more than half teen-aged and from farm families, were accustomed to spending their days outdoors and sharing crowded quarters at night. One visitor to the CP construction sites wrote, "In a little tent, ten by twelve feet, a half dozen or more Chinamen find abundant accommodations for eating and sleeping." Tents went up at the facings of each tunnel and at or near the site of grading, putting in sidings, or other work. As noted, the Chinese were divided into gangs of twelve to twenty men, each with a headman and a cook.

They ate healthy, well-cooked, and tasty food, unlike the white workers. The CP provided the Americans with boiled beef and potatoes, beans, bread and butter, and coffee. If they wanted to spend their own money, the company kept stores that offered dried fish and salted codfish, peaches, cherries, raisins, apples, tomatoes, eggs, beets, turnips, pickles, and more.[37] The Chinese paid for all their food. They demanded and got an astonishing variety—oysters, cuttlefish, finned fish, abalone meat,

* It is not true, however, despite persistent myth in California, that most Chinese came to the United States to work for the CP. In fact, in 1866 and 1867 more Chinese left the state than entered.

Oriental fruits, and scores of vegetables, including bamboo sprouts, sea-weed, and mushrooms. Each of these foods came dried, purchased from one of the Chinese merchants in San Francisco. Further, the Chinese ate rice, salted cabbage, vermicelli, bacon, and sweet crackers. Very occasionally they had fresh meat, pork being a prime favorite, along with chicken.[38]

The food helped keep the Chinamen healthy. The water they drank was even more important. The Americans drank from the streams and lakes, and many of them got diarrhea, dysentery, and other illnesses. The Chinese drank only tepid tea. The water had been boiled first and was brought to them by youngsters who carried two pails on a sturdy pole across their shoulders.

Augustus Ward Loomis, a Christian minister who came to observe them, noted that the Chinese set an example for their white co-workers in diligence, steadiness, and clean living. In an article for the *Overland Monthly* he wrote, "They are ready to begin work the moment they hear the signal, and labor steadily and honestly until admonished that the working hours are ended." Loomis approved of their habits: "Not having acquired a taste for whiskey, they have few fights, and no 'blue Mondays.'"[39] They did smoke opium on Sundays, their day off, but they did not "stupefy themselves with it. You do not see them intoxicated, rolling in the gutters like swine."

They took daily sponge baths in warm water, washed their clothes, and otherwise kept themselves clean and healthy. According to contemporary B. S. Brooks, who wrote a pamphlet about the Chinese, the white worker "has a sort of hydrophobia which induces him to avoid the contact of water." In contrast, "the Chinaman is accustomed to daily ablutions of his entire person."[40]

The Chinese were ideal workers. Cheap. Did as they were told. Made a quick study and after something was shown or explained to them did it skillfully. Few if any strikes. The same for complaints. They did what no one else was willing or able to do.

*T*HERE was other good news beyond the Chinese willingness to work and their capability at it. When winter set in at the Summit Tunnel facings, Montague had put them to other work. He continued to get reports from survey teams he had sent as far east as the Truckee River and on into Nevada. From those reports he learned that the location engineers could shave several miles off Judah's original line and, even better, eliminate two tunnels and perhaps a third.

Grading above Colfax and tunneling at the summit meant that the CP was into the battle with the Sierra Nevada in earnest. Stanford wrote to President Andrew Johnson, "The grading between Newcastle and Colfax was very difficult and expensive, increasing as the line was pushed up the mountain slope. The cuttings have been deeper, the embankments higher, and more rock work encountered, as the line has progressed eastward. . . . We have encountered and are now laboring upon the most difficult and expensive portion of the line entrusted to us. This, too, at the very commencement of our efforts."[41]

In general, the men of the CP, including the Chinese, worked like the Irish and other white men working for the UP. The surveyors went first, followed by the engineers, who laid out the exact line. Then came the bridge gangs, so that when the gradings got to the bridge site they could continue. Then there were the men who dug the cuts or who dug and dumped the dirt to make the fills. Next came the track layers with their rails, spikes, fishplates, distance markers, sledgehammers, and ballast. After them the carpenters, who built the roundhouses, depots, and other buildings.

Unlike the UP, the CP was not concisely organized as a military force. Of course, in California it had no Indians to contend with, for they had nearly all been wiped out. But the military manner of organizing complex outfits fit the CP as much as it did the UP—squads, platoons, companies, battalions, regiments, divisions, with separate commanders and staffs for logistics, planning, intelligence, finance, personnel, and more.

The bosses on the spot, where the construction was going on, were Charles Crocker and James Strobridge. Crocker was described by his assistant chief engineer, Lewis Clement: "He was a business man in the full sense of the word—prompt, methodical, fearless and confident. He was decided and firm; yet not obstinate. When he was satisfied that he was in the wrong, he was always ready to concede it and apologize." He kept his word, Clement said. But "he was very quick to act, and sometimes acted too quickly—he acted and then considered it afterwards." He was the manager of construction, which was a job "no ordinary man could have done." He wasn't imposing, despite his bulk: he was less than six feet tall, with a fair complexion, and beardless. "I don't suppose," Clement said, "that there was a mile of road constructed that he didn't go over the ground, either on horse-back or with a wagon; he always wanted to see what had been done and what was being done." He was out in every kind of weather, "and it made no difference whether it was an American horse or a bucking Spanish pony." Clement admitted that Crocker "was a large eater and a man of very strong prejudices."[42]

When the job was completed, Crocker was the only one of the Big Four—indeed, the only Californian—who thought to praise and thank the Chinese for what they had done. The Chinese, meanwhile, were called "Crocker's pets," and he was known to them as "Mistuh Clockee."

Strobridge had lost an eye to a black-powder explosion in Bloomer Cut, but the Chinese respected him without hesitation or stint. Those who had learned English called "Stro" the "One-Eyed Bossy Man." He could see as well with one eye as most men could with two, and when, as happened occasionally, there was trouble among the Chinese workers, Strobridge could pick out the ringleaders with a glance. He confronted them, usually with an ax handle, and they gave way and he prevailed.[43] One white foreman would sometimes spur on his Chinese work gang by clapping a hand over his right eye and striding about as Strobridge did, implying that Stro was about to appear. "Men generally earn their money when they work for me," Strobridge said.

Strobridge appreciated what the Chinese did. After a few months with them, he said, "They learn quickly, do not fight, have no strikes that amount to anything, and are very cleanly in their habits. They will gamble and do quarrel among themselves most noisily—but harmlessly." And Montague reported at the end of 1865, "The Chinese are faithful and industrious and under proper supervision soon become skillful in the performance of their duty. Many of them are becoming expert in drilling, blasting, and other departments of rock work."

Leland Stanford, the governor of California who had won many voters by denouncing the Chinese immigrants, wrote to President Andrew Johnson, "As a class they are quiet, peaceable, patient, industrious, and economical." And he asserted, "Without the Chinese it would have been impossible to complete the western portion of this great National highway."[44]

And what did the Chinese think of their employers? For sure they wanted the jobs. Most if not all of them saved money while working for the CP, and those who went back to China with their savings used the money to live well. Others went to work for the multitude of railroads building new lines west of the Rocky Mountains after the CP was constructed. Many settled in California, where they raised families and became an important part of the population. Still, there is no solid answer to the question. For the most part, we just don't know.

There are indications, of course, including how many went to work with the CP and stayed with it. The CP's successor, the Southern Pacific, kept the workers on a regular pension. In 1915, the newsletter of the Southern Pacific carried a letter from a former worker then living in China, thanking the railroad for sending his pension check each month. Another indication came in November 1917. A half-year earlier, the United States had declared war on Germany. A Liberty Loan was sponsored by the government to raise money to fight the war. A group of about twenty San Francisco Chinese, who were the last of the original crew that helped build the CP, enrolled and purchased the bonds.[45]

BY the end of 1865, Crocker still needed money. The bill for the blasting powder alone was killing him, even though it was less expensive now that the war had ended and Crocker was able to obtain a great amount of government surplus. But the Big Four had borrowed all they could, or so it appeared. Then, on November 29, the government inspectors examined the track from mile 31 to mile 54, from Newcastle to Colfax, and pronounced it satisfactory. At $48,000 per mile, the government had to issue $1,104,000 in bonds to the CP to sell. That helped, considerably, but as always the CP had long since borrowed on that money, and anyway it was far short of what was needed.

Crocker, as head of the construction company, was being paid by the CP in cash, in bonds, and in stock, at the rate of $2 worth of stock for every $1 owed him. The actual value of the stock was about 10 cents per share. He had borrowed, or so he later said, "all the money available, much of it from my personal friends. I owed William E. Dodge & company three and a quarter million dollars." That wasn't quite true: the company, not Crocker, had borrowed the money. The other Big Four, plus E. B. Crocker, were silent partners in the construction company.[46]

Crocker's associates rallied to his side. They agreed to help pay his bills; although they were not legally his partners in Crocker & Company, they would stand or fall together. "Go on!" Stanford assured him. "We will stand by you."[47]

By the end of 1865, the CP had fifty-four miles of working track, to Colfax. Less than twenty miles had been spiked that year. But those few miles had cost an astounding $6 million. Only $3,363,300 in stock had been subscribed (not all paid for), and only one block of government bonds had been received. Earnings were up, with net profits at $280,000, which was the best news. Most of the earnings came from freight. The company anticipated 1866 revenues of nearly $500,000 from freight and just over $200,000 from passengers, plus income from the sale of timber. But whatever the anticipations, the sober truth was that the Western branch of the transcontinental railroad had scarcely penetrated the Sierra Nevada.

Chapter Eight

THE UNION PACIFIC
ACROSS NEBRASKA
1866

*T*HE Union Pacific and the Central Pacific were the first big business in America. Except for the invention of the telegraph, which gave their officials a means of almost instant communication—quite limited because of the cost per word—the railroads had to invent everything: how to recruit, how to sell stocks and bonds, how to lobby the politicians, how to compete, what to build and what to buy, how to order and store necessary items that numbered in the hundreds of thousands. Only the government and armies had organized on such a scale. Where the railroads went, they created stopping points complete with water tanks, repair facilities, boarding terminals, unloading equipment, eating places, hotels. From these grew farms, villages, cities.

Omaha was the first to benefit. In 1865, it doubled in size to fifteen thousand inhabitants, and grew even more in 1866 and each year that followed. During the summer and fall of 1865, small mountains of materials piled up in Omaha. Five of the UP's seven steamships had the exclusive task of hauling ties, iron wheels and rails, rolling stock, and machinery; the others brought more workers and additional supplies. When weather prevented the graders and trackers from working on their main job, they found employment in Omaha, where a great cluster of shops was located, one of which was capable of building nine flatcars at a time. There was employment for everyone willing to work, making bricks, or making UP buildings out of bricks, at the Burnettizers, on the flatcars, as teamsters, and more.

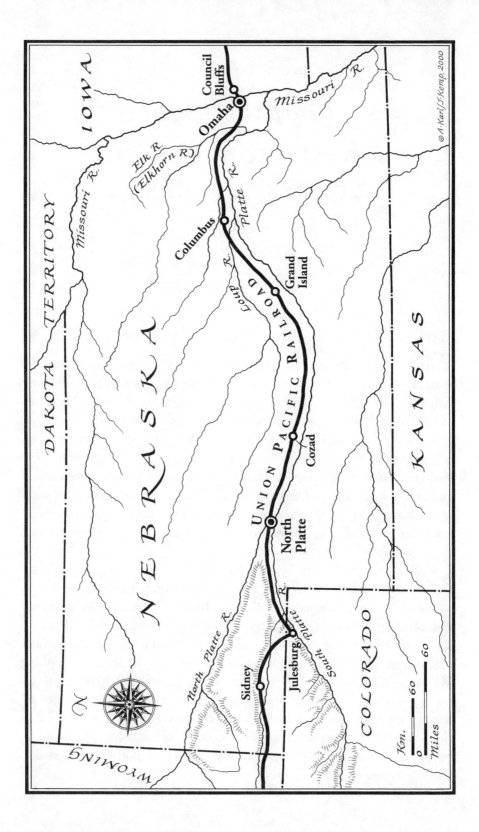

The flood of workers meant a severe housing shortage and a growing number of gamblers and prostitutes. The hotel rooms and dining rooms were crude. One UP employee characterized the town's population as "the closest thing to the Foreign Legion you could find." Jack Casement wrote his wife that there were no good boardinghouses in Omaha and that the hotel in which he was staying was "cram full and kept very poorly. The meals were nothing that a white man wanted." He promised her that he was looking for a house to rent for the two of them.[1]

West of Omaha, settlement was growing, thanks most of all to the prospect of transportation, but also to a reassessment of the Great Plains. Previously, most Americans had accepted as fact that everything west of the Missouri River was the Great American Desert. But in 1866, the well-known Massachusetts editor Samuel Bowles brought out a book based on his 1865 trip entitled *Across the Continent.* The Plains, he said, were "not worthless, by any means." Indeed, they were the nation's pasture, capable of growing grass that fattened livestock. In time, he said, the railroad would carry eastward beef and leather, mutton and wool, and more. "Let us, then, not despise the Plains, but turn their capacities to best account."[2]

Moses Thatcher, a Mormon crossing Nebraska in June 1866, noted in his diary that "the country is one vast green ocean." And it was more than the national pasture. "There are some fine farms recently located here," he wrote. "The small grain such as wheat, oats, barley & corn are looking finely." A well-known travel writer, Bayard Taylor, saw the countryside a month later and called it the most beautiful he had ever seen. He wrote that "Mr. Horace Greeley's 'vanishing scale of civilization' has been pushed much further west since his overland trip in 1859." Taylor said Nebraska constituted the largest unbroken area of excellent farming land in the world.[3]

A correspondent from the *Cincinnati Gazette* commented, "The soil is very rich, and the mind falters in its attempt to estimate the future of such a valley, or its immense capacities." He went on to say, "The grain fields of Europe are mere garden patches beside the green oceans which roll across the Great Plains."[4]

I N January 1865, the three government commissioners came to examine the track already laid. Accompanied by Durant and other officials of the UP, plus the governor of Nebraska and others, on what the *Omaha Weekly Herald* called "one of the loveliest winter mornings that ever dawned on the word," in cars pulled by the *General Sherman*, they rode to the end of track (at Fremont). The *Herald* reported that the return trip was made at an average speed of thirty-five miles per hour. The commissioners accepted on behalf of the government the first forty miles of track, and on the return to Omaha, they wired the secretary of the interior that they had found the road "in superior condition." President Andrew Johnson accepted the report the same day, and on January 27 the government issued the bonds, each carrying 6 percent annual interest, payable twice a year.

According to the *Herald*, the commissioners were astonished at Durant's "personal omnipresence in every department of the work, his vigilant and untiring watchfulness of all details, and the energy and effective push which he had imparted to the Colossal enterprise."[5] The *Herald*'s praise for Durant was wondrous to behold. In March, the newspaper called him "the Great Manager, who is to railroads what Napoleon was to war."[6]

Perhaps, but Napoleon's reputation rested on more than forty miles of track. Durant needed to prove the comparison apt. To do that, he first of all needed to establish a solid organization, one with forceful, trustworthy, and capable men to run the company in its many operations, men far better than the ones he had already hired. At the beginning of 1866, he set out to do that. To begin with, he let go his brother Frank, along with Herbert Hoxie and Joseph Henry. He pulled Samuel Reed off his surveying job and put him in charge of construction. Durant gave Reed, forty-seven years old at the time, the title of "superintendent of construction and operations." Reed was a quiet, likable, methodical man who was a conscientious worker, skilled in his methods. He would supervise all grading, track laying, bridging, and tunneling—a tough, demanding position for which he was perfectly suited.

In February 1866, Durant put the Casement brothers in charge of track laying. John ("Jack") Stephen Casement, thirty-seven years old, although only five feet four inches tall, had earned an impressive reputation as a track layer in Ohio. He had risen to brigadier general in the war as a division commander. Stocky, muscular, fearless, "General Jack" could handle anything, and if he couldn't his brother could. Only five feet tall ("five feet nothing," according to one wag), Dan Casement was also a veteran. According to a diary kept by one of his UP workers, Dan may have been short and stocky, but "once he lifted a 30 foot rail off the ground without any trouble. It weighed about 600 pounds."[7] Between them the brothers had formed the firm of J.S. & D.T. Casement, which Durant hired and put in charge of laying the track. It was an inspired choice.

Durant made other adjustments, but by far his best choice, the one that made the UP possible, was to stick to his determination to lure General Grenville Dodge away from the army. At the end of February 1866, having failed to get Dodge to sign on with the UP, Durant sent him a telegram suggesting that Dodge might want to take the field as a surveyor. Dodge declined, but in his telegram of reply (dated March 2) he did offer Durant some advice, based on what he had heard about the disorganization and demoralization in Omaha.

"Let me impress upon you the importance of commencing the years work by placing at Omaha a chief in whom you have confidence," he opened, "who in all things you will support and who you can hold responsible that your orders are carried out—and who all connected with the road will know they must obey." He insisted that the heads of divisions would be *"divided interested independent commands."* Dodge insisted that each of the chiefs of a division must be "jealous of his power and rights" and that everything be done to promote *"harmony, energy, economy or celerity."*[8]

Late in April, Durant went to St. Joseph to meet with Dodge and offer him the post of chief engineer of the UP. The general refused to accept unless he received absolute control. He told Doc that his military experience had convinced him that a divided command would never work. As chief engineer he would "obey orders and insist on everyone under me doing the same." Durant agreed.

On April 27, Dodge went to Omaha and wrote to General Sherman (in St. Louis) requesting a leave of absence so that he could go to work for the UP. In his reply, dated May 1, Sherman agreed, with these words: "I consent to your going to begin what, I trust, will be the real beginning of the great road."[9]

It was indeed. Dodge went to work, beginning by cleaning the stables. He put Jacob House in charge of the headquarters in Omaha. He moved the unhappy Hoxie off his job in Chicago to become the transfer agent, operating out of Omaha. "I would rather be at Omaha under you than to be in the city with a much larger salary," Hoxie told Dodge. He had been doing many tasks in the city, including freight, and added, "I am heartily sick of this living at hotels, without my wife, and both ends pushing me for freight. I can't make the river higher."[10]

With these and many other changes, Dodge put the working end of the UP on a military basis. Nearly all his chief subordinates had been in the Union Army, and with but a few exceptions his graders and track layers had been participants in the war. There were thousands of them, with more coming. Military discipline came naturally to them, for they were accustomed to giving or receiving and carrying out orders. Without that military organization, it is doubtful that the UP could have been built at all. The UP had farther to go than the CP, and hostile Indians to contend with, plus shortages and the nonexistence of timber, water, and other necessities.

Dodge said later that the changes in the railroad world had been caused by what had been learned during the Civil War. "The great principles then evolved have taught the American people that there was no problem in finance or relating to the development of the country so great that its people did not feel able to grasp and master it."[11] Dodge and his subordinates had learned in the army how to deal with problems.

It wasn't easy, and it wasn't all done at once. Durant retained the title of "vice-president and general manager," which meant that Reed, Hoxie, and others still reported to him. Meanwhile, Dodge had to deal with Silas Seymour, whose title was "consulting engineer." Seymour had no authority, but he answered only to Durant and was able to—and did—create a great deal of mischief.

The Indians out on the Great Plains posed their own threat. With the Civil War over and the UP building, settlers were moving out into what they regarded as their land. The Homestead Act, giving a quarter-section of land to each settler, was a magnet. Nebraska gained population so fast that in 1867 it became a state, much earlier than expected.

The Pawnee, living in eastern Nebraska, were "Hang around the Forts," as the hostile Indians called them. Surveyor Bissell wrote that "the Pawnees were normally friendly," but also that they "were more degraded in their habits and ways of living than almost any tribe."[12] They had made their peace with the white men, and many of their warriors had become soldiers in the white man's army.

But west of Columbus, Nebraska, the Sioux and Cheyenne were predominant, and decidedly hostile. They despised the iron rail, which along with providing great benefits to the whites had an additional disadvantage for the Indians in that it split the Great Plains buffalo herd into two parts, because buffalo would not cross the tracks. The Indians wanted the iron rail, and the men who surveyed for it and the men who were building it and the farmers who were following it and the travelers who were sure to come on it, out of their country. And they had plenty of men, young and even old, who were ready to follow a war chief on a raid, against either the settlements or the surveyors or the graders or the road builders. Thus the UP needed protection from the army, but the army had nowhere near enough men or posts beyond the frontier to provide it.

This meant the UP's workers would, in most cases, have to protect themselves. Dodge ordered it. He wanted every man armed. He wanted them all drilled too, if they needed it, but since they were veterans he decided they didn't. They had to keep their rifles always within easy reach, however—life on the frontier.

It meant doom for the Indians' way of life. No longer could they be free and independent, living off the buffalo herds. They could either follow the way of the Pawnee and live on reservations, cared for by the white man, or get killed. As General John Pope, who was replacing Dodge, observed, "The Indian, in truth, no longer has a country. He is reduced to starvation or to warring to the death. The Indian's first demand is that the white man shall not drive off his game and dispossess him of his lands. How can we promise this unless we prohibit emigration and settlement? . . . The end is sure and dreadful to contemplate."[13]

Dodge, by contrast, was in agreement with General Phil Sheridan. He had no sympathy for the plight of the Indians, and believed, "There were really no friendly Indians." That was wrong—the Pawnee surely were—but it set the tone for the UP and, in truth, could hardly have been helped, considering the scope and events of the Sioux and Cheyenne actions.

The Indians were one problem; the weather was another. The Missouri River could not be navigated until late March or early April. Jack Casement had his crews ready by the first day of spring, more than three thousand of them, and the boarding cars nearly ready for them, but the river was too low for the cars to be sent to Omaha, and besides, the rails could not be shipped until the spring rise deepened the water. By mid-April, the supplies began pouring into Omaha, and the Casement broth-

ers went to work, with Dodge's full backing. Dodge had long argued, correctly, that nothing would give the UP more credibility than the laying of
track with trains running on it. The Casement brothers built it. By June
4, the track layers had reached the hundred-mile post (although the
bridge over the Loup River was only a temporary pile trestle), and by late
July, the gangs had passed Grand Island (153 miles from Omaha) and
were headed for Fort Kearney, two hundred miles from Omaha. The
graders, meanwhile, were beginning to grade the third hundred miles. So
far the Indians had left both groups alone.

In May, to anticipate their depredations, Sherman formed a new department, designating it the Department of the Platte. He put General
Philip St. George Cooke in command, with headquarters in Omaha, and
expressed the hope to Grant that President Johnson and the secretary of
war would "befriend this railroad as far as the law allows."[14]

*T*HERE is nothing connected with the Union Pacific Railroad that is
not wonderful," wrote the correspondent of the *Cincinnati Gazette*. "In
one sense the road is as great an achievement as the war, and as grand a
triumph." Continuing the image, the reporter went on, "Go back twenty
miles on the road, and look at the immense construction trains, loaded
with ties and rails, and all things needed for the work. It is like the grand
reserve of an army. Six miles back are other trains of like character. These
are the second line."

Going forward to the end of track, he wrote, "are the boarding cars and
a construction train, which answer to the actual battle line." The boarding cars were each eight feet long, some fitted with berths, others with
dining halls, one a kitchen. The construction train carried forward all supplies—ties, rails, fishplates, sledgehammers, shovels, rope of various sizes
and length, more than a thousand rifles, and much more.[15] It was indeed
comparable, in many ways, to an army moving across the landscape.

Samuel Reed, in Omaha, was responsible for keeping the army supplied. Before Dodge signed on, and even after, he cleared his decisions
with Doc Durant in New York. His telegrams to Durant, sent once a day
or more, are today in the UP Archives in Omaha, and they constitute a
remarkable collection that speak directly to the question, How did the
UP do it?

Here are some examples, all from 1866. Reed to Durant, February 5:

"Can change line second Hundred miles will reduce bridges one half [in] timber. . . . Have ordered the change if you do not approve countermand." February 15: "Shall I contract for one hundred thousand cottonwood thirty five dollars and plans for car shop." February 19: "Shall we deliver ties on new line west of Loup fork sixty to eighty teams ready to commence hauling as soon as decided." February 26: "Notified Harry Creighton to build telegraph line to end of road [but he] will not do it without order from New York." March 1: "The new line will be better than the old one less bridging less grading and four to six miles nearer fuel and ties." March 12: "Must have three spans Loup Fork Truss[.] Can make temporary bridges for balance[.] Single pile bents will not stand in channel[.] Piles drove east abutment & three east piers[.] West abutment & west pier half drove." March 13: "McManus & Hornby propose to build engine house ten stall for twenty thousand [dollars] and car shop for thirty five thousand [dollars] shall I close. Can I contract Loup Fork masonry." March 20: "Navigation open first boat just arrived."[16]

The last telegram in the preceding sample marked a big moment for Reed and all who worked for the UP. Supplies could now get to Omaha by steamship. This allowed Durant to embark on a bold experiment. He had been told that barges were unsuitable in the shifting water of the river, but he nevertheless had two built and purchased a steamboat, the *Elk Horn*, to haul them. The boat and the barges made it to Omaha from St. Louis in less than ten days. Durant had opened a new era for shipping on the Missouri River.[17]

Reed to Durant, April 7: "I have contracted for 500 cubic yards of stone for foundations and small bridges at $4 per yard delivered on the line of the road. Also for 50,000 ties. Mr. Davis is sawing the timber for Loup Fork Truss bridge [the bridge was to be seventeen hundred feet long]. There is a little more than one third of the piles drove for the temporary bridge over Loup Fork. Grading contractors are commencing their work, [although] the frost is not out of the ground yet. We have just received two rafts of logs the first of the season. There is a good stage of water and I think we shall receive ties and timber rapidly via river from this time. Twelve hundred tons of iron rails have been received. We have more than one hundred thousand ties on the line of the road, inspected and paid for. I can contract for 50000 hard wood ties to be delivered twenty to twenty five miles west of the west end of the second hundred miles." And so on.

Reed's telegrams to Durant are remarkable, partly because of the detail Durant insisted on holding in his own hands, even after Dodge signed on, also for all the details Reed had to handle, and most of all for the scope of the enterprise. And by mid-April, Reed was reporting on the speed of the construction. On April 17, he took government commissioners over the completed track: "We left Omaha at 9:20 am and arrived at the 40 miles post at 10:40 then run slow over the road to end of track, 63½ miles from initial point. The Commissioners appear to be well pleased with the work and expressed themselves accordingly. I intend to have the track laid to the 65 mile stake before six o'clock tonight. We are laying ¾ of a mile each day. The boarding cars will be completed Saturday and sent to end of the track after that we can lay one mile per day."

May 28: "Track laid to west end of station at Columbus [across the Loup River, at 86.5 miles from Omaha]. No track laid Saturday on account of storm." May 31: "Eight thousand feet track laid today. Ninety-seven and quarter miles laid [from Omaha, counting sidings]. Columbus hard place men had big drunk two days lost." Despite Reed's disapproval, one should hope so for the sake of these young lions, Columbus being the first village they had come to since leaving Fremont, at the beginning of the season, that had beer or whiskey for sale.

I N August, a correspondent of the *New York Times* wrote that one of the new railroad towns, Kearney, was "small, but vigorous and promising." He predicted that "she will be a rich and busy city someday" and commented on "these numerous towns which spring up so suddenly on the Plains. They remain in constant and fierce rivalry, each eagerly clutching at every straw of trade to keep itself afloat and to swim ahead of its neighbors." He found that, with the track completed to Kearney less than a week ago, the first train came in from Omaha yesterday, "and tomorrow shall see the first eastward bound train! Yet already the road has been built two miles further on. This in one day!" He considered it "extraordinary" to see in how short a time "the smooth, grass-covered prairie, unworn by wagon-tracks and undented even by hoof-prints, has been converted into a grand iron highway." Occasionally a dip in the surface had to be filled with a few shovels of dirt, "but beyond this, it needs only that the ties be laid, the rails spiked on them and the spaces filled in with earth."

Summing up, the reporter said that what he was witnessing "is the genuine American genius—the genius of the West especially, which welcomes obstacles and looks on impossibilities as incentives to greater exertion."[18]

There were thousands of the young lions, five hundred or more working on the grades, then a thousand, then three thousand by 1868, in order to keep well ahead of the track layers, who eventually numbered more than seven thousand. The men came to Omaha on their own, or in response to a UP advertisement that promised good pay, good food, lots of work, and a free ride. Many were Irish and so the whole gang was labeled, but in fact they came from all over Europe and the United States, including a few newly freed African Americans. Jack Casement had a former slave with him as a servant. His name was Jack Ellis and he had been with Casement during the last year of the Civil War. Some three hundred freed slaves worked on the UP all together.

What the workingmen had most in common was their age, most of them teenagers or just into their twenties, and their status as veterans. One diarist noted, "Nearly everybody wearing a long blue overcoat with brass buttons, the regular U.S. soldier uniform left over from the Civil War, with one or two revolvers strapped to their sides."[19] Others wore gray coats. This is perfectly clear in group photographs taken in 1867–69. "It was the best organized, best equipped, and best disciplined work force I have ever seen," Dodge wrote of these men. "I used it several times as a fighting force and it took no longer to put it into fighting line than it did to form it for daily work."[20]

Their food was served on long tables in a dining car. They sat on benches, as at a picnic table. The meals consisted of coffee, potatoes, and boiled meat (usually beef; Jack Casement kept a herd of five hundred cattle marching along with the advance of the rails). It took about nine bushels of potatoes per meal to feed the men on a dining car. Good butter was kept at hand, when possible, and occasionally even ice water. Sometimes there was variety: a diarist wrote that at one dinnertime "a Negro mammy appeared with a huge basket full of fried chicken, bread and butter, doughnuts, bottles of milk and other food. We bought her out at once, basket and all."[21]

The men got their board and room at a cost of $5 per week. The "room" consisted of a space in one of the flatcars, or on top of it after the summer heat began. The cars were eighty-five feet long, ten feet wide, and eight feet high. They contained seventy-eight bunks, three tiers high and capable of sleeping two hundred men. The graders' beds were in dugouts half beneath the ground, perhaps roofed with sheet iron—the same kind of hut used in the Wilderness and at Vicksburg. The men bathed only when they were near enough to the Platte to make it possible, and that wasn't often. They almost never washed their pants, shirts, and jackets. About a quarter of them had mustaches, another quarter had beards, a quarter had full facial hair, and the rest were clean shaven (at least when the photographer showed up). The hair on their heads was generally long, down to the shoulders. About half seem to have smoked, mainly pipes.

They were paid from $2.50 to $4.00 per day, depending on what they did. Only one in four was a track layer. Some put in the ties or filled around them or handled the rails or spiked them down or attached the fishplates to them. Others were graders, teamsters, herdsmen, cooks, bakers, blacksmiths, bridge builders, carpenters, masons, and clerks or telegraph operators. Most had to be taught their jobs, but they were quick learners, and the work was so specialized they seldom if ever made a mistake.

How hard they worked is an astonishment to us in the twenty-first century. Except for some of the cooks and bakers, there was not a fat man among them. Their hands were tough enough for any job—one never sees gloves in the photographs—which included pickax handling, shoveling, wielding sledgehammers, picking up iron rails, and using other equipment that required hands like iron. Their waists were generally thin, but oh those shoulders! Those arms! Those legs! They were men who could move things, hammer things in, swing things, whatever was required, in rain or snow or high winds or burning sun and scorching temperature, all day, every day. Nebraska can be hotter than hell, colder than the South Pole. They kept on working. They didn't whine, they didn't complain, they didn't quit, they just kept working.

They had taken on a job that is accurately described as backbreaking. It was in addition a job that experts said could not be done in the time allotted (ten years), if ever. But they were building a railroad that would tie the country together, a railroad that almost every American wanted built as fast as possible, a railroad that required much of the skill and ingenuity and organizational ability and manufacturing capacity and stick-to-it determination of all Americans, a railroad that every American—most of all those men who were working on it at the cutting edge—was damned proud of.

A day's routine was something like this: In the morning the men were up at first light. After their toilet they went to wash faces and hands in a tin basin, had a hearty breakfast, and went to the job, whether plowing, shoveling, placing ties or rails, spiking them in, or putting on the fish-plates at the junction of two rails. At noon, "Time" was called and they had an hour for a heavy dinner that included pitchers of steaming coffee, pans of soup, platters heaped with fried meat, roast meat, potatoes, condensed milk diluted with water, sometimes canned fruit and pies or cakes. There was little conversation: the men were there to eat, and they made a business of it.

Afterward, they sat around their bunks smoking, sewing on buttons, or taking a little nap. Then back to work, with the bosses cursing and excoriating to overcome the noontime lassitude. "Time" was called again an hour before supper, to allow some rest. The evening meal was more leisurely. Then to the bunkhouses, for card games, a smoke, lots of talk ("railroad talk" was said to consist entirely of "whiskey and women and higher wages and shorter hours"), perhaps a song, such as "Poor Paddy he works on the railroad" or "The great Pacific railway for California hail." Then to bed, the whole to be repeated the next day and the next and the next.

During the spring of 1866, Jack Casement offered each man a pound of fresh tobacco for every day he laid a mile or more of track. Bissell, who was there, noted, "This was done." Dan Casement went out in the early summer to offer time-and-a-half pay to ensure that the UP reached the hundredth meridian before any other line. He also offered double wages for two-mile workdays. Henry Morton Stanley, the reporter who found Livingston in Africa and who was reporting for two American papers, was impressed by the results: the workers, he said, "display an astonishing amount of enthusiasm" for their jobs.[22]

*T*HE snakily undulating double row of glistening rails stretched on to the west. Side tracks were filled with supply trains bearing hundreds of tons of iron and thousands of ties, fishplates, and more. The end of track, the last terminal base, was brimming with riotous life. There the Casement brothers had a huge takedown and then put-up-again warehouse. There were the boarding cars, the dining cars, the combined kitchen, stores, and office car. There were dusty lines of wagons bearing ties, hay, rails. A construction train would run up, men quickly unloaded its material, and the train started back, to bring on another load.

The wagons, drawn by horses, plied between the track layers and their supplies. Here was where all the work paid off. One wagon took about forty rails, along with the proper proportion of spikes and chairs, along the rails already laid. The horse started off at a full gallop for the end of track, running between the rails. A couple of feet from the end of the rails already down, metal checks were placed under the wheels, stopping the wagon at once. On each side of the wagon there were rollers to facilitate running off the iron rails. Parties of five men stood on either side. Two men seized the end of a rail with their tongs and started forward with it, while the other men took hold with their tongs until it was clear of the car. They all came forward at a run. The chairs had, meantime, been set under the last rails placed. At the command "Down!" they dropped the rail in its place.

Every thirty seconds there came that brave "Down," "Down," from either side of the track. The chief spiker was ready; the gauger stooped and measured; the sledges rang. Two rails every thirty seconds, one on each side. Four rails to a minute. These were the pendulum beats.[23]

As the rails went down, they were gauged by a measuring rod exactly four feet eight and a half inches, as Lincoln had designated in 1863. Ere the rail's clang in falling had ceased to reverberate, the wagon moved forward on the new track and another pair of rails was drawn out. When the wagon was empty, it was tipped over on the side of the track to allow the next loaded wagon to pass it. Then it was tipped back again and sent down the track for another load, the horse straining at a full gallop.

The lead horse, always, was Blind Tom, a noble, venerable, full-blooded horse who pulled the front wagon. His name came from his condition—he couldn't see. The workers pronounced him "perfect" in his role. No one claimed less sagacity for Blind Tom than that for any of the humans around him. When his wagon slipped and got stuck in a gap between the joints, he tugged with herculean force to drag it through. He became something of a celebrity from being mentioned in so many newspaper accounts of the construction.

Behind the wagon there was a man dropping spikes, while another settled the ties well under the ends of the rails. There was no ballast for the ties other than sand, which was added later. For now, they were simply put on the grade. The attitude was, as with the cottonwood ties, that it could be fixed later, when trains would be going down grade from the mountains where the material—gravel or hardwood ties—could be sent, to where it could replace the sand or cottonwood. It would be much cheaper, and would get the road built all the faster.

There were thirty men driving in the spikes, on the outside and on the inside, with three strokes of the sledgehammer per spike, ten spikes to a rail, four hundred rails to a mile, eighteen hundred miles to San Francisco.* Twenty-one million times those sledgehammers had to be swung. This was the beginning of what would be called assembly-line work. The pace was as rapid as a man could walk. Such a pace was attained because each man had a certain thing to do, and that only. He was accustomed to doing it and had not to wait on the action of anyone else.

In 1866, there were some one thousand men working at or near the end of track, out of a total force of eight thousand. There were four locomotives with ten cars each running between the track head and the last siding. It took forty cars to bring on the rails, ties, bridging, fastening, fuel, and supplies for the men and animals. Everything had to be transported from the Missouri River.

Ahead of the four construction trains came a locomotive pulling a general-repair car that held a blacksmith shop, cables, rope, winches, barrels, boxes, switch stands, iron rods, and more. Then the feed store and saddler's shop, then a carpenter shop, then a sleeping car or two, then a sitting and dining room for foremen, then a long dining room, then a car that contained a kitchen in front and a counting room and telegraph office in the rear, then a store car, then six cars that were all sleepers.

Two locomotives powered the work train. The crew included two foremen, two engineers, two conductors, a financial manager, a storekeeper, a physician, a civil engineer and seven assistants, a draftsman, a telegrapher, the chief steward and sixteen assistants, and the workers. The physician had broken bones and mashed fingers to repair, and sometimes Indian arrows to extract.[24]

All the cars were hauling material. There were tie layers, who needed seventy-five teams of horses and wagons to haul the ties forward along

---

* Ten spikes to the rail provided only enough stability for moving the construction cars ahead with more materials. Following gangs had to put in the proper complement of ties, or about 2,250 per mile. Then spikes were driven for all ties, averaging between nine and ten thousand per mile.

the side of the track. Then the track layers, the gaugers, the spikers. Keeping up with everything were the herd of cattle, along with a butcher and helper to kill daily for consumption, and herders to care for the cattle. There was a baker and helper to bake the bread, and more.

It was the very embodiment of system. Henry Morton Stanley was in Nebraska to write about the Indian uprisings and massacres for a St. Louis and a New York newspaper. After a breakfast with Casement, Stanley watched the men laying track. He noted: "All this work is executed with great rapidity and with mechanical regularity. Captain D. B. Clayton, superintendent of laying the track, showed your reporter a specimen of what could be done. He gave his men the order, and in the space of exactly five minutes, as timed by the watch, they laid down the rails and spiked them, for the distance of seven hundred feet. There were fifty rails laid down, one on each side of the track. At that rate sixteen miles and a half of track could be laid down in one day."[25]

*T*HEIR slang was expressive. An engineer was a "hogger." The fireman was the "tallow-pot." When the engineer wanted the brakes set, he whistled a signal called the "whistle down brakes." Setting the handbrakes was a "tie-down." A drifting railroad worker was a "boomer." A "bumper" was a retaining post at the end of a spur track. A "car toad" was a car repairer. "Cushions" were passenger coaches, of which the workers saw few to none. To "dance the carpet" was to appear before an official for discipline. A "fly light" was a man at work who had missed a meal. A "drone cage" was a private car, also seldom seen by the workers. A man asleep on the job was a "hay." And so on. A phrase universally known was "gandy dancer," for a track laborer.

It took an immense force to support the end of track, just as it took an immense force to support the front line in a battle. Twenty miles back of the end of track stood construction trains, loaded with ties and rails and all other things needed for the work. It was like the grand reserve of an army. Ten to twelve miles ahead of it were other trains of like character— the second line.[26] One reporter wrote, "Sherman, with his victorious legions, sweeping from Atlanta to Savanah, was a spectacle less glorious than this army of men, marching on foot from Omaha to Sacramento."[27]

On May 11, as the Casement-led force was getting under way, the *Omaha Weekly Herald* put it exactly. "The question of time is of such moment that minutes and seconds even are estimated when interruptions occur in the work of track-laying. The great machine must move in every part; every wheel must be in constant motion; so many rails must be put down and so much done every minute of every working hour of every working day, or loss accrues."[28] No minutes, or even seconds, were wasted on the UP. On August 2, the *Omaha Weekly Herald* reported that the previous day the government commissioners had accepted thirty-five miles of the track after being "surprised almost beyond measure at the rapidity with which the work is being pushed forward—thirty-eight miles having been built in twenty-eight days and in one instance 2 miles in one day."

On their ride, the commissioners uttered expressions of wonder "at the extent and amazing fertility of this Valley of the Platte." One called it "the finest Valley in the world." Their train, meanwhile, sped forward at a speed of thirty-five miles per hour, "not spilling a drop of water from the well-filled goblets, so smooth is the track." The commissioners arrived at the end of track toward the end of the day, when the men were seated in the dining car having their meal. Together with the kitchen and sleeping cars, and the construction supplies and cars, the total constituted "almost a city in itself." On the return trip to Omaha, the train made the last thirty-two miles in thirty-seven minutes.[29]

At this time Dodge and Reed made a trip over the road, then continued on to see how the graders were doing. Their biggest worry was crossing the North Platte at the Nebraska city (now named North Platte) at the junction of the North and South Platte Rivers. Reed sent a telegraph to Durant on August 4: "General Dodge was with me at crossing of North Platte and decides that pile bridges will be suitable for crossing that stream. Can reach there before January with track. Shall I close contract or wait until I can send you plan." Why he had to have Durant's approval for something Dodge had already decided on doing isn't clear.

On September 17, Reed wired that he had on hand two hundred thousand ties, which had reduced the price to 60 cents per tie. "If the grading can be done and iron delivered we can lay the track to Julesburgh before spring. Did you send spikes? Fish joints? Or is all the iron to be laid with chairs! The above has been written on the supposition that the men employed on the work are not molested by the Indians. We lost 98 mules 50 miles west of end of track. The men are very timid and on the first appearance of Indians would all leave the work. Sherman promised protection if there were troops in the country to be spared."[30]

At the end of August, the commissioners wired President Johnson that they had inspected an additional forty-five miles of the UP and accepted them. Their telegram concluded, "The cars now run two hundred and five miles west of Omaha; or fifteen miles beyond Kearney."[31]

THE men were really hopping for the Casement brothers. On September 21, the *Omaha Weekly Herald* was able to announce that the UP had printed a timetable. It was now running twice a day from Omaha to Kearney, a distance of two hundred miles. The passenger train, with first-class coaches and newly completed freight cars, left Omaha at 1 P.M. and 7 P.M. and arrived at Kearney at 5:10 A.M. and 11:10 A.M. Turned around, the trains got back to Omaha at 2 P.M. and 8 P.M. At Kearney, coaches met the train and moved passengers and freight to Colorado, Utah, Wyoming, and California.[32] The *Rocky Mountain News* had reported a few months earlier that all horse-drawn coaches had been withdrawn from Omaha.[33]

General Sherman went for the ride. He was impressed beyond measure. He wrote to Grant that he hoped the line would be complete to Julesburg, Colorado, by April 1867. "This will be a great achievement," he ventured, "but perfectly possible when we see what has been done." He confessed that he was puzzled about what to do with Fort Kearney: because of the railroad, it was of no further military use.[34]

Sherman's puzzlement illustrated one of the main purposes of building the UP. The army was spending millions of dollars in building forts on the Plains and across the Rocky Mountains, and in getting the soldiers to them and supplying them. But it was critical that it be able to do so, because, with the end of the war and the rapidly increased immigration to the United States, families were moving out onto the Plains at a fast pace. The hostility of the Plains Indians required the army to get out there to protect the immigrants. But stationing companies and even regiments at frontier posts did little good, since the troops could never mount up and go out to catch marauding Indians in time—the Indians would have long since departed the scene of their outrage. With the railroad, and its ability to move troops faster and safer from one place to another, the army needed fewer men and fewer forts, which made it much cheaper to maintain. Thus did the government get an immediate payoff from its investment in the UP. Sherman had anticipated this, which was one of the reasons he and Grant were great friends of the railroad.

Early in 1866, Sherman wrote to the editor of the *Omaha Weekly Herald*. "You know how outspoken I have been in the matter of befriending the Great Pacific Railroad," he opened, "as also on all subjects calculated to develop the vast natural resources of the Northwest." Then he pointed out, "You can hardly create a more lively interest than already prevails in the whole civilized world on the subject of a Pacific Railroad."[35]

How right the general was can be seen in the coverage given the railroads, from newspapers in Sacramento, San Francisco, Omaha, Chicago, Denver, Salt Lake, New York, and elsewhere. The public was fascinated by the construction of the transcontinental railroad. In part this was due to the magnitude of the undertaking, in part to its usefulness, not only to the military and the settlers but to all Americans. Everywhere people agreed that the coming of the railroad meant a new day was at hand.

Another factor: the Civil War was over, and the great corps of reporters and editors that had come of age during the conflict suddenly had little of national significance to write about, except for national politics. This meant that sophisticated reporters and editors, who were savvy about what people wanted to read, were at loose ends. Many of them decided that the railroad was the news to cover. As each month went by, more and more of them started doing so. In a short time it became the big story.

A s of October 6, 1866, the end of track had reached the hundredth meridian, 247 miles west of Omaha. Doc Durant decided that this was the big story of 1866. He invited scads of people for his grand excursion, to ride west on the "sumptuous Directors' car" which he had purchased from the Pullman Palace Sleeping Car Company, built to his exacting and extravagant specifications. There were other Pullman cars in the train, called by one newspaper "the most sumptuous and resplendent, not only in America but all over the world." Then there was the "Lincoln Car," which had been built for President Lincoln but used only for his funeral, which Durant had purchased with the UP's money, along with five coaches and a freight train bearing food, liquor, tents, and other articles.

The guests included Senators Benjamin Wade, J. W. Patterson, J. M. Thayer, F. W. Tipton, and John Sherman, twelve representatives, and others, along with Robert Todd Lincoln, son of Abraham Lincoln, Mr.

and Mrs. George Francis Train, Mr. and Mrs. Silas Seymour, George Pullman, John Duff, and many others. Reporters from every daily in the United States were invited, and many came.

In Omaha they got to see a part of what the UP had constructed, including a roundhouse capable of sheltering twenty locomotives at once (there were already twenty-three locomotives on the line; one hundred were expected in 1867), a blacksmith shop with twelve forges, a two-story machine shop, extensive car shops turning out nine cars per week, and more.

The first night was spent at Columbus, where some went to see Casement's men laying track on a siding while others visited a prairie-dog colony or went hunting for buffalo and antelope. In the evening, Dodge had a huge bonfire lit in the center of a great circle of tents. A grand feast of game was accompanied by champagne (the breakfast and lunch on the dining cars had been meals to write home about too). A party of Pawnees, recruited by the same Dodge who had expressed his belief that there were no friendly Indians, gave the party a scare that night when they raced through the camp, wearing war paint. After Dodge had reassured the shrieking ladies and the timid gentlemen that these were friendly Pawnees, the crowd gathered to watch a few war dances and a mock battle complete with fake scalping. It all lasted until 2 A.M.

While on this trip, Dodge was elected to Congress by the people of Council Bluffs and its district. Later he figured himself to be the only man "elected to Congress who forgot the day of election." He never campaigned for the office and hardly ever went to Washington to serve.

At 132 miles west of Omaha was the last farm to be found until Salt Lake City. At the one hundredth meridian, the train turned around and started back toward Omaha. Durant was ecstatic and resolved to have excursions whenever the UP had something to celebrate. Dodge, at first wary, began to get into the spirit of the thing as he slowly realized how much good it was doing for the company. On the last night, he treated the guests to the spectacle of a staged prairie fire set at a safe distance. He also conducted what amounted to a continuous press conference. He answered all reporters' questions. He later confessed that he had sprinkled his remarks with "a great deal of romance" of the sort reporters dote on. Despite the cost, which was huge, he decided that, "from a sight-seeing point of view, it may be considered as very successful."[36]

As Maury Klein puts it, "The selling of the West had begun in earnest," even though, at what is today Cozad, Nebraska, the tourists were not very far west. But as Klein says, "Even at this early stage the market value of self-parody had been discovered."[37]

SHORTLY after the excursion, the UP announced that it would convert one of its construction trains to a passenger car so that the line could run out to Lone Tree Station, forty-one miles west of Columbus. Soon after that, the line ran daily service to Grand Island. By late August, it was "Open to Kearney," near the military post of Fort Kearney. The service was sometimes irregular and the passage sometimes problematical, but it was a start.

The fuel was cottonwood poles, which were green. The firemen insisted they sprouted when placed in the firebox. Still, they generated enough steam to haul a small train of cars across the countryside at twenty miles per hour. In historian Robert Athearn's words, "It was such an improvement over travel by jolting, wearying prairie schooners that to the postwar traveler it must have seemed he was moving through another world, in another age."[38]

Exaggeration is endemic to railroad historians. Athearn later quotes a young Danish girl whose father, in 1867, paid the UP $10 each to carry his family to North Platte. They sat on benches without backs and were jolted by the movement of a springless car over new track. It was a tiring experience, she wrote, one that she remembered years later as quite unpleasant.[39]

DODGE spent far more time working than entertaining. He arranged for military escorts when and where he could, dealt with the government commissioners who came west to examine the track laid by the UP, ordered supplies of all kinds, and handled land matters for the company. He was in ultimate charge of the bridge building. It was Dodge who decided, as Reed telegraphed Durant, that the North Platte was tame enough for a twenty-three-hundred-foot-long trestle built on cedar piles. He was in charge of the Loup Fork Bridge, completed in 1866, fifteen hundred feet long.

Dodge was also in command of the company's land and mineral interests. He arranged for the first lands received from the government along the completed road. He founded twelve depots and made a town around each one of them, where he had lots recorded and the best ones taken up by the company. At such critical points as Kearney and North Platte, he reserved a large acreage for railroad shops, sidings, and other needs. His working theory was that it was best to "take all the property needed or that ever would be needed while the land was vacant." He sold lots to settlers at anywhere from $25 to $250, one-third in cash and the balance over the next two years. The purchaser had to plant shade trees. In addition, Dodge kept a sharp lookout for coal, iron, and other minerals.[40] He had Jacob H. House doing a hydrographic survey of the Missouri River to find the best place for a railroad bridge. If in the process Nebraska didn't become an appendage of the UP, it was close.

Also in 1866, Dodge sent out his surveyors to find the best route over the Black Hills, through Wyoming, to Salt Lake, and beyond, to the California state line. In a May 1866 letter to surveyor James A. Evans (with more or less similar copies to the other surveyors), Dodge said, "You know that a railroad can be built where a mule or man can hardly travel." He told Evans what to survey—how to get over the Black Hills, for the company was "anxious to determine beyond a doubt where we shall pass them." To that end he wanted all lines examined, not excluding the one Dodge had found out of Cheyenne. Dodge said he wanted Evans to write him "as often as possible." Further, he wanted from Evans a report on "the geology, mineralogy, and the mineral and agricultural resources of the country." He concluded, "Time is everything with us. Use economy in all expenses."[41]

To Dodge's delight, Evans pronounced the line headed west out of Cheyenne as the best. To the south, the route west from Denver was impossible, just as Dodge had thought. To go north on the North Platte to the Laramie River was also impossible. Evans "pushed through, taking three weeks to run 25 miles—a narrow, wild, precipitous gorge, and never before passed by man," according to Dodge. It was therefore "impracticable." So were the other three routes Evans ran, except for the Lone Tree line Dodge had discovered. It was shorter, had gentler grades, less curvature, no canyons, was relatively free of snowfall, and required fewer bridges.

Indeed, the surveys westward from North Platte, Nebraska, all the way to the probable meeting with the CP pleased Dodge no end. As he put it in his 1866 report, "The surveys this year have connected our lines, settled the location over the Rocky Mountains and from that point westward. We have demonstrated that a line can be built from the Missouri river to the California state line without meeting any mountain barriers, impassable snows, or great deserts that it is not practicable to overcome; that we have a line for directness, distance, alignment, grades and work, that is not equaled by any other road of the same length in the world. That we have, in fact, the best general route across the continent."

There were mountain ranges, to be sure, but Dodge said the UP could overcome the Black Hills, Medicine Bow, and the Wasatch Range "without extraordinary expenses, with comparatively light grades, with but a few miles of maximum grades, and with an alignment that is extraordinary." In those mountains there was "plenty of timber—cedar, mountain pine, and hemlock—rock in cuts, and the whole country is underlaid with valuable mines of silver, iron, copper, and gold." Between the Black Hills and the Wasatch Range, "coal begins to crop out, and it extends west to Salt Lake, along with sandstone and limestone." Dodge did admit that on the western slope of the Rocky Mountains it was "desolate, dreary, not susceptible of cultivation or grazing. The country has no inviting qualities." Still, there was produce for road building "and labor to build this portion of the road exists there to-day [by which he meant Mormons from Salt Lake City] without importing a single man or mechanic."

Dodge's 1866 report constituted the first clear description of the country from the western part of Nebraska all the way through to the Sierra Nevada, along with the first description of the best route for a railroad over that country. He was quick to praise his surveyors for all that they did, nor did he neglect to add that they had "all the time been in a hostile Indian country, unceasingly dependent upon military escorts, every mile having been located under guard, the party perpetually apprehensive of attack. The engineers performed their work much better than could have been expected."[42]

What pathbreaking work the surveyors were doing was illustrated by the information they got. One of them, L. L. Hills, talked to the "oldest inhabitant" on the Platte River. "Oldest" is relative here, for he could not have been there more than a couple of years. Anyway, the old-timer said the Platte "never flooded over at the Loup Fork." Hills's own observations were more accurate: "I have no doubt that this valley will make one of the finest stock-raising countries in the world."[43]

While Dodge worked on his report, the graders and track layers and other workers were busy. Reed wired Durant on November 13 that he had iron to lay track as far as North Platte, but the next day he had to tell the Doctor that there had been a "severe snow storm at end of track." When the Casements were shut down by weather—the ground froze—Jack stayed in North Platte, building a blacksmith shop, icehouse, slaughterhouse, wash house, and stock pens.

Meanwhile, Reed was out front with the graders. On November 29, he wired Durant that he hoped to keep the grading going through December. "The grading on the 4th hundred is not as well advanced as it should be," he admitted. Then he explained, "The Indian scare and severe storms has drove most of the men off of the line, [but] I have used every effort to get as much grading done as possible." Meanwhile, "the Truss bridge over Loup Fork, is completed."[44]

*B*ACK in New York, at 20 Nassau Street, the Union Pacific Railroad Company needed money. The government bonds it had received for completed sections could be sold—nothing could be easier, since the government stood behind the twice-yearly interest payments at 6 percent—but despite the fulsome favorable publicity Durant's excursion to the hundredth meridian had brought forward, the UP bonds had no market value and could be used only for loans at ruinous rates of interest. The stock was so worthless it could be sold only "to people who would take a risk as they would at a faro-bank."

Oakes Ames solicited subscriptions for Crédit Mobilier stock from his fellow congressmen. Two representatives bought five hundred shares each, and Senator James Grimes of Iowa took 250. But many others refused, not because of any question of ethics but because they did not consider it a good investment. Except for two, the businessmen Ames approached to buy shares also turned him down. The Ames brothers and their Boston friends now owned more than half of Crédit Mobilier's twenty-five thousand shares (Oakes and Oliver Ames had 16 percent of the total, with 4,025 shares). Durant was the largest individual holder, with 6,041 shares, and was president of the company.

In late November, the UP directors met in New York. Their first order of business was to adopt the line Dodge had proposed in his report, which they did. No wonder, for the line from Cheyenne began at the point where the government loan jumped from $16,000 per mile to $48,000, but, as Dodge's description made clear, it would not cost the company anywhere near that much to build. That it was also the best and shortest route made the choice easier.

At that same meeting, the directors had to deal with the position of president of the UP. General John Dix had been appointed minister to France, but he did not resign as head of the UP; instead, he took a leave of absence. The board was no longer willing to allow Durant to run things to suit himself and decided to elect a temporary president. Durant wanted the office, but to his dismay he received only one vote, against thirteen for Oliver Ames. The board then adopted a resolution denying the authority of any individual to act for the board, a blunt message to Durant: the UP was no longer his to run as he saw fit.

Doc wanted to fight but was in no condition to do so. He was exhausted, as might be expected after the year he had put in. His friend George Francis Train told him to see a specialist, warning, "Do it or you will have a stroke. You can't strike the Almighty in the face as you do without getting a lick back."

Oliver Ames and his friends, meanwhile, insisted that the UP change its ways. Like the men working for it in the field, it had to be reorganized. Durant's careless way with records had to go. They insisted that proper books be kept and made available to the entire board. The office staff had to be refashioned. There had to be an audit.[45]

Dodge concluded his 1866 report with praise for his surveyors and also for their assistants. He said the latter were "young men, as a general thing, and far above the average, many of them of fine education, and who not only perform the duty well, but intelligently."

The road itself, Dodge said, was by the end of November 1866 "built and running 305 miles, commencing at the Missouri river and extending 10 miles west of the North Platte river." During the period between April 1 and December 1, some 254 miles of track had been laid, "more road than was ever before built in the same length of time. It challenges the attention of the world." In its grades, alignments, superstructure, stations, water tanks, turnouts, and equipment, "the road is a first-class American road."[46]

That last phrase was at best a forgivable exaggeration. The road needed lots of work—new ties, stronger rails, gravel to ballast the rails, new bridges, fewer curves, and more—but none of that mattered at the time.

All that mattered was getting the thing built, getting locomotives hauling cars from New York or Chicago all the way to San Francisco over a continuous track. In 1866, the UP had made a big stride forward to that goal. It had laid over three hundred miles of track, figured out the route for the run to the Salt Lake and beyond to California, learned through experience how to manage its affairs, how to survey, how to make grade, how to lay track, how to build towns and cities, depots and shops. Whatever the worries of the board on the East Coast—and for sure there were many—out at the working end the UP had laid more than seven times as much track in 1866 as it had in 1865. It was on its way.

Abraham Lincoln and Dodge at the time of their first conversation, in 1859. Lincoln was a politician and a railroad lawyer running for president. He met Grenville Dodge in Council Bluffs, Iowa. His first words were, "Dodge, what's the best route for a Pacific railroad to the West?" From then on, until his assassination, Lincoln was the number-one proponent and supporter of the railroad.

Theodore D. Judah (1826–1863). He founded the Central Pacific and discovered the way over the Sierra Nevada mountains. He and his wife, Anna, persuaded the U.S. Congress to fund the railroad with loans of bonds and gifts of alternate sections of land (no photograph of Anna has been found). More than any other individual he made the CP railroad a reality, although he did not live long enough to see a single rail spiked.

General Grenville M. Dodge (1831–1916). He was a Civil War hero and then chief engineer of the Union Pacific. He was the most influential person in building the railroad from Omaha to Promontory Point and was the man who found the line for it to go across the Black Hills and through Wyoming and Utah. In 1859, Dodge convinced Abraham Lincoln to build the road up the Platte River Valley and later got the President to support the 1862 and 1864 bills that made the road possible.

The Big Four of the Central Pacific (clockwise from top left): Leland Stanford (1824–1893), Collis P. Huntington (1821–1900), Charles Crocker (1822–1888), and Mark Hopkins (1814–1878). They were as stern and determined as they look, but they took great risks with their money and their time and energy to build the line. Stanford was president and the chief politician. Huntington borrowed the money for capital expenses in New York, Boston, and Washington, and lobbied Congress for more help. Crocker was in charge of construction. Hopkins handled the books. Together they reaped where they had sown.

General Jack Casement in Wyoming in 1868 poses on horseback in front of one of his construction trains. The Casements were in charge of laying the Union Pacific's track and were simultaneously feared and respected by the workers.

Samuel B. Reed in Echo City, Nevada, in 1869. Reed was chief of construction for the UP, in charge of keeping the men building the road supplied with everything from food to rails, ties, spikes, and everything else. He was also responsible for keeping the graders, barge builders, tie cutters, and tunnel builders supplied.

The surveyors of the UP pose at their camp in Echo Canyon, Utah. They are formally dressed for the occasion. The surveyors came first. They laid out the line. Most of the time, they slept on the ground and did their best to avoid hostile Indians.

General and Republican presidential candidate Ulysses S. Grant and party at Fort Sanders, just south of Laramie, Wyoming, in 1868. Grant has both hands on the fence. General William T. Sherman, in profile, is in front of the door. Thomas "Doc" Durant, the sixth man from the right with his hands clasped, bends forward.

General Dodge and party crossed the continent in 1867. Back row: Lt. J. W. Wheelen; Lt. Col. J. K. Mizner; Dr. Henry C. Terry, assistant surgeon; John E. Corwith. Front row: David VanLennep, geologist; John R. Duff; General G. M. Dodge; Brigadier General John A. Rawlins, chief of staff; Major W. McK. Dunn, ADC to General Rawlins.

Some of the directors of the UP meet in their private car at Echo City, Utah. Silas Seymour is seated at the table, on the left, with Sidney Dillon seated beside him. Doc Durant is beside Dillon, with John Duff on the right. They were on their way to Promontory Summit for the driving of the last spike.

Burnettizing works of the UP at Omaha. This was one of three. Cottonwood ties went through the Burnettizing machine, which treated them by draining the water out of the lumber and putting a zinc solution in its place—otherwise the ties were too soft and perishable. The timbers about to go in are bridge timber; the men at the right are loading one into the works.

The first big bridge
built by the UP was
across the Loup River
at today's Columbus,
Nebraska, where the
Loup flows into the
Platte River. The tim-
bers were cut in
Chicago. On top of the
bridge is the telegraph
line. The bottom pho-
tograph shows the inte-
rior of the structure.

Casement's crew laying track in 1866. Sometimes they laid as much as two miles of track per day. For the sake of the photographer, the men are posed—about the only time they stood still.

On October 6, 1866, the UP tracks reach the one hundredth meridian, near Cozad, Nebraska. Some of the UP directors are posed under the sign. Doc Durant organized an excursion of reporters and politicians on the spot to celebrate and publicize reaching it. Bottom: Durant went beyond the end of the track to pose for a picture standing at the cross ties and emphasizing the theme of Westward the Course of Empire.

Hall's Fill near Sherman Summit. At 8,242 feet, the summit was the highest point on the continental railroad. The UP had reached Cheyenne, Wyoming, in November 1867, and got to the summit in early April 1868.

The bridge over Dale Creek, four miles west of Sherman Summit. One UP engineer called it "a big bridge for a small brook that one could easily step over." It was 126 feet above the streambed and 700 feet long, by far the biggest bridge of the UP. The workers had to dig cuts on both sides leading up to the bridge. It was sufficiently strong to carry a railroad (at four miles per hour, tops) and withstand Wyoming's winds. It is gone today—the track runs south of it—but it was one of the greatest engineering feats of the nineteenth century.

A supply train being unloaded at the end of a track, at Mud Creek, near Fort Bridger, Wyoming.

A UP turntable in Rawlins Springs, Wyoming, 1868. All through Nebraska and Wyoming, Grenville Dodge laid out towns that became major centers for railroad repairs and workers, such as today's Rawlins, Cheyenne, Green River, Laramie, and others.

Lewis Carmichael's camp in Bitter Creek Valley, three miles east of Green River, Wyoming. Carmichael was a major contractor for the UP and made camp here because in the Wyoming desert between Rawlins and the Green River, water was a major problem. Below: A cut dug out by Carmichael's crew in Bitter Creek.

Snow on the Laramie Plains, Wyoming, caused many difficulties for the UP. Sometimes—as for passengers traveling to Grant's inaugural as president in March 1869, when this photograph was taken—the snow was so deep the passengers tried to shovel it away, or they attempted to walk along the tracks.

The UP's temporary and permanent bridges cross Green River, Wyoming. Citadel Rock looms over the scene.

Left: A UP construction train at Granite Canyon, Wyoming, chugs its way across what the railroad called the "Big Fill," at Mile Post 536 from Omaha, between Cheyenne and Sherman Hill. The fill was 375 feet long and 50 feet deep, the largest fill on the UP. Middle left: The Petrified Fish Cut two miles west of Green River, Wyoming. Fills and cuts, then more fills and cuts—it seemed it would never end. Bottom left: The engine Osceola passes through Fish Cut. The locomotive had been confiscated by the government during the Civil War and later turned over to the UP.

The UP's steam shovel at Hanging Rock, in Echo Canyon, Utah. This was the only mechanical power used to move earth on the entire line.

A UP construction train passes through the cut at the head of Echo Canyon. The view is to the east.

On January 9, 1869, the UP's track reached one thousand miles west of Omaha, in Weber Canyon, Utah. The railroad put up a sign to mark the achievement. The base of the tree became a picnic spot for tourists.

The UP telegraph corps at work in Weber Canyon. The telegraph line, required by the Pacific Railroad, ran parallel to the road and was critical to keeping New York informed and essential to keeping supplies coming.

Mormon graders at work in Echo Canyon. At the top, they are bringing down rocks for a fill and to make certain no rocks tumbled down to interfere with the scrapers working on the roadbed. In the bottom photograph, they are digging out a cut. Photos taken in 1868.

Mormons dig out the East Tunnel—the second of four. It was 772 feet long and consumed 1,064 kegs of black powder. As it was being dug, the UP built a flimsy eight-mile temporary track over a ridge. Photo taken 1869.

A UP train crosses the Weber River, having just gone through Tunnel 3. Photo taken 1869.

One of the Casements' construction trains near Bear River City, Wyoming. Bear River City was one of the worst Hell on Wheels towns.

The dock of the steamships and the Pacific Rail Road Depot at the Sacramento River Wharf, where the CP began. Here rails, spikes, cars, and locomotives, shipped around South America from New York and other eastern ports, were unloaded and started toward the end of track.

Goods from railroad wharves at Sacramento being unloaded onto railroad cars for the CP. From here the material moved east toward the Sierra Nevada mountains.

The CP built the Long Ravine Bridge in September 1865. It was 120 feet long and fifty-six miles east of Sacramento.

Main Street in upper Cisco, California. The CP had unloaded material to take by wagon to the end of track. Cisco, ninety-two miles east of Sacramento, was reached in November 1866. Photo taken summer 1867.

At Sailor's Spur, a cut is being made in the background and the debris being hauled by one-horse carts to the fill in the area in the foreground. This took enormous patience, since everything was being done by muscle power. Photo taken summer 1866.

Chinese laborers at work from both ends of the Heath's Ravine Bank in the Sierra Nevada—one cartload of rock and dirt at a time. The trees have been cleared away on both sides of the fill; at the top center are trunks piled up to be cut at a sawmill for ties. Photo taken summer 1867.

Chinese laborers at work on the Prospect Hill cut in the Sierra Nevada.

A CP train going through Bloomer Cut, just beyond Newcastle, California. It was 63 feet deep and 800 feet long. Every foot of the way had to be blasted with gunpowder, and the CP used five hundred kegs of powder a day to do it. It was completed in the spring of 1865 and still stands today, although the line now runs through two tunnels to the north.

Fort Point Cut in the mountains. It was 70 feet deep and 600 feet long. The Chinese hauled away the debris layer after layer.

A freight train rounding Cape Horn, California. Cape Horn is just short (west) of Dutch Flat. It was three miles long. The Chinese laborers did the work of blasting out and making the roadbed. The slope was at an angle of seventy-five degrees and the American River was 1,200 to 2,200 feet below the line of the railroad. One magazine commented, "Good engineers considered the undertaking preposterous." Work began in the summer of 1865 and was completed in the spring of 1866.

Top left: *Taken in the summer of 1867, this photo shows a Chinese tea carrier outside one of the thirteen tunnels the CP drilled through the Sierra Nevada.* Left: *Another worker is hauling debris out of the east portal of the Summit Tunnel (length: 1,659 feet), which was drilled through both ends and from the inside out in both directions.* Above: *The tunnel before completion. The CP began drilling in the fall of 1865, and the Chinese worked twenty-four hours a day. The first train went through on November 30, 1867.*

And then the snows came. The winter of 1866–67 was one of the worst ever. The CP tried everything to get through the snow, but even these gigantic plows on the western slope of the Sierra Nevada couldn't buck their way through. Eventually the CP built miles and miles of snowsheds; at left is a photograph taken by Albert Hart of the frame for one of them. This was one of the early, experimental ones, between Cisco and Summit, built in 1867.

Donner Lake as seen from the summit. The west portals of Tunnels 7 and 8 can be seen. The track hugs the mountains and the south side of the lake. Photo taken summer 1867.

In 1868 the CP track got through the Sierra Nevada and down to the Truckee River. This is a Howe truss bridge across the river at Eagle Gap.

Superintendent of Construction James Harvey Strobridge's car at the end of the track. He was the only man on either railroad to bring his wife and all the other comforts of home. Photo taken probably in summer 1868 in Nevada.

By 1868 the CP was laying out track in the Nevada desert. That meant the men, horses, and engines had to have water. Here Locomotive 49, the El Dorado, fills its containers at Humboldt Lake to take water to the end of the track.

The first construction train to go through Palisade Canyon in eastern Nevada, along the Humboldt River. Below: An Indian looks down at the CP from the top of the canyon. Photos taken in late 1868.

The race ended in the spring of 1869. Leland Stanford and his party at Devil's Gate Bridge, east of Ogden, Utah, on Weber River, May 8, 1869. They were just looking around, waiting for the UP to reach Promontory Summit for the driving of the last spike, and for Durant to be released from the workers who had held up his train at Piedmont.

Doc Durant and Strobridge at Emigrant Gap, California.

The UP's Paymaster Car, at Blue Creek, Utah, a couple of miles east of Promontory Summit. The men are happy to pose for photographer A. J. Russell as they are about to be paid, something that the UP didn't do very often.

Noon, April 28, 1869, Camp Victory, Utah. The CP's track layers have just completed putting down and spiking in six miles of track. They would do four more that afternoon, setting a record that still stands.

Done! East and West shake hands in a famous photograph by A. J. Russell. The CP's engine Jupiter is on the left (it is using wood for fuel; thus the smokestack is round and covered by a screen to catch sparks). The UP's Engine No. 119 is on the right (it used coal for fuel and thus had a straight smokestack).

The Great Event poster.

Chapter Nine

THE CENTRAL PACIFIC
ASSAULTS THE SIERRA
1866

*I*N 1866, Collis Huntington followed up on the map he had already had approved by the attorney general, the map that showed the CP going 150 miles east of the California-Nevada border. Now he wanted an amendment to the railroad bill of 1864 that Congress initially approved, ordering that the CP build until it ran into or even past the tracks of the UP. In short, he wanted a race sanctioned by the U.S. Congress.

A race fit perfectly into the business climate of America. The businessmen spoke little and did much, while the politicians did as little as possible and spoke much. In historian Thomas Cochran's words, the businessmen emphasized "time more insistently than anyone since the original creation."[1]

Huntington hired Richard H. Franchot, an ex-congressman and former Union Army general, to represent his interests to Congress. Franchot, probably the first paid lobbyist, set a pattern for the hordes who followed him. He received $20,000 per year, the same salary the Big Four paid themselves. They did not even ask for a receipt, although his expense account may have reached millions of dollars as he dispensed information, cash, good cheer, and favors.

It was an ideal setup for a lobbyist, as the case made itself. All the CP wanted, it said, was the right to compete fairly. How could the Congress give the UP the right to build as far west as possible without allowing the CP to build as far east as it could? How indeed? The argument and the people making the argument were irrefutable.

In addition, the CP was still stuck at mile 54 out of Sacramento, was still chipping away at the Summit Tunnel, while the UP was almost 250 miles west of Omaha and going strong. The UP directors thought that the CP couldn't possibly make it to the California-Nevada border before they got there. There was no point spending time or money to forestall the CP's getting permission to build farther to the east.

Whatever the directors thought, they were up against their match. Huntington later recalled that the 150-mile limitation on the CP "ought not to have gone into the [original] bill, but I said to Mr. Union Pacific . . . I would take that out as soon as I wanted it out. In 1866 I went to Washington. . . . I went into the gallery for votes. I sat right there. I examined the face of every man . . . carefully through my glass. I didn't see but one man I thought would sell his vote." So he let the politicians vote as they saw fit.[2] He knew he had them.

On June 19, 1866, the Senate approved the amendment to the railroad bill by a vote of 34 to 8. A week later, the House assented by 94 to 33, and on July 3, 1866, President Johnson signed it. The amendment authorized the CP to "locate, construct and continue their road eastward, in a continuous, completed line, until they shall meet and connect with the Union Pacific Railroad." Another provision permitted the companies to grade three hundred miles ahead of the end of track. Still another said the railroads could draw two-thirds of the government bonds upon completion of acceptable grade and before track had been laid.[3] Congress reserved the right to name the exact site where the two lines would connect. That would be decided later.

Meanwhile, the great race was on, exactly as the Congress and the President and the people they represented wanted. Or, as the *Sacramento Union* put it in a January 1866 article, "It is the duty of the Government to urge the construction of the road with all possible speed."[4] The *Omaha Weekly Herald* wrote, "American genius, American industry, American perseverance can accomplish almost anything."[5]

It was indeed such an American thing to do. A race, a competition. Build it fast. The company that won would get the largest share of the land and the biggest share of the bonds. The cost to the country would be the same if it took ten years or twenty years or five years to build. People wanted to get to California, or back east. They wanted to see the sights, to ship the goods. The road could be fixed up later. Build it. Nail it down. And there was no better way than to set up a competition.

This was democracy at work.

• • •

*H*OPKINS and Huntington's correspondence, handwritten, is long, even voluminous letters, full of detail. They had no other means of communicating, except by telegraph—which cost so much per word that they thought it outrageous and refused whenever possible to use it—or by a conference, nearly impossible when they were on different coasts. So they wrote, handsome letters, quite legible, well written, covering all the points. In the middle part of the nineteenth century, before the typewriter and the telephone, businessmen did so as a matter of course. So did the politicians, come to that, and the doctors, lawyers, schoolteachers, generals and enlisted men, housewives, nearly everyone.

Hopkins to Huntington on January 23, 1866: "It will require all the means and good management that we are master of to build the road over the mountains at the rate we are going." February 16 (in reference to getting teamsters to pick up freight at the end of track to carry on the Big Four's wagon road from Dutch Flat): "We are powerless to get freight taken unless we pay the teamsters $1.25 a ton—and even at that it was difficult to get them from the Pacific Road, for no better reason than because there were more taverns on the Pacific Road—more waiting girls and Bar maids and from long acquaintance that road was more familiar and homelike."

In the same February 16 letter, after a discourse on the difficulty of building the railroad from Dutch Flat over the summit and down to the Truckee River, Hopkins wrote: "Snow prevents work about 5–6 months in the year, so we need to get it done this season if possible. . . . We're pushing hard. For as we see it, it is either a six month job or an eighteen month job to reach a point where the road will earn us a heap and where in construction we can make a *pile*." By that last phrase he meant that, when the track laying reached the desert in Nevada, the company could build more in a day than it could in months in the mountains, and thus receive more government bonds.

"This winter only pack mules can transport the stage passengers to Virginia City [Nevada]. Crocker's camp supplies and much of his forage for his work animals are packed in at a cost of one cent per pound," he added. February 24 (following a long discussion of water resources): "We need the right to take water for construction and operation. Without this grant from Congress we are entirely at the mercy of a set of water speculators—real water sharks—known as ditch companies. They go ahead of the RR and buy up all the water to make us, the farmers and the miners or anyone else pay them hugely for it. We have already paid $60,000 in construction costs to go over, along, and around these ditches."

There is a great deal about money, and when the government will turn over bonds, and what price Huntington is getting for the bonds in hand, and what he is paying for rails, locomotives, cars, and other supplies. And a great deal on various dealings of the Big Four with regard to West Coast railroads. Plus personnel problems and hopes.

Hopkins again on May 5: "Our cuts weakened the support of the natural hillside formation, so at Tunnel hill, just above Secret Town, where the original intention was to make a tunnel, the material was too soft to tunnel without being lined by expensive masonry, so it was decided to make an open cut in the spur, which is near 100 ft thick. The cut was nearly done when in March it broke back several hundred feet and slowly continued to slide—imperceptible to the eye, yet continually moving. All the space that 500 men could make during the day with their carts and wheelbarrows would be filled the next morning." And so on, as he recounted the perils of building a track in the mountains.

On July 9, Hopkins said that Crocker was suffering from a powder shortage because the powder company "can't make it fast enough." Then, turning to the good news: "It is a great consolation to know that you whipped out the UP at Washington [by getting Congress to approve the amendment]. They thought to Lord it over us, and get well paid. They must be in a bad fix if they have mortgaged a road up to within 150 miles of our state line. Send me a copy of the UP's first mortgage. I will perhaps get some new ideas for the next mortgage we make."

There were other problems. On July16, 1866, Hopkins wrote to Huntington: "The ship Hornet burned at sea. Even using the invoices/schedules/and letters, it can not be determined what RR material went down with her. Our invoices show only 1182 bars of iron, 100 kegs spikes and 65 ball chains. But the bills you sent in have many other things listed, but for which we have no bill of lading."

On July 21, Hopkins said that he was satisfied that each of the Big Four was doing what he ought to be doing—Stanford with the politicians, Crocker running construction, Huntington making loans and buying all equipment and supplies, and he himself in charge of finance. He felt he was useful "here, while I am sure no one of us could do so well as yourself there [New York, Boston, and Washington]. Until we can hear a locomotive whistle scream on the other side of the summit, so as to feel ourselves well *out of the woods,* I don't intend to ask or suggest any change."

Huntington agreed. "If it had not been for you and I," he wrote back, "my opinion is that the Central Pacific would have gone to the Devil before this." Huntington confessed, "I have gone to sleep at night in New York when I had a million and a half dollars to be paid by three o'clock on the following day, without knowing where the money was coming from, and slept soundly. I never worried." He practiced more rigorously than man of any previous age the self-denial of conventional pleasures today in return for wealth and power tomorrow. CP lawyer Alfred Cohen later said, "I have seen Mr. Huntington trudging about from office to office trying to get people to lend him money. . . . They were put to terrible straits to get money to get over the mountains."

The correspondence wasn't all business. "Mrs. Hopkins will probably go east this spring, as the advanced age of her father and his feeble health induces her to change her promise never to make the voyage without me."[6]

*T*HE winter of 1865–66 was the wettest in years. On the lower slopes, below Colfax, the rains were heavy enough for the *Sacramento Union* to complain that the railroad's "embankments are so miserably built that they give way under the soaking rains of this climate, and long delays are occasioned."[7] The soil was thick, spongy, a mucky trap for vehicles. Crocker got hundreds of mules to carry food, powder, tools, and their own forage to the camps beyond the end of track. A stagecoach setting out from Dutch Flat for Virginia City got so mired in mud near Gold Run that it was stuck for six weeks. Heavy landslides spread mud and boulders across the completed track, often blocking the road. The snows higher up hampered work on the tunnels. There were five feet of snow on New Year's Day, 1866.

From then until March, as often happens in California, the skies were clear and calm. But in March, the storms came again, bringing sleet and snow which lasted until the end of May. Indeed, from May 20 until June 1, the weather was almost one constant snowstorm. Strobridge later said, "The winter made the roads on the clay soils of the foothills nearly impassable for vehicles. The building of the railroad was prosecuted with energy but at a much greater cost than would have been the case in the dry season. . . . All work between Colfax and Dutch Flat was done during this winter in the mud."[8]

Crocker and Strobridge stayed with it. By the spring of 1866, they had hired and put to work the largest number of employees in America. The CP had over ten thousand men working on the railroad, eight thousand of them Chinese. Some one thousand of these labored for Arthur Brown, who had charge of the company's trestling, timbering, and bridging. He had his men felling trees, shaping timbers, and driving piles for bridges. The track-laying foreman, Henry H. Minkler, had his men spiking in rails in early May up and around Cape Horn.[9]

Charlie Crocker rode up and down the line with a leather saddlebag holding gold and silver coin to pay the men. "Why, I went up and down the road like a man bull," he told an interviewer. He was inspecting, criticizing, or roaring with anger. Once he told Stro, "Rule them with an iron hand." That was after he saw a group of white men talking excitedly in a group. "There is something breeding there," he told Strobridge.

"They're getting up a strike," Stro replied. After Crocker had paid off the other men, Strobridge said, "There, they are coming. Now get ready."

When the men got close enough to hear, Crocker said, "Strobridge, I think you had better reduce wages on this cut. We are paying a little more than we ought to. Reduce them about 25 cents a day."

Hearing this, the men stopped and talked. Finally, one of their leaders stepped forward and said to Crocker, "We thought, sir, that we ought to have our wages raised a little on this tunnel. The tunnel is very wet, and the cut is wet." Crocker replied that he had just been talking to Stro about lowering their wages.

"We thought we ought to get an advance," said the worker, "but you ought not to reduce it, certainly." Crocker asked Stro what he thought.

"I wouldn't make a fuss over it. We had better let them go on at the same figure."

"All right," said Crocker, and that was that.[10]

S T R O B R I D G E lived in a manner that all the others, even Crocker, envied. His wife, Hanna Maria Strobridge, and their six adopted children were with him, living in a standard passenger car pulled by the headquarters locomotive, which stayed right behind the end of track. Strobridge had it made over into a three-bedroom house on wheels. Mrs. Strobridge had an awning fitted to her front porch, and when the train was halted she hung houseplants and a caged canary around her entrance. People wiped their feet before entering. She was the only woman on the CP line, and Stro was the only man with a family life.[11]

WORK on the Summit Tunnel went slowly at best. Montague decided it would be worth the cost to sink a shaft from the top so that the Chinese could work on four facings at once—the ones at each end, and two others going in opposite directions from the middle. The shaft would be eight by twelve feet wide, and seventy-three feet deep.

By hand, the Chinese began to cut it through, haul the debris (mainly granite chunks) up from the bottom, and lower the timbers into place to shore it up. The bosses decided some mechanical aid might speed things up. An old locomotive, the *Sacramento* (one of the first locomotives in California), was cannibalized and sent to the top of the digging, to serve as a hoisting engine. Minus its cab, wheels, and turning shafts, the *Sacramento* was loaded by a winch onto a reinforced freight car and hauled to the end of track, near Colfax. There a mule skinner named Missouri Bill took over. His job was to drag the twelve-ton engine, now called the *Blue Goose*, to the summit, fifty miles away as the crow flies, seventy-five miles on the mountain trails. The wagon the *Blue Goose* traveled on, specially designed, had wooden wheels two feet wide. Ten yokes of oxen pulled it, spurred on by Missouri Bill's profanity and whip. When the oxen encountered a team of horses pulling wagons, the horses kicked, bucked, and otherwise created havoc. Bill sent one man ahead to blindfold approaching horses.

Going downslope, Bill put blocks under the wide wheels; heavy logging chains were attached to the largest trees nearby and, with a few feet of slack, attached to the wagon. Bill then knocked out the blocks, and the wagon and the *Blue Goose* slid a yard or so. Then the process was repeated. He used the chains to climb, too. This went on for six weeks, until the summit was finally reached. After the engine was set up in a building fifty feet square that had been built for it, and placed on a bed of huge timbers at the top of the tunnel shaft, it began to haul up the granite and lower the timber. Work went faster, as much as a foot a day. But it wasn't until December 19 that the bottom was reached and the Chinese could get started drilling and blasting.

Crocker then decided that he wanted more experienced men for the tunneling. He sent an emissary to Virginia City, Nevada, to persuade some of the best Cornish miners to come to his site, with the lure of higher wages. They came, but instead of giving them exclusive charge of excavating the tunnel, Crocker faced them in one direction and Chinese workers in the other. "The Chinese, without fail, always outmeasured the Cornish miners," he recalled. "That is to say, they would cut more rock in a week than the Cornish miners did. And there it was hard work, steady pounding on the rock, bone-labor." The Cornishmen quit. "They swore they would not work with Chinamen anyhow," said Crocker. After that, "the Chinamen had possession of the whole work."[12]

In the mid–twentieth century, a Hollywood firm tried to duplicate Missouri Bill's feat of hauling a dismantled locomotive to the summit, using a smaller engine. The engine was moved up the mountain for a total distance of five hundred yards. The firm gave up the task as impossible.[13]

AT the tunnels, especially Summit Tunnel, the Chinese were using great amounts of black powder, up to five hundred kegs a day. Despite the end of the Civil War, the price had gone steadily up, from $2.50 per keg to $15 a keg. This was a seller's market, for real. As Stanford explained, the CP spent its money with the greatest of economy "except in the matter of speed, and then we never hesitated to make a sacrifice."[14]

Crocker and Strobridge decided to experiment with nitroglycerin, which was brand-new (and spelled as two words). Said to be an extraordinary explosive, it had been invented in Italy in 1847, then refined in the 1860s by demolitions engineer Alfred Nobel in Sweden. It was five times more powerful by bulk than black powder, and thirteen times more destructive. The Railroad Record in August 1866 said that "its storing and transport involve no danger."

Would that it were so. There were terrible accidents, ignored for the most part by the CP but nevertheless more than enough to force most companies to swear off it. The Dutch Flat Enquirer, a booster of the explosive—"the work of blasting has been greatly facilitated," it reported that spring—said that in one explosion in New York City "nobody is to blame, it is perfectly safe and harmless and simply blew up from maltreatment and in self-defense."[15]

The CP found that, when they got to drilling holes of fifteen to eighteen inches into the granite, poured in the liquid nitroglycerin, capped the hole with a plug, and fired it with a percussion cap, the nitroglycerin did a far better job than powder. The work progressed at nearly double the speed, and the granite was broken into far smaller pieces. But the accidents proved too much. In one, after a number of charges had been set off simultaneously, a Chinese worker hit a charge of nitro that hadn't exploded with his pick. It exploded and killed him and the others working near that spot.

Strobridge declared, "Bury that stuff." Crocker said to get it out of there. And even though Nobel perfected dynamite in 1866, it was never tested or used by the CP. In 1867, the CP ignored the dangers and did make and use its own nitroglycerin, but except at Summit Tunnel did not make a practice of it.[16]

According to Henry Root, Strobridge spent most of his time that fall near or at the Summit Tunnel—No. 6, as it was called. He had assistants who traveled over the work and were known as "riding bosses." Root said, "More powder was used by the rock foremen than was economical, but time was the essential of all operations, so there was a good reason." Thus did the CP imbue even their modest assistants with the spirit of the enterprise—nail it down! "In the vicinity of Cisco," Root wrote, "the rock was so hard that it seemed impossible to drill into it a sufficient depth for blasting purposes. Shot after shot would blow out as if fired from a cannon."[17] Clement told Stanford, "Perseverance alone conquered."[18]

The CP would not wait for the Summit Tunnel to be cut and tracks laid through it. The company would push on beyond the Sierra Nevada by outflanking the Donner Pass. Partly this was to keep the enormous workforce employed, but mainly it was to get into Nevada and head east before the UP could get to the Salt Lake and head west. The Big Four had not set up the race in order to lose it.

The CP sent three exploring parties prodding through Nevada to look for routes for the railroad between the Big Bend of the Truckee River, some thirty miles east of today's Reno, and the Salt Lake Valley, five hundred miles beyond. The leaders were survey engineers Butler Ives, William Epler, and S. M. Buck. The direct route, straight east, had a series of mountain ranges, including the Clan Alpine, the Desatoya, the Shoshone, the Towabe, the Toquima, the Monitor, the White Pine, the Shell Creek, and the Snake—all in Nevada—and the Needle, the Wah Wah, the Confusion, and others in Utah. Still, it had to be explored.

East of Reno, according to one observer, "desolation began to assume its most repulsive form. Miles on miles of black, igneous rock and volcanic detritus. Outcrops of lava, interspersed with volcanic grit," were the main features. Another traveler said that the country was "so destitute of vegetable and animal life, as not to rise to the rank even of a *howling* wilderness." There was no water. The desert was filled with the bones of thousands of animals who had not made it to California.[19] The second route, to the north of the Humboldt River, was just as bad.

Samuel Bowles, who had just crossed the continent, declared that "the Humboldt route would be more easily built" than going across central Nevada. "It goes through a naturally better country as to wood, water, and fertility of soil. It is generally conceded to be the true natural roadway across the Continent. The emigration has always taken it."[20] He had it right. Even today the Humboldt is, as it was for Charlie Crocker and his group in 1850, a narrow but wonderful oasis. The grass is green and high, the ducks, geese, herons and eagles, the grazing horses and cattle, are numerous. So are the deer. The water is clear and plentiful until the river gets to the Sinks, where the grass grows in great meadows but the river sinks into the earth.

Butler Ives led the exploration of the Humboldt Valley for the CP. When he got to the Humboldt Wells, where the river rises in northeastern Utah out of the East Humboldt Range at the northern edge of the Ruby Mountains, he tried two approaches to Salt Lake City. One angled southeastward across the Great American Desert and around the bottom of Salt Lake to the city. No good. Then he returned to the wells and set off in a northeasterly direction, across the top edge of the desert, across the Promontory Mountains, around the north shore of the Great Salt Lake, across Bear River, and then southward along the western base of the Wasatch Range to Weber Canyon. That was the way to go.[21]

*I*N the meantime, Crocker was having shacks for laborers and warehouses for materials constructed along the Truckee River, twenty miles east and considerably below the Donner Summit. He would send gangs of workers there when the snows fell on the Sierra, to make grade and lay track while waiting for the Summit Tunnel to be completed. He began with a thousand men; another thousand soon followed. They started to make grade back toward Donner Pass.

The editor of the *Virginia City Territorial Enterprise* was delighted to learn of Crocker's plans. "What a joyful day it will be," he declared, "when the shrill whistle of the locomotive shall be heard as the train of cars from across the mountains shall go rattling down the Truckee. And that day is not two years distant."[22] Freight trains from Sacramento were pulled up the Sierra in a steady procession. "A 116-foot grade, with a dozen heavily loaded freight cars, is no sardine," said the *Dutch Flat Enquirer*, "but they manage to do it somehow." At Colfax, later at Dutch Flat, eventually at Cisco, the cars were unloaded and the supplies put onto wagons, to go up and over the Sierra Nevada, then down to Nevada.[23]

On November 5, the CP laid its track to Emigrant Gap, eight miles west of Cisco, twenty-one miles west of the summit, and five thousand feet above sea level. It was now only two thousand feet or so below the summit. It expected to reach Cisco in ten days.

That November, the stage-line owner Ben Holladay arrived in Alta, after riding the train from New York to Fort Kearney, Nebraska, then proceeding in a special horse-drawn coach. He brought with him the chilling news that the UP was on the march. It was coming on. In October, it had laid sixty-five miles of track. The editor of the *Sacramento Union* was not impressed. "The building of one mile of road anywhere between Newcastle and Cisco involves more labor and expense than the construction of 20 miles on the level prairie," he wrote.

Two weeks later, Montague was able to send a telegram from Alta: "Track will be laid tonight within 4,500 feet of Cisco depot. Ties will be distributed tonight and track laid tomorrow. Can run passengers to Cisco Thursday [November 29]. Snow at Crystal Lake this morning 8 inches deep and 12 inches at Cisco. Temp. 28."[24]

The tunneling went on, up and down the line. Lewis Clement declared, "No matter what the cost, the remaining tunnels would be bored in the Winter."[25]

On November 24, 1866, the first trains arrived at Cisco Station. They were loaded with ties, rails, chairs, fishplates, and measuring rods. It took three engines to pull the freight up the mountain. Strobridge had wagons and carts to meet the train, with hundreds of Chinese aboard. All night they loaded rails and the rest onto the wagons and carts. They also pulled two locomotives off the tracks and put them atop skid sleds. (These were logs split down the middle and rounded at the ends. They were greased with fat on the bottom to help them slide.)

At dawn, the procession toward the summit began. Carts went first, followed by the wagon train. At the rear, hundreds of Chinese tugged at ropes alongside mule teams and horse teams to skid the locomotives over the summit. And then the snow came.

The workers on the CP, from the bosses down, believed that there was more rain and snow in the winter of 1865–66 than had ever before been seen in California. This winter of 1866–67 was much worse. The snow came early and stayed late. There were forty-four separate storms. Some deposited ten feet of snow, some deposited more. At the summit the pack averaged eighteen feet on the level.* Strobridge put hundreds of the Chinese to work doing nothing but shoveling the snow away to keep open a cart trail to the tunnel opening. If it had not been for the race with the UP, the CP would have closed down that winter, but the fear of losing all Utah and Nevada to their rival drove them on.

The Chinese laborers dug snow tunnels from fifty to five hundred feet long to get to the granite tunnels. Some were large enough for a team of horses to walk through. Alternatively, a temporary railbed was placed on top of the snow and material was lowered from the surface by steam hoist, sometimes as much as forty feet. The waste was hauled out the same way.[26] Windows were dug out of the snow walls, to dump refuse and let in a bit of light. Also chimneys and air shafts. But for the most part the Chinese worked, ate, drank their tea, gambled, smoked opium, and slept in the remarkable labyrinth they were building under the snow.

This was cruel work, dangerous and claustrophobic. Still, they pressed on, drilling the holes in the granite, placing the black powder and then the fuse, lighting the fuse, getting out of the way, then going back in to clear out the broken granite. At four facings. They made six to twelve inches a day, at each end and toward the two ends from the middle.[27]

There were accidents of all kinds, mainly from blasting powder. Sometimes the heavy explosions started avalanches, and entire camps of workmen would be buried alive. Near the Summit Tunnel an avalanche carried away some twenty Chinese, whose bodies were found after the spring thaw. The CP eventually sent their bodies to their homeland for burial. How many died we don't know. The historian Thomas W. Chinn has written that, without doubt, the "loss of life was heavy."[28] On Christmas Day, 1866, the *Dutch Flat Enquirer* reported that "a gang of Chinamen were covered up by a snow slide and four or five died before they could be exhumed. The snow fell to such a depth that one whole camp of Chinamen was covered up during the night and parties were digging them out when our informant left."[29]

---

* More snow falls there than anyplace in the United States south of Alaska.

J. O. Wilder, a young surveyor,* wrote, "There was one large snowslide at Camp 4, where there were two gangs of Chinese for Tunnels 11 and 12, also a gang of culvert men. The slide took it all, and one of the culvert men was not found until the following spring. At our camp the snow was so deep we had to shovel it from the roof and make steps to get to the top. We were snowed in, and our provisions got down to corn meal and tea. Had it lasted one week longer we would have been compelled to eat horse meat, for there were two hundred or more men in my camp. . . . The cuts were filled by landslides, which had to be removed by gangs of Chinese. A Push Plow loaded with pig-iron to hold it to the rails, with three engines behind, would back up and take a run at the snow and keep going until it got stuck, and then back up and take another run."[30]

The plow was a monster—ten feet wide, eleven feet high, and thirty feet long. It was square and sheer in the rear; in the front it looked like a big wooden wedge laid on its side, with iron plates reinforcing the forward edge that slanted down almost to the rails. Just back from the forward edge, a sharp iron prow rose like a ship breasting a wave. The idea was that the wedge should scoop up drifts like a spade and the prow would part them, tossing snow up onto both sides of the track. Sometimes it worked.

AND still it rains," reported the *Sacramento Union* in late December. "The roads become sloughs, through which stage horses stagger, or in which they break down altogether. . . . The rain washes and the swollen streams sap the high embankments over which the locomotive has ascended to the region of snow."[31]

The editor of the *Union* wrote that, "within five hours ride of Sacramento, where roses still bloom and the air is balmy, snow has fallen to a depth of three feet on a level, and the sleigh-bells are making music along white highways. . . . The locomotive makes this concentration of the seasons—this transition from Spring flowers to Wintry delights—on the same day. . . . Each puffing engine is armed with a snow plow. And this suggests the beginning of that battle of the railroad men with the white storms of the Sierra."[32] The next day Cisco reported the worst

---

* He worked for the CP-Southern Pacific railroads for fifty-four years, finally retiring in 1920.

storm in ten years. Strobridge's prediction was that the railroad, now shut off, would be back in operation in ten days.

On December 22, Charlie Crocker's brother E.B. wrote Huntington about the "terrible storm that has given our RR a severe trial. We do not know the exact extent of the damage as Charlie and Montague are up on the road and have not reported. Those deep cuts and fills are sliding in and settling." He could not get particulars, because the telegraph above Colfax had been down for nearly a week. Still, "on the whole it has not been as bad as we expected for we had great fears about a good many of the banks and cuts standing a heavy storm." The snow, E.B. said, "is the least of our troubles and we no longer fear it. Since the storm I have greater confidence than ever in successfully working our road in the winter."[33]

On the last day of the year, the CP was able to announce that it was "in daily operation from Sacramento to Cisco." That was ninety-two miles, within twelve miles of the summit and 5,911 feet above sea level—the highest altitude yet reached by a railroad in the United States, or anywhere else. Some ten thousand men had been engaged in construction on the track. Much of the masonry and heavy rock excavation had been done beyond Cisco. Twelve tunnels were being constructed, night and day, by three shifts of men, a total of eight thousand, mostly Chinese, at work. Except for the Summit Tunnel, they would be completed by the spring of 1867—and the Summit Tunnel by September.

A large force of laborers was at work in the Truckee Canyon. The graders were almost three hundred miles beyond the end of track. Grain for the horses and food for the men, plus supplies, had to be hauled by teams pulling wagons over the desert for that great distance. Water for men and animals was hauled forty miles. A. P. Partridge, a white man working for the CP, recalled that the snows came early that year and drove as many as three thousand Chinese out of the mountains and down to Truckee, "where they filled up all the buildings and sheds. An old barn collapsed and killed four Chinese. A good many were frozen to death."[34]

Still, the CP expected that by the end of 1867 the end of track would be beyond the California-Nevada border, and that it would be building at a mile per day once it got into Nevada. The railroad was well into its assault on the Sierra Nevada and on its way east.[35]

Chapter Ten

THE UNION PACIFIC TO THE
ROCKY MOUNTAINS
1867

WEATHER dominates everything. No matter if it is D-Day at Normandy, or the launching of a rocket into space, or an outdoor wedding, or the building of a transcontinental railroad, everything depends on the weather. The winter of 1866–67 was terribly severe in California, so, even though there were tunnels to dig, which the Central Pacific could pretty much do whatever the conditions outside, the weather stopped the forward progress of the railroad.

The winter from the Sierra Nevada all the way to the Atlantic was one of the worst in the whole of the nineteenth century. In the Rocky Mountains, it was severe beyond any living memory. In western Nebraska, there were "fantastic drifts" and the temperature dropped to forty degrees below zero. In New York City, the East River froze solid. In Chicago, the firemen had to give up, because the water froze in their hose lines. In Omaha, the Missouri River froze over. The weather stopped the Union Pacific in its tracks.

The Casement brothers wanted to go to work in February, but that month and nearly all of March were far too cold with too much snow, so they sat and waited at North Platte. The Missouri was still frozen as late as March 25. Samuel Reed wrote home on March 27 that he had just received a telegram from Grand Island: "We are out of luck in this country, wind blowing and snow drifting worse than ever, half men either blind or frozen, looks bad." Reed wrote further, "There is an immense quantity of snow on the plains and in the mountains. I expect very high water and we may lose some bridges."[1]

Reed's telegrams to Durant are a nearly constant weather report. February 22: "Heaviest storm of the season. Road blocked." March 21: "Severe snow storm strong wind road blocked badly." March 23: "Six inches snow since last evening with strong north west wind road badly blocked still snowing."

Then, in early April, came the rains. They destroyed twenty miles of the road east of Grand Island and damaged far more. Reed to Durant, April 9: "Flood whole length of line immense damage to road. Track at Loup fork repaired track washed away near Fremont, North Bend, Shell Creek, Lone Tree, Grand Island, Wood River and Willow Island."[2] General Jack Casement put his crews to work repairing track that he had already counted on. "We are all in a heap, generally," he wrote.[3]

How big a heap was Arthur Ferguson's concern. The young surveyor reported to work on April 15, 1867. The railroad was not running and he was stuck in Omaha. A week later, he was still there. "Water in the river still rising," he wrote in his diary. "Track in places entirely out of sight— a good prospect of the depot grounds being drowned out." A day later, "Water has risen four inches since last night. The bottom now presents a vast sea of rushing waters." On April 24, he finally got out of town but was delayed at the Elkhorn River, where there was damage to the bridge. He and his party had to be ferried across the river, to a new engine that was waiting for them. "Road at places in very bad condition."

The train was pulling baled hay in its cars. The morning of April 25, one of them caught fire from a spark from the engine. "It was a grand sight to see an engine rushing madly across the plains, followed by a car wrapped in flames and streaming sparks and fire in its path." Then two other cars caught fire, "and we had to run with these burning cars some ten or twelve miles. Arrived at North Platte about 1 p.m." On April 26, Ferguson got to the end of track on the "first through train from Omaha."

The previous day, Reed had written his wife that no grading or track laying had yet been done. "Before the break, there was a prospect of rushing ahead more rapidly than last year. It gives me to blues to think that our road, which was in such good shape, should be at this season of the year so badly cut up."

On May 1, Ferguson finally set off in a wagon to do his job, but "until nearly dark we were stuck in mud holes and had to unload and reload."

Finally, he got so badly stuck that he sent his man back to fetch more livestock to help pull him out. "I felt very lonesome. Alone with a loaded wagon, which was deeply imbedded in the mud—the dark and gloomy shades of night fast gathering and with the vast expanse of prairie, I felt truly desolated. There is an indescribable something, a feeling unspeakable, an utter desolation which creeps over a man on these vast plains."

There was more. In a couple of days he got started on his work, mainly running levels for the graders. Among his diary entries for May are May 15: "About half-past one it commenced snowing and continued to snow hard for several hours. News was brought to camp this evening that the Indians made a descent on the ranches east of us yesterday and ran off with the stock." May 17: "The weather is quite cold. I put on my greatcoat, draw my feet up to the fire, and read 'Pickwick.' About 2 p.m. the party returned, the weather being too inclement. While I now write, Clark is sitting by the stove with his greatcoat on. It has commenced to drizzle. The wind blows very hard and very cold, though we are very comfortable in our tent, with the exception of a few places where it leaks."

May 22: "The Indians have killed four men. When the men go to work, even if they are in full sight of the camp, they go well armed. I counted ten guns, most of them breech-loading. Something like the times of 1776." May 23: "Last night were startled by the howling of wolves. . . . There is reported to be a camp of 700 Sioux lodges on the North Platte. Indians are reported to have been seen in the bluffs today." May 25: "A party of Indians dashed into the camp below us and ran off three head of stock, and then they came charging towards our tents but turned off into the bluffs in plain view of camp. The Indians were pursued and the stock retaken, with one head in addition, which was captured from the savages."[4]

E. C. Lockwood was a lad in his teens working as a paymaster for the Casement brothers out on the line. One day he saw seventeen Sioux Indians under the leadership of Spotted Tail ride up to the tracks. Jack Casement received them cordially and showed them the process of track laying. At one point he took them through one of the cars with U.S. Army rifles stacked horizontally on one of the walls. Lockwood found it "interesting to see the expressions on their faces." But then the impression turned; Casement had Lockwood put up a shovel sixty feet or so away, then challenged the Indians to show what they could do with their bows and arrows. Lockwood later wrote, "Sixteen of the Indians put their arrows through the hole in the handle, while the seventeenth hit the handle at the hole, knocking the shovel over. He felt quite disgraced."

Next came a race between the Indians on their ponies and the locomotive. Spotted Tail got into the cab of the engine along with Casement and Lockwood, while the warriors lined up four abreast for the word to go. "Away they went. At first the Indians outdistanced the locomotive, which so pleased them that they gave their Indian war whoop. But presently the engine gathered speed, then overhauled them. The engineer as he passed opened his whistle, which so startled them that all, as if by word of command, swung to the offside of their ponies. Of course this ended the race."[5]

DESPITE the weather and the Indians, Dodge had big plans for the railroad in 1867. So did Durant. In April, from Omaha, he telegraphed to Nebraska Senator John Thayer, "I will pledge myself to complete two miles a day for the first one hundred working days after the frost is out of the ground." By April 20, the Casements were at work preparing for and laying new track. Their workforce was as big as and more complex than that of the CP.[6]

Dodge expected to push the end of track as far as Fort Sanders, Dakota Territory,* on the Laramie River, between the Black Hills and the Medicine Bows, west of the mountains and 288 miles beyond the North Platte River. The track would surmount the summit of the Black Hills at an altitude of 8,242 feet (the CP's highest point was twelve hundred feet or so lower). Then down the mountains' western slope, across Dale Creek, and a descent to the Laramie Plains.

When Dodge outlined his plan to Sherman, the general expressed wonderment: "It is almost a miracle to grasp your purpose to finish to Fort Sanders this year, but you have done so much that I mistrust my own judgment and accept yours." He also told Dodge that, after the railroad

---

* When the track got beyond Laramie, Congress removed Wyoming from Dakota Territory and gave it a territorial status of its own. At the beginning of 1867, Wyoming had fewer than a thousand white inhabitants; by early 1868, thanks to the railroad, it was estimated to have forty thousand white people. The original idea was to name the territory "Lincoln."

had gotten across Nebraska and into Wyoming, Indians such as the Sioux and Cheyennes "must die or submit to our dictation."[7]

"I hope you will have troops to give us ample protection," Dodge wrote back. "We are going to be short of labor, and any lack of military protection, when Indians are at war, would render it almost impossible to keep men on the line." Dodge knew the problems Grant and Sherman had, what with demobilization and reconstruction in the South and demands from all over the Western United States for protection, but "what you and I know is going to be hard to make a lot of Irishmen believe. They want to see occasionally a soldier to give them confidence." Sherman wrote back, "I give you all that I possibly can."[8]

One of Sherman's handicaps was the slackness in enlistment. He had a demand for soldiers everywhere, but few were signing up. The army tried to get the newly freed slaves to join, but Sherman said they were slow to do so, which "limits our ability to respond." Still, he signed off, "So far as interest in your section is concerned, you may rest easy that both Grant and I feel deeply concerned in the safety of your great national enterprise."[9]

*I*N mid-April, the Casements had started their armies west. The numbers—from 3,500 graders working as far as 200 miles in advance of the end of track, to 450 track men, 350 men of the train force, 100 surveyors, several thousand tie cutters and lumberjacks, and as many as 1,000 shop men—approached 10,000. In addition, L. B. Boomer, owner of the Chicago Howe Truss Bridge Company, with well over 1,000 working for him, was supplying the UP with prefabricated sections for bridges. These were made of 12-inch-by-12-inch-by-16-foot lumber, sent out from Chicago, according to specifications sent to the bridge company by the UP engineers.[10]

Durant arrived in late April, to do an inspection. With him were the UP's Acting President Oliver Ames and Director John Duff, and a government director. Reed, who picked them up on the east bank of the Missouri, wrote his wife, "I do not feel any trembling in my boots. Let what will, come. I have a clear conscience."[11]

Dodge joined them and took them out on the line, and Durant said he and the others were "well pleased" with the road. Still, Oliver Ames was appalled to discover what Nebraska looked like west of Fort Kearney. He thought it a miserable waste, and said that if it were up to him he wouldn't take *all* the land along the railroad as a gift.

The directors told Dodge to begin selling lots belonging to the railroad, and he did, with some success, matching the government's price of $2.50 per acre. His best argument was that rain followed the tracks. Dodge thought that the rain belt moved westward at the rate of eight miles per year behind the tracks. Twenty-five years after the UP went through Nebraska, he declared that it now rained as much in the Plains as it did east of the Mississippi, and to such an extent that farmers in Colorado or Nebraska could raise fine crops without irrigation, "right up to the foot of the mountains." This had been predicted, he claimed, by a "Prof. Agassis in 1867," who said it would come by "the disturbance of the electrical currents, caused by the building of the Pacific railroad."[12]

Durant and Ames were in the midst of a gigantic struggle. Durant believed that the road would never make any money, that the only chance for a profit in return for all their work and investment was in construction—i.e., with the Crédit Mobilier. Ames thought the opposite. Durant wanted to cheapen the construction as much as the UP could get away with, and lengthen the mileage. Ames wanted to make money from the road itself. Durant called him a "damn fool."

On May 6, Reed told his wife that Durant and the other men had "broken up in a row and no one knows what will be the end."[13]

The Casements and their men, meanwhile, continued to lay track, quickly making more than a mile per day. "That slender line of iron," reported the *Chicago Tribune*, "goes constantly onward."[14] One mile per day, sometimes one and a half, even two miles a day. They were going across western Nebraska, toward Julesburg, just a couple of miles into northernmost Colorado, where they would break away from the Platte River and follow its tributary, Lodgepole Creek, into present-day Wyoming.

The crew chiefs lived as did their men. A *Chicago Tribune* reporter wrote: "The chiefs intend to have their men do a fair day's work—that is business. But they also intend to make them as comfortable as possible. If a man is sick, they take care of him. If he dies, they bury him. He is as well fed as those who employ him, and is as well housed. He undergoes no more risks than they do."[15]

The Casements and their men never let up, except on the day of rest. The construction train and wagons were twenty miles long. At the end of track, the cry of "Down!" rang out every thirty seconds. The wagons, when empty, were tipped over, and a teamster barked out his orders and his horse jerked forward, hauling the next load forward. Behind the men pulling off the rails and putting them into place came the gaugers, then the spikers and bolters, who all swarmed to the rail in rapid succession, measuring and squaring and pounding it into place. The drumbeat was the sledgehammers on the spikes. It was always there, monotonous but thrilling. The railroad was being built.

Alongside the various crews the foremen paced restlessly, spitting out orders, exhorting, pleading, cursing. Up ahead—sometimes far ahead, as much as a hundred miles—the grading parties worked, linked to the others only by the thin tentacles of telegraph wire, also far in advance of the work. Ahead of the graders, the surveyors were laying out the final line.

Arthur Ferguson was one of them. He recorded in his diary the way he and the others operated. July 24: "This morning, our party proceeded to change a portion of the line, opposite our present camp, for the purpose of avoiding some exceedingly rough and expensive work. After completing this we went to the end of our division for the purpose of changing the line which we completed this afternoon." July 25: "Worked hard all the morning at staking out and running levels." July 28: "After breakfast we staked out several hundred feet on the curve on the change of line opposite camp. We then recommenced work on our estimate of the 1st Div., 5th 100 mile and finished all with the exception of figuring out the cubic yards over a portion of it. We are now located in a wild and beautiful region. I finished reading the New Testament through this morning. Mr. Shannon sits by my side reading one of Sir Walter Scott's works."[16]

"What unites them all," Maury Klein wrote, "is a fierce determination not to let down those coming on behind." They were like an army in so many ways, but most of all in this epitome of friendship: they all knew and accepted that every man was dependent on every other man. "Every party is bent on holding up its end. The men will not be outstripped by those pushing on ahead or chasing from behind." Like sergeants or junior officers, the crew chiefs knew their men's determination and took full advantage of it. In Klein's words, "No one will know the names of those thousands who provided the brawn, but the greatest accomplishment of all will be theirs: they built the railroad."[17]

• • •

*T*HE weather slowed the railroad down, and even stopped it for some time. The Indians threatened to put it out of existence. What the construction crews had, the Indians wanted. Livestock, rifles, ammunition, hats, jackets, food in cans. Much of it could be easily captured by a raiding party. Then there were scalps. Most of all there was the land, which the Indians regarded as theirs. One quick dash on the Casements' working gangs, one pile of rails or ties set over a completed track, would bring riches such as never before known on the Great Plains. There for the taking. The soldiers seldom if ever could detect, prevent, or defeat an Indian raiding party.

On May 1, 1867, the Cheyennes eliminated a four-man mail party just west of Laramie. That was just a start. On May 18, Ferguson saw an Indian war party sweep by as it "pulled up one mile of Railroad stakes in sight of the party," stakes he had helped place. The Indians cantered away without loss.[18]

Two days later, Dodge wrote to Sherman pleading for more protection. The Sioux had "cleaned out two of our subcontractors of everything they had and scared the workmen out of their boots, so they abandoned the work and we can not get them back." The Sioux had also raided tie men cutting trees in the Black Hills, killing several, and hit a survey team, killing a soldier and a surveyor. After other complaints, Dodge told Sherman, "I have smothered all the recent attacks and kept them out of the press."[19]

But Dodge was not so successful as he wished in keeping the Indian raids out of the newspapers. It became a major story, played up in all the papers, especially the New York, Chicago, and other big-city dailies. The scalps taken, the wounds inflicted, the savages' practice of firing arrows into dead bodies or mutilating them in other ways, and many more atrocities were widely reported, with full details, some of them made up by the reporters. In a pretelevision era, the reports took the place of smoke, burning buildings, weeping victims, stabbing or shooting wounds, and other outrages that grab and hold the American viewing public in the twenty-first century.

As the weather improved, the raids increased. On May 25, 26, and 27, the Sioux and Cheyennes struck the line at various points, derailing a work train near the end of track, killing four UP workers, taking UP livestock. At another place a war party killed four graders and at yet another a six-man section gang. Dodge was traveling to the end of track with three government commissioners that spring when about a hundred Indians swept down on a grading party. Dodge's standing orders to "every surveying corps, grading, bridging, and tie outfit was never to run when attacked." The graders had their arms stacked on the cut where they were working. They rushed to them to begin shooting, but the Indians managed to run off some stock first. After that experience, according to Dodge, the commissioners "on returning to the East dwelt earnestly on the necessity of our being protected."

Sherman did what he could to help. He visited the work site several times each year. Dodge wrote to him once a month or more. Dodge also wrote the commander-in-chief, General Grant, who "had given full and positive instructions that every support should be given to me."[20]

Given the army's size, that support often meant little or nothing. Or, as one trooper said, "It's awkward as hell for one soldier to surround three Indians." Indeed. On June 2, Ferguson recorded: "This morning, shortly after sunrise the camp was aroused by the cry of here they come! Here they come boys!" He and his tent mates grabbed their rifles and rushed out, "and there we saw the Indians charging down upon us from the northern bluffs." The white men fired and the Indians pulled back, then retreated. "One of the engineers captured from the Indians a white woman's scalp, which was quite green having been killed but a few days."[21]

A few days later, Sherman was in Nebraska examining the line and pondering the Indian raids. He wrote to Grant. The Indian country was large, he said, as large as the whole settled United States. It posed enormous problems. But the railroad, when completed, would settle many of them. Supplies could then be hauled west in sufficient quantity to mount a real offensive action against the Indians. Military posts would be unnecessary, because the train could move the troops around.

The Indian guerrilla war continued. Two of Dodge's surveyors, L. L. Hills in the mountains and Percy Browne west of the Rockies, were killed. They had been caught unaware. They should have been looking out for themselves, but there was something in the nature of these surveyors that made them careless of danger. Both men and their parties were entranced by the country around them. In June, it was in full bloom. Thick grass flowed in the wind, delicate white lilies sprouted through the grass. Even the cacti were covered with red and golden blossoms.

On June 18, Hills wandered away from his party and was caught by a band of Arapahos. He was riddled with arrows. One of his young helpers, nineteen-year-old axman J. M. Eddy, rallied the men and drove off the Indians. When Dodge learned that Eddy had served under him during the war, after enlisting at the age of sixteen, he promoted him and put him to work directly under himself. Eddy stayed with the UP until it was constructed, and continued to rise; eventually he became a general manager of the railroad, a position he held for the rest of his life.[22] Hills had evidently ignored, or forgotten, Dodge's orders, which were that "the chief of the party must absolutely command it, and at all times be ready to fight." Another was "the importance of never slacking their vigilance no matter where they were, never being off their guard." According to Dodge, those who followed his orders "generally took their parties through."[23]

A month after Hills's death, Browne was looking for the Continental Divide, west of Nebraska, but he found that he was in a great basin five hundred feet lower than the surrounding country. He and his party set off across it in search of water flowing west. The Sioux caught them. A long skirmish followed. Browne was hit by a ball in the abdomen. He staggered a few hundred feet before falling.

He begged his assistant to "Shoot me first," before riding off. But his men would not abandon him. They let the horses go, hoping the Sioux would follow. They did, and Browne's men improvised a litter by lashing their carbines together. They trudged down a ridge. Browne never groaned or complained. A half-hour after reaching a stage station, he died.[24]

Dodge could not afford to lose his best surveyors.

*F*IRES were another hazard. Engineer Robert Miller Galbraith ran a UP train from Sidney, Nebraska, west. He was burning a combination of cedarwood and Iowa coal, and pulling among other things two carloads of baled hay, uncovered. After a short run, he discovered that sparks from the fuel to run the boiler had set the hay on fire. He tried to ditch the burning cars by cutting them loose from the remainder of the train, but one of them fell onto the track. He ran the locomotive to the next station, where with a cold chisel and a hammer he cleaned out the grates on the engine, throwing the clinkers out onto the deck, which set it afire.

Meanwhile, his brakeman took a pine tie out from under the track and cut it up for kindling wood. That enabled Galbraith to get up steam.

He set off, and had come to a little trestle bridge when a car loaded with mules jumped the track and tipped over. Galbraith ditched the car and went on to the end of track. After sleeping on the ground, he woke up and "found I had a fine herd of cooties." He was called back to North Platte to pick up Dr. Durant and bring him west. And so it went for the early engineers. Galbraith would not have taken any other job.[25]

A s the end of track moved on west, it was accompanied by a scene that greatly pleased the workingmen and would later excite Hollywood and the book writers who made epics out of the Union Pacific, led by Cecil B. DeMille. Hell on Wheels—the man who came up with the phrase, which was universally adopted, is unknown—began at North Platte. The village had grown from almost nothing to five thousand inhabitants since the track stopped there for the winter of 1866–67. Most of the residents were workers waiting for warm weather. The village bulged with gambling dens, houses of prostitution, taverns, music halls, hotels, and an occasional restaurant. These establishments were run by sharks, from Chicago mainly, who had put up a small investment—canvas for a tent or for some split lumber, a bar full of liquor, some money for dancers and dealers, a little more here and there.

The sharks took in large amounts. Their customers consisted of young men with whatever they had saved from their wages, whether last year's or last week's, with nothing to do, far from home and family constraints. Their chief entertainment came from getting drunk, getting laid, and losing all their money to the gamblers. What the hell, there was nothing else to spend money on, and anyway they had a place to sleep and eat, and during the working season they would make more money the next morning.

Many of them, perhaps most, were young Irishmen. Stephen Vincent Benét wrote about them in his 1935 fable "O'Halloran's Luck." He opened, "They were strong men built the Big Road and it was the Irish did it." The grandfather of the protagonist was "a young man then, and wild. He could swing a pick all day and dance all night, if there was a fiddler handy." He and his buddies "had left famine and England's rule behind." He "liked the strength and the wildness of it—he'd drink with the thirstiest and fight with the wildest—and that he knew how to do. It was all meat and drink to him—the bare tracks pushing ahead across the bare prairie and the fussy cough of the wood-burning locomotives and the cold blind eyes of a murdered man."[26]

They had served in the Union Army, for the most part, and were accustomed to the life. Whether many of them, or only a few, or none suffered from shell shock or other forms of postcombat trauma is not known, but for certain they were accustomed to pistols and rifles and artillery going off, to losing everything on one roll of the dice, to wounds and death.

Henry Stanley wrote of North Platte when it was at the end of track: "Every gambler in the Union seems to have steered his course here, where every known game under the sun is played. Every house is a saloon and every saloon is a gambling den. Revolvers are in great requisition. Beardless youths . . . try their hands at the 'Mexican monte,' 'high-low,' 'chuck-a-luck,' and lose their all."[27]

Sometimes they protested about being cheated. When they did, they were shot. One a day, or more. Hell on Wheels moved as the end of track moved. It could be taken down and set up again in a day. Its population numbered two thousand or so. By June, Hell on Wheels was in Julesburg, a town that, according to Samuel Reed, "continues to grow with magic rapidity. Vice and crime stalk unblushingly in the mid-day sun."[28] It had grown from forty men and one woman to four thousand.

Stanley visited the place and was amazed at what he saw: "I walked on to a dance-house. Gorgeously decorated and brilliantly lighted. I was almost blinded by the glare and stunned by the clatter. The ground floor was as crowded as it could well be. . . . Mostly every one seemed bent on debauchery and dissipation. The women were the most reckless, . . . expensive. They come in for a large share of the money wasted. . . . Soldiers, herdsmen, teamsters, women, railroad men, are dancing, singing or gambling. There are men here who would murder a fellow-creature for five dollars. Nay, there are men who have already done it. Not a day passes but a dead body is found somewhere in the vicinity with pockets rifled of their contents."[29]

These places were built of the "most perishable materials," Samuel Bowles wrote. They consisted of "canvas tents, plain board shanties, and turf-hovels." The population was scum. "One to two thousand men, and a dozen or two women were encamped on the alkali plain. . . . Not a tree, not a shrub, not a blade of grass was visible; the dust ankle deep as we walked through it, and so fine it irritated every sense and poisoned half of them." Hell on Wheels was "a village of a few variety stores and shops, and many grog-shops; by day disgusting, by night dangerous; almost everybody dirty, many filthy, and with the marks of lowest vice; averaging a murder a day; gambling and drinking, hurdy-gurdy dancing and the vilest of sexual commerce the chief business and pastime of the hours."

Where these people came from, where they went to later, "were both puzzles too intricate for me," Bowles confessed. "Hell would appear to have been raked to furnish them; and to it they must have naturally returned after graduating here, fitted for its highest seats and most diabolical service."[30]

The so-called "Big Tent" was a hundred feet long and forty feet wide, covered with canvas but with a wood floor for dancing. The right side was lined by a splendid bar with every variety of liquors and cigars, with cut-glass goblets, ice pitchers, splendid mirrors and pictures. A full band played, apparently day and night. Gambling tables surrounded the dance floor. Fair women, in light and airy garments, mingled with the throng. Men paid 50 cents for a drink for their girl, 50 cents for themselves, with a dance thrown in. The whiskey for the men was watered, and it was tea for the girls, but no matter. Down it went.

One reporter noted that in such places "Madam Rumor has full sway. It reminds one of Washington during the war. There are as many reports as then. Every stage driver, every passenger, every ranchman, every railroad employee, has his little legend to tell."

The UP officials tried to hold things down, however they could. Occasionally they would send out a Columbus priest named Father Ryan, who would put up a tent and ties for the congregation to sit on. According to the reporter who witnessed the scene, they listened devoutly to the sermon and shared in Communion, and sang a hymn or two. Then Father Ryan "talked to them about their profanity, their drunkenness, and their general waste of money. He urged them to be true to their faith, and to their employers, and to take a pride in their work on the great railroad."[31]

Julesburg got so bad that Grenville Dodge, who had seen a lot of young Americans downing a lot of drinks during the Civil War, stepped in. He heard that gamblers had taken over and refused to obey the local UP officials. What bothered Dodge the most was that they had taken up lands he had set aside as belonging to the UP and refused to pay for them. He called Julesburg "a much harder place than North Platte." Dodge told Jack Casement to take his train force into town and clean the place up.

Casement, who was a teetotaler, was ready. He marched into town that night with two hundred men. They met with the gamblers, who spat contempt at him and refused to pay up. With a quiet voice, Casement ordered his men to open fire, "not caring whom they hit." When Dodge came to town and asked what had happened, Casement led him to a nearby hill full of fresh graves. "General," he told Dodge, "they all died, but bought peace. Julesburg has been quiet since."[32] Among those with Dodge were engineers Evans and Reed, and General John A. Rawlins. Grant had asked Dodge to take Rawlins, who served as his aide and was one of Grant's closest friends, along with him, in the hope that the pure mountain air would cure Rawlins of his consumption. Others included a geologist who was hoping to find coal on the lands given the UP by the government. Sherman provided two companies of cavalry and two of infantry for protection. Jack Casement joined the party.

One of Dodge's first tasks was to get a surveying party to work. He discovered that the men who had been working for L. L. Hills were waiting for a leader. Dodge placed Evans in charge and put him to work on the land west of the summit of the mountains. Then he began to look over the ground around his camp. He had the authority to lay out town sites and take lots for the company's use as depots, repair shops, sidings, and so forth. On this one, he came immediately to the conclusion that the railroad's main shops should be precisely where his tent stood. So he laid out a town, claiming 320 acres for the railroad's use. He honored the dominant tribe in the region by calling the town Cheyenne.[33]

On July 4, Rawlins gave a well-received speech. The next day, a band of Indians sprang on a grading crew and killed three men. Rawlins was astonished to see the Indians attack when there were four companies of U.S. troops camped in the area. Dodge had the dead men buried on the site of his new town, and Cheyenne had its first cemetery.

The city of Cheyenne is where the mountains meet the plains, on the southeastern edge of Wyoming, at an elevation of 6,062 feet. It is a natural crossing place. From Cheyenne today, one train track leads west across the state and on to California, another north to Montana and south to Denver; so too the interstate, with I-80 going east-west and I-25 north-south.

The Union Pacific is the main corporate employer in town. To the uncountable number of train buffs in the United States, and indeed around the world, Cheyenne is a Mecca. There the last steam engines purchased by the UP are housed. They were made during World War II and used well into the 1950s, and today they haul passenger trains to special events. The old depot has been turned into a railroad museum. Dodge's tent site has a marker on it. Everyone with any connection to the UP or to trains knows the simple fact that Dodge picked well, and that Cheyenne remains, as it has been for nearly a century and a half, one of the premier railroad towns in the world.

DODGE stayed in Cheyenne for three weeks, long enough to see another Hell on Wheels roll into it. The army established a post just north of town, called Fort A. D. Russell. Dodge rode over the summit and on to Dale Creek, on the edge of the Laramie Plains. While his men went trout fishing, he studied the creek. It was a tiny stream that in July just barely trickled through a gorge that was 130 feet deep and 713 feet wide. It would take a trestle bridge 125 feet high and 1,400 feet long to cross it, plus some cuts before the bridge could be reached. Dodge studied it for several days and could find no other way to get across. It was a mighty puny creek to require such a terribly large bridge, but that could not be helped.

Dodge went on to Fort Sanders, where he stayed long enough to lay out another town, to be called Laramie (and eventually to be the site of the University of Wyoming). It was here at Fort Sanders that Dodge learned for the first time that Browne had been killed by Indians. Now he needed a new surveyor to mark out the region to the west.

He was tired, overworked, shorthanded, sick, and he had just lost two of his best engineers and surveyors. On the trip west he had suffered "everything but death from my rides—how long I can stand it God only knows." But he had to continue, in order to do Browne's work and lay out a line west of the Rockies. "I must push West," he wired the company. "The Indians hold the country from here to Green River [in today's western Wyoming] and unless I get out there, we will fail in all our plans for 1868."[34]

That would not do. The railroad had captured the public, to the point where it dominated the news. Horace Greeley's paper, the *New York Tribune*, declared that Casement's men "are working upon a scale never before approached in railway history."[35] *Harper's Weekly* pronounced, "No road of its length and magnitude was ever before contemplated, much less attempted. . . . The work is now one of such national importance that the people insist upon its vigorous prosecution as positively as they insisted on the prosecution of the late war."[36]

The railroad to the Pacific may have been of the greatest importance, but riding on an 1867 train imposed a terrible price on passengers. Back east, and not infrequently in the West as well, at least according to *Harper's Weekly*, the railroads used "abominable old-fashioned, low-roofed cars and there are still passengers who ignominiously submit to this and to every other kind of railroad tyranny." The cars were subject to a constant "jerking and thumping." Sometimes during this ordeal, "a brakeman thrusts his head into the car, shouts something, slams the door, and leaves the excited passenger to the wildest conjecture." In addition there was the "misery of summer railway travel, including the heat, the glare, the dust, the cinders and the rattle, plus the flies."[37]

Through the summer, the Indians continued to dispute the road. Ferguson noted on July 8, "In the past 48 hours, they have made dashes on both sides of us. Everything indicates lively times on the Lodge Pole line as regards Indians." July 9: "Last night about midnight, three Indians rode up within gunshot of our tent." August 5: "I have cleaned my carbine out today and got my ammunition, 74 rounds, in readiness." A climax came on August 11: "The report has reached us that the Indians have thrown a train of cars off the track and after killed all on board except the conductor, piled ties around the engine and cars and destroyed them by fire. It is also reported that the Indians have carried off two white women."[38]

That wasn't rumor. On August 7, a party of forty or so Cheyennes led by Chief Pawnee Killer went after the railroad. Operating near Plum Creek, in central Nebraska, they cut the telegraph, then removed the spikes and bent the rails and waited for the next train to derail itself—just as the Confederates and Yankees had done to each other's trains during the war. When the train hit the damaged rail, over the engine went. The engineer, fireman, two brakemen, and three telegraph repairers were killed. Behind that train came another freight train. It crashed into the wreck and was overturned. The conductor ran back down the track and stopped a third train, which backed up to the Plum Creek station. The Cheyennes meanwhile burned the trains and cars; they killed and scalped seven or eight people and threw their bodies into the flames.[39]

A relief train carrying workers armed with carbines went back to the scene before dawn. As the train approached, the engineer and others saw that the Indians had found some barrels of whiskey, got drunk, and set the wreck on fire. A *Chicago Tribune* reporter noted that the fire "lit the prairie for a considerable distance around. The dark forms of the savages were plainly seen dancing triumphantly around the scene of their atrocious work, while their fierce yells were borne savagely back to the train." It was horrifying. The *Tribune* wrote: "The railroad men in Omaha, fresh from Cheyenne, filled with alarming rumors . . . have an infallible remedy for the Indian troubles. That remedy is extermination. These men, most of them tender and gentle with the weak of their own race, speak with indifference of the 'wiping out' of thousands of papooses and squaws."[40]

It wasn't just the ordinary railroad workers who felt that way. So did their leaders. "We've got to clean the damn Indians out," Dodge declared, "or give up building the Union Pacific Railroad. The government may take its choice." For his part, Sherman wrote at this time, "The more we can kill this year the less will have to be killed the next year, for the more I see of these Indians the more convinced I am that they all have to be killed or be maintained as a species of paupers."[41]

A FTER going over the pass (called Sherman Pass by Dodge, a name it retains), examining Dale Creek, and laying out Laramie, Dodge and his group pushed on west, looking for water flowing toward the Pacific as a sign that they had passed the Continental Divide. After crossing the North Platte River (which flows out of the Medicine Bow Mountains nearly straight north as far as today's Casper before it turns east), they set out to the west, "endeavoring to find running water."

They were now in the Great Basin. The streams running into it sank, and one of Dodge's party said the dry creek beds looked to him like the "shallow graves of deceased rivers." (This area is today called the Red Desert. Here was where the Sioux had caught and killed Browne.) There Dodge discovered and helped a party of UP surveyors who had been without water for nearly a week. They were headed straight east, by compass, looking for water, and were in Dodge's words "in deplorable condition."

Dodge discovered a spring in a draw. General Rawlins, grateful for the drink, pronounced it the "most acceptable of anything he had had on this march." He drank again and said that, if some spot was ever named for him, he hoped it would be a spring of water.

Dodge instantly replied, "We will name this Rawlins Springs." And so it is to this day.* Dodge told his wife that Rawlins was "one of the purest, highest minded men I ever saw. That he must die with that dread consumption seems too bad."[42]

*T*HOMAS Hubbard was a surveyor helping make a line across Wyoming. His diary entries, although short, are vivid descriptions of the land. August 5, 1867: "The country over which we passed was a barren desert of alkali composition. There was not a spear of grass or a drop of water in the whole distance." August 6: "Run about ten miles and quit work at six P.M. The country through which we run was if possible more barren than yesterday. There is no water within ten miles of our line. We have to haul our water in barrels. The team started tonight to get a fresh supply. The weather suffocatingly hot." August 7: "The team returned with casks filled with water. But it was so full of all kinds of poison that we could not use it. It was as red as blood and filled with all kinds of vermin. The horses and mules as dry as they are would not drink it. We were compelled to return twenty miles to our old camp to get water."[43]

Dodge went on to the Wasatch Range, then Salt Lake City, where he conferred with Brigham Young. In the Wasatch he had found Weber Canyon and marked it down as the place to get through the mountains and on to Salt Lake Valley. The geologist with him found immense coal deposits at a place Dodge called Carbon.

Dodge further discovered that he could follow any one of a number of streams into the Snake River Valley in southern Idaho. Thus "the entire feasibility of a railroad from several points on our line to Snake River Valley, and thence to Montana, Idaho, Oregon, and Washington Territory, was fully demonstrated." That was the line he wanted to build. "It would be by far the best line from the Atlantic to the Pacific, would avoid the high elevation of the Wasatch and Sierra Nevadas, with their heavy grades and troublesome snows, and no doubt ere long it will become the great through route."[44] He did eventually build along that line.

* "Springs" has been dropped; the town is now Rawlins.

The UP called it the "Oregon Short Line." But in 1867, he was stuck with the Weber Canyon, around the Salt Lake, to meet up with the CP coming from the Sierra across Utah. That was the route dictated by Congress, and that was the route that was going to be.

DODGE found something else in Weber Canyon. There were CP surveyors there doing preliminary work for their railroad. It appeared that Huntington and his partners thought the CP would reach the Salt Lake first and take over the Mormon business, then extend to the Green River (which Dodge had just crossed). For his part, Dodge wanted the UP to get as far as Humboldt Wells. He had thought the CP had hoped to get as far as Ogden, on the east side of the Salt Lake forty miles or so north of Salt Lake City, but now he learned it was planning to go farther east than Ogden. The race was well under way.

Best of all for the UP, what Dodge found between Laramie and Utah was an open prairie of comparatively low elevation (about seven thousand feet). In two months his party had covered fourteen hundred miles on horseback. He had laid out a preliminary line for the surveyors from Julesburg to the Salt Lake, and in the process made the first map of the Great Basin and southern Wyoming. It was a country in which the UP could sink artesian wells to a great depth and keep the water tanks full by using windmills. "The work of building the road there was unexpectedly light," Dodge later wrote, "and it almost seems that nature made this great opening in the Rocky Mountains expressly for the passage of a transcontinental railway."[45]

The Sioux and Cheyennes thought the Basin and the Great Plains to the east had been made for them. They continued their raids, although nothing quite so big as the Plum Creek affair.

President Johnson appointed a Peace Commission, with Sherman on it. The commission went from tribe to tribe to parlay with the chiefs and sign treaties. A big conference was held in September at North Platte, with the railroad as the main subject. Pawnee Killer and others were there, and Sherman made a speech. He told the Indians, "This railroad will be built, and if you are damaged [by it] we must pay you in full, and if your young men will interfere the Great Father, who, out of love for you, withheld his soldiers, will let loose his young men, and you will be swept away." That was blunt enough. So was what followed: "We will build iron roads, and you cannot stop the locomotive any more than you can stop the sun or the moon, and you must submit, and do the best you can."

Pawnee Killer, who had stopped two locomotives, stomped out of the council in a rage. He swore to end the railroad building. Sherman was as determined as the Cheyenne chief. "Whether right or wrong," he wrote his brother the senator, "those Roads will be built, and everybody knows that Congress, after granting the charters, and fixing the Routes, cannot now back out and surrender the country to a few bands of roving Indians."[46]

T H E Casements and their men were almost at Nebraska's western border, near mile 440. The company's rolling stock had grown to fifty-three locomotives, eleven hundred freight cars, ten passenger cars, five baggage cars, and sixty handcars, plus one paymaster's car, one cooking car, twenty-five caboose cars, twenty-five coal cars, one officers' car, and one president's car (the old Lincoln Car). The UP had 350 mechanics and carpenters working in Omaha and North Platte who could turn out twenty cars a week and do all the railroad's mechanical repairs."[47]

All this cost money. The UP had it. Commencing in July 1867, the promoters found a ready market for UP bonds. The Casement brothers and their workers, after all, had laid 260 miles of track in eight months and were surging forward. No such railroading had ever been dreamed of. Further, when the UP got to the mountains, not very far distant that summer, the government loan of bonds would rise to $48,000 per mile. In addition, the UP announced at the end of August that its earnings during the three preceding months alone had been nearly three-quarters of a million dollars; deducting expenses of a quarter-million dollars, the net operating profit was almost a half-million. The UP's own bonds, equal in numbers and price to those loaned by the government, sold well.[48]

Also encouraging was that the Ames brothers and their Boston allies held 52 percent of the Crédit Mobilier stock, and had used their control to oust Durant from every office in the company. And Henry V. Poor, editor of the *American Railroad Journal*, had just written, "There is nothing connected with the Union Pacific that is not wonderful." In an editorial, he added, "The Union Pacific bonds are the safest and best investment at the same price in the country. Their security is absolute."[49] Durant did hold on to his UP stock and his office there, but he and the Ames brothers remained at loggerheads, with Durant looking to milk the government through the construction charges while they wanted to build a railroad that would return profits of its own.

Bond sales continued to be solid. In October, $672,000 were sold; in November, it was $700,000; in December, $2,450,000, or a total for the three months of $3,822,000. The U.S. government had accepted 240 miles of track at $16,000 per mile, to a total of $8,160,000 in loaned government bonds, and the price per mile was about to go up. The UP earned $3,465,000 for the year 1867, with operating expenses, including taxes, at $1,404,000, making $2,061,000 in net earnings.

The profit went to the Crédit Mobilier, whose trustees on December 12, 1867, declared the firm's first dividend: each holder of ten shares (at $1,000 per share par value) got $600 of the first mortgage bonds and six shares of UP stock, for a total cash payment of 76 percent on the investment. A handsome payoff, with more to come. Oakes Ames started to get congressmen to buy Crédit Mobilier stock. His motive, he later said, was: "We wanted capital and influence. Influence not in legislation alone, but on credit, good, wide, and a general favorable feeling." He placed the stock with nine U.S. representatives and two U.S. senators, amounting in all to 160 shares for $16,000. Not much, considering the amounts the company was working with, but enough to threaten to set off the biggest scandal of the nineteenth century.[50]

*A*T the beginning of November, the Casements and their men had reached within a few miles of Cheyenne. The town had already held an election on August 10 and set up a city government. On September 19, Cheyenne's first newspaper, the *Daily Leader*, had been printed. By October 12, the end of track was at Dead Pine Bluffs (now Pine Bluffs), within thirty-five miles of Cheyenne. By October 29, it was within seventeen miles, and the anticipatory tension mounted. The UP was nearly five hundred miles from Omaha.

Jack Casement, like Grenville Dodge, had hoped for more. He wanted to get over Sherman Pass and beyond Dale Creek down to Laramie, but it wasn't to be. The biggest holdup was ties. Indians had chased tie cutters out of the canyons on the North Platte, so Reed had to buy ties from the Missouri River Valley and have them—inferior cottonwoods—shipped west by train.

Some directors boasted that the UP would finish by 1870 and a man could go from New York to San Francisco in a week. Horace Greeley's newspaper commented, "It is hard to realise that so great a distance may be accomplished in so short a time."[51] But to the men on the spot, that 1870 promise sounded more like boast than fact. The supply line was longer and growing, thus the flow of material was tricky to coordinate and time. Dodge was hoping to pile in supplies at Cheyenne during the winter to prevent supply problems in the spring, but no one knew what the winter would be like.

On November 16, 1867, the lead article in the *Chicago Tribune* read: "Dated Cheyenne 11/14/67; Yesterday, at 5 o'clock in the afternoon, track-laying on the UP was completed to the city of Cheyenne, and in a few moments the whistle of the locomotive was heard above the noise of the hammers and the rattle of wagons all over the bustling city." The entire population "rushed wildly to the railroad track," where there was a banner, "Honor to whom honor is due; Old Casement we honor you." Jack Casement made a speech. "Before nightfall Cheyenne was left half a mile in the rear. Cheyenne is now connected by rail with Chicago and the rest of mankind."[52]

Shortly thereafter, Casement went into winter camp, with Cheyenne as the end of track. Julesburg began moving its tents. Dodge quickly decided that Cheyenne was an even worse Hell on Wheels. He called it "possibly the greatest gambling place ever established on the plains and it was full of desperate characters."[53] But he had his own report to the directors of the UP for 1867 to work on, and cleaning up the town could come later. Much of his work was centered on the exploring he did west of the Black Hills and east of the Salt Lake, where he was the first to make maps, and for which he has never received the credit due him.

Nor has Dodge or his men received credit for what they did to improve the UP in the face of the storms and floods of the winter of 1866–67. But Dodge knew what had been accomplished. In his report he wrote, "The track has been raised, new bridges constructed, larger waterways built, and the old structures enlarged, as shown [necessary] by the floods of this year, the highest and most extensive ever known in the country, and it can now be safely said that a repetition of these floods will not materially injure the road or delay the running of trains."[54]

A large part of his report was on the valley of the Snake River and how easily the UP could turn it to advantage, but when Dodge was writing, in

1867, most Americans would have been glad to have one line crossing the country, and few of them dared to think of any others. Not Dodge. And he never hesitated to point out why. "The Pacific slope to-day has less than 1,000,000 inhabitants," he wrote, "and they are yielding $50,000,000 to $60,000,000 of bullion yearly, with grain plus immense yields of wool, hides, wines, timber, and everything that can be produced in that delightful climate and fertile soil." He further stated that "the best vegetable productions of the Mississippi and Missouri valleys are dwarfed in comparison with those of California. The wheat crop of California and Oregon for 1867 was 25,000,000 bushels, and far exceeded in value the gold product of both States." Just think, he concluded, what the product of those states would be when the railroad was completed. Why, they would need two, three, four railroads. "No man to-day can even estimate it." Finally, he concluded: "Without the Union Pacific railroad the country west of the Missouri river would be a burden to the government, and almost an uninhabitable waste; with it, it will soon be an empire, and one of our principal elements of power and strength."[55]

Dodge had never been a man to brag or exaggerate or try to sell something through inflated words. Here, to the men of his time, he appeared to come close, or actually to go over the line. To readers at the beginning of the twenty-first century, however, he appears modest. The reality far outstripped his prediction.

The same issue of the Chicago paper that announced the arrival of the first train to Cheyenne also noted that Mrs. Elizabeth Cady Stanton and Miss Susan B. Anthony had come by train to Omaha, where they gave lectures "in favor of woman suffrage."[56]

In politics, economics, culture, where and how people lived, America was changing.

Chapter Eleven

THE CENTRAL PACIFIC
PENETRATES THE SUMMIT
1867

IN 1867, the UP was coming on, a mile a day, two miles a day, sometimes three miles in a day, racking up miles, collecting the government bonds and selling its land grants. Before the year was over, it was penetrating Utah with surveyors, its grading crews were well into Wyoming, and its track layers were past Cheyenne. The company hoped that before 1868 was out it would have its end of track into Utah. Along with Durant and Dodge, its directors, surveyors, supervising engineers, construction bosses, and multitude of workers thought that the UP would lay track all the way to the California-Nevada border, where it would meet the CP and thus win the race.

In 1867, the CP was still short of the summit of the Sierra Nevada. Its progress was measured in yards, not miles. It was collecting no government bonds, it was not selling land grants, it could not sell much or even any of its own stocks and bonds. Meanwhile, it was spending tons of money. It looked likely that the UP would win the race.

The reason was obvious to any observer. The UP was laying track over a relatively flat country, while the CP was in some of the roughest mountains on the continent. The UP had to haul in ties, rails, food, forage, and more, upstream on the Missouri River, but from Omaha out to the west, it carried the supplies forward on its own railroad line. The CP had plenty of water and wood, but it had tunnels to drive through granite mountains. The UP could draw on the settled portions of the country for its workers. The CP had to rely, for the most part, on the Chinese. But if and when the CP emerged from the Sierra Nevada, it would be on the Truckee River and then the Humboldt, where it could make time in grading and track laying just as the UP was coming up against the Wasatch Range.

By 1868, both railroads would be far from their base. As Henry Poor, editor of the *Railroad Journal,* explained, "The operations of a railroad company are like those of an army, the cost and difficulty of the maintenance of which increase in inverse ratio as the scene of its action is removed from its base." Only a completed railroad could supply the road under construction with its materials and labor force. Thus, Poor said, a given amount of work would cost "thrice as much and occupy thrice the time" for a railroad west of the Mississippi River as for one on the east side.[1]

In the first few months of 1867, the Chinese worked for the CP in gangs, in eight-hour shifts or sometimes longer, around the clock. They lived in quarters dug in the snow, going to work surrounded by snow. They usually operated in teams of three at a time at the tunnel facing, with four teams working side by side. Of the men who held the drills, one reached as high as he could, another held it at waist level, another down at his toes. The fourth team worked from stepladders that allowed the men to reach the top. Two men pounded. The man with the drill was turning it constantly while holding it firm and in place. The men who were pounding did so with sledgehammers weighing from fourteen to eighteen pounds each. They swung, hit the drill at its far end, dropped the hammer, brought it up again behind them, and swung once more. Alternately, at many times a minute. They could drill four inches of holes, one and three-quarters inches in diameter, in eight hours.

They stopped only to drink some tea, or when the hole got deep enough—one and a half to two inches in diameter, a foot and a half or more deep—for another man to put in the black powder, then the fuse. When the three or four holes were filled, the fuses were lit and everyone retreated down the tunnel to a safe distance. After the explosion, the three-man crew trudged back to the facing to do it over again. The crews were bossed by white foremen, usually Irish, who worked a twelve-hour shift. The progress at each facing toward the middle was between six and twelve inches per day. This was done by all three shifts working around the clock. How many fingers or hands were lost to the hammers we don't know.

Another break for the teams came when the blasted rock at the base had to be removed. At a signal from the foreman, the remainder of the gang—thirty or so men—moved in with their shovels and wheelbarrows. They would load up the rock, wheel it out of the tunnel to a windowlike opening in the snow, and dump it down the mountain.

More than a dozen tunnels were cut this way through the granite mountains. Most were in curves, laid out by Lewis Clement. When the faces met, they were never more than an inch off line, showing the remarkable accuracy of his calculations and instrument work under the most difficult of circumstances. *Van Nostrand's Engineering Magazine* said in 1870 that the undertaking was preposterous, but Clement did it.[2] The Summit Tunnel was sixteen feet wide at the bottom, eleven feet high at the top of the spring line, which was nineteen feet high to the top of the arch, a semicircle sixteen feet in diameter.[3]

Tea was brought to the workers by young Chinese employees, carried on a yoke over their shoulders, one keg on each end of the yoke. They used kegs that had originally been filled with black powder and were washed clean before the tea went in. In California it was known as "powder tea." The men ate before and after their shift, excellent Chinese food, expertly prepared. The remainder of their time off was spent, besides sleeping on mats in the snow tunnel quarters, in washing themselves and their clothes, gambling, talking, reading. They seldom saw the light of day or a blue sky: they walked to and from work inside the snow tunnels, and there they endured their long, grueling shifts in a dim, dank world of smoky lights, ear-ringing explosions, and choking dust.

I N the High Sierra in the winter of 1866–67, there were forty-four storms. Some were squalls, others much bigger. The one everyone recalled began at 2 P.M. on February 18 and didn't let up until 10 P.M. on February 22. It added six feet of new snow to that already on the ground. The wind raged on for five more days, building huge drifts.

The wind was so strong men and animals could not face it. Engineer John R. Gilliss, who worked on the tunnels, recounted the time when three of his men were walking with the storm at their backs in order to get to their shack. "Two got in safely. After waiting a while, just as we were starting to look for the third, he came in exhausted. In a short, straight path between two walls of rock, he had lost his way and thought his last hour had come."[4]

A storm would begin with a fall in the barometer and a strong wind from the southwest. The thermometer was rarely below twenty degrees at the beginning, and usually rose to thirty-two degrees before its close. That meant the last snowfall was damp and heavy. Then the wind shifted, which scattered the clouds, raised the barometer, and dropped the temperature all at once. The lowest temperature of the winter was five degrees above zero.[5]

On February 27, the snow began falling again, and it continued until March 2. This storm added four more feet of new snow. At the eastern approach to the Summit Tunnel, the Chinese had to lengthen their snow tunnel fifty feet in order to get to their quarters and on to work. One of the engineers said that whenever he returned to his shack he had to shovel it out before he could enter. Twenty Chinese were killed in one snowslide. Individual workers simply disappeared. Often enough their frozen bodies were found in the spring, sometimes upright in the melting snow, with shovels or picks still gripped in their hands.[6]

In early March 1867, the *Sacramento Union* reported that nineteen Chinamen had been killed by a snowslide on the east side of the summit, but that wasn't so bad—a much larger number had been reported lost, and in any event the road from Emigrant Gap to Virginia City was open for stages drawn by horses. It was believed this road would stay open.[7]

COMMUNICATION over the mountain was kept up via the Dutch Flat and Donner Lake Wagon Road, five or six hundred feet below the grade and the tunnels. The rocky sides of Donner Peak quickly became and remained smooth slopes of snow and ice. Even the tops of the telegraph poles were buried by drifts. Up to one-half the CP's labor force was kept busy shoveling. Sometimes after storms the entire labor force was engaged in removing snow.[8]

Engineer Gilliss found the scene from the Dutch Flat road to be "strangely beautiful at night." He was drawn by the sight of "tall firs, which though drooping under their heavy burdens pointed to the mountains that overhung them. The fires that lit seven tunnels shone like stars on their snowy sides. The only sound that came down to break the stillness of the winter night was the sharp ring of hammer on steel, or the heavy reports of the blasts."[9]

To those who were struggling to get more blasting powder, drills, food, and other supplies to the men working in the tunnels, the sight was much more daunting than inspirational. The teamsters and their oxen had to make their way through new snow that was soft, powdery, and up to their waists or higher, even to their shoulders. The falling snow or the drifts would cover their tracks. Into this the oxen would flounder. Often they would lie down, worn out, to be roused by teamsters twisting their tails. Bellowing with pain, they scrambled to their feet and went on. Gilliss saw one team so fortunate as to have had their tails twisted clear off and thus to have been spared further agony.

The teamsters at first used Canadian snowshoes, but soon learned to abandon them for Norwegian skis. These strips of light wood—ten to twelve feet long, four inches wide, and tapered in thickness from the center to the ends—were turned up in front and grooved on the bottom. They had a strap in the middle, and the men carried poles in each hand in order to steady, push, and brake. A good man could cover as much as forty miles a day on them—that is, with no oxen to urge on.[10]

The storms cost the CP time and money, and which was more expensive cannot be said. In January, one snowstorm caused drastic damage to a trestle a hundred feet high about two miles below the end of track, at Cisco. A small lake above the trestle, with a dam at the downslope end, was put under great strain by the snow piling up on it. One warm day started a melt which caused the dam to give way. A thunderous surge of water rushed down the ravine and carried away the center section of the trestle.

The bridge had to be repaired. It was difficult to get to it because of the fifteen feet and more of snow in the woods around it. Loggers and oxen went to work. Swarms of workers cut down huge trees, then whipsawed them into shape for the carpenters, who rebuilt the trestle. In less than a month, by February 4, trains were crossing the trestle once again, bringing on rails and hardware for the three thousand track builders forty miles away on the Truckee River and supplies for the Chinese.[11]

A T this time, the directors made a costly but necessary decision. One day, over lunch with Crocker, Stanford took out his pencil and began estimating the cost of covering the track with snowsheds in its most vulnerable parts. That meant putting a roof over the track that led through the snow belt. Arthur Brown, superintendent of the bridges, thought the cost to be "almost appalling, and unprecedented in railroad construction." Yet he confessed that "there seemed to be no alternative." Huntington was also appalled. "It costs a fearful amount of money to pay all the bills," he protested to Hopkins, and added, "I sometimes think I would change my place for any other in this world."[12] But it had to be done.

Brown later said, "although every known appliance was used to keep the road clear from snow that winter of 1866–67, including the largest and best snow plows then known, it was found impossible to keep it open over half the time and that mostly by means of men and shovels, which required an army of men on hand all the time at great expense."[13]

Lewis Clement designed the snowsheds, which ended up covering almost fifty miles. One of them extended for twenty-eight miles without a break. About five miles were covered in 1867, the rest mostly in 1868.

G UNPOWDER and Chinamen were the only weapons of combat the road builders had with which to fight the earth and stone through which they had to pass, laid in their path centuries ago by the Creator," according to one of the engineers.[14] But the black powder was too slow for Crocker and Strobridge. On January 7, 1867, Crocker wrote to Huntington, "We are only averaging about one foot per day on each face—and Stro and I have come to the conclusion that something must be done to hasten it. We are proposing to use nitroglycerine." They had read about it in a recent article in the *Scientific American*.[15]

As we saw, they had tried nitroglycerin once in 1866, but put it away as too dangerous. It was greatly feared by the workers, except by the Chinese, who had become skillful in using it. Crocker and Strobridge thought it was not proper for general use, and anyway the black powder had certain advantages on rock other than granite. But on the Summit Tunnel, and the next two to the east, nitroglycerin was necessary. Among other things, the nitroglycerin required smaller holes; it was costing the CP $1.19 per Chinese worker for each eight hours, and it took three men an hour to drill one foot. "We are bound to use it," wrote Crocker, "if we find it will expedite the Summit Tunnel."

Crocker had it brought up the mountains in its separate ingredients— glycerin and nitric and sulfuric acids. He hired James Howden, a Scottish chemist, to mix them where the nitro would be used. Howden's brew was a yellow liquid, light and oily, which he made up each day at a cost of only 75 cents per pound. As the Chinese became more accustomed to handling the brew, they grew careless. Consequently, one of the engineers wrote, "many an honest John went to China feet first." But John Gilliss calmly observed that the accidents "would have happened with powder."[16]

Gilliss estimated that nitroglycerin was eight times as powerful as the same weight of powder. And the tunnel cleared of smoke faster than when powder was exploded in it. At the facings, inward progress increased by 54 percent, from 1.18 feet per day with powder to 1.82 feet per day with nitroglycerin. At the bottom of the tunnel shaft, where the workers had their backs to each other as they moved outward, the average daily progress jumped from 2.51 feet with powder to 4.38 feet with nitroglycerin, a 74 percent increase.

Mark Hopkins told Huntington, "Charles [Crocker] has just come from the tunnel and he thinks some of them are making three feet per day. Hurrah! For nitroglycerine."[17] E. B. Crocker wrote that as of early May there was "only 681 feet left between the headings. Last week they made 60 feet—more than three feet per day. Nitroglycerine tells."[18]

Crocker also wanted to use the power of the engine he had transported to the top of the mountain, the *Sacramento*, to run drills. "We are all alive to the need to get through the Summit Tunnel," he wrote in January. They had been at it since the fall of 1866 and had so far made only 290 feet, with 1,367 feet of drilling and exploding and carrying out the blasted rock to go. "We have got Strobridge, who lives right up there, roused up. He has talked with the foreman and they are ready to give a steam drill a trial."[19]

On February 12, E. B. Crocker told Huntington, "We've tried nitroglycerine and it works well." Drilling smaller holes saved time. "We are beginning to use an electric battery to fire off charges," he wrote, "and that too at once effects a great savings in time." And the company was replacing chairs with fish joints to tie rails together. "The section men are delighted with the fish joint."

Not all the newfangled devices worked. Strobridge had to abandon the electric battery. He also refused to allow steam to be taken from the *Sacramento*'s boiler to run the drilling machine. His reason was that he didn't want to stop the engine to make the necessary connections for the drilling machines. Told that it would only take two hours, he replied that he didn't have two hours to give. E. B. Crocker told Hopkins, "The truth is things have got to such a pass that there can't be a thing done unless it suits Strobridge."

A part of the trouble was with Charles Crocker. E.B. said of his brother, "Whenever a man gets Charles' confidence, he swears by him and all he says or does is right." Stanford wrote Hopkins, "I fear the drilling machines will prove useless. There does not appear a will that they should succeed, and usually where there is no will there is no way."[20]

"Charley says to wait until we reach the Summit before we haul iron over to the Truckee," Stanford wrote to Hopkins on February 5, 1867. There were about eight thousand Chinese working on the tunnels, but there was also a crew of about three thousand Chinese east of the summit, and they could be laying track. Crocker, however, wanted them to grade, then to lay rail when good weather made it possible to get the rail over the summit.

Construction worker A. P. Partridge spent much of the winter on the Truckee, building grade. He recalled the coming of the Chinese, who took up the old buildings and sheds in the area. One heavy snowfall collapsed an old barn and killed four. Further, "a good many of them were frozen to death." Once he went up to Donner Lake for a dance at a hotel. When the sleigh returned to Truckee in the morning, "we saw something under a tree. We stopped and found a frozen Chinese. We threw him in the sleigh and took him into town and laid him out by the side of a shed and covered him with a rice mat, the most appropriate thing for the laying out of a Celestial."[21]

Through February and March, Partridge worked on putting up bridges over the Truckee River. He and his crew put up two 204-foot spans and one two-span bridge of 150 feet per span. The Chinese, meanwhile, were moved east to get the heavy grading done well in advance of the main force. Some three thousand men with four hundred horses and carts were sent out, a distance of three hundred miles in advance of the track. Hay, grain, and food for the Chinese, plus all the supplies they needed, were hauled by teams of horses over the desert. Water for men and animals was hauled forty miles.[22]

*T*HE surveyors for the CP were way out in front of the graders, all the way to the east of the Salt Lake, working their way up Weber Canyon, then through Echo Canyon, across the Wasatch Range and on to Fort

Bridger, on the eastern slope of the range. By the spring of 1867, they were setting up their flags and stakes right beside those of the UP surveyors. The CP intended to get to Fort Bridger, whereas the UP boasted that it would meet the CP at the California-Nevada border.

E. B. Crocker wished the two lines could work together, but it wasn't to be. "Our surveys run to Weber," he wrote, "so we're confident that we'll reach Ft. Bridger before they do. It can be done in spite of Durant's frantic efforts and boasts."[23]

The CP was trying to get government approval of its proposed route from the California-Nevada state line to Humboldt Wells in northeastern Nevada, but President Johnson's secretary of the interior, Orville Hickman Browning, refused to issue the permit. The Crocker brothers wanted it done as soon as possible, and immediately after Browning had approved, they were ready to present him with a route from Humboldt Wells to the Salt Lake, and then with another route from the Salt Lake eastward into Wyoming. "That will be so much gained," E. B. Crocker commented dryly.[24]

There was big money at stake. As Stanford wrote to Huntington, "Our real profits lie in the road beyond the Sierra Nevadas and to secure the line to Salt Lake if necessary we can afford to make great sacrifices in getting over the mountains."[25] Salt Lake City was the only settled establishment between the two ends of track, the only place that needed to import goods that could be carried on trains, and the only one that had products to export. Then there was the government loan of bonds for every mile constructed to go to the railroad company that built it. And the government gift of alternative parts of land (which in truth wasn't worth much if anything in the desert, where most of it was never sold) would increase as more track was laid.

Perhaps most of all, there was the prestige to be considered. Bragging rights were to be had by one or the other of the railroads. That was the way the Congress had set it up. Congress had reserved to itself the right to pick the spot where the roads would meet, but it had not yet done so and showed no inclination to do so. It wanted the roads built as fast and as far as possible. The spot would be chosen after the grading crews had passed each other, and as the rails at the end of track approached each other. Where that would be, no one knew. So the surveyors kept surveying, the graders kept grading, the rail layers kept laying.

•   •   •

BOTH companies were trying, with some success (the full extent of which is not known in any detail), to place moles, or spies, in the other railroad's camp. The UP sent two engineers to Colfax to snoop around and see what they could pick up. The Crocker brothers knew about this effort and showed them around, filling their heads full of nonsense. The UP engineers "were quite inquisitive" and took in whatever they were told. What they were told was that the tunnels were terribly long and progress was disappointingly slow and it would take a long time to blast through the granite. They went back to Omaha to report to Durant that there was nothing to worry about, that the CP would be blasting away for years. They convinced Durant that it would take at least two more years to get through the Summit Tunnel. E. B. Crocker told Huntington, "While the engineers were here we led them to think that it would take us a long time to get over the mountains. We thought that Durant, while laboring under that idea, would not be apt to be in so great a hurry."[26]

Then one of the UP spies told Durant that the CP wasn't going to wait for the Summit Tunnel to be finished, but was going to haul tracks over the mountains and begin working east from the Truckee. "This news was probably a small bombshell in Durant's camp," E. B. Crocker wrote to Huntington. "He saw that if we dodged around the summit in this way that his hopes were dashed." On the spur of the moment, Durant wrote his spy and told him that he, Durant, would slap an injunction on the CP to prevent any such dodging of the summit. But Crocker commented, "This is ridiculous."[27]

The CP, meanwhile, was planting its own spies on the UP. "I have a way," boasted Huntington, "of finding out what is done in the Union Company's office."[28] In April 1867, E. B. Crocker heard that "the Union Pacific has had a good deal of trouble with snow this winter—full as much if not more than we have had. The fact is that after this year while they are building between the Black Hills & Salt Lake, they will only be able to work on construction during the summer months. They will be such a high latitude that the snow will fall early and stay late and from now on they will find themselves in the fix we are now in."[29]

Still, the UP was so far winning the race. Charlie Crocker said he "felt about like resigning" at the time. He got after Strobridge, told him to hurry up.[30]

• • •

*I*N mid-May 1867, General James Rusling of the army's Quartermaster Department got on a CP train at Sacramento, bound for the mountains and beyond. He was going to inspect army posts. When he left, the day was hot and humid, but as he got to Cisco, the chill signified that the train was in the mountains. "We were shivering in winter garments," commented the general. But the track impressed him and his companions, who were surprised at how well built it was and also at its "audacity."

Rusling observed grades of over a hundred feet to the mile, "and in many places the track literally springs into the air, over immense trestlework bridges or along the dizzy edges of precipices that seem fraught with peril and destruction." When the general and his party reached Cisco, the snow reached to the eaves of the hotel.[31]

Rusling took a "mountain mud-wagon" out of Cisco, through a mixture of slush, mud, and ice. He changed to a sleigh and "then came a long and dreary pull for several miles till we got well across the summit of the Sierras." Everywhere he looked, there were Chinese at work. They had pigtails coiled around their heads and were wearing blue cotton blouses. Rusling talked to a few of their foremen, who "spoke well of the almond-eyed strangers and praised them especially for their docility and intelligence."[32]

One week later, Charlie Crocker was frustrated in his strenuous efforts to put more Chinese on the CP payroll. His brother explained to Huntington that "*a want of men*" had struck the railroad. "We are scouring the state for men to put on the Truckee, but they come in very slow." The Chinese had been discovered by the owners of mines and other employments; the CP's use of Chinese laborers "has led hundreds of others to employ them so that now when we want to gather them up for work, a large portion are permanently employed at work elsewhere that they like better."

Getting enough Chinese to work on the grades and track was so "very important" that the directors of the CP "concluded to raise their wages from $31 to $35 per month and see if this will not bring them." It would cost the CP $20,000 more per month, but with the Chinese going to Idaho, Montana, and elsewhere, it had to be done.[33]

In late May, unbelievably and unacceptably, the Chinese went on strike. "This is the hardest blow we have had," E. B. Crocker reported. He wanted Huntington "to see what you can do about getting laborers from the East."[34] Initially it was the Chinese who were employed in grading, but they were soon joined by those engaged on the most critical part of the work, the tunnelers. The spokesman for the tunnelers said the Chinese wanted $40 per month rather than the $35 they were collecting, and they wanted the workday reduced to eight hours—which it was supposed to be, but the foremen had not been enforcing that rule. Further, in what was a shock for those (including Crocker and Strobridge) who thought the relations between the CP and its workers were excellent, the *Sacramento Union* reported that the Chinese wanted to eliminate "the right of the overseers of the company to either whip them or restrain them from leaving the road when they desire to seek other employment."[35]

Charles Crocker was convinced that agents of the UP had inspired the strike and issued its demands. The UP's motive was "to keep us in the mountains while they were building the road over the plains." But he couldn't prove it, for the good reason that the UP had nothing to do with the strike, which was inevitable given the shortage of Chinese workers and the manifest need of the CP for more of them.[36]

The CP tried to entice workers, but it wouldn't pay $40 per month or reduce the hours. "Charley will go up and attend to it," E. B. Crocker assured Huntington, because, "if they are successful in this demand, then they control and their demands will be increased." The CP didn't want to lose "too much time on the work." But he also knew that, "when any commodity is in demand beyond the natural supply, the price will tend to advance." So he had sent a CP agent to the South to try to recruit "5,000 Freedmen. I hope it will be successful and they will come soon."[37]

It wasn't to be. The following day, E.B. wrote, "the truth is the Chinamen are getting smart. The only safe way to beat them is to inundate this state and Nevada with Freedmen, Chinese, Japanese, all kinds of labor, so that men come to us for work instead of us hunting them up." Good luck on that one. The next day, E.B. wrote, "Since my last letter all the Chinamen on the whole line have struck for $45 and a shorter working day." He still was opposed to paying the expenses of men coming from the East to work, and thought that "a Negro labor force would tend to keep the Chinese quiet as the Chinese have kept the Irishmen quiet."[38]

It couldn't be done. The CP was going to have to deal with the Chinese. Fortunately for the bosses, the Chinese were not militant. Charles

Crocker later said, "If there had been that number of whites in a strike, there would have been murder and drunkenness and disorder. . . . But with the Chinese it was just like Sunday. These men stayed in their camps. They would come out and walk around, but not a word was said; nothing was done. No violence was perpetrated along the whole line."[39]

Crocker cut off the men's provisions. No food got through to them. E. B. Crocker reported, "They really began to suffer." On July 1, 1867, after a week of such treatment, "Charles went up to them and they gathered around him and he told them that he would not be dictated to—that he made the rules for them and not they for him." He said that, if they went to work right away, "all would be well, but if they did not, then he would pay them nothing for June."

The Chinese leaders protested. "They tried hard to get some changes" —a reduction in hours, for example, or an advance of even 25 cents per month. Charlie told them, "Not a cent more would he give." Most said that they would go back to work, but some of their leaders threatened to whip those who did and burn up their camps. "Charles told them that he would protect any who worked and his men would shoot down any man that attempted to do the laborers any harm." He would bring on the sheriff and a posse if necessary.

Four days later, E. B. Crocker noted, "The Chinese are working harder than ever since the strike." They were, at least according to Crocker, "ashamed of the strike. I don't think we will ever have any more such difficulties with them."[40] Thus did Charles Crocker and his partners show other employers around the nation one way—theirs—of how to deal with strikers.

*T*HE UP and the CP continued to tell tall tales to each other. "I met Durant yesterday," Huntington wrote to E. B. Crocker, "and he told me that the UP had a tunnel 2,600 feet in length and that it would take two years to get through it. Of course it was a lie."[41] The UP also wanted to talk to the CP about jointly building a great central city at the point of meeting of the two roads. But as E. B. Crocker said, "Cities don't thrive unless there is a big, prosperous country around. It might happen in 30 or 50 years. You can give them all that great city and not give up much."[42]

Both sets of directors and engineers were telling lies to Brigham Young. They needed his Mormons to help make grade and lay track, and they knew he wanted the line to come through Salt Lake City, and they further knew that it never would do so, because to go south of the lake was to get into terrible desert. But even as their surveyors assured them that there was no such possibility, they told Young to hang on, that they would do their best to get to his city.

E. B. Crocker held out an intriguing possibility to Huntington. "I have an idea that in six months or a year from the time the roads are completed," he wrote, "the two companies will be consolidated. This central city matter is an interesting thing to trade on." It was almost 130 years after the roads were completed before the two lines consolidated, and the great central city never was built.[43]

"They [the UP] have been pretty smart in building their railroad," Crocker said at one point, "but they have never yet come up to their bragging." They said they would be in Cheyenne by September 1, 1867, and they didn't make it until November 8. Still, "it would not do for us to trust in their laziness." Thinking about it, he added, "What a loving crowd the Union Pacific men must be."[44]

STANFORD had run for governor advocating a stoppage of all immigration from China to California, and in his inaugural address in 1862 had denounced the immigration of Asiatic people. The CP's need for labor changed his mind. In the summer of 1867, the CP was sending agents to China to recruit laborers. A great many of them, in fact, according to E. B. Crocker. "The [Chinese] agents go to get a large immigration to come over and work. They know all about the work and can explain it to their countrymen. They will induce thousands to come over. We shall follow this up and get others to go over to China to hurry up the immigration." The CP sent handbills and made arrangements with the steamboat company to provide favorable rates for the passage. "We want 100,000 Chinamen here so as to bring the price of labor down." He further reported, "The new arrivals from China go straight up to the work. It is all life and animation on the line. Charles and Stro feel greatly encouraged."[45]

Leland Stanford loved the idea. So did Collis Huntington, who wrote Charlie Crocker on October 3, 1867, "I like your idea of getting over more Chinamen. It would be all the better for us and the State if there should be a half million come over in 1868."[46]

*I*N August 1867, E. B. Crocker sent a telegram to Collis Huntington: "Summit Tunnel broke through at 4 P.M. Toot your horn. Locomotive on the Truckee is in running order. Track laying commences Monday on the Truckee."[47]

The breakthrough was seen by only one single light, and that not the sun but a lantern. There was much broken rock still to be removed from the bottoms. The breakthrough had to be extended up, down, and sideways to complete the whole tunnel. The grade had to be built, the ties put down, the rails laid and spiked.

But that light was exactly where it should have been. Clement had achieved a triumph of the first magnitude in engineering. The Summit Tunnel was 7,042 feet above the sea. This was the highest point reached by the CP. The facings were off by only two inches, a feat that could hardly be equaled in the twenty-first century. Clement had done it with black powder, nitroglycerin, and muscle power. He had not used electric or steam-driven drills, steam engines to power scoop shovels, or any gas- or electric-powered carts or cars to haul out the broken granite. There were no robots, no mechanical devices. Well over 95 percent of the work was done by the Chinese men. They and their foremen and the bosses, Clement and Crocker and Strobridge, had created one of the greatest moments in American history.

The Sierra Nevada had been pierced. The CP had gone through the mountains at exactly the point where Theodore Judah had said it should be done, following a line that he had laid out. Work on the tunnel had begun in 1866. The shaft had been started on August 27, 1866. A year later, the *Sacramento Union* reported that what "many predicted it would require three years to accomplish has been done in one."[48]

Even though they were through the summit, the CP had not a single aid-worthy twenty-mile stretch of continuous track laid. The line east of the summit was not yet connected and would not be until 1868. The UP had built five hundred miles of track since 1865. The CP was 370 miles behind its rival. In 1867, the CP had laid only some thirty-nine miles of track. Although it was beyond the Summit Tunnel, it was only by two and a half miles. There was a seven-mile gap down the mountain to Tunnel No. 13. Crews could not complete the gap until the snow melted. After that gap, there were twenty-four miles laid to the state line. Crocker had managed to get locomotives over to the east side of the summit, and some flatcars and track material. But that was all. Meanwhile, in October 1867, Huntington wrote E. B. Crocker, "I am sorry to hear your doubts about reaching the Truckee with a continuous line this fall." Still, he said he realized "that all will be done that can be done, and I think Charles can do a little more than any man in America. And if it is not done, I shall know it could not be."[49]

The Big Four were telling reporters that the line would close the gap "in two weeks, if the weather holds good." Charles Crocker told Huntington at the end of October, "The weather is splendid now and the Wise People say we are going to have an open winter, which they also said last winter—from such a winter as last the good Lord preserve us."[50]

A few days earlier, Huntington had written to "Friend Stanford" that he had just spent days in Washington getting bonds due the CP from the government. "I had to go to the Interior Dept., then to the President, and then to the Treasury."[51] He was asking for $320,000 in bonds, due the CP since its 1866 report. But the railroad had not laid enough track to justify an examination by government engineers or a grant of bonds. Huntington said, "I was determined to have the bonds if I could. I got a report from the attorney-general that I was entitled to those bonds. I got one from the solicitor of the treasury. I got two cabinet meetings in one week [where] the majority voted that I should have the bonds."

Huntington stayed at it for nearly a week. "Well," one Treasury official said to him, "you seem entitled to them, but I can't let you have them." Huntington went to see him every day to demand his company's bonds. He said if he did not get them "I will sit here a fortnight." After more wrangling, the CP got its bonds.[52] But of course they had already been borrowed against, and they could not be sold at par. The CP general counsel Creed Haymund later put it, "I have grown sick and tired of hearing of the generosity of the Government. We built it for them." Charles Crocker said he would "never have anything more to do with anything that had to be managed in government style."[53]

In other words, as was so often the case, the CP was out of money. And it had enormous expenses. Building the snowsheds, for example. In November, E. B. Crocker wrote to Huntington that "you still sneer at pine lumber being stacked up on the line, but if you knew how much it cost us last winter to shovel snow out of those cuts, you would not say another word. Those snow sheds will pay for their cost in a single winter."

Huntington was also complaining about the cost of keeping the entire labor force at work. Crocker told him it had to be. "All are anxious to complete the mountain work," he explained, "so as to move into the valley and beyond and not have to come back to the mountains in the spring. They all understand it and cheerfully work Sundays to get through."[54]

The Big Four were always looking for another way to make money. Hopkins was thinking about putting out a pamphlet in the German language "to show the value of our land for grape growing." He thought that the Germans would rush to buy up the land once they knew that "there is no doubt that the grapes raised on our foothills make the best wine in the state."

Stanford wanted consolidation and monopoly. He once said he expected "to see the time when there would not be more than five great companies in the United States," and he especially wanted one single railroad. "If all the roads were operated as one road," he said, "they could regulate prices lower than today and make money, while now they don't make money."[55] So, through 1867, the Big Four reached out for a monopoly of railroading in California. By the end of the year, the partners owned five railroads—the CP, the Western Pacific Railroad, the California and Oregon Railroad, the California Central Railroad, and the Yuba Railroad—and were considering adding a sixth, the Southern Pacific Railroad. Most of these roads had little finished construction, but they had federal land grants and could be picked up cheap. With them, the Big Four had a near-monopoly on the railroads in California.[56]

Despite the buying up of other railroads, Charles Crocker & Company was out of money. On October 28, the Big Four plus E. B. Crocker therefore had voted to follow the lead of the UP and the Crédit Mobilier and create the Contract and Finance Company. Charles Crocker became the president. The Big Four hoped to sell some stock in the new company, but as Stanford lamented, "We did not succeed in any quarter in interesting others and finally gave it up." So each man subscribed for one-fifth of the Contract and Finance Company's stock. Huntington told Hopkins to "take as much as you are forced to but as little as you can." The Big Four then signed a contract with the new company that gave it the right to build from the state line to the Salt Lake at $43,000 per mile in cash plus an equal amount of CP stock.[57] In addition, it would build most of the line for the recently acquired railroads.[58]

It was obvious to the Big Four that someday soon the Contract and Finance Company would be making huge profits, so they created phony investors who supposedly owned much of the stock. A half-year later, that stock was "sold" to Charlie Crocker, so that the stockholders of the Contract and Finance Company consisted of Crocker and his brother E.B., Collis Huntington, Mark Hopkins, and Leland Stanford.[59]

ON November 30, 1867, the grading through the Summit Tunnel was finished, the track was laid, and the spikes were pounded in. Also on that date, the first scheduled train from Sacramento arrived on the east side of the Sierra Nevada.

The next day, Mark Hopkins wrote to Huntington. "Yesterday we all went up to see the first locomotive pass the summit of the Sierra," he opened. "It was a pleasant sight to reach such a point where a train would gravitate towards the East. For these years past gravitation has been so continually against us that at times it seemed to me that it would have been well if we had practiced a while on smaller and shorter hills before attacking so huge a mountain." He confessed to feeling that "our UP friends were too highly favored, but still we have worked on up the mountain—the labored and rapid puff of the engine told how heavy and hard the work."

Now, he went on, "we are on the down grade & we rejoice. The operators and laborers all rejoice. All work freer and with more spirit. Even the Chinamen partake of our joy. I believe they do five extra percent more work per day now that we are through the granite rock work." Looking ahead, Hopkins predicted that, from that day onward, "we can trot along toward Salt Lake instead of remaining in each camp so long that the Chinese become sick and tired of it."

Summing up, Hopkins quite rightly said that the Summit Tunnel was "a thing never before done."[60]

What had been accomplished was astonishing. Samuel Bowles, in his book on riding the Central Pacific rails in 1869, says of the portion through California, "These miles of road, ascending and descending the great California range of mountains, are without parallel in expense and difficulty of construction, and in variety and magnificence of scenery, among the entire railroad system of the world." He spoke of the cost—a million dollars in gold for black powder alone—and commented, "This mountain range, with all its doubts and difficulties and cost of construction, reared itself at the very beginning of the whole enterprise on the Pacific side." It had to be attacked first. Therefore, "the courage and the faith of the California pioneers and executors of this grand continental roadway rise to the front rank."[61]

They had transported all their materials around South America or through Central America. They had overcome lawsuits, opposition, ridicule, evil prophecies, monetary uncertainty, and losses. They had organized a vast laboring force, drilled long tunnels, shoveled away snow, set up sawmills, hauled locomotives and cars and twenty tons of iron over the mountains by ox teams. Nothing came easy. But they had done what other capitalists and engineers and politicians and ordinary folks thought impossible, drilled tunnels through the Sierra Nevada, most of all the tunnel at the summit.

Now they were through, and, in Hubert Howe Bancroft's words, they were ready to enter into the competition with the Union Pacific. Not just for bonds and lands but for prestige. "It was the grandest race that ever was run," Bancroft wrote. Compared with it, "the Olympics were a pretty play." The finish line was the completion of "the most stupendous work that men had ever conceived, and one of the most far-reaching in its results."[62]

It was a work that was to change the whole world.

Chapter Twelve

THE UNION PACIFIC
ACROSS WYOMING
1868

As the UP came out of Nebraska to begin its assault on Wyoming and the CP got through the Sierra Nevada, the railroads' race toward each other became the top of the news. The anticipation of a transcontinental railroad, generally predicted to happen in 1870, mounted throughout 1868. Every newspaper in America carried the story nearly every day or week on its front pages. Lecturers filled Chautauqua halls with their "I was there, I saw it" speeches. The illustrated monthly magazines, along with the heavy-think journals, featured it. E. B. Crocker wrote Huntington in April 1868, "There seems to be a perfect mania for transcontinental railroads."[1]

It mattered to every citizen. This was no "isn't that interesting" item but, rather, one that already had, or was destined to have, an economic effect on the entire populace. One Nevada reporter caught this in an article he wrote in the summer of 1868. He opened his report: "The gap in the great span of iron that shall wed the two oceans is decreasing day by day. . . . No longer is the long and drowsy journey by the way of Panama deemed safe or expeditious by the busy man whose time is as coin to him. . . . The long and tedious stage ride grows less each day. . . . The Overland route is preferable even in winter for all practical purposes of travel." He noted, "Every day sees a huge train of sixty cars laden with timber, ties and railway iron pass Reno [Nevada] on its way to 'the front'"—i.e., to the end of track.[2]

The economic benefits of the railroad (and of the telegraph, with the line being built right alongside the tracks) to the business traveler were obvious. People eager to sell products to the populace of California and the West Coast, and to buy from there fruits and vegetables, and to enjoy the minerals from the mines, could scarcely wait. The California and West Coast residents referred to everything east of the Missouri River (or, increasingly, east of the end of track) as "the States"—or, more poignantly, as "home." They wanted to get there, if only for a visit, and only the railroad made it possible for them to get there in a week rather than months, at a cost of not much more than $100 rather than $1,000 or more.

In August 1868, a correspondent for the *Chicago Leader* wrote that it might even be possible in the year 1869 that "old men, who predicted that the road would be built, but 'not in our time,' may have an opportunity of bathing in the Atlantic one week and in the Pacific the next—or sleigh-riding in New York on Christmas, and pulling ripe oranges in Los Angeles on New Years."[3]

The story of the building of the first transcontinental railroad traveled. If it was not the top of the news in Western Europe, it was close, especially in Germany and even more in Ireland and Britain. In France, Colonel W. Heine, a Civil War veteran currently serving as secretary of the U.S. Legation at Paris, gave a lecture on the railroad to the French Geographical Society. At the urgent request of the society, Colonel Heine repeated it to a public gathering that drew a large and enthusiastic audience. He spoke of the "intelligence, the liberality and the foresight of the American Government in having taken the initiative in the creation of so grand an enterprise." To widespread approval, he paid homage to Lincoln, "who had the honor of signing the land-grants of the greatest railroad of the world with the same pen that had decreed the abolishment of Slavery." Throughout his speech, Heine drew cheers and ovations from the audience, who only wished that their government had the land to give away and the foresight to follow the Yankee lead. One of his remarks that drew a loud response bore testimony to "the perseverance of the men of the North, who at the time when all the world thought them lost, lost no time in organizing victory across three mountain ranges as well as on the field of battle."[4]

Nearly everyone in the United States knew that, like winning the war, building the railroad was not easy. A reporter for the *New York Tribune,*

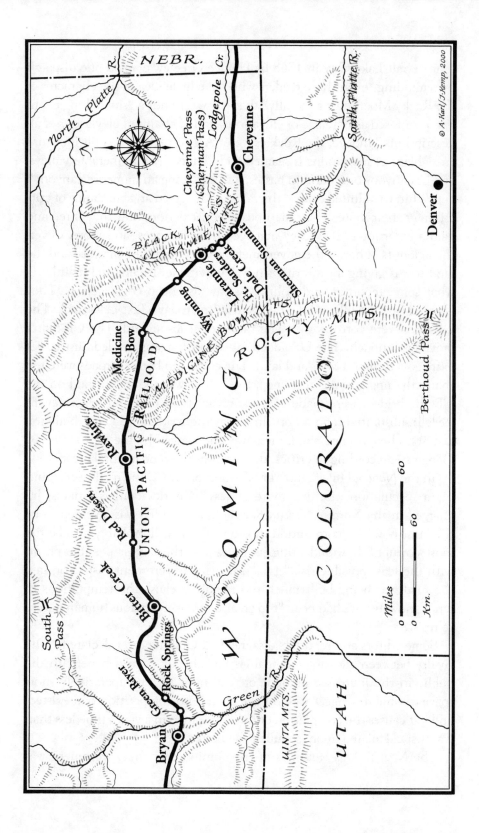

sent to Salt Lake City in 1868 by Horace Greeley, opened one dispatch by reminding "even those readers who have little idea of the character of the Rocky Mountains generally" that they were not a "single long chain but a confused assemblage of elevations, and of chains of elevations of all descriptions." Indeed, the Rockies were "Alps on Alps. . . . This immense assemblage of mountains is seamed and divided by innumerable valleys, and by canyons or mountain passes, a valley being an immense canyon."[5]

Within the United States, the railroads received an abundance of criticism for their routes, their methods of construction, how they hired and paid a labor force, how they managed their finances, and more. Given the amounts of bonds the government was loaning the railroads, and the land it was giving away, criticism was inevitable. It centered mainly on what some reporters and politicians saw as cheap construction. They charged that the UP and the CP were failing to lay a first-class track. The UP's ties were cottonwood. The rails were substandard. The CP didn't move fast enough. The UP added miles to what was needed, just to get extra government bonds and land. The curves on both railroads were too sharp, the upgrade was too steep, the ballast was too much sand on the UP, the bridges were made of wood rather than iron and in any event were insubstantial, and so on. In short, the roads were being built too fast, too cheaply. The shoddiness was encouraged by the race set up by Congress. According to critics, the race was the fundamental error.

To the *National Intelligencer* of Washington, D.C., the roads were "simply a speculation, nothing more or less." Charles Francis Adams, Jr., charged in the *North American Review* that the UP "was destined to be the most powerful corporation in the world; it will probably also be the most corrupt." It would bring its investors "the largest possible profit, with the least possible risk." Isaac Morris, a government inspector, said the road was being built much too rapidly because the temptations in lands and subsidies had been "too great for poor, avaricious human nature to resist."[6]

Some editors and reporters disagreed. A Utah reporter declared: "The rivalry between the two Companies has already been a benefit to the public in the increased amount of road built in a comparatively short space of time to what it would have been if no competition had existed; and if it causes the completion of the entire road in a year's time less than was first calculated upon, so much the better."[7]

The *New York Tribune* was of the opinion that the government was saving money on the railroads, not giving it away. In an 1868 editorial, the *Tribune* calculated that, whereas the government was accustomed to paying as much as 40 or 50 cents per ton per mile to haul supplies to troops in frontier outposts, the UP had reduced that rate to less than 10 cents per ton per mile. That meant that, though the cost of government supplies in 1867 was $699,698, it would have cost $2,625,536 had the supplies been transported by wagons. The government had saved nearly $2 million in one year alone, and that in a year when the track had only reached the Nebraska-Wyoming border. Meanwhile, the value of its public lands alongside or near the railroad had gone up far more than what the government would have received for *all* its lands had there been no railroad. The *Tribune* reflected the optimism of the vast majority. "We shall look for a great stream of travel over the Pacific Railroad next year," the paper declared, "and its completion will give a wonderful impetus to mining, settlement and industry throughout the new Territories, as well as on the Pacific coast."[8]

MOST of the men who built the UP had participated in winning the war. They and a vast majority of their fellow countrymen in the North were well aware that during the conflict a great deal had been learned about how to build and maintain a railroad. They understood that the lessons were now being applied to the transcontinental railroad. Those lessons—or principles, as Dodge called them—had, in his words, "taught the American people that there was no problem in finance or relating to the development of the country so great that its people did not feel able to grasp and master it."[9]

No problem. Not mountains, not deserts, not Indians, not finances or swindlers, not distance, not high interest rates or a scarcity of labor, not politicians whether venal or stupid, not even a civil war or its aftermath. Americans were a people such as the world had never before known. No one before them, no matter where or how they lived, had had such optimism or determination. It was thanks to those two qualities that the Americans set out to build what had never before been done.

GENERAL Dodge was one who had helped bring about victory in the Civil War. He was also instrumental in getting the Pacific Railroad Bill of 1862 and its amendments in 1864 through the Congress. He had then become the chief engineer of the UP, and as such he was going into 1868 full of hopes, plans, and ambitions. Dodge said he wished to build the way to the Salt Lake, almost five hundred miles from the end of track on the last day of 1867, and then endeavor to meet the CP at Humboldt Wells, which was 219 miles west of Ogden, and to do that in the spring of 1869. Maybe—perhaps—who knew?—the UP track layers could meet the CP at the California state line.[10]

That was hubris. But for the most part, Dodge had prepared the UP for 1868. To the west, he had surveyed across Wyoming, Utah, and Nevada, right up to the California state line. To the east, the Chicago and Northwestern Railroad had reached Council Bluffs, Iowa, and with a temporary bridge over the Missouri River supplies could be gotten to Omaha at a much faster rate than ever before. Dodge and his subordinates had piled up an immense amount of rails (sixteen hundred carloads of track iron from the Chicago and Northwestern alone), spikes, fishplates, ties, and other supplies in Omaha, and had shipped enough to Cheyenne to keep the Casements and their men busy for a long time. And they in turn had plenty of men. Further, the railroad, in reaching the Black Hills, was now close to ample supplies of good timber for bridges and ties, which could be floated down mountain streams to the work itself, thus providing great relief to the strain on transportation from Omaha.

Ahead of the UP through Wyoming, there was relatively easy going. Even better news for the directors, who were as always concerned about money, was that, for the next 150 miles from Cheyenne onward, the company would be receiving $48,000 in government bonds for each mile of track laid and accepted. From there on it would be $32,000 per mile. From Omaha to Cheyenne, they had received only $16,000 in bonds per mile.

Greatly encouraged by all this welcome news, the directors told Dodge "to build as much road as possible in 1868." He and the men working for him and thousands working for them set out to do just that.[11] In January 1868, Dodge wrote his construction superintendent, Sam Reed, "You must do more hard work in 1868."[12]

D ODGE'S plans, like those of the CP, rested on a clause in the law (put into it in 1866) that allowed each company to grade three hundred miles in advance of a continuous line of track and collect part of the government bonds for each twenty-mile segment graded. If Dodge could lay track to within one hundred miles of Ogden, then the UP could send its grading crews as far west as Humboldt Wells.

The CP, for its part, if it could get track into Ogden, could advance three hundred miles eastward, well into Wyoming. Its problem was that the gap between the end of track at Donner Lake was still several hundred miles short of Humboldt Wells, which is what gave Dodge the thought that the UP might make it to the California state line before the CP got east of it.

Huntington had his own plans. In April 1868, he drew a red line across a map of a preliminary survey and sent it to Secretary of the Interior Browning. The line ran north of the Salt Lake, across the Promontory Mountains to Ogden, then eastward into the Wasatch Range and up a northern fork of Echo Creek. The map was fraudulent, but Huntington backed it up with a letter that lied about where the CP had its end of track. If Browning would approve, CP grading crews could occupy the ground in and east of the Wasatch. It helped that one of Huntington's lobbyists was Thomas Ewing, Jr., a former associate of Browning. It also helped that Browning had an intense hatred of the UP, or at least of Doc Durant, which he regarded as one and the same. On May 15, he approved Huntington's line as far east as Monument Point, Utah, but withheld his decision to Promontory and beyond.

Possession of Utah was at stake. "It is an *important matter*," Huntington told Stanford. *"We should be bold and take and hold possession of the line to Echo."* Oakes Ames, meanwhile, stressed the UP's need "to build 3 miles a day until next Dec. or Jany and get to Salt Lake before the Central." Whether the UP could do that was to be seen. The CP crowd relied on the divided counsels of Durant, Dodge, the Ames brothers, and other officials of the UP. "Ha! Ha!" E. B. Crocker told Huntington. "What a time the Union Pacific folks have. That is a trouble we do not have [because] we are all united."[13]

President Johnson's Cabinet reached no firm decision on how far the grading could go. The Congress stayed aloof from the controversy. The railroads went ahead surveying as far as they could and making grade as fast as possible. Soon enough they were making grade beside each other in Utah, the CP going east and the UP going west, on parallel roads.

• • •

255

*P*ush is the word for this season," Sam Reed proclaimed at the start of 1868, and, like most of the leaders in the field for the UP, he pushed himself hardest of all. His telegram copy book, in the UP Archives in Omaha, shows just how hard. The copies cover all types of work and consist in large part of the kind of telephone conversations a twenty-first-century businessman would have with his superiors and subordinates. What follows is a tiny selection.

January 28, Reed to J. Lathrop at the end of track: "If you want anything from Omaha you will have to send it here to be approved." Same day, Reed to G. W. Frost in Omaha: "Send for Dale Creek bridge four sets blocks for one inch line and one coil of seven-eighths line, two clamps that will span thirty inches to clamp timber for bolting Congdon will explain, three one and one quarter inch augers."

Same day, Reed to M. F. Hurd at the end of track: "Put the station house on the north side of main track west of turntable track." Same day, to Lathrop: "I have ordered ten dozen shovels and six dozen picks and handles for Carmichael." Same day, again to Lathrop: "Is there any dirt cars at the station. Mulloy picked up some Sunday if there send one with ox for dumping to Miller and Co." Same day, to Hurd: "On section 288 estimated 4000 yards earth instead of 6500 as you telegraphed look into it."

Same day, to Frost in Omaha: "Send my bridge timber in preference to iron. Eighteen to twenty cars of Iron intended here daily must be cars enough to load timber in Chicago if there is any instead of sending it forward." Same to same, also January 28: "Have you paid Bent and CO for 50 tons of hay furnished me some time since."[14]

Here is another sample, all telegrams dated March 13, 1868. Reed to H. Bissell at Dale Creek: "Send a man over and count the boxes of bolts that have been received at the Bridge soon as possible and give me the answer." Also to Bissell: "Has Butterfield put on another gang of raisers. How is he getting along raising the bridge." To Frost in Omaha: "There was received here yesterday a lot of three inch plank. I have not ordered lumber of that description." To Lathrop: "How many boxes of Dale Creek Bridge bolts have you received since February 1ˢᵗ and are there any at your place." To H. M. Hoxie in Omaha: "Are there any boxes of Dale Creek Bridge bolts at Omaha. If so send them forward. 109 boxes have passed Chicago. 83 received here." To Lathrop: "Were the bolts shipped by team from your place or sent to end of track and shipped from there. We are short at bridge, not all received."

On it went. To Lathrop again, also March 13: "In Reynolds and Dowling bill for supplies, I find 300 pounds whole pepper. Does he want that amount." To Bissell at Dale Creek: "There is a man in Omaha that represents that he is hiring men for Hall. Send a man to Hall's Camp and find out if he wants the men." Again to Bissell: "There has been sent from Carmichael to Dale Creek 109 boxes of bolts and washers if not received let me know immediately." To Lathrop: "How much hay received from Casement since January 1ˢᵗ to March 1ˢᵗ. How much from McDonald. How much wood used in Casement's boarding car and sent to them at Cheyenne since January 1st." To Bissell: "Have you received the 109 boxes or only the 86 boxes of bolts and washers." To Lathrop, same day: "Bissell reports only 86 boxes bolts and washers received at the bridge. Where are the balance." To W. Snyder, Omaha: "Michael Haley is authorized to hire men for Hall. Send good rail road men only men wanted." Also on March 13, Reed sent a thousand-word telegram to H. C. Crane, the UP's secretary in New York.[15]

*R*EED was "talking" to men in New York, Chicago, Omaha, and at the end of track. That the telegraph would keep up with the end of track was a requirement of the Pacific Railroad Act, and in any event absolutely necessary to the building of the road. There was a regular work gang for the telegraph. The poles were brought to the front on the material trains and distributed by wagons. One gang fastened the cross-arms to the top of the poles while another group, under a foreman, dug the holes. A third gang erected them. A wire was brought forward in a wagon and unwound from a reel as the wagon moved ahead. A wire gang raised the wire and fastened it to the insulators.

There was an intense rivalry between the telegraph gangs and the track gangs. Sometimes the telegraph workers were delayed by a lack of poles, but when that happened they connected the wires to a temporary telegraph set. That way, communication between Cheyenne, Omaha, Chicago, and points east and the end of track was never lost.[16] Or, rather, almost never: the buffalo had a way of using the poles as scratching posts and would sometimes knock them down.

Besides the buffalo, Reed's problems included liquor. On March 28, he sent a wire to Secretary Crane: "As soon as a party of men commence at work a lot of tents are put up on the vicinity and whiskey furnished to the men." As a result, robbery and murder were commonplace. "Whiskey ranches interfere materially with our men. Two men were shot Thursday night. Can something be done through Congress to stop the indiscriminate sale of whiskey in the vicinity of our work."

*M*ORE examples of how the telegraph was used by the men making the line, the following all from April 9. Reed to L. Carmichael at Dale Creek: "I have written you this morning to put on night gang on cut west of bridge. Keep as many men on them as can be worked night and day." To Reynolds and Dowling at Dale Creek: "Put night gang on first cut west of bridge. Keep as many men on as can be worked night and day there are plenty of carts you can have if you want more to surface road bed." To M. Hurd in Cheyenne: "Can you let us have an engine and 2 empty box cars for an hour or two." To Furst & Bradley in Chicago: "Send me one hundred more scrapers." To G. W. Frost in Omaha: "Send on No. 3 tonight for immediate use 6 relays, 6 sounders, 6 keys, 6 switches, 2 coils insulated copper wire 6 clip boards." To Hurd: "Have you the level notes from Sta 1500 west. Want to start engineering party out with Creighton Saturday."

To M. F. Seymour at Dale Creek: "Have 9 boxes bolts from Pittsburgh will send them up to Summit tomorrow noon will send to Snyder for 500 extra." To W. Snyder in Omaha: "Please send me on express train as soon as you can have them made 500¾ inch bolts 22¾ inches long answer." To A. L. Thompson: "There are three cooking stoves at Mulloy shanties near Summit. You can have one. You will have to take down some of your shanties at Dale Creek for what lumber you want." To J. E. Boyd in Omaha, with a copy to Gustavus Ames in Omaha: "When will you have a force on your work west of Little Laramie." And, finally, the last one of the day, to G. W. Frost in Omaha: "Pay bill just received. You have charged for shovels $20 per dozen. I can buy them in Cheyenne for less."[17]

Just before going to sleep that night, Reed wrote his wife, "I have too much for any mortal man to do."[18] So did nearly every man working for the UP, although it would be difficult to imagine anyone working more hours or harder than Reed. Still, he kept his optimism. On March 18, he had sent a telegram to his rival, Charlie Crocker. "My men have stuck stakes in the Humboldt Mts. We'll meet you there."

Crocker laughed at the audacity. "He won't find his stakes when he arrives," he told a reporter. "I'll have trains running that far by the end of this year."[19]

Reed was living in Cheyenne, as were the Casements and the workers. Dubbed the "Magic City of the Plains," the town had grown from nothing, when Dodge platted and staked it out in July 1867, to a town of a few thousand that was selling lots at a record pace. Frame buildings were replacing tents. Leigh Freeman, the son of a UP employee, had been a telegrapher at Fort Kearney when he founded a newspaper, the *Frontier Index* (later in Cheyenne). In 1866, he moved his printing press (and thus the newspaper) by wagon to North Platte. He continued to follow the railroad westward, setting up in the Hell on Wheels towns and providing the UP's workers with news and entertainment.[20]

*T*HROUGH the winter of 1867–68 and indeed up to and even beyond the beginning of spring, the storms had kept most of the crews from working. On February 28, 1868, for example, Reed sent a telegram to Secretary Crane saying he had "just returned from the mountains [Sherman Pass] where I have been storm bound since last Monday. The storm has been more severe than any other this season. All the cuts were full of snow and it will take ten days to two weeks to clear them."[21]

By the beginning of April, the worst seemed to be over, and the frost was leaving the ground. The Casement brothers and their men were eager, or, in the typically American phrase, "raring to go." By April 5, the track-laying crews had covered ten miles and had nearly reached Sherman Summit at 8,242 feet of altitude, the highest point of any railroad anywhere. Or, as Reed put it in an April 7 telegram from Cheyenne to Secretary Crane in Omaha, "Track laid over highest railroad summit on the Continent. S. B. Reed." Graders meanwhile had started down the west slope toward Dale Creek, four miles beyond Sherman and thirty-five miles west of Cheyenne.

*A*T Dale Creek, the engineers and the crews had to build a bridge over the creek. To support the effort, Dale City had come into existence. In December 1867, the *Frontier Index* had noted its presence: "We are informed that this is a right pert place, just now; contains about forty buildings, with a population of about six or seven hundred railroaders, tie men, teamsters, wood choppers, etc., and a good prospect of a steady increase for some months to come." The workers were there to make grade, dig the cuts, and otherwise prepare for the coming of the bridge trusses, most of all to build masonry foundations for the big trestle. In March 1868, a post office came to Dale City.[22]

The bridge would be 126 feet above the streambed and seven hundred feet long, making it by far the highest bridge of the UP, ever. To stand at the site today, or to look at its photograph by Andrew Russell, is to be filled with astonishment. How could they possibly even imagine such a thing, much less do it? A bridge, built entirely of wood, 126 feet above the creek bed and seven hundred feet long? Sufficiently strong to carry a locomotive, a tender, a string of passenger or freight cars, while swaying in the Wyoming mountain winds? With a mile of cut on the west side and nearly as much on the east, through solid rock? Daunting at best, quite probably to most engineers impossible. Yet the UP did it, in what was one of the greatest engineering feats of the nineteenth century.

All this to get the tracks over Dale Creek. Engineer Hezekiah Bissell called it "a big bridge for a small brook that one could easily step over." When the track got near Sherman Summit, the *Cheyenne Daily Leader* said the next day that "a vast and varied amount of freight and passengers went to the end of track today. There were five car loads of iron and spikes, twenty-five dirt scrapers, twenty quarters of fresh beef, patent plows, men's boots, gunnies of ham, cases of pepper-sauce, sacks of grain, bales of clothing and working men with Winchester rifles, carpet bags, blankets and every other conceivable article of tools, food and wearing apparel."[23] Meanwhile, the grading crews were moving on west.

As Reed's telegrams show, the construction superintendent and the men working for him made the bridge a top priority. Reed especially stayed after the company supplying the trusses. The wood was cut in Michigan, then shipped to Chicago, where it was fashioned to specification into double-framed trestles with bents spaced forty feet apart. Then it was shipped by rail (across the temporary bridge over the Missouri River from Council Bluffs to Omaha) to the end of track.

Except for the Russell photographs, the UP made no record as to the detailed plans of the bridge and the actual work of building it. In October 1946, the only description the Engineering Department of the UP could find was: "Dale Creek is crossed by a pine timber trestle ridge of 40-foot spans, with double bends resting on piers of granite masonry raised only to a small height. The roadway is suspended by a low truss frame resting on these bents. . . . The timber trestle was replaced in 1876 with an iron bridge known as the 'spider web,' it appeared so slender, 707 feet long, 127 feet high at the deepest point."[24]

Progress on the bridge was enough to make even Reed indulge in a little smile now and then, but on April 14, when the bridge was half finished, a storm came up. Reed sent a telegram to the Chicago firm, "Wind blowing a gale, no work being done on bridge. Do not ship the truss bridges until further orders." He ordered a transit and levels sent to the bridge, and the bridge wired for more cables, then more, then even more.[25]

Engineer Bissell was there to see the near-catastrophe. "The bridge men were scared out of their wits," he wrote in his diary, "and doing nothing to save the thing." Bissell sent men to the contractors, telling them "to bring every rope and chain they could get hold of to the bridge as soon as possible. When the ropes first came, no one dared to go and put them on to guy the bridge. I finally induced two or three to go, and soon there were plenty of others. I probably saved the bridge."[26]

Two days later, April 16, Durant, Dodge, and a party of big shots arrived in Wyoming. They were there to watch the first train go over Sherman Summit. "In the presence of such a large number of distinguished army officers and citizens," Dodge told Secretary Browning in a telegram, Durant insisted on pounding in the last spike on the final rail at the summit. After that was done, Dodge reported, "the Union Pacific Rail Road crossed the Summit of the mountains this day, the highest elevation reached by any rail road in the world."[27]

What a day! What a week! On April 23, Reed wrote his wife, "Bridge finished." The track was over the bridge, the cuts through the rock on either end were nearly done, which meant a "great load off my mind." Meanwhile, James Evans had already surveyed a location from Fort Sanders, just west of Dale Creek, all the way to Green River. Two weeks later, on May 6, he had completed the final line and was able to telegram Dodge triumphantly, "We save considerable in distance and altitude both over the preliminary lines."[28] By then the graders were approaching the Green River, and Reed planned to go to Salt Lake City to convince Brigham Young to get the Mormons started grading east up the Weber Canyon.[29]

*T*HE Casements were pouring it on. The railroad was over the divide of the Black Hills and had nothing to impede it from there all the way to the Wasatch Range. On April 21, Jack Casement wrote his wife, "I have never been hurried up more in my life." He loved it. "Have crossed the high Bridge [at Dale Creek] today and want to commence laying three miles a day at once." He, his brother, Dodge, Durant, all the workers on the railroad were on the march with clear objectives in front of them— Weber Canyon, Ogden, Promontory, Humboldt Wells. At three miles per day, maybe even more, nothing could stop them.

"We are now *Sailing*," he wrote on May 2.[30] A few days later, the road ran down the Black Hills' western slope all the way to Laramie. With the grade ready for track clear to Green River, more than half the way through Wyoming, the Casement construction train and the crew were ready to roll. Many others were ready to follow. Leigh Freeman moved his printing press to Laramie and set about publishing the *Frontier Index* there. In its first issue, May 5, the paper predicted that Laramie would soon rival Chicago. When it was only two weeks old, the *Index* boasted, "Laramie already contains a population of two thousand inhabitants." The UP was now building the ramshackle Union Pacific Hotel beside the tracks and a $10,000 windmill to pump water for its men and engines (it was the largest ever erected).[31]

The grade went nearly straight north out of Laramie. Then, just past Rock Creek it turned straight west across the Medicine Bow River, up to and across the North Platte River.* Fort Steele was on the western side of the North Platte River, then, a bit farther west, a town founded by the UP and called Benton, then Rawlins Springs (today called Rawlins). The most important work, after the Dale Creek Bridge was operating, was to get the bridge up and the tracks over it ready for trains at the crossing of the North Platte River. Arthur Ferguson was one of the surveyors as-signed to that duty.

On Saturday, April 25, 1868, he and others left Omaha at 5:30 A.M. on

---

* The North Platte River comes out of the Sierra Madre range, flows north until it receives the Sweetwater River, then turns northeast to skirt the Medicine Bow Mountains, then southeast out of Wyoming into western Nebraska, until it joins with the South Platte River at the Nebraska town of North Platte.

a train headed west. After a delay of two hours on account of reported Indians ahead, the train arrived in Cheyenne at 6 P.M. Thus did Ferguson cross Nebraska in one day. In Cheyenne, he "witnessed strange sights. The whole city was the scene of one high carnival—gambling saloons and other places of an immoral character in full blast—streets crowded with men—various houses illuminated—vice having unlimited control, making the Sabbath evening a sad and fearful time." He went to bed early.

The next day, a construction train took Ferguson to the end of track, at that point five miles west of Dale Creek. Then on by wagon to Fort Sanders, where he and his party slept three to a bed. Continuing the next day along the grade, Ferguson was struck by the land, a "dismal and desolate country, a terrible country, awful, all sage brush and grease weed." He and four others were in the wagon, with three hundred rounds of ammunition and lots of fear of Indians, especially after passing a short distance from what he called "a camp of several hundred hostile Indians."

On Sunday, May 3, Ferguson got to the North Platte, but not at the site where an army contingent was camped. So everyone turned out for guard duty, all night long. In the morning it began to snow, and not until May 6 could he and his party get to the proper site and begin their work of measuring, leveling, surveying.

On Tuesday, May 12, Ferguson opened his diary entry, "This has been a fearful day." He had begun by running the line west of the river, but found that he had lost the tape line and started back over the river to search for it. Everyone piled into the wagon, but the driver didn't know the ford. "The first thing we knew was that the water was floating in the wagon box, and our mules were out of their depth and being swiftly carried down stream by the terrific violence of the current." The wagon box capsized and all the men were floundering among the waves. Ferguson retained the leveling instrument in his hand but he got tangled up in the wagon box, which was pressing him down. "I immediately saw that it was for me a struggle for life or death and therefore dropped the instrument." Eventually he got out, but two of his companions were drowned. He said he would never forget "the look of awful terror and despair that had settled on their countenances." Attempts to locate the leveling instrument, plus the three guns that had gone down, not to mention the bodies of the drowned men, were unsuccessful.[32]

• • •

WHILE Ferguson's party was putting up the bridge, men, mules, horses, and wagons went over by ferry. There was quite a bit of horror, including mules and horses drowned, wagons tipped into the river, and so on. On May 17, Ferguson noted, "Two more men drowned in the river yesterday. Quite a number of grading camps are here waiting to cross the river." But, no matter the death toll, the engineers were concerned with the bridge and, not incidentally, with making some money on the side. Thus Ferguson recorded that on May 20 he and two others bought three lots in the town of Benton, which was not yet founded. Five days later, they sold the lots (for which they had paid $2.50) for $25 each.

Mainly they worked. Measuring, leveling, putting in pilings, staking out bents, then setting in rails and putting sidings on each side of the bridge.

THERE was more excitement, primarily from Indians. Ferguson's diary contains numerous references to their war parties. For example, May 24: "The Indians made a dash on some pilgrims who are camped on the opposite side of the river and succeeded in capturing 19 head of stock." June 4: "At about sunrise, were attacked by Indians and succeeded in shooting one." June 20: "The Indians made a dash on the camp and captured some stock and killed one man." June 21: "Indians killed two men. Both had been horribly mutilated about the face by cuts made by a knife or a tomahawk. They captured one hundred head of stock." June 30: "Four men were killed and scalped today about two miles above camp." July 2: "Indians ran off 70 head of cattle and killed two more men last night within three miles of here."

Ferguson also recorded rumors that had little or no foundation in fact. As one example, July 16: "Out of a party of 25 men who were on the Sweet Water, 24 of them are said to have been killed by Indians." He also recorded death by accident or by shoot-outs among workers, which in truth were nearly as serious as the Indian threat. June 7: "Two men were shot this evening in a drunken row—one was instantly killed, and the other is not expected to live." June 26: "This evening another man was shot." July 7: "This afternoon one man was shot and wounded in the knee and another killed." July 11: "One of the workmen was killed within five feet of me by the falling of a bent. In falling he was struck on the head and then fell through the work into the water and was drowned before my eyes. This evening another man was shot and killed, which was occasioned by some personal difficulty." July 14: "Another man shot this evening." July 18: "Another man shot last night." July 19: "Another man and four mules drowned in the river today."

It was an arduous job that was not finished until July 15, when "the first locomotive crossed the bridge, with two more following directly afterwards." They were construction trains, pulling freight cars loaded with rails, fishplates, ties, and more. Still, Ferguson could write, with considerable pride, "The bridge is a success." On July 21, he could record that "the first passenger train that was ever west of the north fork of the Platte crossed the ridge about noon today. Men commenced digging the water tank today. They will work all night."[33]

On August 3, Ferguson himself was almost caught by flying bullets. He commented, "It is owing to the carelessness of individuals in our vicinity whose reckless disregard of life and limb in their promiscuous shooting is perfectly outrageous and alarming."[34]

Life came cheap on the Union Pacific Railroad, as Ferguson knew as well as any. Nevertheless, he directed his emotions not at the workers who shot their fellows and who were more dangerous than the Native Americans, but at the Indian boys who sometimes killed and often stole from the whites. In fact, the Indian outrages were exclusively committed by teenage boys. The threat of war parties, so severe in 1867, had gone away. This was thanks to the resolution of the veterans who were working for the UP, and to the five thousand troops stationed along the line of the UP between Omaha and the Salt Lake.

Another factor was the quality of the rifles. The Sioux, Cheyenne, and Arapaho were using muzzle loaders, with loose powder, balls, and percussion caps. The U.S. Army soldiers were not much if any better off until 1867, when the Springfield rifle was first issued to the infantry on the Great Plains. It was a breechloader, made from the old Springfield musket, sighted for a thousand yards maximum range. On two occasions in the fall of 1867, the Sioux lost some of their best warriors to the quickness and range of the Springfield, which was a splendid weapon.

Further, the Pawnees protecting some of the graders and others were getting better at their task. In truth, they were living what they regarded as a joyous life. The army furnished them with arms and ammunition, food, clothes, and pay, all this to do what they wanted above all other things to be doing, fighting their enemies. And if their enemies proved to be too strong for them, they could always retreat to the nearest white troops for protection. In addition, they were now much farther west than they had ever been or would have dared to go by themselves.

David Lemon was an engineer for the UP. Fifty-six years after the event, he wrote a reminiscence of one of his experiences on the railroad. During the first week of October 1868, at night, he was in the cab of a locomotive on the line, with two boxcars of oats and corn followed by twenty-three cars of railroad iron. Sioux Indians had removed bolts and fishplates from the rail joint and torn down telegraph poles to pry apart the rails.

Lemon crashed. "You can well imagine the ugly wreck." Not until daylight did a relief crew arrive to assist him. Pawnee troops gave chase to the Sioux. When they returned, they had seven scalps. They said the scalps were all from Sioux, "although one of them had long red hair, which was probably that of an escaped white convict who had taken refuge with the Sioux tribe." That night the Pawnees had a grand scalp dance.[35]

*I*N the eyes of the men of the UP, the Indians deserved extreme punishment and even more. President Oliver Ames came west and raged, "I see nothing but extermination to the Indians as the result of their thieving disposition, and we shall probably have to come to this before we can run the road safely."[36]

General Sherman hoped it wouldn't come to that, but he was ready if it did. British reporter Henry Stanley had been at North Platte, Nebraska, in the fall of 1867, for a peace council. He heard Sherman say to the Indians: "We built iron roads, and you cannot stop the locomotive any more than you can stop the sun or moon, and you must submit, and do the best you can. . . . If our people in the east make up their minds to fight you they will come out as thick as a herd of buffalo, and if you continue fighting you will all be killed. We advise you for the best. We now offer you this, choose your own homes, and live like white men, and we will help you all you want."[37]

Ferguson was more rabid. "I have no sympathy with the red devils," he wrote in his diary on August 17, "notwithstanding the halo of romance by which they are surrounded by the people of the East, who, secure in their happy and peaceful homes, know naught of the wild and awful horrors of the West." He added that, for his part, having been "surrounded by too many perils, and knowing too much of the savage details of Indian warfare," he wanted them eliminated. "Let the savage strength of the demoniac Indian be broken," he wrote. "May their dwelling places and habitations be destroyed. May the greedy crow hover over their silent corpses. May the coyote feast upon their stiff and festering carcases, and the sooner the better."[38]

As bloodthirsty as that was, Ferguson had the same kind of mixed emotions as most of his fellow surveyors and engineers. To a man, they loved the wild life, the scenery, the game, the swift and clear-flowing streams, the untouched prairie and forest, the flowers and trees, the birds, the opportunity to ride across an unfenced country. And they also loved Indians, as long as the Indians stayed out of the white man's way.

But they were also aware that, as the first white men other than the mountain men ever to come into this paradise, this Eden, this unspoiled country, they had the job of wiping it out by bringing to it the very thing that had brought them into the wilderness, the railroad. Much as they loved the wild country, they were going to tame it. Thus Ferguson observed, "The time is coming and fast too, when in the sense it is now understood, THERE WILL BE NO WEST."[39]

That was partly right. The West was not going to be eliminated from the maps or from American territory or from people's imaginations. But it surely would be changed. One such change was in fact already evident. In the summer of 1868, a herd of eight hundred Texas cattle was trailed into the vicinity of North Platte. The first Nebraska cow town was born. In the next year, seventeen hundred head arrived and were put out to graze on the prairie. By 1870, the total cattle herd was up to seven thousand, with a smaller number of sheep. And this was just the beginning.[40] The cattle and sheep were displacing the buffalo even as Ferguson was helping build the UP.

The tame was replacing the wild. As Ferguson understood, there had to be a price. One that he recorded but apparently did not understand was accidents. To UP workers they were just a part of the job, bound to happen. Moving all those iron rails, throwing down fishplates and spikes also made of iron, swinging sledgehammers all day long, and all the other movement of goods and supplies, meant accidents. How many could not be said. Nor is there an accounting of how many men lost a limb or their lives.

Accidents involving locomotives were another matter. First of all, they cost money—even by the standards of the UP or the CP, big money. Second, it was thought that locomotives would last, if not forever, at least through a man's lifetime. That a locomotive accident could cost lives was taken for granted, but the trouble was that they often cost valuable or even irreplaceable lives—namely, the engineers running the trains.

That there would be accidents with locomotives was inevitable. They were the biggest moving things ever built by man, and they moved faster than anything ever built. Even the fastest animal—say a cheetah—could outrun them for only a short distance. They could go farther pulling a heavier load than anything else.

Morris Mills, an early employee of the UP, noted in 1926 that more radical change in operating practice for the railroads came in the 1870s than in any other decade before or since. This included advancing from hand to air brakes, from a coupling hook to automatic couplers, from iron to steel rails, from eight-wheel locomotives to ten-wheelers, from ten-ton capacity for freight cars to forty- or even sixty-ton capacity, from snow-plows of the wedge type to the rotary plow, and more. But none of those and other improvements had been made before 1870. Indeed, as Mills pointed out, "Railroading in the days of hand brakes, soil ballast, light power, and mountain grades, entailed hardships that produced a type of employee that were a veritable survival of the fittest."[41]

Accidents were so common they hardly got reported. The *Chicago Tribune* gave one paragraph to an incident in which a construction train in eastern Nebraska, near Fremont, ran over a cow. The accident threw several cars off the track. Five men were killed, twelve wounded (and two of them died the following day). "Several ladies were badly mangled."

Another report, dated July 15, 1868, dateline Laramie City, said that a westbound freight train that had just passed over the Dale Creek Bridge ran into a car carrying gravel. The car had become detached from an eastbound train and ran down the grade toward Laramie "at such fearful velocity that it demolished the rear car of the freight train, which contained a number of persons." One man was killed, another seriously injured, and others were cut or bruised.[42]

After the track got up to and beyond the second crossing of the North Platte, a boiler malfunction, sometimes even an explosion, became commonplace. This was because, throughout the Wyoming desert, from Rawlins to Green River, the water was an alkaline concoction that destroyed the boilers faster than they could be replaced. It looked like water but, according to Morris Mills, when heat was applied to it "it became a law unto itself and defying the ingenuity of man it would shoot out through the smoke stack like a miniature geyser." Engines headed east rolled into Cheyenne looking as if they had been whitewashed. Eventually the UP learned how to apply a chemical process to the water to make it behave.[43]

*T*HE region west of Rawlins was an "awful place," according to Jack Casement. It consisted of "alkali dust knee deep and certainly the meanest place I have ever been in." Surveyor James Evans said, "It is not a country where people are disposed to linger."[44] But the railroad, and those who worked on it and those who worked on them, had to get across it.

On June 21, 1868, Arthur Ferguson recorded in his diary, "Large numbers of wagon teams, men and women, the latter principally prostitutes, are now crossing the [North Platte] river, bound as far west as Green River, which they say is quite a town."[45]

The sharpers, the cooks, the bartenders, the musicians, the girls, and the women were leaving Benton for the next end of track to boast a city, or at least a railroad establishment. Leaving Benton was no problem. A Cheyenne, Wyoming, reporter described the place as reminding him of "the camps of the Bedouin Arabs, [because it] is of tents, and of almost a transitory nature as the elements of a soap bubble." Novelist J. H. Beadle was there in the summer of 1868 and, tramping through the alkali in his black suit, he said he came to resemble "a cockroach struggling through a flour barrel." He found "not a green tree, shrub or patch of grass. The red hills were scorched as bare as if blasted by lightning."

Samuel Bowles, the travel writer from Massachusetts, described Benton as "by day disgusting, by night dangerous, almost everybody dirty, many filthy, and with the marks of lowest vice; averaging a murder a day; gambling, drinking, hurdy-gurdy dancing and the vilest of sexual commerce." He thought the inhabitants a "congregation of scum."[46]

A month or so later, they were all gone. There was not a single house or tent, only the rubble of a few chimneys and the sole surviving institution, the cemetery. This was because, as Ferguson noted, Hell on Wheels was on the move. Like the UP Railroad, Green River was the next stop.

• • •

*T*HERE was money to be made out of the railroad. Among the many who knew that basic fact were Doc Durant and his fellow stockholders in the Crédit Mobilier. Dodge might want to build a first-class railroad, one that would last. Durant was for that, in his own way, but meanwhile he wanted to make money, not from any dividends the UP might pay from profits earned down the line, but from the construction phase. So he and his fellow trustees began handing out the Crédit Mobilier profits to none other than themselves, as UP stock- and bondholders. On January 4, 1868, the dividend was 80 percent of their CM stock, paid in UP first-mortgage bonds, and 100 percent in UP stock. Then, in June, they made three distributions to CM stockholders who also held UP shares. The first distribution amounted to 40 percent in stock of the UP, amounting to $1.5 million in face value or $450,000 at the current price of $30 per share, plus 60 percent in cash, or $2.25 million. The second was 75 percent in UP bonds, worth $2,812,500. The third was a cash allotment of 30 percent, or $1,125,000.

A man holding a hundred shares of Crédit Mobilier stock, which had cost him $10,000, received in 1868 alone $9,000 in cash, $7,500 in UP bonds then selling at par, and forty shares of UP stock worth about $1,600 in cash, or a total of $18,100. Added to the earlier dividend, he received $28,200 for his $10,000 investment, or 280 percent in one year.[47]

No one could accuse Doc of thinking small. Indeed he was thinking of much more than money. Though money was nice to have, and his lever for power, he also wanted every American to know his name and his accomplishments. At forty-eight years of age, he had time to make that happen, but he knew that just making money would never get him there. He wanted a place in history. Not from politics: he was contemptuous of politicians, a feeling common to the men of the Gilded Age. Durant wanted what such contemporaries as John D. Rockefeller and Andrew Carnegie and Cornelius Vanderbilt had, or something like what Collis Huntington or Leland Stanford would have. Doc wanted, above all else, to be remembered as the Man Who Built the Union Pacific Railroad.

Doc's competition for that title was Grenville Dodge. Durant knew that Dodge had a sizable lead on him, one that perhaps could not be overcome. Dodge was the one who told Lincoln where the railroad should run, the one who had pushed Lincoln on the 1862 Pacific Railroad Bill and the 1864 revision, the one who had brought Grant and Sherman into play. Durant knew—better than anyone else, since he was the person who had insisted on bringing Dodge into the company as chief engineer—that Dodge had been indispensable. He knew in addition that Dodge was the one who had found the route out of Omaha, the route up Lodgepole Creek to Cheyenne, the route to Sherman Summit and beyond to Laramie, and then to Green River and beyond. Plus which, all the employees, from the Casement brothers, Evans, Reed, and so on down to the lowliest Irish laborer, reported to Dodge. Back in New York, or even in Boston, people might think of it as Durant's railroad, but not west of the Mississippi.

Yet, even if Doc couldn't compete with Dodge on the ground, he could send in the "interfering engineer," Silas Seymour, to fight for him. From the beginning, that had been Seymour's role, to work for Durant by second-guessing Dodge. From Omaha westward, Seymour had questioned Dodge's route and often tried to change it, primarily to add more miles, so that the UP would collect more government bonds and land grants. In most cases, Dodge was able to overrule Seymour.

On April 23, 1868, Dodge met with Doc and the UP's Dillon and Seymour at Cheyenne. They had what Dodge called "a very plain talk." Doc assured Dodge that "he had no desire to interfere with the work or delay it, but only wanted to help." For his part, Dodge vowed that "nobody could go over his work superficially and change it."

Less than two weeks later, Durant, from Fort Sanders, issued his "General Order No. 1" (a nice way for Doc, who had never been in the military, to steal a military phrase from one of the heroes of the Civil War). He took advantage of the multitude of duties that descended on Dodge, who was not only a member of Congress but also chief engineer, surveyor, the man in charge of selling the land grants, and more, duties that involved him in much travel. So Durant declared, "In order to prevent unnecessary delay in the work during the absence of the Chief Engineer from the line of the road, the consulting engineer [Seymour] is hereby invested with full power to perform all the duties pertaining to the office of acting Chief engineer and his [Seymour's] orders will be obeyed accordingly by everyone connected with the engineer department. Any orders heretofore given by the chief engineer conflicting with orders that may be given by the consulting engineer are hereby rescinded."[48]

Seymour had told Durant that Dodge's line from Green River to the Salt Lake was all wrong, that he had laid out a new one and it was much better, and longer. That was one of the causes of General Order No. 1. But more important was Durant's desire to be the man who built the railroad.

This, and other disputes between the vice-president and the chief engineer, came to a head. On July 26, the Republican nominee for the presidency, General Ulysses S. Grant, along with Generals Sherman and Sheridan and others, including Durant, was going to be in Fort Sanders. Dodge had been in Salt Lake City when he received word that he too was expected. He took a chartered stagecoach to the UP's end of track, then a train to Laramie, arriving on July 25. Grant was there as part of a campaign tour whose purpose was to shake the hands of as many Union veterans as possible. Sherman, who was with him, wrote his brother the senator, "Of course Grant will be elected. I have just traveled with him for two weeks, and the curiosity to see him exhausted his and my patience."[49]

Dodge took Grant, Sherman, Sheridan, and the other generals to the end of track, then at Benton, 124 miles beyond Fort Sanders and Laramie. In his own words, he "took great pains on this trip to post them thoroughly about everything connected with the Union Pacific." What an opportunity for a reporter! Or, come to that, for a tape recorder! But neither was there. Still, one can imagine General Dodge, the top railroad man in the Union Army, the man on whom Grant, Sherman, Sheridan, not to mention Lincoln had relied to keep the trains running or to lay new track for them, telling his confederates about the progress and prospects for the longest railroad in the world. And one can imagine how hard the generals listened, the questions they asked, and how impressed they were.

At one point Dodge declared that he was ready to quit his job if Durant, Seymour, or anyone else changed his final location. Grant heard him, thought for a moment, then exacted a personal promise from Dodge that he would not resign until the railroad was finished.[50]

The men rode the train back to Fort Sanders. July 26 was a baking-hot day. At the Officers' Club at the fort, a big log bungalow, the generals met with Durant and Seymour. Durant took the floor. He was bold enough to attack Dodge, telling Grant and the others that Dodge had selected extravagant routes, wasted precious time and money on useless surveys, ignored the sound judgment of Silas Seymour, was about to by-pass Salt Lake City, had neglected his congressional duties, and more.

Grant turned to Dodge. "What will you do about it?" he asked.

"Just this," Dodge answered. "If Durant, or anybody connected with the Union Pacific, or anybody connected with the government, changes my lines, I'll quit the road."

There was a tense, but momentary, hush. Then Grant spoke. "The Government expects this railroad to be finished," he declared, speaking as if his election was assured. Then he turned to Dodge. "The Government expects you to remain with the road as its Chief Engineer until it is completed," he said.

Doc Durant took it all in. He pulled at his goatee, then managed to mumble, "I withdraw my objections. Of course we all want Dodge to stay with the road."[51]

Three days later, after traveling from Fort Sanders to Omaha on the UP, Dodge entertained Grant, Sherman, and Sheridan in his house in Council Bluffs. They talked about the war, and the coming election, and of course about Durant and the UP. Dodge managed to get in some digs against the CP.

The showdown at Fort Sanders has gone into the history books as decisive, but Dodge was not yet clear of Durant. The vice-president fired off from New York a series of telegrams to the men in the field. He wanted more speed. To Reed: "Work day and night. . . . Increase track-laying to 4 miles a day." To Evans: "Notify Casement that 16,000 feet of track per day won't do." To Casement: "What prevents your doing 5 miles per day."

On August 8, Dodge wrote Ames, president of the UP, that Seymour was still in command on the line while Durant controlled company headquarters in New York. He charged that Durant's orders were "to skin and skip everything for the purpose of getting track down, & your temporary Bridges will now hardly stand to get trains over them."[52] Meanwhile, Seymour was trying to ruin "the finest location *that was ever made*" with his excessive grades and curvature. And he warned, "Somebody will have to answer for the *swindle*. I doubt whether a mile of Road will be accepted, with such a location."[53]

DESPITE all the harassment, the Casement brothers and the men under them continued to move west. The undulating double row of glistening rails stretched on, on, on. Every twenty miles or so the Casements laid a side track. One of their workers said, "There we sorted material for the front and our engine went back to bring up material needed at the front. Then it would go back to the end of track and throw off iron, ties, spikes and bridge timbers on both sides of the track." The side tracks were filled with supply trains bearing hundreds of tons of iron and thousands of ties.

The last terminal base, by late summer well past Rawlins, was brimming with riotous life, grotesque with makeshift shacks and portable buildings. There too was the Casements' takedown warehouse with dining room. Toward the end of track, the construction trains waited their turn, among the dining cars, the bunk cars, the combined kitchen, stores car, and office car, each eighty feet long. Among them there was, sometimes, the Lincoln Car, for Durant or other notables.

At the end of track, Casement directed the work of a thousand and more men. The track layers were the elite of the force, experts in their job, selected by the Casements for their physical strength, endurance, coordination, and ability to learn. The supply teams, three or four hundred of them, plodded back and forth along the grade, covered with desert dust, red with pulverized granite, white with soda and alkali, blue with Irish dudeens. The line of wagons toiling on, bearing ties, hay, and other supplies up the interminable grade, stretched out. On the grade, ahead of the track layers, tiny antlike figures delving, plowing, scaling, cursing as they finished the grade. Scattered throughout there were three hundred or more African Americans, former slaves. The *Salt Lake Daily Reporter* noted that, out in the Wyoming desert, "as the successive gangs of graders advance in this direction they close together until it seems as if every inch of ground was covered with men, and that there would be no room for any more."[54]

Everyone worked fast, at top speed, partly because that was what Dodge, Durant, and the Casements wanted, partly to stay ahead of the track layers or the telegraph men or to keep up with the crews making the bridges, or to satisfy an eager public and to realize the full utility of the road once finished, or just to get the hell out of that infernal desert, or most of all to beat their rivals on the CP. But, no matter how fast they went, they did their best. By 1868, for example, there were almost no cottonwood ties, and the crews were rapidly replacing existing ones.

By the end of the summer of 1868, the *New York Tribune* asserted that the railroad project was, and would continue to be for years to come, "the great absorbing fact of the West."[55]

For sure it drew the reporters. Durant put out a call for them to come see for themselves, and that summer they did so, in a party headed by Charles A. Dana of the *New York Sun*. They dubbed themselves the Rocky Mountain Press Club. It was a rousing success, and led to two months of good stories as well as increased sales of UP stocks and bonds. A few weeks after their tour, Schuyler Colfax, Grant's running mate, toured the road. After him came a band of professors from Yale. They were all impressed, although Jack Casement complained that the visitors were "a great nuisance to the work." But his men laid four miles of track in one day, which mightily impressed the professors. They, like everyone else in America—or, indeed, the world—had never seen anything like it.[56]

In August 1868, the track was thirty miles past the bridge over the North Platte River, almost seven hundred miles from Omaha. On September 21, the end of track was just outside Green River.* In a few days, the town had become another Hell on Wheels. A month later, it had been left behind. From July 21 to October 20, seventy-eight working days excluding Sundays, the Casement crews had laid 181 miles of track, an average of 2.3 miles per day. They often did three miles, sometimes five, and once (October 26, 1868) set a record of almost eight miles in one day, for which they got triple pay. They did all this in altitude as high as most mountains, in scorching sun or freezing nights, with ill-tasting water. Durant was so pleased he wired the news of eight miles in one day to Oliver Ames, declaring that the feat "has the *ring* of work in it" and was "the achievement of the year."[57]

A reporter for the *Western Railroad Gazette* told how it was done through a "barren alkali desert, with nothing but distant mountains to invite the eye or cheer the hope." He wrote that, in the process of laying track, "there is no limit to its speed except the ability of the road to bring up the ties and rails. For the track laying a picked force of about four hundred men are employed." The ties were carried ahead a mile or two from the supply train by horse-drawn wagons and laid by a special team. The rails were brought forward "to the very edge. Two are dropped to their

---

* Professor John Wesley Powell, on his way to his epic journey of exploration down the Colorado River, arranged to take the UP from Omaha to Green River. There he put into the river and descended to the Colorado.

places, the car pulled by a trained horse over them, and two more dropped, and so on, while the moment they fall men adjust them exactly, others follow with spikes and rivets and others still with shovels and bars to level and straighten the whole work." When the car was empty it was tipped off the track and sent back for another load while a fresh one came to the front. And so it went, without pause.[58]

More good news followed. Secretary Browning had appointed a three-man Special Commission to look at the charges of scandal and defects in construction, charges that were widespread and widely believed. But on November 23, the commission, composed of Brigadier General Gouverneur K. Warren, Jacob Blickensderfer, and James Barnes, reported that the line had been "well constructed." The members unanimously agreed that Dodge had picked "the most favorable passes on the continent" along with "favorable alignment unsurpassed by any other railway line." Further, "so few mistakes were made and so few defects exist" as to be "a matter of surprise." Overall, "the country had reason to congratulate itself that this great work of national importance is so rapidly approaching completion under such favorable auspices."[59]

In early November, the end of track was 890 miles west of Omaha. Another Hell on Wheels was born, Bear River City. It was typical. Brigham Young assured the shocked Mormons that it wouldn't last long. Bear River City was just short of the Wyoming-Utah state line, on the Bear River, on the eastern side of the Wasatch Range. Meanwhile, Jack Casement reported that he was "straining every nerve to get into Salt Lake Valley before the heavy snows fall. Thirty more days of good weather will let us do it."[60]

AT the other end of the line, at Omaha, the UP was also moving ahead in giant strides. In late November, the *Western Railroad Gazette* reported, "The first corps of workmen have arrived for building the great Union Pacific Railroad Bridge." The contractor was L. B. Boomer of Chicago, who had built so many of the UP's bridges and was generally thought to be one of the best (if not *the* best) in the country at his job. The location would be from Council Bluffs to Omaha. When it was finished, it was hoped within a year, and the UP had hooked up with the CP (at a point yet to be determined), there would be a continuous line of rails running from the Atlantic to the Pacific. The bridge work, the *Gazette* said, would "be prosecuted with all the energy which money, men and skill can impart to it." The bridge would be "an immense structure" and would cost about $2 million.[61]

SUCH progress alarmed the men of the CP. Collis Huntington was the only man among the Big Four who had met Durant, and in 1868 he had sent his appraisal to Mark Hopkins: "You have no ordinary man working against you. Durant is a man of wonderful energy, in fact reckless in his energy, and it looks to me now as though he would get to Salt Lake before we can."[62]

That was certainly accurate. But even as the Crédit Mobilier paid out nearly 300 percent in one year's dividend, the UP was desperate for cash. "Money is awful tight and we have large amts to pay," Oliver Ames moaned. "We hope to get through but things look Blue." To Durant he wrote, "The demands for money are perfectly frightful." Undaunted, the trustees of the Crédit Mobilier on December 29 declared a 200 percent dividend payable in UP stock, even as Ames ordered Durant to "cut off all useless expense and economize everywhere." Ames took the sting out of his message with the qualifying phrase "where it will not delay work."[63]

Durant was unfazed. He was determined to beat the CP not only to Ogden but beyond, at least to Humboldt Wells if not farther west. To do that, he needed to get the UP track through Echo Canyon, Utah, down to Ogden and, he hoped, beyond, before the winter froze the ground and covered it with snow. To that end, on December 18 he sent a telegram to Casement: "How fast are you sending men to head of Echo? We want 2,000 as soon as can be had."[64]

The race was into its final stretch. The men working for the UP and for the CP, from the top on down, were in sight of each other. In late September 1868, Frank Gilbert sent a dispatch to his newspaper, the *Salt Lake Daily Reporter*, stating that General Dodge had just made a trip from Promontory to Humboldt Wells. In the area between the north end of the Salt Lake and Humboldt Wells, the UP had "four locating parties, and two construction parties of engineers, while the Central Pacific Company also have six parties of engineers between the same points. We understand that the lines of the two companies are being run nearly parallel, and everything now seems to indicate that there will be two grades if not two roads, between the Lake and the Wells."[65]

Chapter Thirteen

Brigham Young and the Mormons Make the Grade 1868

*H*E was a man noted for his firmness, intelligence, fairness, decisiveness, good looks, and ability to put the long-term interests of those in his charge ahead of their short-term gain. Like the top politicians, he had a remarkable memory for facts and figures, geography, who owed what favors or money to whom, the names of his competitors and his followers and their wives. He knew who had taken what position on this or that issue, and when, and what his own position had been.

That these are the qualities of a leader needs no elaboration. He was the perfect man to say to his brethren, when they were a thousand miles away from any settlement, "This is the place," and make it into a garden. His people said to him that they were ready to follow him wherever he chose to lead. Had it not been for his generally feared or despised religion, he quite possibly might have been a president of the United States, and, depending on the time, a good or even a great one. As it was, he founded Salt Lake City and made it and his Mormon religion into a great city and religion. In the process, he played a major role in building the UP and the CP.

Brigham Young was a six-foot, two-hundred-pound individual, quite tall and heavyset by mid-nineteenth-century standards. He had a commanding presence. The *New York Tribune*'s reporter Bert Richardson described him as someone who had "secretive eyes, an eagle nose, and a mouth that shuts like a vise, indicating tremendous firmness."[1]

He had become head of the Mormon church when its founder, Joseph Smith, was assassinated, and he led the faithful members to near Council Bluffs, Iowa, in 1846. From that point, where Grenville Dodge later lived and Lincoln visited in 1859, Young had led the first party up the Platte River Valley, then through what became Wyoming and on to the Salt Lake, where he founded the city.

In 1863, in the middle of the Civil War, right after the UP was founded, Doc Durant communicated with Young about the best route across America. Young sent one of his many sons, Joseph A. Young, with a party of Mormons, to do some surveys. So eager was Young to have a railway come to Salt Lake City that he paid the expenses of the party. Joseph Young reported on a number of routes, but the one he liked best, and the one eventually picked by Dodge, was up Weber Canyon and then Echo Creek. When Samuel Reed came to check this out the next year, 1864, he reported that the line was much more favorable than had been anticipated.[2] Brigham Young was thus involved from the beginning with the route to be followed by the Union Pacific. He was also one of the original shareholders. He bought five shares and, wonder of wonders, actually paid in full for them. So from the first he had been an enthusiastic promoter.

But there was a widespread rumor among the "Gentiles" (as Mormons called non-Mormons) that Young's opposition to commercial intercourse with outsiders, along with his disapproval of efforts to mine precious metals in Utah, made him a railroad opponent. That was the opposite of the truth. According to a contemporary Mormon historian, during the original Mormon crossing of the plains to Salt Lake Valley, Young had pointed to where the railroad tracks would one day run. In 1852, he had signed a memorial to Congress asking for a transcontinental railroad. In a December 1853 letter to Congress, he remarked, of the prospective road, "Pass where it will, we cannot fail to be benefitted by it." He became a friend of Samuel Reed, and helped the UP do its surveys, and referred to the telegraph and the railroad as the two "great discoveries of our age." In January 1866, he told the Utah legislature that the want of a railroad was "sensibly felt" and that its completion was "to be viewed as very desirable."[3]

In August 1866, he wrote to Reed to congratulate the UP. "We watch its progress Westward with great interest," he said in his telegram, "as every mile of track which is laid lessens the weary distance which stretches on every side of us." Dodge sent Young a query about the route.

Young replied that it was "impracticable" to run a line through the desert in the winter. Dodge had asked what had happened to the camels Jefferson Davis had imported when he was secretary of war, hoping to use them as pack animals for the construction. "There are no camels here," Young replied (they had gone wild and were living in New Mexico), but he would do whatever he could to help the railroad.[4]

In 1867, as the railroad got closer to Salt Lake City, Young said, "This gigantic work will increase intercourse, and it is to be hoped, soften prejudices, and bind the country together."[5]

A s the head of the church and the power behind politics in a state that was heavily Mormon, Young had nothing to fear, as he well knew. If it was not true that nothing happened in Utah until Young had given it his blessing, it almost was. He had, for example, long emphasized the value of a community that combined agriculture with manufacturing. He wanted commodities made at home, and for the most part got them. He urged his people to strive for independence, and they did.

As a religious leader he had a gift. He sent his disciples out to recruit, especially in England. He urged the converts to come to Utah to participate with the community of Saints in a full life, and they did. In 1867 alone, for example, some five thousand adults came to Zion, mainly from England. By that time, they could ride from New York City to Omaha for $25 for each adult, and from Omaha to North Platte for $10. There Young had wagons pulled by oxen waiting for them (in 1868, when the UP track ran past Laramie, a record number of wagons, 534, were sent forward from Utah to bring them in). Young estimated the total cost per immigrant from Liverpool to the UP's rail terminus to be $65, much lower than the cost of crossing the Plains before the railroad.[6]

Besides bringing in converted immigrants at the lowest price, the railroad made it possible for Utah residents to go back east to shop, buy, visit, convert others. In addition, they could import heavy or difficult-to-make manufactured goods and thereby lower their price too. In this they were just like Californians, or for that matter anyone living west of the Missouri River. And they could ship their products to a ready, indeed eager, market. In 1867 alone, for example, the people of Utah harvested eighty thousand acres of cereal crops, along with seven thousand acres of root crops, and a thousand acres of orchard produce.

So Young was keenly aware of the benefits the railroad would bring his people. In February 1868, he told the legislature that, if all went well, within two years "the solitude of our mountain fastness will be broken by the shrill snort of the iron horse." But although he clearly wanted the road and as soon as possible, critics back east of the Missouri River predicted that the coming of the railroad to Utah would bring a much-desired end to the Mormon way of life—namely, polygamy. In the spring of 1868, the *Chicago Republican* had a lead editorial entitled "Mormonism Doomed." The newspaper said the country would soon see that "happy time" when polygamy was gone from the land, thanks to the railroad, which would bring in Gentiles who would soon "overflow and engulf Utah slowly and surely." The *Deseret News*, commenting on the editorial, thought it cheeky if not worse for a Chicago paper to teach morality to the citizens of Salt Lake City. Like Young, the editor of the *Deseret News* had no fear of the outside world, and was ready to welcome it.[7]

REASONS to welcome the railroad went beyond getting converted immigrants to Salt Lake City faster and cheaper, beyond importing bulky manufactured goods at less cost, beyond shipping agricultural products to market, beyond making it possible for Utah residents to pay visits to family and friends back east. There was, in addition, the hope that when regular train service east and west was inaugurated Salt Lake City would become a major tourist center.* There were other factors, but most of all there were two needs that came together. The lack of circulating medium (cash money) in Utah meant that the Mormons badly needed work that would be paid for and the cash that went with it, and the lack of labor in the West meant that the UP and the CP badly needed workers.

In the summer of 1867, Brigham Young, Jr., and his family returned from a trip to Europe. In Chicago, at the end of July, some officials of the UP invited him to ride with them to the end of track. They included Sidney Dillon, a director and head of the Crédit Mobilier, Senator John Sherman, and investor Jacob Cox, governor of Ohio, so naturally Young, Jr., accepted. Of course they talked while riding the rails, and Young

---

* The hope was realized. In the first summer of regular service, more visitors stopped at Salt Lake City during the travel months than at any time since its founding.

noted in his diary that Dillon "wants our assistance in laying out the U.P.R.R. and building the road." Sherman and the others "were anxious to awaken a real interest in the minds of our people to push this railroad through our Territory."[8] No agreements were reached, or even broached, but a positive contact had been made.

BY the spring of 1868, the UP was beginning its push across Wyoming while its surveyors were well into Utah and even beyond. The track had reached Evanston (named for UP engineer and surveyor Evans), on the edge of the Utah border, which had been picked by Dodge as a division point for the railroad. The UP's need for competent, trustworthy workers was critical. Without them, the company might as well give up on any thought of beating the CP to the Salt Lake. For the Mormons, meanwhile, with lots of young men who were eager for work and desperately short of money, the spring brought with it another plague of grasshoppers. The insects were consuming the newly planted crops.

On May 6, 1868, Durant sent a telegram from Fort Sanders to Young in Salt Lake City. With that telegram, the Doctor saved himself and the company from the ignominy of losing the race so badly as to become an object of derision. Of all the countless things Durant did for and against himself and the UP, for all the wonders he wrought, for all his meddling and interference and mistakes, nothing could match this telegram. Doc knew whom he needed and how much he needed them and he didn't care what it cost. He was willing, even eager, to bet all in order to win all. Not that he ever had any intention of paying up on the debt he encountered when his bet was taken.

The telegram to Young began, "Are you disposed to take contract for a portion or all our grading between head of Echo Canyon and Salt Lake if so please name price per cubic yard." The UP would provide the Mormons with "powder, steel and tools as you require at cost and transportation. Work to be done this season." If Young's reply was affirmative, Doc said he would send Reed and Seymour to Salt Lake City to arrange details, "so that work may be commenced at once."[9]

A remarkable offer. Young could name his price and set other conditions. What Durant wanted was work, to be started "at once." Doc was leading one of the two biggest corporations in the United States. He was engaged in a construction campaign that had no parallel. Nothing built in America—or, indeed, in the world—had ever been done on such a scale. Furthermore, the race with the CP was like a war. Every effort by Durant and the UP bosses, as every effort by Huntington and the other CP bosses, was bent to winning. Neither the directors nor those who worked for them or, come to that, those who put up the money cared what it cost. Win now, pay later, was the motto, just as it had been for the North in the Civil War.

Young answered Durant's telegram within an hour of its receipt. Yes, he said.[10]

Seymour and Reed went straight to Salt Lake City and negotiated. Young agreed that the Mormons would grade from the head of Echo Canyon toward the Salt Lake (some fifty-four miles). Work was to commence in ten days and be completed by November 1. The UP would carry men, teams, and tools from Omaha for free, and provide powder, steel, shovels, picks, sledges, wheelbarrows, scrapers, crowbars, and other necessary tools at cost plus freight charges.

The Mormons would receive 30 cents a cubic yard for excavations when the earth was hauled less than two hundred feet away, and 50 cents for longer hauls. Cuts made through hard materials were scaled at higher prices. Tunneling was $15 a yard. The UP would pay labor costs on a monthly basis (with 80 percent paid on the 20th of each month). Young wanted $2 and up per day per worker, depending on their talents.

The contract was drawn, and on May 19, Young gave Seymour and Reed a letter. In it he said he had "carefully examined the figures you are accustomed to giving to grading and masonry work" and was ready to sign if the UP would add 10 percent to the figures, but only if the UP was prepared to give him the contract for building the grade from the mouth of Weber Canyon around the Salt Lake, whether the railroad went south or north. He also wanted Reed to make a depot at the mouth of Echo Canyon to handle the supplies. In return, he promised as many as five thousand men, all ready to take orders and go to work.[11]

The contract was signed. Young put notices in the two Salt Lake City newspapers (the *Daily Reporter* and the *Deseret News*) calling on all the men who wanted work to report to three of his sons, who were ready to hire. Commenting on a surplus of labor in and around the city, caused mainly by the grasshopper infestation, Young said it was a godsend that the Mormons could turn a surplus of labor into money. The *Deseret News* stressed that Mormon boys could now find work close to home, and another commentator remarked that the contract would "obviate the necessity of some few thousand strangers being brought here, to mix and interfere with the settlers, of that class of men who take pleasure in making disturbance wherever they go."[12] Some few days later, four thousand men had responded to the call. However, rumor had it that as many as ten thousand would be needed, and the Mormons continued to show up.

They came from the farms around the Salt Lake. Orson Hyde of Springtown, Utah, wrote Young on May 27, 1868: "Much of our wheat in this settlement is eaten off by the grasshoppers; consequently, several are ready to go to work on the rail road." From Spring City Ward, Andrew Jenson wrote, "Crops destroyed by grasshoppers and people to R[ail] R[oad]." Lewis Barney wrote that the "country was full of grasshoppers and every thing devoured by them and not a morsel of bread to be had to sustain life. Consequently [I went] to work for the railroad." A good thing too, for Barney was cutting timber for ties and bridges and "I cleared 500 dollars through the summer."[13]

Young sent a telegram to Reed (then at the UP's end of track in Wyoming) asking him to send "at your earliest convenience" such additional supplies "as your judgment may deem necessary for putting a large force of hands at work at once, for I am anxious to complete the work in time, and the days are passing."[14] They were burning daylight, wasting time, and he wanted to get going.

On May 31, from Weber Canyon, Reed sent a telegram to Durant demanding "tools for five thousand men from Salt Lake Valley, men ready to commence work as soon as tools are received."[15] A week later, the first group of westbound Mormon converts from Liverpool came to New York and got on the train; they arrived in Wyoming before June was out. By then another group was en route, with yet another to follow. The total emigration from Europe for Salt Lake City in 1868 was 3,232, mainly from Great Britain, and nearly all ready to go to work.[16]

YOUNG had his critics, although few lived in Utah. In the East, they charged that Young was favoring his sons and closest associates as subcontractors, that he was getting a tithe from every laborer, supposedly for the Mormon church but, as one editor of a newspaper knew, that was "just another name for Brigham Young," who was otherwise enriching himself. The *Cincinnati Commercial* charged that, whereas Young's contract called for 30 cents per yard for work done, he gave only 27 cents to his subcontractors "and the Prophet [Young] pockets the odd million." The *Cheyenne Daily Leader* on June 15, 1868, charged that the contract between Young and the UP was "outright slavery." It claimed that Young called for manpower from each Mormon settlement according to its population, and the draftees had to work at wages set by Young. Further, the *Leader* believed the UP had denied work to Wyoming residents because it was "the settled policy of the railroad company to give large contracts to Brigham."[17]

That was not true. Although at the time there was a widely held impression that Young would undertake all the grading in Utah for the UP, actually the contract for the work for fifty miles east of Echo Canyon, in the direction of Wyoming, was held by Joseph Nounan and Company, a Gentile firm. With Nounan as with Young, there were misunderstandings and miscalculations in the contract, and a good deal of acrimony resulted between the contractors and the railroads. This was usually the case in the construction of railroads at the time.[18]

Young had three of his sons—Joseph, Brigham, Jr., and John W.—and Bishop John Sharp hiring and directing the men. Sharp, close to Young, was also his lawyer, and would remain a major Utah railroad leader for decades. Together Joseph Young and Sharp became associated in a firm known as Sharp & Young that took on grading contracts and the boring of several tunnels. The partners soon had fourteen hundred men working for them in Echo Canyon, and working well. Young said they improved rapidly because "they have got used to the labor."[19]

In early June, Young was the principal speaker at a mass meeting in the new Tabernacle in Salt Lake City. He said he had always wanted the railroad and that the Mormons would help to build it. One of his followers wrote, "We felt much better after he did that; we feared he might not be willing and we'd never have a road." Young also said he expected the line to run through the city, for which the *Cheyenne Daily Leader* jumped on him. The newspaper pointed out that the line north of the city would be sixty or seventy miles shorter, but it admitted that Young would probably have his way, because "there is more political strength and influence united in him than in any other one person in America."[20]

Well, perhaps, sometimes, in some places, but not always even in Utah. Early that summer, Dodge came to Salt Lake City. Young knew the UP's workings well enough to know that, though Durant had considerable power, and Reed had power, and there were other men who had to be dealt with, in the end it was Dodge who got what he wanted. Clearly, wherever Dodge sat was the head of the table. He was a man of such strong personality that even such men as Durant gave way—and even such men as Young.

On this occasion, Dodge had come to tell Young that the UP was going to go around the north end of the lake and would run not through Salt Lake City but, rather, through Ogden. Though Young put what Dodge called great pressure on him to go south instead of north, Dodge held firm. His own surveys and those of others had convinced him that north was the best way to go.

Young would not quit, not yet. According to Dodge, "He even went so far as to deliver in the Tabernacle a great sermon denouncing me, and stating a road could not be built or run without the aid of the Mormons."[21] Young then approached the CP to accept the southern route, but to no avail, for their surveyors had come to the same conclusion as Dodge.

Dodge stood firm. He told Young that the Mormons would have to build their own spur line to Ogden if they wanted rail service in Salt Lake City. Young finally, unwillingly, but as gracefully as he could, accepted the decision. A few weeks later, in another Tabernacle sermon, Young said that wherever the railroad went around Salt Lake, "it is all right because God rules and He will have things as He pleases. We can act, but He will over-rule."[22]

At the beginning of June, the Mormons were at work. The *Deseret News* exclaimed, "We live in a wonderful age." Admittedly, the railroad would bring in Gentiles, but it would also carry them out.[23] Dodge took one look and from then on he couldn't have enough Mormons working for the UP. They were, he said, teetotalers to the last man, tolerated no gambling, were quiet and law-abiding, said grace devoutly at meals, and concluded each day's labor with communal prayers and songs.

One of their songs, a favorite of Dodge's, written by James Crane, a Mormon railroad grader, ran:

> At the head of great Echo
> The railway's begun
> The Mormons are cutting
> And grading like fun.

They say they'll stick to it
Till it is complete,
When friends and relations
They're longing to meet.[24]

By June 9, they had broken ground for the masonry and grade at Devil's Gate in Weber Canyon. John Sharp could put only eighty men to work there. He could set no more at the job because the defile in which the men worked was so narrow it couldn't hold any more. Once he was clear of Devil's Gate, he used as many as five hundred men on a single job. Through the canyon, Mormon gangs worked as hard and as faithfully as did the Chinese for the CP. They cut timber for bridges and ties, or made grade, or built bridges, or dug tunnels, and more.

The July 22, 1868, *Deseret News* said, "A birds-eye view of the railroad camps in Echo Canyon would disclose to the beholder a little world of concerted industry unparalleled." Historian Clarence Reeder, in his dissertation on Utah railroads, summarized the Mormon construction efforts: "A people working together in harmony under the guidance of their religious leaders to accomplish a temporal task which they treated as though it were divinely inspired."[25]

Samuel Schill was a twelve-year-old that summer. His dad was a teamster hauling supplies for the UP. In June, when the Weber River was high and running very fast, someone asked young Sam if he could swim. Sure, was the answer. Well, then, swim the river, and while you are at it carry over this rope to the engineering party on the other side. The engineers need it to start establishing a ferry here.

Sam did it, for 50 cents. That was the first money he had ever earned. He earned more working for the railroad, by hauling ties cut by his dad down to the roadbed.

At night, he later recalled, he would sit around the campfire with the grown-ups, singing such songs as:

Hurrah, hurrah, the railroad's begun.
Three cheers for the contractor, his name Brigham Young.
Hurrah, hurrah, we are faithful and true
And if we stick to it, it's bound to go through.[26]

• • •

287

*H*OW good were these Mormons in a job that began with daylight and lasted until dusk, or sometimes went through the night? The authoritative voice is that of Hubert Howe Bancroft in his 1890 history of Utah: "It was acknowledged by all railroad men that nowhere on the line could the grading compare in completeness and finish with the work done by the people of Utah."[27]

In addition to grades and bridges, the Mormons and other UP workers had to drive tunnels. All together the UP had four tunnels. One was in Wyoming, at Mary's Creek, in the Rattlesnake Hills, a short one of 215 feet, and straight. It was driven through brown sandstone that had to be timbered. The second tunnel was at the head of Echo Canyon. At 772 feet, it was the longest on the line, with long cuts leading to it. The tunnel was driven through weak clay rock that required it to be lined with timber. Work started in July 1868, but it was not finished until May 1869. The railroad ran a temporary track eight miles in length around it. Tunnels 3 and 4 were in Echo Canyon, three-quarters of a mile apart, some twenty-five miles from Ogden. Tunnel 3, on a curve, was 508 feet long, driven through a sharp spur of black limestone and dark-blue quartzite. Begun in September 1868, it was completed in April 1869. Tunnel 4, also on a curve, was 297 feet long, and it was completed by January 1869. In all of these tunnels, the UP gangs used nitroglycerin. No one protested. It was obvious to everyone working on the railroad that the need for speed was paramount, if the race was to be won.

The several crossings of the Weber River were made with trestles. These were temporary structures. In the judgment of historian John Debo Galloway, in his book *The First Transcontinental Railroad*—published in 1950 and still a definitive work—"The use of the temporary structures on the rapid advance westward was fully justified by the desire to get the road into operation, since the bridges serve the purpose for which they were erected. Permanent stone and masonry work could be added later. The procedure that was followed by the Union Pacific in its original construction was entirely proper for a railroad building into a new territory."[28]

*T*HE CP watched, worried, and acted. In mid-1868, the CP's end of track was more than five hundred miles west of Echo Summit, but it was there that Stanford and the other members of the Big Four wanted to go. They were determined to begin the Utah grading at once, and in the process to use the best workforce they could possibly get, the Mormons. So, in the first week in June, Stanford set out by rail and stage for Salt Lake City. But Seymour and Reed had beat him there, and Reed had Brigham Young's friendship, and a contract with him. Young told Stanford he had all he could do at present to complete the work he had taken on for the UP. After that was done, he intended to make new contracts with Reed, which would take the UP one or two hundred miles west of Salt Lake City.[29]

Stanford went into action. At first he found Young to be "cold and close," but he managed to break down the defenses. Young wanted a railroad to come through his city, but Stanford "found good reasons why they [the Mormons] would be most benefitted by the northern route." He told Hopkins to "tell Charley [Crocker] to double his energy, and do what is necessary to secure what labor is required to push the road to its utmost. Anything less will end in defeat." Shaken by the experience of dealing with Young, Stanford confessed to Hopkins, "It has been pretty difficult navigating here, and it requires care now to avoid getting into breakers, which are devilish close, but I think I see the way out."[30]

When Stanford asked Young what he would want for his workers, Young replied that the supplies he required were "flour, beef, bacon, beans, dried fruit, molasses, sugar, small quantities of rice and hospital supplies, tents or lumber for quarters, short-handled shovels, assorted picks, medium and breaking plows, scrapers, wheel-barrows and plank, carts and harness."[31] To Stanford that sounded reasonable, a lot more reasonable than the food the CP had to provide the Chinese.

Stanford wanted Young to agree to a contract for grading west of the mouth of the Weber River, but the Mormon leader wouldn't do it. Finally, Young agreed, or at least seemed to agree, to send workers all the way to Humboldt Wells to do grading toward the east. Stanford in any case was more interested in the area just north of Salt Lake City. On July 28, he sent a telegram to Young: "We want to let you a contract for grading two hundred miles west from Weber Canyon. Would you prefer contract to proposition I made?"

Young wired back the next day that when his work for the UP was done he was ready to make a contract "upon the proposition you made, but some one must be sent here [Stanford had returned to California] authorized to contract, and the work must be ready and kept ready, that hands may not be hindered from time work begins."[32]

Like Dodge, Reed, and others, Stanford was learning what a shrewd, practical businessman Young was. On August 10, Young told Stanford by telegram that the CP's delays and problems with the UP had "caused such a scattering of our surplus laborers that I am unable to make a contract. Soon after you were here great numbers were inquiring for work west, but the delays have been such that they are now out of reach. I am unable to give any encouragement at present."[33]

Young did try. On September 5, he sent a telegraph to "all the Bishops south of this City," in which he asked them "to send me all the help you possibly can, as quick as possible, to work on the railroad. We wish to rush it through to Monument Point. . . . The pay will be sure, and in money at liberal rates."[34]

THE contract with the CP was not made that summer, or even in the early fall. Durant had meanwhile sent some of his toughest Irish graders all the way out to Humboldt Wells to begin grading west. "Durant was going to the Pacific Ocean, I believe," Huntington later said. "He started for there, at any rate."[35] But in November, Stanford, by then back in Salt Lake City, met Durant, who was also there to put pressure on Young. "We had general talk in the main," Stanford told Hopkins. On November 9, 1868, however, Stanford finally managed to get Young to agree to a contract calling on the Mormons to build from Ogden west to Monument Point, north of Salt Lake.

The subcontractor was the Mormon company of Benson, Farr & West. Brigham Young had a quarter-interest in the firm. The company had already built a hundred miles west from Monument Point. The partners were bishops in the Mormon church and at the top of Mormon society: Ezra Taft Benson was a member of Young's original Council of Twelve (and great-grandfather of a future secretary of agriculture); Lorin Farr was mayor of Ogden; Chauncey West was a Mormon bishop.

Another Mormon bishop, John Sharp of Sharp & Young, at that moment grading west for the UP, was practically alongside the Benson, Farr & West workers. Durant told Stanford, "If we hired his men, he could play the same game."[36] A bidding war began, as each side tried to hire laborers away from the other. This drove the wages up drastically, but the competitors kept at it.

Threats and counterthreats, bluffs and actions aside, Benson, Farr &

West were making progress on the CP roadbed between Ogden and Monument. So were the UP workers. The two railroads were now grading within a stone's throw of each other for much of the long distance between the mouth of Weber Canyon and Humboldt Wells. The graders were even working at night, in the desert country north of the Salt Lake, by the light of big bonfires of sagebrush. It was madness, but it was done, and continued to be done.

Beginning November 1, Stanford made his headquarters in Salt Lake City. Among other objectives, he wanted to spy on the UP. He had Lewis Clement with him; Acting Chief Engineer Montague had put Clement in charge in Utah, along with Consulting Engineer George Gray. The three men went out to inspect the preliminary line run by Butler Ives in 1867. They agreed that the line required an eight-hundred-foot tunnel through solid limestone that would cost $75,000 to blast and would delay track laying in the home stretch of the race. A new line laid out at the expense of alignment in order to avoid the tunnel would require a fill of ten thousand yards of earth, with rock cuts leading up to it that would consume more than fifteen hundred kegs of black powder. Stanford ordered it done anyway.

Stanford also wanted to convince his Mormon contractors to start grading toward Monument Point as soon as they completed the hundred miles to the west of that place that they had contracted to do. They expected to be finished in about a month. Stanford wanted them to start the new grading in Ogden, working west toward Monument Point. His thought, apparently, was to establish Ogden as the meeting point for the two railroads. Congress had not yet set the place, and others, including his own partners plus Durant and the other big shots from the UP, had other plans.

By the next month, December 1868, the CP was in apparent control of a line from Monument Point to Ogden. It had finished about two-thirds of its grading, although blasting and filling at Promontory went slowly. The contractors, Benson, Farr & West, gave many excuses, but Stanford "started Brigham after them," and they began to work faster.[37]

One of the Big Four who had other plans was Huntington, who was obstinately in favor of the CP's going as far east as Echo Summit and meeting the UP there (the UP had graded from the summit west through most of Echo Canyon, thanks to the Mormons, but its track was still in Wyoming in 1868). Stanford saw nothing to be gained by parallel grading in Echo Canyon, but still he wished all the bad luck in the world on the UP. "One good storm," he wrote Hopkins on December 10, "would settle the question of their coming through the Weber Canyon this winter."[38]

*T*HE use of codes and of code-breaking goes back to the beginning of writing. It was usually used by governments to hide what they were doing. President Thomas Jefferson had a code system used by Captain Meriwether Lewis to report on the political views of other army officers, and another for Lewis to use while exploring the Louisiana Purchase and the Northwest, in order to fool the Spanish should they happen to intercept Lewis's messages. Sometimes Civil War generals used codes, although, it must be said, not often enough (George B. McClellan's uncoded orders were captured by the Confederates before the Battle of Antietam, giving Robert E. Lee a chance to read them).

The first use of codes by businessmen to prevent detection of their doings known to this author was by the CP and the UP. It was inaugurated in 1868, just as the race between the two corporations was headed toward a climax. The purpose was to baffle any wiretapper. A reasonable fear, since all a spy had to do to find out what the opposition was up to was to tap into the telegraph line. (The UP, apparently, couldn't keep a secret; one of its engineers, F. C. Hodges, wrote to CP engineer Butler Ives telling all he knew about the UP's plans and progress. Ives sent the information on to the Big Four.)

The CP's code consisted of symbolic words. "Yelp" was Brigham Young's code name. "Riddle" stood for William Ralston, of the Bank of California. Mark Hopkins had one key to the code, now at Stanford University in his handwriting. He was the only one of the Big Four who habitually used the code. He didn't bother with it on some occasions, as in his one-word reply in 1868 to a Huntington inquiry, "No." He evidently felt that was sufficiently cryptic.[39]

The Big Four, especially Huntington and Hopkins, used codes to hide important numbers, like profits, costs, and the like, most of all totals. This may have been to hide the figures from the UP, but there is also a strong possibility that another purpose was to fool government regulators and inspectors. And it worked.

• • •

Brigham Young and the Mormons Make the Grade

MILANDO Pratt was a Mormon farmer near Ogden who had lost his crops to grasshoppers ("Great clouds of grasshoppers flew over these inter-mountain valleys and would darken the sun like a misty fog, and when night overtook them they would alight upon the ground and devour the crops whenever within their reach") and thus became a subcontractor for Benson, Farr & West. He helped make the grade to the west of Monument Point, but he still wasn't free of grasshoppers. "Those pestilential things were no respecters of places when night overtook them," he remembered, "for they would settle down upon the waters of the Great Salt Lake which pickled them in its briny waters by the hundreds of thousands of tons and then cast their carcases ashore until a great wall of these inanimate pests was formed for miles along the lake's shore." They put forth a "great stench" when the sun hit them the next morning "and cast the aroma of this slowly melting putrid wall upon the windward breezes to be wafted earthward toward our suffering camp."

Until the grasshoppers came to die, Pratt and his fellows had been taking their bath in the lake each night, "in its refreshing soothing waters." They quit doing that when the pests came, and began using kerchiefs dipped in camphor solution, which was kept on hand in the camp to battle gnats and mosquitoes. But they soon found they missed the bath so much they decided to bring into action "our railroad implements of warfare and force a gateway through the dormant remains of our insufferable common enemy." Using horses and scrapers, they forced a way to the lake through the barrier of putrid grasshoppers so that they could again enjoy "the freedom that this great inland salt sea afforded."

There being no grass around the lake, and with hay selling for $75 per ton, Pratt had to send the horses into the hills with night herders to graze. Such was the life of a Mormon grader.[40]

For engineer James Maxwell, the grasshoppers posed a special problem. First he lost a black Newfoundland dog, who could not be seen through the swarm of grasshoppers from fifty yards away. Next his train was stopped by grasshoppers. "This seems like a big story," he admitted, "but it is true and easily explained." The grasshoppers were so numerous they "covered the rails," so when he was headed up a grade, his driving wheels slipped on them. And if that seemed unbelievable, consider this: "The chickens seemed to think that they had a bonanza, but very soon they didn't care for any more grasshoppers, and crawled into the tents or wagons, anywhere at all to get shelter." A cow nearby who was pestered by the grasshoppers "would run away, whenever an opportunity was offered."[41]

WORSE than the grasshoppers was Doc Durant. Always eager to enter into a contract that would be good for the UP, he was also always slow, or unwilling, or unable to pay. Not even Brigham Young could get what he had earned. Here is a sampling of the telegrams Young sent Reed in the last half of 1868. July 31: "Men who have completed or nearly completed their jobs are anxious for their pay. When will you be here." August 5: "When will you be in this City. Answer immediately." September 22: "The men are exceedingly anxious to get their pay for day work performed last June and since."[42] None of the messages got any reply.

By October, Young warned Durant that the men were so angry many of them were walking off the job. The *Cheyenne Daily Leader* sneered that the workers were deserting because some of them were "weak in the faith," but mainly, the newspaper said, they would stay at their posts, because "Brother Brigham holds the whip as well as the reins, and whither he would drive they go."[43]

Whatever kept them at work, Young's pleas left Doc unmoved. The UP had, Young declared, paid only a third to a half of the value of the work done. Many subcontractors had borrowed money at 2 percent a month to pay their workers, and Young himself had put out $46,860 of his own money, but neither expedient was enough. He told Durant, "I need money very badly to carry on the work and do not know how to get along without it. Two or three hundred thousand is needed." He got $100,000.[44] Durant put that money to Young's credit in an account in New York, but Young informed him that he had already drawn checks for nearly that amount and he was still $130,000 in arrears. "I have expended all my available funds in forwarding the work," he wrote Durant, "and if I had the means to continue would not now ask for any assistance. These explanations must be my apology for troubling you in the matter."[45]

Young did all he could to pay the men out of his own pocket, but it wasn't enough, and the problem continued into 1869 and beyond. It should not be thought that only Young and the Mormons had to beg, badger, plead, threaten to sue, and otherwise try to force Durant to pay up. Joseph Nounan and another Gentile contractor, J. M. Orr, had to wait and beg and plead for what they had earned, and been promised, as well.

*A*T the beginning of 1869, Young praised Durant for his "energy and go-ahead-ivness."[46] By then the UP had tracks into Utah and almost down to Salt Lake Valley. That could not have been done without Durant and Dodge and many, many others, but neither could it have been done without the Mormons.

They worked without letup. For sure they wanted their money, but even more they wanted the railroad. The energy they put out could not be measured, but how they did it and what they did were observed. On December 15, 1868, an unsigned reporter for the *Deseret News* had described what he saw along the line. "All the ground not graded east of Echo is covered with men," he wrote, "who are working night and day. At night huge piles of sage brush make fires by which the work is prosecuted. The frozen ground is drilled, kegs of powder are emptied in the holes, and a long section of frozen earth is blown up almost simultaneously."

He went on: "The road up Weber canyon is crowded with teams hauling ties, which are deposited about a mile below the mouth of Echo." Here they were taken up by other teams and distributed on the grade up the canyon. The pile driver was at work for the culverts and bridges. There was a cut in the making that was ninety feet deep and five hundred feet long, on which men were working day and night. "Deep drills are being driven, into each of which a few kegs of powder are put, and huge masses of rock are thrown out and loosened for the crowbar to detach."

As for the tunnels, "But a faint idea can be conveyed. Sleepless energy is unceasingly occupied drilling, blasting, rending the foundations of the earth, and cutting a passage through rock harder than granite." The reporter compared the blasts coming from the tunnel facing to "the loud reports of heavy artillery; and the old mountains reverberate from base to summit, ringing back with thundering echoes, as if in anger."

*T*HERE were many teenagers among the Mormon workers. One of them was Bill Smoot, who was fifteen years old and worked at the head of

Echo Canyon for nine months in 1868. "Boys at my age in those stirring times did a man's work," he wrote over fifty years later. "We were hardened by the open life we lived and were brought up to work and did, that we might keep body and soul together. There were no drones. Each has his assigned work." For himself, he wrote, "I caught the railroad fever, even though I had never even seen a picture of a railroad or a train of cars." He had a team of horses, and with them he hauled ties. In the course of his stint, he earned $1,600, which was "a greater sum than my father had earned in cash money during his previous twenty-two years residence in Utah."

Smoot lived in a camp not far from another UP camp that held five hundred men, mainly Irish. "They were good workers," he recalled, "and a jolly bunch of men, but often got the worse from drinking bad whiskey and when they laid off work for a good old Irish wake, they sure let everybody know it for many miles around."[47]

The UP and CP graders were working almost right next to each other north of the lake, according to the December 12 issue of the *Salt Lake Daily Reporter*, "in a seemingly fraternal embrace." But "the frozen ground in the mornings makes work difficult, and unless plowing is done in the afternoon for the scrapers to work at during the next day, progress is tedious and damage to the plows considerable." Although foremen were talking about giving up the work while the ground was so hard-frozen, their bosses were after them to keep going: the line from Ogden to Promontory Summit could be reached in twenty days if the weather remained favorable. But of course it would not, could not. Men working north and west of Ogden told the newspaperman that nothing could be done until spring, because "they cannot open the ground, it is so hard frozen already." The reporter concluded, "Notwithstanding the herculean efforts made by both companies, work may have to be suspended on a large portion yet to be done. The elements are obstacles which even railroad enterprise and energy sometimes cannot overcome." The time had come to call it quits for 1868.

Chapter Fourteen
THE CENTRAL PACIFIC GOES THROUGH NEVADA
1868

CHARLES Crocker promised his partners in the CP that he would build a mile per day in 1868. They hoped so. But Collis Huntington thought Crocker could aim higher. On January 1, he wrote to E. B. Crocker, "I think you do not know the importance of extending the Central Pacific east of the [Salt] Lake to the Wasatch Mts." If he were in charge of construction instead of purchasing materials and raising money, Huntington said, "I would build the cheapest road that I could and have it accepted by the [government] Comm[ission] so it moves ahead fast."

Three weeks later, Huntington told Charlie Crocker to build as fast as he could. "When a cheap road will pass the Commission, make it cheap." He wanted Crocker to "run on the maximum grade instead of finishing making deep cuts and fills, and where you can make time in construction by using wood instead of stone for culverts and pilings, use wood." If the road washed out, Huntington advised, fix it later.

E. B. Crocker told Huntington a day later, on January 22, that he had heard the UP had set a goal for itself of four hundred miles in 1868. The CP intended to do as much, but "there are four essentials: 1st money, 2nd labor, 3rd ties, 4th iron and rolling stock. The 2nd and 3rd we got here, and the 1st and 4th depend on you." The iron that was supposed to be coming wasn't "coming on fast enough," Crocker complained. "What you ship after June 1st will not reach the terminus of the track in 1968. We need you to send more iron, fast."[1]

Huntington's letters and telegrams to the other members of the Big Four, and theirs to him, would fill volumes. He wanted them to make track faster, to get farther east, to defeat the UP at whatever cost. He would sell bonds or borrow to get the necessary money, he would buy the material and ship it to California. They wanted him to be reasonable, but meanwhile to speed up the shipments of material and to sell more bonds and bring in more money. What follows is a small sample of the exchange, from January 1868.

Huntington to E. B. Crocker, January 3: "You have been hurrying me up to sell bonds but it turns out that I am selling them faster now than you can print them. I want 3 million in the next 3 months."

Charlie Crocker to Huntington, same date: "Everything was done that could be done with the labor we could get and we used every exertion to procure more labor the whole season [of 1867]. Therefore I console myself & say *well done*. I am confident that the same number of men and horses never accomplished more work than was accomplished on the CP in the year."

Huntington to E. B. Crocker, January 5:

You write that you don't think that there are enough fish plates for all the iron as though that was a new idea to you. I wrote you early last summer asking about fish plates and *you* wrote back that you would not need them before 1868.

You wrote me some months ago that Charlie would write soon with an order for the number and kind of locomotives we'll want for 1868 and I have not seen it. Next week I will finish buying 24 locomotives: 12 with 8 wheels, 5 ft. drivers and 16x24 cylinders; and 12 with 10 wheels, 4 ft drivers and 18x24 cylinders, and I hope to have all of them on the way by the first of May.

Huntington to Mark Hopkins, January 6: "I have just received a dispatch from Crocker which reads 'send immediately 300 flat cars, we are going for 300 miles in '68; must have rolling stock.' I hope you will make the 300 into 400 miles."

E. B. Crocker to Huntington, January 8: "I met with one of the officers just in from China. He says that right after Chinese New Years (which is Feb. 5) every steamer which leaves China monthly will have from 800 to 1,000 men and he intends to send them all on to our work. Thousands more will come by sail, so we should have enough."

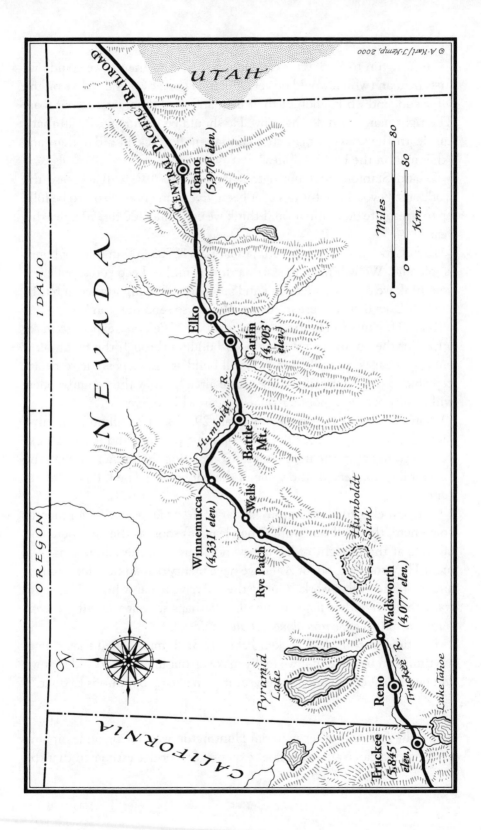

© A. Karl / J. Kemp, 2000

UTAH

IDAHO

NEVADA

OREGON

CALIFORNIA

CENTRAL PACIFIC RAILROAD

Toano
(5,970' elev.)

Elko

Carlin
(4,903'
elev.)

Battle Mt.

Humboldt R.

Wells

Winnemucca
(4,331' elev.)

Rye Patch

Humboldt Sink

Wadsworth
(4,077' elev.)

Pyramid Lake

Reno

Truckee R.

Truckee
(5,845'
elev.)

Lake Tahoe

N

Miles
0   80

Km.
0   80

Huntington to E. B. Crocker, January 13: "And then if we could find first the man (which would be very difficult) to go over and to live on the UP Road, and work amongst their men and send them over to our road. The right man could do that now. He should be found out. By all that I can learn they have a man that can lay more track in a day than any other man in the United States."

Leland Stanford to Huntington, January 16: "We will increase the workforce beyond what it has ever been. Every one now seems to be fully up to a resolute determination. I think we can build 300 to 350 miles this year."

E. B. Crocker to Huntington, January 22: "$705,000 in sales of bonds is splendid. We will have to start a printing mill to keep you supplied. If you think we do not understand and appreciate the importance of reaching Salt Lake first, you are mistaken. We do, so send the iron."

Mark Hopkins to Huntington, January 27: "We don't expect to make a road of the character we have been building through the mountains, but the cheapest possible one. We will build as fast as possible to be acceptable to the commissioners. And we already know the commissioners will readily accept as poor a road as we can wish to offer."

Huntington to E. B. Crocker, January 29: "I sold 2 million of our first mort. Bonds today and got the price up to 98 per cent and interest. I expect to go to par in the next weeks. [Completing the tunnel through the summit did wonders for the value of the CP bonds.] The UP is at 90 per cent."

E. B. Crocker to Huntington, January 31: "As far as paying for men to come here, that will not work. They leave as soon as they get here and chuckle at the thought of having swindled us. No, the Chinese are our men. They cost only about ½ and we have plenty of men here for foreman and to do the skilled work. You say the UP have a man who will lay more track than any other man in the U.S. Perhaps so, but we will see next summer. *You send the iron along fast and in time.*"

Huntington to E. B. Crocker, February 3: "I am satisfied that almost anything can be done that we really make up our minds to do and that we can build to Weber Canyon this year if we make up our minds to do it."[2]

A LL the iron and other material Huntington was buying and shipping to California came at tremendous expense. Strobridge estimated that the railroad line would have cost 70 percent less than it did had economy been a consideration, but the line was built "without regard to any outlay that would hasten its completion."[3]

Almost twenty years later, Lewis Clement wrote to Leland Stanford on the subject of the cost of building the line, a letter that Stanford submitted to the U.S. Pacific Railway Commission, which was investigating the finances of the UP and the CP. Clement said that in 1863 iron rails cost $41.75 per ton. But Congress had required both railroads to buy American-made rails only, and by 1866 the cost was up to $76.87 and by 1868 to $91.70 per ton at the rolling mill. The rails had to come around Cape Horn or via the Isthmus of Panama to get to San Francisco, then were lightered (taken by smaller ships) to Sacramento, then taken by rail (and, until 1868, by wagon or sled over the summit after Cisco) to the end of track. Cape Horn was cheaper than the Isthmus but it took longer, so in 1868 all the rails came through Panama. It cost $51.97 per ton to ship the rails through the Isthmus, which put the cost of rail delivered to San Francisco at $143.07 per ton, with more expenses to come to get the rails to the end of track.

In 1865, Clement wrote, two engines cost $70,752 at the factory, then almost $16,000 more to ship. "But their power was absolutely necessary to supply materials needed for construction; without those engines there would be delay."

In 1868, the costs remained high, or were up. Building the snowsheds was one factor, but there were many others. It cost money, for example, to ship the men and materials around the break in the track just east of the summit. In Nevada, "everything was expensive." Barley and oats for the horses and mules was $280 per ton, hay $120. "Water was scarce after leaving the Truckee and Humboldt Rivers" and had to be hauled for steam and general use. "There was not a tree that would make a board on over 500 miles of the route, no satisfactory quality of building stone. The country afforded nothing. The maximum haul for ties was 600 miles and of rails and other material 740 miles."[4]

Of course, the UP had the same or similar problems and difficulties until it got to the Wasatch Range, but for the CP, despite the handicaps, it was heavenly to be out on the desert making a mile or more per day instead of in those accursed mountains making a foot or a few yards per day.

• • •

A major expense, and a task that kept Clement working in the mountains for long periods in 1868, was making the snowsheds. It had to be done. In the winter of 1866–67 and again in 1867–68, half—and sometimes all—of the labor force had to be used to shovel the snow. Beyond the danger of the work, there was the constant threat of avalanches. Clement would send men hauling black-powder kegs to reach the threatening combs of great masses of compact snow leaning over the granite bluffs. "It required courage and determination and the call for volunteers for this daring undertaking was always answered."[5]

In 1867, Crocker and Stanford had discussed the problem of snow. Stanford had taken out his pencil and begun estimating the cost of covering the vulnerable sections of the track with snowsheds. The cost was appalling, but as Arthur Brown, the CP's superintendent of bridges and buildings, said of the winter of 1866–67, "It was impossible to keep the road clear from snow or open over half the time and that mostly by means of men and shovels, which required an army of men on hand all the time at great expense." So Stanford and Crocker decided to do it. In the summer of 1867, Brown, then thirty-eight years old, got started. That year he had built about five miles of experimental sheds, primarily above and below Cisco, wherever the track ran through a deep cut and was thus even more vulnerable.

In June 1868, when some of the snow had melted or been removed, permanent construction began. Brown had twenty-five hundred men working for him. He kept six trains constantly busy bringing on timber and spikes and bolts. He kept every sawmill in the Sierra busy and used sixty-five million feet of timber and nine hundred tons of bolts and spikes. Workers were paid top rates, $4 per day for carpenters and $2.50 to $3 for common laborers. The total length of the sheds was thirty-seven miles. Nine miles west of the summit and four miles east of it, the sheds ran almost continuously. The cost was over $2 million. "It costs a fearful amount," Huntington said. Brown called the cost "unprecedented in railroad construction."

There was no alternative, as Brown later said. "As the road was then rapidly progressing up the valley of the Humboldt, it became a matter of the most vital importance that the sheds should be so far finished that the supplies and building materials for construction ahead should not be interrupted" when the snows returned in the fall. The expense was increased because Brown had to keep the track clear for the traffic of con-

struction trains going to the front, and because of the number of men kept busy shoveling snow all through June and into July.[6]

On June 16, Mark Hopkins wrote to Huntington about the men doing the shoveling. "This work was commenced as early in March as the storms would permit," he said, "and has been continued by all the men who could be found willing to work themselves blind & their faces pealed and scared [sic] as though they had been scalded in the face with scalding water."[7]

When the snow was cleared away to make room for work, the CP built two types of sheds. First, where the gallery was exposed to the terrible avalanches of snow and ice from the steep and rocky slopes, it was extended back up the slope of the mountain several hundred feet from the center line of the road. Thus the galleries were built along the side of the mountains in such a way that the slope of the roof conformed with that of the mountain, so that the snow could pass over easily. Second, massive masonry walls were built across ravines to prevent the snow from striking the sheds at right angles. They were strengthened on the downside by boulders. There it was necessary to build the sheds of enormous strength by bracing them against the mountainside, framing them and interlacing them with beams and crossbeams.[8]

The job wasn't completely finished until 1869. The CP thought it up and did it, though other railroads, most notably in the Alps, later copied it. It was an engineering feat of the first magnitude—"the Longest House in the World." The biggest one ran twenty-nine miles, which made it "The House Without End." It had one hundred million board feet of lumber, and it withstood the Sierra snowfalls; in one season, sixty-five feet piled up.[9]

One of the problems was sparks from wood-burning locomotives that would get into the timber and set it afire. Initially the locomotives burned pinewood. The link-and-pin coupling was in use. The crews would "wood up" the tenders, from three to five cords at a time. The woodsheds were mainly beside the sidings. They were filled in September and October with a full winter's supply. Chinese gangs on work trains did the loading and unloading. When a fire got a start in one of those woodsheds, it was impossible to stop it, and it burned for hours, sometimes days. Fire was always the archfiend, because not only were all the station buildings and sheds built of lumber but of course all the trestles and truss bridges.[10]

Constant spraying with water helped keep some control of the fires in the snowsheds, but after many years all the wood had to be replaced with concrete. The sheds remain one of the wonders of the CP. They were, until replaced with concrete, one of the wonders of engineering with wood. The timbers were fifteen feet or longer, almost as big as big tree trunks. Photographs of them continue to astonish and amaze. Except for their vulnerability to fire, the thirty-seven miles of sheds would still be there, being used.

In July 1870, *Van Nostrand's Engineering Magazine* said of the work first planned by Stanford and Crocker, then laid out by Clement, then made under Brown's supervision, that the men of the CP "just roofed in their road. They took the giant branches of the pines and braced them against the mountain side, framing them and interlacing them with beam. They sloped the roof sustained by massive timbers and stayed by braces laid into the rock, covered by heavy planks up against the precipice so that descending earth or snow would be shot clean over the safely housed track into the pine tops below. They have conquered the snow."[11]

*T*O the east, out where the desert met the foothills of the Sierra Nevada, CP engineer Joseph Graham was in charge of building the road through Nevada. As he recalled, "On the first day of April, 1868, I set the first stake of the survey of the boundary for Reno. The original town-site comprised about 35 acres extending for about a quarter of a mile between the Truckee River as the south boundary and English Ditch as the north boundary." Charles Crocker pulled the town's name out of a hat. It was named for Jesse Lee Reno, a Civil War general and hero killed at the Battle of South Mountain in September 1862. The CP sold lots at auction. Because Reno was to be the trade center for the relatively nearby Virginia City, Washoe, and Carson City country, there was a rush of buyers, and choice twenty-five-foot lots sold for $1,200 apiece.[12]

*H*UNTINGTON had played a leading role in getting the 1866 Railroad Act amendment passed. The bill authorized the CP to "locate, construct, and continue their route eastward, in a continuous completed line, until they shall meet and connect with the Union Pacific Railroad." As noted, with no point of junction specified by Congress, the roads were free to build

as far as they could. The race that was therefore set up inspired the directors, the supervisors, the surveyors and engineers, the foremen, and the laborers of both the UP and the CP to go as far and as fast as they could.

There were some requirements. One permitted the companies to grade three hundred miles ahead of the end of track; another permitted them, upon completion of acceptable grade, to draw two-thirds of the government-subsidy bonds before the track had been laid. But first there had to be continuous track—not a problem of any magnitude for the UP, but a big one for the CP.

By 1868, the CP had been under construction for five years, but it had only 131 miles of track in place, and they were not continuous. There was a seven-mile gap on the eastern slope of the Sierra, just east of the summit. To the west the Chinese had laid sixteen miles from Cisco to the summit, but although track had been laid and spiked the line had been abandoned when the heavy snows came. In January, Secretary of the Interior Orville Browning had approved the CP's proposed line from the Truckee River to Humboldt Wells. But the CP still had to get a continuous line from the summit down to the Truckee, and from Cisco up to the summit. It wasn't going to be easy getting that done.

In mid-April, Strobridge moved a large number of Chinese from Nevada back to the still-snowbound region above Donner Lake and to the west and put them to work shoveling out the surveyed line of the unfinished track and on the grade west of the summit. Snow had covered it to depths of ten to thirty feet, with ice on the grade below the snow. Cuts made between Tunnels No. 8 and 10 were simultaneously buried under snowdrifts twenty to sixty feet high. Meanwhile, the completed track running up from Cisco to the summit lay beneath snow so firmly impacted that snowplows couldn't get through. On both sides of the summit, thousands of men had to clear the track. Besides shovels, they used picks and blasting powder.[13]

As the finished track progressed, California (and national) politicians were getting after the CP for its freight and passenger rates. On April 14, Huntington wrote Hopkins, "I notice that everybody is in favor of a railroad until they get it built and then everyone is against it unless the railroad company will carry them and theirs for nothing."[14] Despite Huntington's complaints—which he most certainly regarded as legitimate, and which would continue and increase, as would the political attacks on the CP and the UP—the work went on.

"Keep right on laying rails just as though you did not care for the snow, and we're bound to get to Weber Canyon before the Union Company," Huntington told Charlie Crocker in a letter on April 15. "If you do that I will forever pray that you will have your reward!"[15]

By May 1, 1868, the CP line from Reno to Truckee was completed. The crews were meanwhile clearing the snow near the summit so that the track layers could re-lay the track between Cisco and Tunnel No. 12 and complete the last seven-mile gap to open the line to Nevada.

On May 15, Huntington filed with Secretary Browning a map of the definite location of the CP's proposed line from Humboldt Wells to Weber Canyon. Browning's approval was necessary before the crews could start clearing the grade. At that time, the CP's tracks were five hundred miles west of Echo Summit, yet that was where Huntington hoped to reach. The Pacific Railroad Act forbade the builders to draw subsidies on work done more than three hundred miles ahead of their continuous track, yet the CP officials still wanted to get to grading in Utah. The CP chief engineer, Montague, had his surveyors running lines north of the Great Salt Lake and east of Ogden, in the Wasatch Range, where they were working next to the flags of the UP surveyors near Fort Bridger, Wyoming. The UP surveyors were simultaneously staking out a line across Utah and Nevada to the California border.

It was about this time that Stanford went to Salt Lake City to try to talk Brigham Young into putting his Mormon shoulders to the plow. Brigham had not immediately agreed. Stanford told Hopkins, "Have Charley [Crocker] double his energy and do what is necessary to secure what labor is required to push the road to its utmost. Anything less than the most that can be done will very likely end in defeat."[16]

On June 15, 1868, six days after Stanford's telegram to Hopkins, the CP's gap between Cisco and Truckee was finally closed. Crocker sent a triumphant telegram to Huntington: "The track is connected across the mountains. We have one hundred and sixty-seven continuous miles laid."[17] A day or two later, he sent three thousand of his Chinese graders, with a fleet of four hundred horse-drawn carts, to Palisade Canyon, on the Humboldt River, three hundred miles in advance of the end of track. Getting supplies and food to them was frightfully costly, but he got to work on it anyway.

On June 18, 1868, the CP ran its first through passenger train from Sacramento to Reno, a distance of 154 miles.* A reporter for the *San*

* The run meant rapidly rising revenues for the line. By the end of 1868, Mark

Francisco Daily Alta California was aboard. He wrote that the train, which departed at 6:30 A.M., consisted of one boxcar stocked with freight, one baggage car with freight and the U.S. mails, and three of the CP's new passenger cars. The locomotive was the *Antelope*, which had just been overhauled and painted, with bright-red wheels, a walnut cab, shiny brasswork, and a portrait of an antelope painted on the headlight. A truly fitting picture for the first locomotive ever to cross the Sierra Nevada.

Hank Small was the engineer. He checked out the locomotive, oilcan in his hand. Then he got started. After Roseville, California, "we proceeded on our way and now the mountains appeared so close that it seemed that we could put our hand out of the window and touch them. . . . The engine blows and wheezes, with short, sharp aspirations and the feeling of weight as we ascend a steep and increasing grade." At 9:50 A.M., the train had gone up 2,448 feet, to Colfax. Then came the jaws-to-the-floorboard passing around Cape Horn, with passengers looking "anxiously and with evident trepidation into the depths below." Then came Secret Town and an elevation of nearly three thousand feet.

"Up and up, onward we climbed skyward." Then came Dutch Flat. Two miles farther, it was Alta at 3,625 feet. The first tunnel, five hundred feet long, was seventy-five miles from Sacramento and forty-five hundred feet above the sea. The snow levels came down to the road. "Chinese are swarming everywhere. They have nearly finished their work in this vicinity and are packing preparatory to passing over the summit into the great interior basin of the continent."

At 102 miles from Sacramento, "we stand 6,800 feet above the sea. Two miles more and the cars reach the entrance of the great summit tunnel, 1,659 feet in length. We have scaled the great Sierras at last and a plus ultra might be written on the granite walls of the great tunnel before us. We are 7,043 feet above the sea."

On the west side of the tunnel, "a swarm of Chinese are busy shoveling away the snow, which has come down in great slides bringing with it huge granite boulders upon the tracks." It took two hours to clear the track. The passengers waited with whatever patience they could muster until conductor George Wood called out "All aboard!" On the trip down to the Truckee, "the snow banks come down so close to the track that the eaves of the car rake them on either side." The road wound around the precipitous mountainside, almost encircling Donner Lake as it de-

---

Hopkins found that the CP had its biggest net profit ever, more than $1,250,000.

scended, making a circuit of seven miles to gain not more than a quarter-mile.

On it rolled, to the Great Basin of Nevada. "The mighty task is accomplished. Words cannot describe it." The Chinese onlookers did, in their own way. The *Alta California* reporter watched them as they watched the train. He called them "John," and wrote: "John comprehending fully the importance of the event, loses his natural appearance of stolidity and indifference and welcomes with the swinging of his broad brimmed hat and loud, uncouth shouts the iron horse. With his patient toil, directed by American energy and backed by American capital, John has broken down the great barrier at last and opened over it the greatest highway yet created for the march of civilization."[18]

Theodore Judah, who did the original surveying, had thought it could be done. He had convinced the Big Four, then Congress, then the President that it could be done. Now that it had been done, he must have looked down from heaven and smiled.

A T the lush Truckee Meadows, the wild grass grew two to three feet high. The California pioneers had stayed there to fatten their horses and cattle before pushing over the Sierra. When the track was open from Sacramento to the meadows, Crocker sent fifty carloads of supplies to Strobridge per day, divided into five trains each hauled by two locomotives. Crocker told Bancroft that those trains "were the heaviest that ever went over the road and the heaviest that ever will probably."* He said the trains went over the seven miles of completed track just past the summit "and went safely. If the track had not been good, it could not have been done."[19] As quick as the supply trains were unloaded, they started back over the mountains for another load.

The CP was on the move. The Truckee's Lower Canyon headed east, going through a narrowing meadowland that lay between great bare brown hills, until the river swung left some thirty-five miles past Reno and headed north, toward its outlet at Pyramid Lake. As the end of track moved east, the construction superintendent's headquarters train, along with dormitory cars, stayed right behind. J. C. Lewis, editor of the week-old *Reno Crescent*, described it. "A locomotive came rushing down the

---

* Not true, but close enough for the nineteenth century.

track having in tow a string of boarding and lodging houses. One and four-story houses, which we called the Hotel de China. In the lower deck was cooking apartments; the second, third, and fourth decks were sleeping and eating rooms. Next several houses of a superior quality for the officials of the company. . . . Altogether a novel sight and one we shall long remember. We are prepared for anything Charlie Crocker may do in the future."[20]

On July 1, 1868, Huntington wrote to Crocker to tell him that he had sent 60,146 tons of rails from New York, all on fast ships, and he expected to raise the figure to ninety or a hundred thousand tons by the end of the year. Then he added, in a near-perfect expression of his many exhortations and therefore perhaps the most widely quoted of all his words, "So work on as though Heaven were before you and Hell behind you."[21]

The same day, July 1, engineer Graham got to the Big Bend of the Truckee, where he set the stakes to found the town of Wadsworth. Crocker came up a bit later and walked over the site, and after a half-hour he pointed to where he wanted the engine house and the station buildings for the town. This spot, 189 miles from Sacramento, became the base of supplies for the remaining five hundred miles of construction.

After Wadsworth, where the crews said good-bye to the Truckee, and until the track got to the Humboldt Sink, the route was northeastward across the Great Desert, a vast waste of sand and sagebrush and white alkali deposits, with high mountain ranges to the south and bleak hills to the north. The desert ran nearly a hundred miles, without a tree, without water, without anything that could be used for construction. A popular saying was that "a jack rabbit had to carry a canteen and haversack" to get across it.[22]

The CP spent big money trying to drill wells, but to almost no avail. Clement remarked, "Tunnels were bored into the mountains east of Wadsworth to develop small springs and when water was found, it was carefully protected and conveyed, in some cases, over eight miles in pipes to the line of the road."[23] The water for men, horses, and locomotives came from the Truckee River and was carried in huge, semiconical wooden vats on flatcars. The vats had big spouts that worked like the spouts of railroad water towers. At the end of track, much of the water had to be transferred to barrels and sent ahead by wagons to the graders. Timbers and boards for ties, bridges, station houses, and other structures, plus wood for fuel and rock for retaining walls and other masonry, came from the Sierra Nevada, where such materials were boundless. It was still expensive to bring them east, but it was done.

That year the CP had a most unusual but major problem with its Chinese workforce. Charlie Crocker explained it to Huntington. "The most tremendous yarns have been circulating among the Chinese," he wrote. "We have lost about 1,000 through fear of Indians out on the desert." It seemed that they had been told "there are Snakes fifty feet long that swallow Chinamen whole on the desert, and Indians 25 feet high that eat men and women for breakfast and hundreds of other equally ridiculous stories." Crocker solved the problem by sending twenty-two Chinamen taken from different groups "up the Humbolt [sic] to see for themselves and they have just returned and things are more quiet since."[24]

The track layers were making great strides, while the graders ahead of them moved even faster. The *Alta California* described the way the thousands of men at work moved their residence each day. "Camp equipage, work shops, boarding house, offices, and in fact the big settlement literally took up its bed and walked. The place that knew it at morning knew it no more at night. It was nearly ten miles off and where was a busy town of 5,000 inhabitants in the morning, was a deserted village site at night, while a smooth, well built, compact road bed for traveling stretched from the morning site to the evening tarrying place."[25]

One good thing about the desert—it was flat. Wadsworth, where the Truckee River turned north, was a bit more than four thousand feet in altitude. From there the route moved up in about as gentle a grade as the Nebraska plains. For 275 miles it gained only a thousand feet of altitude. So, in July and early August, the track layers put down and spiked forty-six miles of iron, or an average of one and a half miles per day.

FROM the beginning of the summer of 1868 to the end, Charles Crocker kept in much closer personal touch with the men. "I used to go up and down that road in my car like a mad bull," he told an interviewer, "stopping along wherever there was anything going amiss, and raising Old Nick with the boys that were not up to time." When he slept, which wasn't often, it was on the train. When he woke, he could tell from the movement of his car exactly where on the line the train was. When Mrs. Crocker complained that he talked to her too roughly, he would reply, "Well you know that I don't mean anything when I am abrupt with you."

"Well," she replied, "your manner is overbearing and gruff. That is the way you talk with me and with everybody."

Crocker told his interviewer, "I got so that I was really ashamed of myself. That sort of bearing was entirely foreign to me."[26]

O N September 3, government commissioners rode from Sacramento to the end of track to make their inspection. W. H. Rhodes, correspondent of the *San Francisco Chronicle*, accompanied them. Some excerpts from his long dispatch:

> Really, the speed is terrific. . . . Truckee is a young and flourishing town, full of people, who all seem to be busy in the great lumber trade. Hundreds of saw-mills are at work and millions of feet of timber are daily flatted out into boards. . . .
>
> We arrived at Reno and here beheld another new town. The noise of hammer, and plane, and saw re-echoed on all sides, and the city rises like an exhalation. It is a complete mirage on the desert, and will probably be as magnificent.

After spending the night at Wadsworth, the inspectors set out again, one of them scrutinizing the ties, rails, and grade with a spyglass, another lying down to sleep.

> The argument being this, that if the passengers could sleep the track must be level, easy and all right. He slept profoundly and did not wake until we overtook the end of the road just 307 miles from Sacramento.
>
> Here we found a very large number of men at work—principally Chinese—laying the track. The scientific part of the job is superintended by white men, but the rough work is done by the Chinese.

Shocking to modern readers, taken for granted by readers in the nineteenth century, the white superintendents of the Chinese were called "herders."

Rhodes got a horse, "and I rode on a gallop to the front. The grading is completed several hundred miles in advance so that there is no delay in placing the rails. It would be impossible to describe how rapidly, orderly and perfectly this is done, without seeing the operation itself. There are just as many employed as can conveniently work, and no more. Vehicles laden with ties are always in advance, and Chinese with gauge and leveling rod place them across the grade, almost as quick as thought. The car with the rails is brought up at a gallop, and six white men—three at each rail—roll the iron off the car, and drop it upon the track, with the velocity of steam. The empty car is lifted off the track, and then one fully loaded is drawn to the front, and the same operation repeated ad infinitum."

Rhodes pulled out his watch to time the last half-mile being laid. It was done in "a little less than twenty-eight minutes. . . . It is a fact, beyond dispute, that this company has laid over six miles of track in a single day."[27] The inspectors judged the final twenty-mile section of the line to be acceptable, and the bonds were issued.

By this time, the crews were picking up speed to a fare-thee-well. "They can and do lay the track now at the rate of four miles a day," another reporter wrote. He had just talked to Charles Crocker, who told him that, if the additional fifty locomotives then on ships en route to San Francisco arrived soon, the CP would be into Salt Lake City by December. The company already had seventy locomotives at work. The reporter's conclusion was apt: "This is railroading on a scale surpassing anything ever before conceived."[28]

Far to the east, Butler Ives, with a party of twelve men, was making the final location from Humboldt Wells to the Wasatch Range. "They keep me out in these infernal regions of salt and desolation," he wrote his brother, "because I am familiar with the country & don't fear the Indians." Montague had told surveyor Ives that "the necessity for *pushing ahead* will compel us to sacrifice good alignment & easy grades for the sake of getting light work. Make temporary location by using sharp curves and heavy grades wherever you can make any material savings on the work. The line we want now is the one we can build the soonest, even if we rebuild immediately. Keep this in mind."[29]

On October 21, Huntington wrote to Crocker, "Why doesn't Stanford go to Salt Lake and stay until the roads meet?" Stanford did, and stayed for almost three months. Huntington went on, "I have got the new line to Echo Summit approved," which wasn't quite true. "You must lay tracks to the tunnel. By God, Charley, you must work as man never worked before. Our salvation is you."[30]

By the end of October, the line was open to Winnemucca, Nevada. According to the *Humboldt Register,* the town was "improving rapidly. Several large stores had opened." The CP made Winnemucca into a division point and intended to build roundhouses and machine shops there, along with other buildings. So, the *Register* concluded, "the town may yet survive and become an important place."[31]

That remained to be seen.* Engineer Graham noted the scarcity of inhabitants in northern Nevada and commented on the sight of empty land: "What settlements were there when the line was being built? Winnemucca was a small town, there was a wayside hotel at Humboldt station, there was a little store at Mill City. I don't remember any habitations until we touched Corinne [Utah], 20 miles east of Promontory."[32]

*T*HAT October, Huntington filed with the Interior Department maps and profiles of the CP's proposed line from Monument Point to Echo Summit. Secretary Browning accepted the documents, but he was about to become a lame duck, since Republican candidate General Grant was the almost certain winner of the 1868 election. So, when Huntington filed an application for an advance of $2.4 million in subsidy bonds for grading that had been done on the line, on the grounds that the CP's was the only line, the true line, the one on which bonds could be issued, Doc Durant and Oliver Ames protested mightily. Browning then decided to do nothing until January 1869, after the election, when he would appoint a special commission headed by General Gouverneur Warren to go to the site to determine the best route through the disputed territory. The UP then got Secretary of the Treasury Hugh McCulloch to agree that he would not issue any bonds until Warren's commission had reported.

Another government commission, out to inspect tracks already laid and in use, traveled by rail from Sacramento to the end of the CP's track in mid-November. On December 3, they sent a highly favorable report to Secretary Browning. "On the new portion of the road," they said, "through Humboldt Valley, cross ties, bridges, and rails are up to standard. Minor defects can be remedied at small cost when hurry of pushing forward the road is over. Heavy trains of rails, ties and fuel are running

---

* Actually, it eventually came true: Winnemucca went into the twenty-first century a thriving town.

safely to the extreme end of the road, 445 miles from Sacramento. The road is being constructed in good faith, in a substantial manner, without stint of labor, materials or equipment, and is worthy of its character as a great national work."[33]

ON November 9, 1868, a reporter from the *Alta California* explained how Strobridge and his men could make that great national work press east so rapidly. He wrote that Strobridge was comfortably established in his camp train, which contained hotel, telegraph office, store, kitchen, sleeping quarters, and a "home that would not discredit San Francisco." In the train were the officials, the clerical force, and some Caucasian workers. Mrs. Strobridge was there, in her boxcar, which was divided into three small rooms, with windows and a narrow, recessed porch on the right side, plus a ventilator in the roof.

Mrs. Strobridge was the only white woman who "saw the thing through from beginning to end." The men called her "The Heroine of the CP." Her car was "neatly fitted up and well furnished." An awning veranda, with a caged canary bird swinging at the front door, gave it a homelike appearance.

The reporter noted long lines of horses, mules, and wagons near the train. At dawn the stock was eating hay and barley. As the sun came up, trains shunted in from the west with materials for the day's work. Foremen were galloping about on horseback shouting out their orders. Swarms of laborers—Chinese, Europeans, and Americans—were hurrying to their work. There was a movable blacksmith shop with a score of smiths repairing tools and shoeing horses. Next to it was a fully equipped harness shop, hard at work on collars, traces, and other equipment.

Down the track, a line of telegraph poles "stretched back as far as the eye could reach." The telegraph wire from the last pole was strung into the car that was the telegraph office. Its last message the previous evening had been back to Sacramento to report on the progress made that day.

To the east stretched the newly disturbed earth, the grade for the ties and rails. By the side of the grade were the campfires of the Chinese, blue-clad laborers who were waiting for the signal to begin. "They are the vanguard of the construction forces. Miles back is the camp of the rear guard—the Chinese who follow the track gang, ballasting and finishing the road bed." The reporter judged that the Chinese were "systematic workers, competent and wonderfully effective because tireless and un-remitting in their industry." Divided into gangs of thirty men each, they worked under American foremen.

When the sun cleared the horizon, the signal to begin rang out. "What at first seemed confusion to the visitor soon resolved itself into orderly action." A train of some thirty cars carried ties, rail, spikes, bolts, tele-graph poles, wire, and more. These were thrown off the train as near to the end of track as possible. There the rails were loaded onto low ironcars and hauled by horse to the end of track. Then came the rail gang, placing the rails on the ties, while a man on each side distributed spikes, two to each tie. Another distributed splice bars, and a third the bolts and nuts for the fishplate. Behind them were the spikers, two to each side. Two more men followed to adjust and bolt the splice bars.

Simultaneously, wagons were distributing telegraph poles along the grade. Men nailed cross-arms onto them, while another gang dug holes for the poles and a third gang erected the poles, keeping pace with the rail gang. "At times lack of wagons make it impossible to keep up the sup-ply of poles, and the telegraph gangs, who pride themselves on never let-ting the track get ahead of them, utilize sage brush, barrels, ties—surreptitiously taken from the track—or anything else that would keep the wire off the ground until the supply of poles again equal the demand." Then came a wagon bearing a reel of wire. As the wire uncoiled, it was carried up on the poles and made fast to the insulators.

Twice a day the camp train moved to the end of track—at noon, to give all hands a hot dinner, and at night, to give supper and sleeping ac-commodations. Through the telegraph (there was a battery on his car and an operator to work it), Strobridge would order his supplies for the next day. "Thus hand in hand on their sturdy march," the reporter wrote, "go the twin giants, the railroad and the telegraph, linked mailed purvey-ors of civilization which is ere long to wrest from its pristine wilderness a continent."

Altogether, it was a great modern army, moving forward with a will and a plan, unable to stop, determined to win the battle.[34]

ON November 13, Huntington wrote Stanford, in Salt Lake City, "If it is within the power of God, man, or the devil to get out rail laid to within

300 miles of Echo by, say the tenth of December, it should be done."[35] Echo was four hundred miles away. To get to within three hundred miles would require more than three miles per day in the month of track laying still ahead, a record beyond any previous accomplishment of the CP.

Stanford was much more interested in getting the Mormons to build west from Ogden in order to connect with Crocker's graders moving east. He was sending Benson, Farr & West crews up to Promontory to "take possession." He wrote Huntington on November 21 that the UP was retreating, because Durant also wanted to get control of Promontory and had therefore ordered UP men to come off the work at Humboldt Wells to work at Promontory.

Plus which, Stanford pointed out, the UP "have the grading substantially done from the mouth of Weber [eastward] to their track," which was just short of Echo. They had built the grade and laid the tracks on the exact line Huntington had handed in to the Interior Department on his maps. So the CP had nothing to complain of, and it was hopeless to try to build all the way to Echo. In any event, the UP was "making desperate efforts to get into Echo before the winter storms and cold shall shut them out."[36]

At the end of November, Stanford and Lewis Clement went to Promontory, where they spent several days looking around. Stanford had earlier decided that the line laid out by the CP surveyors would not do, because it required a tunnel of eight hundred feet through solid limestone. On this occasion he and Clement decided to lay out a new line, "somewhat at the expense of the alignment," but it would eliminate the tunnel and thus save $75,000. The new line would also require a fill of about ten thousand yards.

Stanford also noted that the UP had surveyed a line that ran very close to the CP line, often within a hundred feet. Neither company had yet built a grade over Promontory. On December 4, he wrote E. B. Crocker: "Clem [Lewis Clement] has sent me a profile of the line at Promontory avoiding the tunnel and it looks better than I expected. During the next week the Mormon contractors say that they will have the whole work covered from Ogden to Monument Pt." That is, they would have graders at work on it. "Then, if I have the right of way secured, I shall assert our line to be the only one of the Pacific RR and that others must keep off our right of way."

That last remained to be seen. So too the hope Stanford expressed at the end of his letter: "I have strong faith in our being first to the mouth of Weber. I do think there is ground for hope." Four days later he ended another letter, "Could not Charley, by staying out on the track, push forward faster?" But there were other worries, to the west of Promontory. Stanford said, "At Humboldt Wells I think the true policy is to follow our own line disregarding entirely what the UP has done there, using their grade or not just as our line may make it necessary."

With regard to Huntington's hope to reach Echo, Stanford thought it "such utter folly in every way" that it had to be disregarded. The UP was already there.[37] Huntington, knowing Stanford's objections, told Hopkins in a December 15, 1868, letter, "I think it a terrible mistake that we have made in letting matters run as they have at Salt Lake"—that is, with Stanford in charge. "I sometimes swear terribly about it, but that doesn't do any good."[38]

*I*N 1868, the CP had constructed 362 miles of road. That was virtually the mile per day that Charles Crocker had promised. Both lines were about to enter Utah. There they had completed as much as two-thirds of the grading, but still had track to lay and more grades to make. In Utah was by far the biggest city between Omaha and Sacramento, Salt Lake City. Up to that time, the westward-building UP and the eastward-building CP had been going into a land nearly without people. The roads had been setting a precedent. Instead of building a railroad that would connect one town or city with another, they had been building into a void. They were not striving to take over trade routes; instead they hoped to attract settlement.

The UP and the CP had a lot at stake in Utah. Government bonds, land grants, the sale of their own stocks and bonds, future trade, and more. But what mattered most was winning. Far more so than gamblers, card players, athletes wrestling or boxing or running or playing games, brokers dealing in stocks and bonds, lawyers trying a case, bankers making or calling a loan, whoever else or whatever other competitors, the directors, superintendents, surveyors, engineers, foremen, grade makers, rail layers, ballast men, cooks, telegraph builders and operators, and everyone one else connected to the road wanted to win. In fact, they were all desperate to win and would do whatever winning required. And the final act would be played out in Utah.

Chapter Fifteen

THE RAILROADS RACE
INTO UTAH
January 1–April 10, 1869

DOC Durant had spent far too much money to get through Nebraska and Wyoming fast, and had promised even more to Brigham Young and the Mormons to beat the CP through Utah. It was not possible for the company to sell enough stocks and bonds, or to collect enough loans in the form of 6 percent bonds from the government, even to come close to paying its due bills. It had no hope of paying off longer-term debts. The company owed around $10 million. Meanwhile, in December 1868, the Crédit Mobilier had paid a huge dividend to its stockholders. It amounted to nearly $3 million, which brought the total paid out in 1868 to $12.8 million in cash, plus over $4 million in UP stock (at par value of $100 per share), bringing the total of stock distributed since 1867 to $28.8 million.[1]

To Brigham Young, this was outrageous. Beginning in January and continuing through the year, he would dun Doc to pay up. "I have expended all my available funds in forwarding the work," he wrote on January 16. If he could he would continue to do so, but he was out of funds. "These explanations must be my apology for troubling you in the matter."[2] More followed, with supporting details. "The men are very clamorous for their pay," Young informed Durant. There was some three-quarters of a million dollars yet due them. They had done and were doing the work and "have now waited from half to three quarters of a year for their pay." Six months later, Young was still trying. "To say the least," he

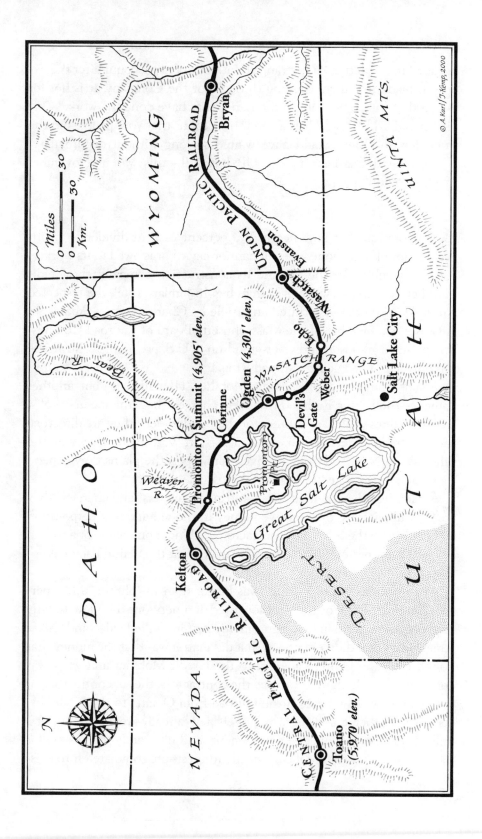

declared in one letter, "it is strange treatment of my account after the exertions made to put the grading through for the Company. It is not for myself that I urge, but for the thousands that have done the work." One UP official told Young, "It is a good thing for us that your people did the work, for no others would have waited so long without disturbance." Young quoted this back to the UP, but still—this was in November 1869!—couldn't get paid.[3]

A corporation that pays nearly 300 percent cash in dividends on invested capital in just one year but cannot pay what is owed to its workers is in big trouble. For the UP and its construction company, the Crédit Mobilier, the trouble was bigger than big. In January 1869, the respected *North American Review* printed an article by Charles Francis Adams, Jr. Adams was a member of the Massachusetts Board of Railroad Commissioners and a grandson and great-grandson of U.S. presidents. The article was entitled "The Pacific Railroad Ring."

Adams's target was the Crédit Mobilier. He called it "but another name for the Pacific Railroad ring." He charged that "the members of it are in Congress; they are trustees for the bondholders; they are directors; they are stockholders; they are contractors; in Washington they vote the subsidies, in New York they receive them, upon the plains they expend them, and in the 'Crédit Mobilier' they divide them."

Adams described them as "ever-shifting characters" and charged "they are ever ubiquitous; they receive money into one hand as a corporation and pay it into the other as a contractor. . . . Under one name or another, a ring of a few persons is struck at whatever point the Union Pacific is approached."[4]

At that time, Adams's "ring" was bigger than his phrase "a few persons" implied. The stockholders consisted of ninety-one individuals, only seven of whom were in Congress (including Grenville Dodge and Oakes Ames).[5] But that didn't matter. What did matter was that the money that flowed from the Union Pacific into the Crédit Mobilier and what was done with it—which wasn't to pay the contractors, the subcontractors, or the laborers who had gotten the railroad from Omaha to the Utah border—was further enriching a relatively few already wealthy men who milked the corporation, the government, and ultimately the people for their fat and ill-gotten profits. "Greedy interests are stimulated into existence," according to Adams, and they "intrigue and combine and coalesce, until a system of political 'rings,' legislative 'log-rolling,' and organized 'lobbies' results; and then, at last, the evil becoming intolerable, the community sluggishly grapples with it in a struggle for self-preservation."[6]

Or so at least Adams wrote. In the process he was preparing the ground for the planting of a seed that might someday sprout and could then grow into the largest scandal in nineteenth-century American history. He was pointing the way and providing the means for politicians, some of them venal, others upright and genuinely and rightly concerned, to go after the Crédit Mobilier, potentially to ruin the shareholders and perhaps the UP itself.

Which was only fair. It was democracy that had made the UP possible. If the company was to be attacked without mercy, even after it built more than half of the road that everyone wanted, it was fitting that the representatives elected in the democratic system do it.

By no means was it just Adams who went after the UP. As its moment of triumph approached, there were many others ready to launch an assault.

*T*HE CP had its own severe problems. Money, of course. Huntington could never sell enough of the company's own stocks and bonds, or gather in enough of the government bonds for grading and tracking, to pay the bills. Questions abounded. Would the company's rails get to Ogden before the UP? Could they go east from Ogden up the Weber River Canyon? Up Echo Canyon? More realistically, could the CP rails reach Promontory before the UP? How much of the grade the company had built and was building in Utah would it be able to use?

The corporation was also vulnerable to the kind of charges Adams had brought against the UP. Charlie Crocker's Contract and Finance Company was like the Crédit Mobilier in so many way that the firms were like two peas in a pod, except that the Big Four plus E. B. Crocker held all the stock of the Contract and Finance Company secretly. As to Adams's implication that the UP had been involved in bribery (how else to explain why so many congressmen held Crédit Mobilier stock?), the CP could hardly stand a close examination of Huntington's accounts.

Huntington had been in Washington with large sums of money at his disposal whenever Congress took up a question in which his railroad had a consuming interest. He had left Washington considerably lighter in his pocket, but with a favorable vote. An investigation of the UP's finances would only help the CP. But what if the politicians, having gotten into the matter, decided to broaden the inquiry to include the CP?

*T*HE two corporations shared other problems. One was material. On January 1, 1869, the CP had thirty-five ships bound for San Francisco. They were bringing essential construction materials, including eighteen locomotives. As the *Salt Lake Daily Reporter* noted, "There is not a rail on the CP line of the road that has not been brought a distance of six thousand miles."[7] In Truckee, the sawmills worked around the clock to meet the CP's orders for a million ties. In Omaha, UP ties were piled up in the yards, awaiting shipment. One of Casement's orders for ties alone required hauling six hundred flatcars a distance of four hundred miles. Even after the ties were delivered along the grade, it took six or more carloads to supply enough material to lay one mile of track.

There were always shortages on both sides. Some were caused by the vagaries of ocean travel. "We have in Cal. 183 miles iron and only 89 miles spikes," Crocker telegraphed Huntington on January 20, "and 81 miles iron and 75 miles spikes to arrive in sixty days. It is very unsafe to half-spike the track at this season of the year." That same day, Hopkins asked Huntington by telegraph, "Will you send spikes by steamer to make up deficiency?"[8] That would cost more, but then, Huntington often said he never did anything until he had Mark Hopkins's approval.

*S*TROBRIDGE had a talk with Charlie Crocker. "I don't like to have those Union Pacific people beat us in this way," Strobridge declared. "I believe they will beat us nearly to the State Line"—that is, between Nevada and Utah.

"We have got to beat them," Crocker replied. He thought it could be done.

"How?" Strobridge asked. "We have only got ten miles of iron available." But Crocker would not give up his hopes. When Jack Casement's men of the UP laid four and a half miles of track in a single day, Crocker said that "they bragged of it and it was heralded all over the country as being the biggest day's track laying that ever was known." He told Strobridge that the CP must beat it, and Stro got the materials together and laid six miles and a few feet. So Casement got his UP men up at 3 A.M. and put them to work by lantern light until dawn and kept them at it until almost midnight, and laid eight miles. Crocker swore he would beat that.[9]

WEATHER was against both companies, although this was mainly their own fault, because they insisted on building through the winter. The CP's grading and track laying were at altitudes of up to five thousand feet and sometimes higher. At Humboldt Wells, Nevada, and to the east into Utah, where Strobridge's graders were at work, temperatures went to eighteen degrees below zero in mid-January and stayed that low for a week. By the end of the cold spell, the soil was frozen solid to a depth of nearly two feet. The graders could not use their picks or shovels. Instead, they blew up the frozen ground with black powder.* The explosion split the earth into big pieces. Crocker called it building grade with "chunks of ice." When warm weather came in the spring, he recalled, "this all melted and down went the track. It was almost impossible to get a train over it without getting off the track."[10]

Thirty-year-old Henry George, the future economist, at that time a re-porter for the *Sacramento Union,* rode over the track in April and wrote that it had been "thrown together in the biggest kind of a hurry." His train, he said, often could move no faster than an ox team.[11]

Sometimes the trains did not move even that fast. In mid-February, a week-long storm came over the Sierra Nevada. The *Reno Crescent* said that up in the mountains the storm was "described as something awful." Two CP locomotives made it across on the front edge of the storm, with enough iron to lay two miles of track, plus "sixteen cars loaded with ties, four cars loaded with bridge timber, a caboose and passenger cars."[12] After the trains arrived, the storm hit, hard—it was the worst of the winter. Back near Cisco, a snowslide knocked out a trestle bridge and caused a blockade. Several passenger trains were snowbound, and not even nine locomotives pushing one of the largest of the CP's plows could get through the drifts.

The slides came in those fourteen miles the CP had not yet covered

---

* In Europe in World War II, American GIs used their hand grenades, or dyna-mite charges, to blast frozen earth apart so that they could dig foxholes.

with their sheds. The good news from the storm was that the snowsheds already built had held up throughout the onslaught. More good news: within a week, the snow had melted and the trains were running again.[13]

For the UP, the weather was equally awful and lasted longer. On January 10, a snowstorm hit Wyoming. The wind was up—indeed, so fierce that snowdrifts covered much of the line. It took a freight train bound for Echo with construction supplies fourteen hours to make the last forty miles. Following the storm came a savage cold wave. For a week the temperature never climbed above zero, and on January 17 it sank to twenty degrees below zero. At Wasatch, a town laid out by Webster Snyder, the UP's general superintendent for operations, which was the winter headquarters for the Casement forces, desperate work was going on to board up the rough-hewn buildings. "The sound of hammer and saw was heard day and night," wrote J. H. Beadle as he tried to drink his coffee in a café whose weatherboarding was being applied as he had his breakfast. But gravy and butter froze on his plate. Some spilled coffee congealed on the table.

Graders worked in overcoats, which slowed them down considerably. They blasted the frozen ground with black powder, just as the CP's graders had done. The results were equally disconcerting. When the thaw came, an entire train and the track beneath it slid off the grade made with "chunks of ice" into a gully.[14] Superintendent Reed wrote his wife how much he was looking forward to completing the job. When that happened, "I shall want to leave the day after for home, and hope to have one year's rest at least."[15]

In February, the storm that had stopped nine CP locomotives in the Sierra came to Utah. "The most terrific storm for years," according to one Salt Lake City newspaper. When it hit Wyoming, the storm shut down ninety miles of the UP line, between Rawlins and Laramie, for three weeks. Two hundred eastbound passengers were stuck in Rawlins, six hundred westbound marooned at Laramie. The eastbound passengers were headed for Washington, D.C., to be there for the inaugural of President Ulysses S. Grant, elected overwhelmingly in November.

On February 15, Dan Casement set out from Echo to rescue them, with a road-clearing crew and a big plow. But he found the cuts filled with twenty-five feet of snow and could move forward only five miles per day at best. Then he and some others decided they would have to walk the rest of the way to Laramie, some seventy-five miles. He almost died—

or, as his brother Jack put it, "came near going up"—before he finally made it. He reported to Jack, "Have seen a cut fill up in two hours that took one hundred men ten hours to shovel out." His men, he said, "are all worked out and frozen." It was "impossible to get through." As for the trains, they "can't more than keep engines alive when it blows."[16]

No one east of the Missouri could imagine what it was like. Webster Snyder said, "New York can't appreciate the situation or the severity of a mountain snow storm." Durant's answer was to wire Snyder to send eight hundred flatcars to Chicago. "If you can't send the cars," he warned, with his usual gracelessness, "send your resignation and let some one operate the road who can."[17]

On March 4, Grant became president even before the would-be celebrants stuck in Rawlins got as far as St. Louis. When they arrived, one of them said, "Most of us are much the worse for wear, and we think it will be a long time before we take another ride over the mountains on the Union Pacific Railroad."[18]

"Have We a Pacific Railroad?" asked the *New York Tribune* of March 6, 1869. Not if passengers were stranded in the Wyoming desert and mails detained for three weeks by a mere snowstorm.[19] Passengers stranded on the line wrote extremely angry letters to the newspapers. Fifty of them signed a letter to the *Chicago Tribune* which said that the workmen had refused to help them in any way because "for near three months they had not been paid." Further, as far as they were concerned, the UP was "simply an elongated human slaughter house."[20]

Webster Snyder noticed that some of the letters came from employees of the Central Pacific and wrote his own to friendly newspapers, only to discover that in New York the dailies refused to print letters favorable to his company. No wonder, since their journalists criticized the UP without any attempt at balance (it was, after all, the worst storm in memory).

ACCIDENTS on the lines were frequent. On January 18, a new CP locomotive, named *Blue Jay*, chugged into Reno looking "prettier than a spotted mule, or a New York school ma'am," according to the *Crescent*. Three days later, it chugged back up the Sierra, headed west with a few carloads of passengers, only to run into a stalled lumber train. The *Crescent* reported that, "bruised, broken, and crippled, it was then taken limping to Sacramento for repairs." Several cars were smashed, "but fortunately nobody was killed." One construction train uncoupled in the middle as it was coming down the long grade into Reno. The front half of the train got well ahead, but then the aft cars gained momentum and hit the last car of the front half. The collision splintered eleven cars and crushed two brakemen.[21]

On the western slope, two Chinamen cutting ties felled a tree across the track. They were engaged in cutting it into lengths for ties and were so intent on the work that they failed to notice the approach of the loco-motive. The engineer, coming around a curve, failed to notice the Chi-nese. Both were run over.[22]

For the UP, during the great February storm, Engine 112 was over-whelmed by its attempt to plow through the snow. The boiler strained until it could do no more and exploded from the effort. The engineer, fireman, and conductor were all killed, as was a brakeman who was crushed by an overturning car.

A s 1868 drew to a close, for one unit of the great UP and CP armies the war had ended. The survey engineers had completed their task—for the UP all the way to Humboldt Wells, for the CP to the head of Echo Canyon. The survey parties were disbanded to cut down expenses.

Some surveyors stayed on to work with the construction contractors, and others went off to lay out lines for new roads. In Maury Klein's words, "They could take pride in a job well done." Nothing accomplished by ei-ther company "was more impressive or enduring than the final line located through a forbidding, unmapped wilderness bristling with natural obsta-cles." Anyone can see for himself in the twenty-first century by driving In-terstate 80 from Omaha to Sacramento. Nearly all the way, the automobiles will be paralleling or very near the original grade as the surveyors laid it out. "In later years," Klein wrote, most of the surveyors would look back on their time laying out the line of the first transcontinental railroad "as the most exciting chapter of their careers."[23] It was also the best work they ever did. Every citizen of the United States from that time to the present owes the surveyors a debt of gratitude that can never be repaid.

It was almost as exciting for many of the graders and their foremen. And for them, the first month or two of 1869 were the most memorable. Much of that time, the two companies worked within sight of each other, often within a stone's throw. On January 15, Stanford wrote to Hopkins to say he thought the CP should get as far as Ogden. To claim more, as Huntington was doing, Stanford thought was "to weaken our case." Going west from Ogden to Bear River, the grading lines of the two companies "are generally from 500 feet to a quarter of a mile apart, but at one point they are probably within two hundred feet." Between Bear River and Promontory, the UP was close to the CP "and crosses us twice," with other grades running "within a few feet of us."[24]

On the rocky eastern slope of the Promontory Mountains, a large gang of Strobridge's Chinese were grading to the east, while Casement's graders were building to the west. They were frequently within a few feet of each other. They worked fast, hard, all day long, even though it was obvious to them that one side or the other was wasting time, labor, and supplies. The two grades paralleling each other can still be seen, often nearly touching, occasionally crossing.

The UP's crews were mainly Irish. They tried to shake the persistence of the Chinese by jeering and by tossing frozen clods at them. The tactics had no visible effect, so they attacked with pick handles. The Chinese fought back, to the Irishmen's surprise. So the Irish tried setting off heavy powder charges without warning the Chinese, timing them to explode when the CP grade was closest. Several Chinese were badly hurt. The CP made some official protests. Dodge gave an order to cut it out. He was ignored.

A day or two later, when the grades were only a few yards apart, the Chinese set off an unannounced explosion. It deposited a cascade of dirt and rocks on the UP's Irishmen, several of whom were buried alive. That ended the war.[25] The grading crews, however, went on scraping furiously in parallel lines beside each other but in opposite directions.*

The track layers were not in sight of each other, but they were aware of how well the rival line was doing, and they put their entire effort into the job. Never before, or since, has railroad track been laid so fast. By January, the UP's track was in Echo City, only eight miles from the mouth of Echo Canyon. The first locomotive got there at 11 A.M. "And Echo City held high carnival and general jubilee on the occasion."[26]

There was trouble, however. The tunnel just beyond Echo went

---

* Mormon crews were also grading, for both companies, but the author has seen no account of their going after each other, or of Chinese or Irish going after them.

slowly. It was the longest of the three tunnels the UP had to drill and dig in the Wasatch Range, 772 feet long with deep approach cuts. Though work had started in the summer of 1868, it was far from completed. No nitroglycerin was used, but excavating the tunnel consumed 1,064 kegs of black powder. Meanwhile, the UP workers bypassed the tunnel with a flimsy eight-mile temporary track over a ridge.

The two tunnels to the west were less than a mile apart in the canyon, perched on narrow, curving ledges above steep, rocky gorges. On these tunnels, nitroglycerin was used to speed up the work. A fifth of the tunnel men protested vainly and walked off the job. The remainder used the nitro to make the work go faster. Nitro then ripped out the tunnels at a record pace of eight feet a day.

On January 9, the track reached a tall, ancient pine that stood next to the grading in Weber Canyon. That pine marked precisely the point where the tracks were a thousand miles from Omaha. It surely deserved to be memorialized, so a sign reading "1000 Mile Tree" was hung from its lowest limb. Andrew Russell took a picture, often reproduced, and the base of the tree became a picnic spot for tourists.

By the end of January, light shone through the largest tunnel, the one closest to Echo. The headings had met. The bottoms remained to be blasted out, a job not completed until April, and not until the middle of May was track laid through it.

THE CP spent January laying track from Elko toward Humboldt Wells. On the 28th of that month, the tracks were 150 miles west of Elko. After getting to the Wells, the track would run northeastward to the state line, then on toward Promontory. But Humboldt Wells was still 224 miles from Ogden, and the CP had not yet reached it.

Charlie Crocker came, saw, and threatened the Chinese crews. According to one foreman who was there, "He stirred up the track layers with a stick; told them they must do better or leave the road."[27] That got them to working even faster.

One day, at the end of track, a supply train came up. It carried no rails, only ties. Crocker went back to the forwarding station to confront the man responsible, a man named McWade. As soon as he saw Crocker, McWade called out, "Mr. Crocker, I know about it. Mr. Strobridge has telegraphed me, and I know it was all wrong and I am sorry."

Grim-faced, Crocker replied, "Mac a mistake is a crime now. You know what we have been trying to do. You know how I have been going up and down this road trying to get the material to you. And here it is— and you have made a mistake and thrown us out of two miles of track today. Now take your bundle and go. I cannot overlook it."

McWade burst out crying. Finally, he managed to say, "Well it is pretty hard on me. I have been a good, faithful man."

"I know you have," Crocker replied, "but there has got to be discipline on this road, and I cannot overlook anything of this kind. You must go. Send your assistant to me."

Crocker put the assistant in charge. But, having made his point, he relented. "I let him lay off a month," he said of McWade, "and put him back again. But it put everybody on the alert, and kept them right up to their work. And it did good, because everybody was afraid, and when I came along they were all hard at work, I can tell you."

Discussing the incident years later, Crocker added, "It got so that I was really ashamed of myself."[28]

A s always, finance was a special problem for the UP. The track layers struck, for $3.50 per day. The UP had no choice with regard to these skilled workers and paid what was demanded. They, and all other workers, also got double pay on Sundays. The Mormon workers demanded $5 a day for a man and team, $10 on Sunday, and at least on paper got it, though they were not paid. When Mormon subcontractors refused work in spring sinks or heavy cuts, Casement flung his tireless Irish into the breach.[29]

On January 4, Snyder had reported to Dodge, "In construction the waste of money is awful. . . . We are ditching trains daily. Grading is done at enormous expense. The ties cost $4.50 each on the ground. . . . The company can't stand such drafts as I know the Construction Department must be making. . . . Would like to know what I am to be paid." Twelve days later, Oliver Ames wrote Durant: "Everything depends on the economy and vigor with which you press the work. We hear here awful stories of the cost of the work. . . . The contract price for ties is but one dollar."

The bosses had turned on each other. On February 3, Durant had telegraphed Dodge to inform him before issuing orders, as always. "If you cannot find time to report here I shall of necessity be obliged to supersede you."[30] A strange threat to be given to a man who had the President-elect's full confidence, and of whom Oakes Ames had declared, "Dodge is a perfect steam engine for Energy. He is at work night and day." And for Durant, Oakes had his own threat. "We must remove him from the management," he declared, "or there is no value to our property."[31]

Such was the word from company headquarters in New York. In Omaha, the bankers were demanding their money, $200,000 in overdrafts from the Omaha National alone. Herbert Hoxie told Dodge, "We must have $750,000 and it ought to be twice that." Oliver Ames had calls for $2 million with neither cash to give nor collateral to get it. Out on the line, where the work was being done, everyone who counted was upset. "I am afraid the Union Pacific is in a bad way," Jack Casement wrote his wife. Sam Reed, covering forty to sixty miles a day on horseback to oversee the crews, told his wife, "Too much business is unfitting me for future usefulness. I know it is wearing me out." But it wasn't so much the work as the financial strain. Reed added, "The Doctor himself, I think, is getting frightened at the bills."[32]

*I*N Washington, the UP had but to wait before it got ahead of the CP. The Andrew Johnson administration would give way on March 4, 1869, to the Ulysses Grant administration. The President-elect and the high command in the army were as close as could be with Grenville Dodge, and friends with the Casements along with other UP officials. Whereas Johnson's Cabinet had favored the CP whenever possible, Grant's could be expected to lean toward the UP.

It all came down to the government loan of bonds to the railroads for miles graded and track laid, and specifically down to which road would get them for the line between the north end of the Great Salt Lake and Echo Summit. Huntington had filed with the Department of the Interior his guesswork map covering the distance, and Secretary Browning had accepted it. Stanford then proceeded on the assumption that the CP's line on a map, even if little work had been done on it east of Ogden, was the true line of the Pacific railroad, and the only one on which subsidy bonds could be issued. Huntington intended to snatch them. He had filed in Washington for $2.4 million in subsidy bonds, two-thirds of the amount due for that portion of the line.

Dodge and the Ames brothers had hurried to Washington to block Huntington. They were successful, at least to the degree of persuading Browning to hold up issuing the bonds until a special commission had reported to him on the best route through the disputed territory. Huntington responded to Browning's holdup with a curse and a comment, "The Union Pacific has outbid me."[33]

On January 14, 1869, Browning had given the commission his instructions. He ordered the commissioners to "make a thorough and careful examination" of the ground between the two ends of track. If either of the lines was "in all respects unobjectionable," they were authorized to adopt it. If not, they should make a new location. "You will also designate a point at which the two roads will probably meet."[34]

Browning's actions caused delay, which he must have intended and which was probably the best he could do as a lame duck. Oakes Ames came to Huntington's hotel room to see if the two roads could make their own settlement. Why not simply split the remaining distance between the two railheads, Ames suggested. That would suit the UP, since it would put the meeting point west of Promontory.

"I'll see you damned first," Huntington snarled. How about the mouth of Weber Canyon? he countered. That would greatly benefit the CP.

Ames replied with his own curse. The two men broke off, met again, snarled once more, broke off, met again, until Huntington finally agreed to a joining at Ogden. Beyond that point, he swore, he would not budge.

On January 29, Stanford discussed the matter in a letter to Hopkins. The commissioners would begin their examination on February 1, he said, "and from the instructions and straws in the wind I fear this thing is set up against us. The far off distance of our track and slow progress works against us with great force. It is trying to ones nerves to think of it."

Stanford blamed not Ames or anyone else with the UP, or Browning, but Huntington. In Stanford's view, Huntington was "trying to save what a want of foresight has jeopardized if not lost. I tell you the thought makes me feel like a dog; I have no pleasure in the thought of Railroad. It is mortification."[35]

O N February 16, the CP was twenty miles east of the Wells, this at a time when the UP was twenty miles east of Ogden with its track. The CP's biggest problem was not laxness on the Chinese crews' part, but getting supplies up to the end of track, brought on not by McWade's mistakes but by haphazard ship arrival in San Francisco and by the blockage caused by the great storm in the Sierra.[36]

A lack of locomotives was not the cause. Huntington had shipped them to California almost faster than Crocker could use them. The *Reno Cres-*

cent's editor called the roll of the new ones to make their way through his town: *Fire Fly, Grey Eagle, Verdi, Roller, White Eagle, Tiger, Hurricane, Jupiter, Mercury, Herald, Heron.* There was no apparent limit.[37]

By February 29, the CP had made another twenty miles in thirteen days, which for all previous track-laying crews would have been spectacular progress but for the CP was disappointing. The line was forty miles east of Humboldt Wells, almost into Utah, but it was still 144 miles from Promontory. The UP on that date had track up to Devil's Gate Bridge on the Weber River and was thus but six miles from the mouth of Weber Canyon and sixty-six miles from Promontory. But the CP was closing the gap.

PROMONTORY Summit was a flat, almost level circular basin more than a mile in width. It stood a little more than five thousand feet in elevation, some seven hundred feet above the level of the lake. It separated the Promontory Mountains to the south from the North Promontory Mountains and stood at the northern end of the Great Salt Lake, or the beginning of the thirty-five-mile-long rugged peninsula that thrust itself into the lake.

There was no terrain problem in grading and laying track across the summit basin, but getting up to it on either side was difficult. On the west side the approach was over sixteen relatively easy miles, but on the eastern slope the ascent required ten tortuous miles of climbing at eighty feet to a mile, including switchbacks. For the UP this was the last stretch of difficult country. There were projecting abutments of limestone to cut through, and ravines requiring fills or bridges. The most formidable of the ravines was about halfway up the eastern slope.

The CP had got there first. It was a gorge of about 170 feet in depth and five hundred feet long. On either side there was black lime-rock that had to be cut through, sometimes at heights of thirty feet and always as much as twenty feet. In November 1868, Stanford, accompanied by two of his engineers, arrived to see it. He took one look at the projected line and ordered Clement to lay out a new one to avoid an eight-hundred-foot tunnel through solid limestone. Clement said that was going to be an awfully big fill. Stanford agreed, predicting that it would require ten thousand yards of earth.

In early February, the CP put five hundred men, Mormons and Chinese, to work. They were supplemented by 250 teams of horses, to pull the carts that carried the earth to the fill sites. One by one they came forward, tipped the cart, and returned for the next load. One hundred fifty feet above, on each end at the top of the gorge, blasting crews were at work. They used nitroglycerin and black powder to make the cut. They made the holes for the explosive with drills, just as had been done at the tunnel facings, or, if one was available, they used crevices in the stone. After pouring in the powder, they worked it down with iron bars.

Sometimes the bars striking the rocks sent off sparks that set off the nitro or the powder. Huge rocks were sent tumbling down the mountainside. Once a man was blown two or three hundred feet in the air. When he came down he had broken nearly every bone in his body. The same blast burned a few others, and three were wounded by flying stones. On another occasion three mules were killed by an unexpected blast.[38]

It took almost three months to make the fill. It is still there today, still causing viewers to gasp and to shake their heads in disbelief, especially if they are carrying a photograph showing how the UP overcame the gorge.

Had either railroad built a causeway or bridge across the Great Salt Lake, most of the difficult work could have been avoided and many miles saved. Dodge thought about it, put enough energy into it to have the lake sounded, and decided it couldn't be done. In 1868, the lake was fourteen feet higher than it had been in 1849, when first sounded. It was not feasible to build, Dodge decided, because "the depth of the lake, the weight of the water, and the cost of building was beyond us, and we were forced north of the lake and had to put in the high grades crossing Promontory Ridge." By the time the Union Pacific put in the causeway at the beginning of the twentieth century, the lake was eleven feet lower than when the original survey was made.[39]

*H*UNTINGTON labored in Washington. He had called at the office of Secretary of the Treasury Hugh McCulloch almost every day in January, to demand the CP's bonds for advance construction work as far as six miles east of Ogden, but Secretary McCulloch was always too busy to see him. Huntington was sure the CP was entitled, because Secretary Browning had approved his map. And if the CP got the government bonds for the route from Promontory to east of Ogden, obviously the UP could not be entitled, because the government was not going to give away two sets of bonds for a line through the same territory.

Huntington began to "bring different influences to bear on the Secretary." He got a report from Browning's office stating that the CP was entitled to the bonds. He also got the solicitor of the Treasury to sign a similar report.[40] Still no action.

Thanks in part at least to Huntington's lobbying, his request for subsidy bonds was brought up for discussion in a Cabinet meeting on February 26—that is, at a time when the Johnson administration had less than a week to go. Browning appeared before the Cabinet and got McCulloch to agree with him, but the Cabinet put off any decision until Monday, March 1. At that meeting, with Grant to be inaugurated on March 4, the Cabinet voted unanimously to approve the CP's request for bonds and formally directed Secretary McCulloch to release them.

"But McCulloch still refused to let me have them," Huntington later recalled. In his opinion this was due to McCulloch's having had a talk with Oliver Ames, which may have been true: Ames must have felt that once Grant was in office McCulloch would be gone and the vote of the Johnson Cabinet would amount to nothing. Whatever the explanation, Huntington was taking no chances. He went to the secretary of the Treasury's office, demanded to see him, then announced that he would sit in McCulloch's anteroom for two weeks if he had to but he was not going to leave without the bonds. McCulloch consulted with his assistants, then declared, with a sigh, "He shall have them." Huntington went back to his hotel room, and by 8 P.M., "I had the bonds. They amounted to over $2,400,000."

The money covered the line in advance of the completed track from Promontory to six miles east of Ogden. Oakes Ames had just talked to McCulloch, who had assured him that no bonds would be issued in advance of completed track, and President Johnson had told both Ames and Dodge "that no such bonds should be issued." The UP had just lost $32,000 per mile in bonds (a total of $2.5 million), plus the right to issue the same amount of their own first mortgage bonds, plus the grants of land. But the directors didn't yet know that they had lost.

Huntington stuffed the bonds into his satchel and got on the train to New York. "This was the biggest fight I ever had in Washington," he wrote Hopkins, "and it cost me a considerable sum." Three days later, Grant was inaugurated. His first order, released on the evening of his inaugural, was directed to two members of his Cabinet. One was the new

secretary of the interior, Jacob Dolson Cox, formerly a division commander under Sherman during the war and the governor of Ohio. The
other was the new secretary of the Treasury, George Sewall Boutwell, a
former congressman from Massachusetts and a friend as well as colleague
of Oakes Ames. The order was to suspend action on the issue of further
subsidy bonds to the CP and the UP.[41]

Stanford, Huntington, and the other two members of the Big Four had
hoped for more. The $2.4 million was the subsidy from Promontory to
Ogden, but the CP had hoped to go at least as far as Echo Summit. On
March 7, 1869, however, less than a week after Huntington got the
bonds, the UP laid tracks into Ogden, 1,028 miles from Omaha. This
ended the dispute as to which line had the right-of-way east of the town.
(At the time, Crocker's rails were 184 miles away from Ogden.)

On March 14, Stanford in Salt Lake City wrote Hopkins to inform him,
"They [the UP] have laid track about three miles west of Ogden." He did
not have to add what Hopkins already knew, that the delivery of bonds to
Huntington for the grading from Promontory down past Ogden by the CP
had already happened. Stanford did tell Hopkins that if the UP were aware
of what the government had done "they would call off their graders." But
in their ignorance, the UP was going all out on the heavy work at Promontory. Let them, was Stanford's attitude. "We shall serve notices for them not
to interfere with our line and rest there for the present."[42]

GRANT'S order to stop any handing out of subsidies may have helped
the UP, at least for a time, but it was not enough. The company owed the
banks $5.2 million in loans, owed its contractors and subcontractors, su-
perintendents, engineers, foremen, and workers $4.5 million, owed oth-
ers who knew how much. It had not a cent available to pay. Brigham
Young wrote Durant at this time that the Mormons had completed the
fill near the head of Echo Canyon. He recounted that the Doctor and
two of his, Young's, sons had stood at the spot a couple of months ago to
make a contract for the work. As Young quoted him, Durant had said, "If
we would keep on a large force, and rush the work, I'll pay you what it is
worth." On that basis the job was done. All Young was asking was for his
people to be paid, and that at a rate 40 percent below what the CP was
paying for similar tasks.[43]

Good luck to Young on collecting. Durant not only ignored him, but at the same time sent a wire to Dodge that was notable, even for Doc, in its brazenness. "You have so largely over estimated the amounts due Contractors," he said, "that it becomes my duty to suspend your acting as Chief Engineer."[44]

Dodge had meanwhile met with Grant three days before the inaugural. Grant had told him that there was evidence of a "great swindle" in the estimates for UP work done in Weber Canyon. As soon as he became president, Grant warned, he was prepared to force a complete reorganization of the road. Dodge then gave orders that at the next meeting of the board, scheduled for March 10, Durant must be voted out.[45]

Good luck on holding that meeting. James Fisk, known as the "Barnum of Wall Street," had just bought six shares of UP stock at $40 each, a total of $240. He was working with Durant, as he had previously worked with financier Jay Gould. With the assistance of the mayor of New York, Boss William M. Tweed, and Judge George Barnard of the New York State Supreme Court in Manhattan, Fisk and Gould had taken control of the Erie Railroad away from financiers no less renowned than Cornelius Vanderbilt and financier Daniel Drew. Now he was after the UP.

No dividend had been paid on his six shares of the UP. Fisk claimed that he had been deprived of his rights because the Crédit Mobilier was absorbing all the profits of the UP. He got Judge Barnard to declare the UP bankrupt and had the judge appoint a receiver, who was, not surprisingly, William M. Tweed, Jr., son of the "Boss." On March 10, Fisk got an order that let him send in the sheriffs to break up the UP's stockholders' meeting. The officers of the law arrived at the Fifth Avenue Hotel in New York City with warrants to arrest the directors. Oakes Ames claimed congressional immunity and sneaked away successfully, but his brother Oliver was arrested and held until he could produce a $20,000 bail in the morning. This was the meeting at which the officers had planned to vote Durant out of office. So much for that.[46]

The New York newspapers had a grand time with the whole thing. "Prince Erie's War Dance," blasted one headline. But the editors could not keep themselves from supporting Fisk, because of what one called the "peculiar relations" between the UP and the Crédit Mobilier that Fisk was attacking. The theme became the Rogue as Reformer, which seemed to fit the engaging chap named Fisk. All the directors of the UP, meanwhile, believed that Durant was behind the whole thing.

The UP appealed to Congress. It took nearly a month for that body to take up the matter.

• • •

Out in Utah, both lines were laying track as fast as could be done. Hopkins sent a telegram to Huntington, "Roving Delia Fish Dance," which meant when decoded, "Laying track at the rate of 4 miles a day."[47] The UP had laid out the new town of Corinne, five miles west of Brigham City, on the east side of the Bear River. It was a Hell on Wheels built of canvas and board shanties. On March 23, the *Salt Lake Deseret News* wrote, "The place is fast becoming civilized, several men having been killed there already, the last one was found in the river with four bullet holes through him and his head badly mangled."

Photographer Russell took a photograph of Corinne. He must have taken it at first light, for there is but one horse and no people to be seen. The shacks and tents are laid out haphazardly. Not all of them were taverns. Three of the nearest buildings are eating houses: "Germania House, Meals 50 cents," "Montana House, Meals 50 cents," and "Montaine House, City Bakery." Off at the far left is an apparently improbable place of business, the "Corinne Book Store."

Jack Casement, driving the work forward by night as well as by day, had just about had enough. "I am perfectly homesick," he wrote his wife. When the job was over, "I think I would like to work in the garden or build a house."[48] But his spirit revived, because the weather was beautiful, the mud drying fast. Rafts were coming down the Bear River carrying pilings and telegraph poles. The UP had five pile drivers at work preparing for building a bridge over the river, while the CP had one at work. Both lines were being vigorously prosecuted. The *Deseret News* wrote, "From Corinne west thirty miles, the grading camps present the appearance of a mighty army. As far as the eye can reach are to be seen almost a continuous line of tents, wagons and men."

What a scene it was. Even for men who had been in the war, which included most of the UP crews, foremen, and superintendents, and many of the non-Chinese in the CP's camp, it was a striking, never-to-be-forgotten image. Russell and Hart, who had seen and photographed great numbers of men in battle and in camp, were inspired to do some of their best work here. They were up before dawn, setting their cameras, getting their plates ready, taking pictures through the day, and keeping at it until the light faded. Everyone who was there knew that, except for the war, there had never before been in North America, and never would be again, a sight like this one. They all soaked it up.

The area twenty-one miles west of Corinne, where the ascent of the Promontory Mountains began, was "nearly surrounded by grading camps." The blasting crews were "jarring the earth every few minutes with their glycerine and powder, lifting whole ledges of limestone rock from their long resting places, hurling them hundreds of feet in the air and scattering them around for a half mile in every direction. One boulder of three or four hundred pounds weight was thrown over a half mile and completely buried itself in the ground."

The lines were running so near each other that, according to the reporter, "in one place the UP are taking a four feet cut out of the CP fill to finish their grade, leaving the CP to fill the cut thus made." Who was ahead, the reporter (whose pen name was "Saxey") didn't know, or at least didn't want to say. But for sure they were going to meet somewhere.

Meanwhile, between Promontory and Brigham City, "I will venture the assertion that there is not less than three hundred whisky shops, all *developing the resources of the Territory* and showing the Mormons what is necessary to build up a country."[49] Dodge had put engineer Thomas B. Morris in charge of the Utah Division. In his diary Morris recorded, "Rode to Brigham City—found camp there. G.L. drunk—had him arrested—hunted up bed in storehouse. Discharged L. Pratt & Van Wagner—drunk—saw G.L. & left him locked up." A couple of weeks later, "Settled up with George & Walter—the latter I discharged for impudence." Four days later, "Stayed all night at Fields—good supper & bed behind the bar."[50]

*T*HE UP got its bridge built first, and on April 7 its first locomotive steamed over the Bear River to enter Corinne. The CP was still almost fifteen miles west of Monument Point. But the CP had its "Big Fill" completed, whereas the UP had just gotten started (March 28) on its attempt to cross the gorge. Strobridge had decided he could save time by building a trestle bridge, to be called the Big Trestle, about 150 yards east of and parallel to the Big Fill. The UP's line could be made a fill later.

The Big Trestle took more than a month to build and was not completed until May 5. It was four hundred feet long and eighty-five feet high. One reporter said that nothing he could write "would convey an idea of the flimsy character of that structure. The cross pieces are jointed in the most clumsy manner." In the reporter's judgment, "The Central

Pacific have a fine, solid embankment alongside it [meaning the Big Fill], which ought to be used as the track." Another correspondent predicted that riding on a passenger car over the Big Trestle "will shake the nerves of the stoutest hearts of railroad travelers when they see that a few feet of round timbers and seven-inch spikes are expected to uphold a train in motion."[51]

THE race," Dodge had declared on March 23, "is getting exciting & interesting."[52] This was so in New York as well as in Utah. On the East Coast, Fisk got an order from Judge Barnard giving the receiver, young Tweed, the power to break open the safe at the UP's headquarters, 20 Nassau Street. On April 2, he came in with eight deputies armed with sledgehammers and chisels. Tweed announced that they were going to break open the company's safe. It took hours. When the safe finally yielded, it was discovered that most of the UP's records and documents had disappeared.

A different sort of fight was taking place in Washington. Congress debated the railroads. Senator William M. Stewart from Nevada, a staunch friend of the CP, described with gusto and in detail the sins of the UP. He was supported by Senator James Nye, also of Nevada. Picking up on Charles Francis Adams's article on the Crédit Mobilier, Stewart declared, "Leading members of Congress, members of the committee on the Pacific Railroad in the House, were not only in the Union Pacific but in this identical Crédit Mobilier, and were the recipients of enormous dividends." That was surely ominous for the congressmen who held Crédit Mobilier stock, but also for the Big Four and their Contract and Finance Company, if only because the UP had its defenders, including General Sherman's brother, and they might well broaden any investigation.[53]

So, on April 9, Dodge met with Huntington in Washington. Both companies had reason to compromise, at once. Huntington made the initial move. The CP would buy the UP track between Promontory Summit and Ogden for its own use. "I offered them $4 million," he later asserted. Huntington coupled the offer with a threat: if the UP refused, the CP would build its own track into Ogden. Dodge argued but eventually gave in.

The two men agreed that the roads would meet in or near Ogden. That evening, in a night session, the Congress that had created the race to begin with, finally voted to end it. A joint resolution said, "The common terminus of the Union Pacific and the Central Pacific railroads shall be at or near Ogden, and the Union Pacific Railroad Company shall build, and the Central Pacific Railroad Company shall pay for and own, the railroad from the terminus aforesaid to Promontory Summit, at which the rails shall meet and connect and form one continuous line."[54]

The race was over. Who could say who won? Generally, the men involved breathed a sigh of relief. Charlie Crocker spoke for most of them. He had been suffering from insomnia for months, and he later said, "When Huntington telegraphed me that he had fixed matters with the Union Pacific, and that we were to meet on the summit of Promontory, I was out at the front, and went to bed that night and slept like a child."[55]

Of all the people to speak for the UP, Silas Seymour, the interfering engineer, was the least likely. But, wandering out to the end of track west of Corinne a week later, he paused to contemplate how much had been accomplished. Exactly a year earlier, he had watched Durant pound in the last spike at Sherman Summit, in the Black Hills in eastern Wyoming. Since then the UP had advanced 519 miles through desert and mountains. Seymour marveled, "Nothing like it in the world."[56]

When Lewis Clement, who had so much to do with it, heard the news, he wrote his friend and CP surveyor Butler Ives, and signed off with a wonderfully perfect line: he said he was glad to contemplate "the bond of iron which is to hold our glorious country in one eternal union."[57]

Chapter Sixteen

TO THE SUMMIT
April 11 – May 7, 1869

OGDEN would be the terminus for the Central Pacific coming from Sacramento and the Union Pacific coming from Omaha, but the initial meeting point for the two lines would be the basin at Promontory Summit. To signify that the graders and track layers had accepted what their bosses in Washington (meaning Dodge and Huntington, the U.S. Congress, and the President and his Cabinet) had decided, on April 10 the UP stopped grading west of Promontory, and on April 15 the CP stopped grading east of the summit. The companies pulled back their men, their tents, their cooking facilities, their equipment, their wagons, horses and mules, everything.

The workers and their superintendents felt that a diktat had been forced on them. It wasn't their choice, it wasn't their decision. It hurt, it stung, it mattered, but it had to be done, even though it meant abandoning the field of battle. It was a retreat. That was something all the Confederate and most of the Yankee veterans in the two companies had experienced more than once during the war, but they hated it as much now as they had then.

Still, losing the battle wasn't the same as losing the war. The rivalry between the two railroad lines continued.* The competition had become

---

* As it would until the last decade of the twentieth century, when the two lines were merged into one Union Pacific.

a habit. At the end of April 1869, even though the race had been over for nearly three weeks, that competition captured the attention of the people of the United States plus the directors of the two companies. Most of all, for every employee from superintendent down to dishwasher, the climax to the competition, even if meaningless in financial terms, was mesmerizing. There had never been anything like it before and never would be again.

For the UP directors and employees, one of the things that stung the most was that their railroad had become, in effect, no different from Brigham Young's grading crews, a contractor for the CP. The UP grading and track-laying gangs were working not for their own company but for the other guy's, and they knew it. Everything they did on the line between Ogden and Promontory Summit would be turned over to the CP. And the UP's treasury was, as always, empty. Dodge warned Oliver Ames, "Men will work no longer without pay & a stoppage now is fatal to us." Jack Casement added his own warning: the banks and merchants from Omaha to Ogden were "loaded with UPRR paper and if the company don't send some money here soon they will bust up the whole country." Seymour added in his own telegram, "We are being ruined for want of track material."[1]

Despite Jim Fisk's legal maneuvers, the UP directors had managed to get the headquarters out of Nassau Street in New York and up to Boston. But when the officers were let go and the sign was taken down in New York, who else but Doc Durant promptly rented the rooms and took possession of their contents. He didn't get much, because the Ames brothers and their friends had acted first in emptying the vaults, file cabinets, and the rest. "When we can get our Books away from NY and cleaned out from that sink of corruption," Oliver Ames declared while doing the deed, "we shall feel safe and not until then."

By April 22, they were safe. The directors held their long-postponed stockholders' meeting in Boston. The highlight came after a series of speeches, when a telegraph from Dodge in Utah was read: "CENTRAL PACIFIC RAILROAD, EIGHTEEN MILES FROM PROMONTORY SUMMIT. WE ARE TWELVE MILES FROM SUMMIT." There were cheers all around, and the meeting was adjourned.[2]

The troubles were not over. Lewis Dent let the board know that he and his partner expected to be retained as counsel for the UP at $10,000 a year. Each. He had connections. He was Grant's brother-in-law, and his

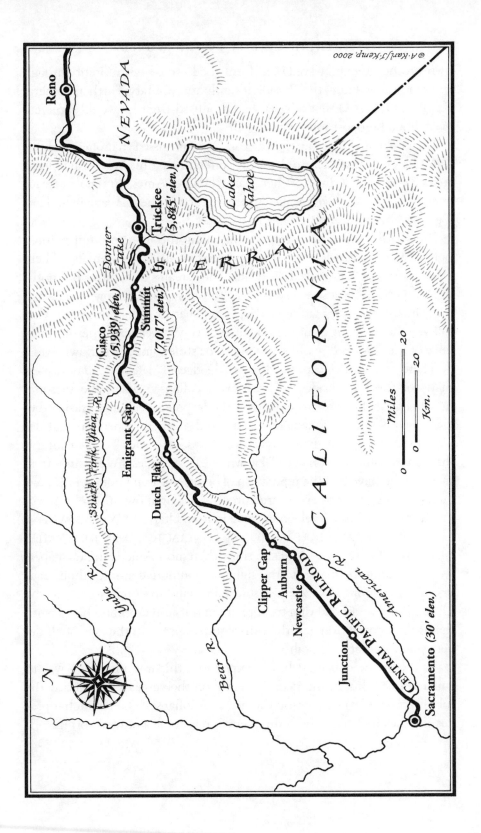

own brother, General Frederick Dent, had served with Grant through the war and was now the President's military secretary. Further, General Rawlins, Grant's closest adviser, had promised Dent he would receive a "very liberal proposition" from the UP.

Dodge said to give him $500 a year. Dent dismissed that offer as an insult. General Dent then told another director that his brother had been treated badly. That director then warned Oliver Ames, "*It is not in the interest of our Co. to make enemies in that direction.*" The UP gave in and put Dent and his partner on the payroll.[3]

Worse followed. The corruption all along the line, so often pointed out by Webster Snyder, was now apparent to all. Cries went up. There were mutters of "Off with their heads" and screams of outrage. But nothing happened, because everyone was too busy with his own concerns. Early in April, Snyder wrote Dodge, "I am heartily sick of this outfit that talks so much about cleaning out thieves & yet weakens when in presence of the thieves & will let thousands be stolen under their own eyes."

There was more. Reports came to Dodge of defective masonry on many of the UP's bridges. Three spans collapsed when the masonry failed. The arches on two culverts at Lodgepole Creek also crashed because of inferior workmanship. Dodge did a quick inspection and declared the masonry at Bear River "worthless." He said, "The backing is dirt and free stone set on edge." He wrote Oliver Ames, "We cannot trust masons who have had the reputation of being No. 1 and honest unless we employ an engineer to every structure to stand right over them."[4]

Shortly thereafter, a telegram came in from Utah: "WE MUST HAVE FIVE HUNDRED THOUSAND DOLLARS TO PAY CONTRACTORS MEN IMMEDIATELY OR ROAD CANNOT RUN." And at a time when most American newspapers were recording the march to the summit in minute detail for their readers, the *New York Herald* ran a sour editorial: "In congress we see the Union Pacific Railroad ring triumphant and its directors and hangers-on flaunt their corruption and their ill-acquired means in the face of all decency and legislative morality."[5]

To the directors it must have seemed that this was a hell of a way to run a railroad. Just as their company was on the verge of completing the job, it appeared to be nearing the brink of collapse. The triumphal procession they had anticipated threatened to become a funeral cortege.

● ● ●

THE CP was moving ahead briskly. Indeed, almost without worries. On April 9, it was 690 miles east of Sacramento and that day laid 4.2 miles of track. The next day, it set down 3.1 miles, and the day after that, 4.6. By April 17, it had reached Monument Point, a quarter-mile north of the lakeshore. There the CP had established three sprawling grading camps. The first had a hundred tents, the second another hundred, and the third seventy-five. "Hustle" and "bustle" were the words that came to people's lips when they saw this hive of activity. As one example, on April 18 a train came from Sacramento. It was thirty-two cars in length. While the Chinese unloaded each car of its rails and ties, others were putting inter-mediate ties under the rails, which were already spiked into place, and still others were putting in additional ballast and tamping it down.

Monument Point was a spot Durant and Dodge had once thought of as a meeting place, after they had given up on the Nevada-California state line or Humboldt Wells. Now none of that was to be. On April 23, the *Alta California* reported that the distance separating the two lines was less than fifty miles. "The CP is laying about four miles of track a day; the UP some days have laid the same, on others only one or two miles, from lack of material—principally ties."[6]

Although the tracks had not yet joined, increasingly emigrants were moving west by rail rather than wagon trains. On April 26, the newspaper reported that immigrants who had traveled from Omaha to beyond Ogden on the UP hired stagecoaches at the terminus and took them to Monument Point, got on a CP train, and were in California only a little over a week after leaving Omaha.[7] There were constant reminders of the change the transcontinental railroad had already wrought. Freight wagons carrying supplies to the end of track from Sacramento and Omaha were constantly rolling past the construction crews. Wells Fargo stagecoaches, which had once spanned the continent, now provided service between railheads. Their run became shorter with each passing day.

The road that was about to be completed had been built, in part, because General Sherman and his army wanted it. So did the politicians, and of course those who settled in the West. Everyone would save time and benefit from its completion, but none more directly than the army. In its task of protecting the frontier and the Far West, the army had sent its units on exhausting marches of sometimes as much as several months just to get to a new post. The expense was terrific, the pain considerable.

But in mid-April 1869, the Twelfth Infantry Regiment, with orders to proceed to the Presidio of San Francisco, took the UP to Corinne, detrained, marched two easy days to the CP railhead, and got on the CP for the trip west.[8] It took a week from Omaha to Sacramento, and for both speed and comfort it was a dream. No American army unit had ever before moved so fast or so far for less money or at such ease.

On April 27, the *Alta's* reporter was at the end of the CP's track, 678 miles from Sacramento. The railroad was fourteen miles short of Promontory Summit, and the UP was within eight miles and was laying a mile per day. The UP was coming on even though it still had to finish the Big Trestle and do some difficult rock-cutting. "They may hurry up," the reporter wrote, "or they may decide to turn to the abandoned grade of the Central Pacific, which is within a few feet of where they are working." That abandoned grade included the CP's Big Fill.[9]

*I*N 1868, Jack Casement's men had laid down four and a half miles of track in a single day. "They bragged of it," Crocker later said, "and it was heralded all over the country as being the biggest day's track-laying that was ever known." Crocker told Strobridge that the CP must beat the UP. They got together the material, talked to the men, and did it, spiking down six miles and a few feet in a single day.

Casement had come back at them, starting at 3 A.M., working by the light of lanterns until dawn, and keeping at the task until midnight. At the end of the day, the UP had advanced the end of track eight miles and a fraction.

"Now," Crocker said to Stro, "we must take off our coats, but we must not beat them until we get so close together that there is not enough room for them to turn around and outdo us." Ten miles ought to do it, he figured.

"Mr. Crocker," Strobridge said, "we cannot get men enough onto the track to lay ten miles." Crocker said it had to be done.

"How are we going to do it?" Stro asked. "The men will all be in each other's way."

Organize, Crocker replied. "I've been thinking over this for two weeks, and I have got it all planned out."[10]

Crocker's plan was to have the men and the horses ready at first light. He wanted ironcars with rails, spikes, and fishplates, all ready to go. The night before, he wanted five supply trains lined up, the first at the railhead. Each of the five locomotives would pull sixteen cars, which contained enough supplies for two miles of track. When the sun rose, the Chinese would leap onto the cars of the first train, up at the end of track, and begin throwing down kegs of bolts and spikes, bundles of fishplates, and the iron rails. That train would then back up to a siding, and while the first two miles were laid another would come forward. As the first train moved back, six-man gangs of Chinese would lift the small open flatcars onto the track and begin loading each one with sixteen rails plus kegs of bolts, spikes, and fishplates. The flatcars had rollers along their outer edges to make it easier to slide the rails forward and off. Two horses, in single file, each with a rider on its back, would be hitched to the car by a long rope. The horses would then race down the side of the grade kept clear for them.

As this operation was being mounted, three men with shovels, called "pioneers," would move out along the grade, aligning the ties that had been placed on the grade the night before. When the loaded cart got to the end of track, right after the pioneers, a team of Irish workers, one on each side, would grab the rails with their tongs, two men in front, two at the rear, race them forward to their proper position, and drop them in their proper place when the foreman called out "Down!"

Ahead of the track layers would be two men to handle the portable track-gauge, a wooden measuring device that was four feet eight and a half inches long. They would stay just ahead of the track layers all day long, making sure the rails laid down were just as far apart as Abraham Lincoln had decreed they should be. The spikes, placed by the Chinese workers atop the rails, would dribble onto the grade as the rails were removed. The bolts and fishplates were carried in hand buckets to where they were needed. When the cart was empty, it would be tipped off the grade and the next one brought on. Then the first would be turned around and the horses would be rehitched, to race back for another load.

Next would come the men placing and pounding in spikes. Crocker told Stro, "Have the first man drive one particular spike and not stop for another; he walks right past that rail and drives the same spike in the next rail; another man follows him and drives the next spike in the same rail; and another follows him and so on." He admonished Stro to have enough spikes on hand so that "no man stops and no man passes another."

After the spikes were driven in place, five to a rail, would come the straighteners. "One man sees a defective place and he gives it a shove and passes on," Crocker instructed. "Another comes right behind him and they get the track straight; none of them stop—they are walking forward all the time." Next would be the crew to ballast the rails. One would raise the track with his shovel placed under a tie. Another would cast a shovelful of dirt under the tie. Then the fillers, one man after another throwing in a shovelful of earth. Crocker told Stro to "have enough of them so that when they are all through you have it all filled and no man stops nor allows another man to pass him."

Finally, the tampers. There were four hundred of them. "Each one gives two tamps and he goes right along and gives two more to the next and does not stop on one rail, so that he will not be in the way of the next man."

The crew placing the telegraph poles and fixing the wire would keep pace with the others. And as the rail layers emptied a car, it would be tipped off the track and another one brought on. The empty car would be replaced and taken back to the pile of rails by the horses at a gallop. When a loaded car was approaching down the track, the crew on the empty one would jump off and lift their car from the rails, then put it back after the loaded car went past with unslackened speed. When all the rails had been laid, another train pulling sixteen cars would come up to the end of track. The Chinese would swarm over it and throw off the rails, spikes, bolts, and fishplates and the process would be repeated.

Strobridge heard everything Crocker had to say, considered it, and finally said, "We can beat them, but it will cost something." For example, he insisted on having a fresh team of horses for each car hauling rail, the fresh horses to take over after every two and a half miles.

"Go ahead and do it," was Crocker's reply.[11]

THEY waited until April 27, when the CP had only fourteen miles to go, the UP nine—and that up the eastern approach to Promontory Summit, heavy work at best, and the Big Trestle not yet done. If Strobridge and his men accomplished the feat, the UP wouldn't have enough room left to exceed the ten miles.

Crocker offered a bet of $10,000 to Durant, saying that the CP would lay ten miles of track in one day. Reportedly, Durant was sure they couldn't and accepted the wager.

On April 27, a CP locomotive ran off the track after the crew had put down two miles of track. The accident forced a postponement of the try for the record until the next day. This was somewhat embarrassing, for the UP had its engineers there to watch, along with some army officers on their way to a new mission, and several newspaper correspondents. Crocker laughed it off. On the morning of April 28, before sunrise, a wagon load of UP officials arrived on the scene, including Durant, Dodge, Reed, and Seymour. They had come to watch Crocker's humiliation and to laugh at him.

What the CP crews did that day will be remembered as long as this Republic lasts. White men born in America were there, along with former slaves whose ancestors came from Africa, plus emigrants from all across Europe, and more than three thousand Chinamen. There were some Mexicans with at least a touch of Native American blood in them, as well as French Indians and at least a few Native Americans. Everyone was excited, ready to get to work, eager to show what he could do. Even the Chinese, usually methodical and a bit scornful of the American way of doing things, were stirred to a fever pitch. They and all the others. We are the world, they said. They had come together at this desolate place in the middle of Western North America to do what had never been done before them.

The sun rose at 7:15 A.M. Corinne time.* First the Chinese went to work. According to the *San Francisco Bulletin*'s correspondent, "In eight minutes, the sixteen cars were cleared, with a noise like the bombardment of an army."[12] Dodge was impressed. By the end of the day, he was ready to pronounce the Chinese "very quiet, handy, good cooks and good at almost everything they are put at. Only trouble is, we cannot talk to them."[13]

The Irishmen laying the track came on behind the pioneers and the track gaugers. Their names were Michael Shay, Patrick Joyce, Michael Kennedy, Thomas Daley, George Elliott, Michael Sullivan, Edward Killeen, and Fred McNamara. Their foreman was George Coley. The two in front on each thirty-foot rail would pick it up with their tongs and run forward. The two in the rear picked it up and carried it forward until all four heard "Down." The rails weighed 560 pounds each.

Next came the men starting the spikes by placing them in position,

---

* All times were local until the four Standard Time zones were adopted in 1878. The railroads demanded it, for uniformity was critical for their operations.

then the spike drivers, then the bolt threaders, then the straighteners, finally the tampers. Keeping pace with the crews was the telegraph construction party, digging the holes, putting in the poles, hauling out, hanging, and insulating the wire.

"The scene is a most animated one," wrote one newspaper reporter. "From the first pioneer to the last tamper, perhaps two miles, there is a thin line of 1,000 men advancing a mile an hour; the iron cars running up and down; mounted men galloping backward and forward. Alongside of the moving force are teams hauling tools, and water-wagons, and Chinamen, with pails strung over their shoulders, moving among the men with water and tea."[14]

One of the army officers, the senior man, grabbed the arm of Charlie Crocker and said, "I never saw such organization as this; it is just like an army marching across over the ground and leaving a track built behind them."[15]

When the whistle blew for the noon meal, at 1:30 P.M., the CP workers had laid six miles of track. The men christened the site Victory (later Rozel, Utah), because they knew they had won. Stro had a second team of track layers in reserve, but the proud men who had laid the first six miles before eating insisted on keeping at it throughout the rest of the day. As they did.

After taking a leisurely hour to eat, the workers lost the better part of another hour as the rails were bent, a tedious job. It had to be done, because the line was ascending the west slope of the Promontory Mountains and on this stretch of line there were curves. Each rail was placed between blocks and hammered until it was in the proper curve.

Then the others went back to work. By 7 P.M., the CP was ten miles and fifty-six feet farther east than it had been at dawn. Never before done, never matched.

Each man among the Irish track-layers had lifted 125 tons of iron, plus the weight of the tongs. That was 11.2 short tons per man per hour. Each had covered ten miles forward and the Lord only knows how much running back for the next rail. They moved the track forward at a rate of almost a mile an hour. They laid at a rate of approximately 240 feet every seventy-five seconds.

Historian Lynn Farrar provided me with the exact numbers. The actual figures were 3,630 feet of level grade, 44,756 feet of plus grade, and 4,470 feet of minus grade. The percent of rise varies from 0.40 percent

(21.12 feet per mile) to a maximum of 1.35 percent (71.28 feet per mile). There were twenty curves ranging from 1 degree to 7 degrees 48 minutes. The beginning of the ten miles at engineer station 549 was on a 3-degree curve. The morning's work contained eleven curves with a total length of 10,848 feet. In the afternoon the work contained nine curves with a total length of 7,512.5 track feet. The morning work had 2,495 track feet of 6-degree curves, and the afternoon work had 827.5 track feet of 7-degree-48-minutes curve. The slower work in the afternoon was partly due to having to curve some rails but also because the "boys" were running out of gas, and they certainly deserved to go more slowly. The net rise in elevation from start to finish was from elevation 4,400 to 4,809.

*T*HERE were many heroes that day. Crocker, to start with, the man who thought it up and planned it out. Strobridge, who organized everything. All the superintendents and foremen. And of course the workers. The eight Irishmen put down 3,520 rails. The CP paid them four days' wages. Others straightened or laid 25,800 ties. The spikers drove into those ties 28,160 spikes, put in place by the Chinese—the spikes weighed 55,000 pounds. The bolt crews put in 14,080 bolts.

The army officer told Crocker he had walked his horse right along with the track layers and they went forward "just about as fast as a horse could walk." He added a supreme compliment: "It was a good day's march for an army."[16]

To demonstrate how well done it had been, engineer Jim Campbell ran a locomotive over the new track at forty miles per hour. Then the last of the five construction trains was backed down the long grade past Victory to the construction camp just north of the lake. There were twelve hundred men piled onto its sixteen flatcars for the ride, smiling, cheering lustily, laughing, chattering, kicking their feet, swinging their arms, breaking into song, congratulating one another. They had done what no men before them had ever done, nor would any to come.

Jack Casement turned to Strobridge. "He owned up beaten," Stro later commented. But Dan Casement was not a good loser. He said his men could do better if they had enough room to do so, and he begged Durant for permission to tear up several miles of track in order to prove it. Durant said no.[17] As far as can be told, Doc never paid Crocker the $10,000 he lost in the bet.

On the CP side of the tracks, it was Huntington who was disgruntled. "I notice by the papers," he wrote Crocker, "that there was ten miles of track laid in one day on the Central Pacific, which was really a great feat, the more particularly when we consider that it was done after the necessity for its being done had passed."[18]

MEANTIME," the *Alta California* reported, "the Union Pacific road creeps on but slowly; they had to build a tremendous trestle-work, over 400 feet long and 85 feet high. But their rock cutting is the most formidable work, and it seems a pity that such a big job should be necessary when the grading of the Central Pacific is available and has been offered to them."[19]

Instead of doing the obvious, as suggested by the correspondent, Doc Durant, riding in a wagon back to Ogden, put out orders to start hauling rails and ties up to Promontory Summit by wagons and begin immediately to lay track toward the east from there. Don't wait for the Big Trestle to be finished, he thundered. Start laying track now. Graders for the UP were working at either end. They were not yet finished, and the rail layers had to wait for them.

The correspondent for the *Alta* described the scene as he saw it. "Standing here, on this rising ground," he scribbled in his notebook and then sent off by telegram to his paper, as he watched from Promontory Summit, "a view of the whole field may be obtained. Along the line of the road may be seen the white camps of the Chinese laborers, and from every one of them squads of these people are advancing." They had to grade four miles and lay track over the ties and spike down before gaining the summit.

On April 30, the CP finished. It had reached the final summit, more than five hundred miles east of the first summit above Donner Lake, all done in less than a year and a half, at a time when all the locomotives, iron, spikes, fishplates, bolts, and more had to come from the East Coast. The *Alta* noted, "The last blow has been struck on the Central Pacific Railroad, and the last tie and rail were placed in position today. We are now waiting for the Union Pacific to finish their rock-cutting."[20] At the summit basin, tents started to go up, to announce the birth of a new town, Promontory.*

---

* It is no longer in existence, but the National Park Service has a splendid interpretive center there.

For the UP, all the cuts were finished but one, and it was grading and laying track in both directions. The Big Trestle was nearly finished, and Casement promised reporters that it would be replaced with a fill in the summer. He didn't explain exactly why the UP would not use the CP's Big Fill.[21]

The UP's accomplishment needs to be noted. From April 1, 1868, to May 1869, Dodge, the Casements, and their workers had laid 555 miles of road and graded the line to Humboldt Wells, making the total distance covered 726 miles. Everything had been transported from the Missouri River, over two ranges of mountains, a task never equaled or surpassed. In Dodge's judgment, "It could not have been accomplished had it not been for the experience of the chiefs of the departments in the Civil War."[22]

Today people can still drive—cautiously—down from Promontory eastward on the surface of curving sections of the original but abandoned UP roadbed.* One drives through high fills and long, deep cuts. There too can be traced the CP's lines. Sometimes the two cross each other. Going west from Promontory Summit, an automobile and a bike trail follow the original CP track, with the UP grading always visible. These are stark mementos of human failure and achievement, monuments to government stupidity and genius, to the competitive instincts and organizing ability of Strobridge and the Big Four and Dodge, Durant, and the other leaders of the UP, and most of all to the men who built them.

*H*ELL on Wheels was into its last flourish. In Corinne and in the camps of the UP to the west, the whiskey sellers, gamblers, and prostitutes continued to do business in a new place but in the same old way. One reporter wrote, "The loose population that has followed the UP is turbulent and rascally. Several shooting scrapes have occurred among them lately. Last night [April 27] a whisky-seller and a gambler had a fracas, in which the 'sport' shot the whisky dealer, and the friends of the latter shot the gambler. Nobody knows what will become of these riff-raff when the tracks meet, but they are lively enough now and carry off their share of the Plunder from the working men."[23]

* Abandoned early in the twentieth century. The new line across Great Salt Lake was opened for traffic on March 4, 1904. The tracks over the summit were torn up in World War II to use as scrap iron.

Colonel C. R. Savage, a photographer hired by Seymour for the occasion, noted in his diary that he went to Casement's camp, "where I had the honor of dining with Jack and Dan Casement in their private car. Very pleasant and agreeable reception." From the car he could see the tent camps, beautiful in the twilight. But they were dangerous. "I was creditably informed that 24 men had been killed in the several camps in the last 25 days. Certainly a harder set of men were never congregated together before."[24]

WHEN the UP workers began building east from Promontory Summit, the two railroads had met—or at least almost, given that the last twenty-five hundred feet were not yet in place. And the UP still had some cuts to make, a bridge to complete, some track to lay, so only the CP's locomotives could get to the site. By mutual consent, the Big Four and the UP's board of directors fixed the date of meeting for Saturday, May 8. Dodge reported that it had been set "far enough ahead so that the trains coming from New York and San Francisco would have ample time to reach Promontory in time to take part in the ceremonies."[25]

Beginning on May 3, the companies began discharging large numbers of men and sending others to the rear to work on part of track that had been hastily laid. The two opposing armies "are melting away," reported the *Alta California*, "and the white camps which dotted every brown hillside and every shady glen . . . are being broken up and abandoned. The Central Pacific force are nearly all gone already, and that of the Union is going fast. Ninety of the latter left for the East this morning, and a hundred more go tomorrow, and the rest will soon follow." Those still on the spot were working day and night to finish the grading and the track laying.[26]

The *Salt Lake Deseret News* had an item that signified the change: "Business at Corinne is very dull. The merchants there are in a state of perplexity as there is no sale in the town. A great many are leaving in disgust, land speculation is at a discount, and this last-born of railroad towns is pronounced the 'greatest bilk of any.'"[27]

The men were not being discharged and sent back soon enough to please everyone. Colonel Savage wrote in his diary, "The company would do the country a service in sending such men back to Omaha, for their presence would be a scourge upon any community." He watched as returning men "were piled upon the cars in every stage of drunkenness. Every ranch or tent has whiskey for sale." Then he pronounced his own judgment, one that has been quoted countless times since: "Verily, men earn their money like horses and spend it like asses."[28]

Dodge, generous in his remarks about the Chinese, sneered at the ten-miles-in-one-day record. "They took a week preparing for it," he declared, "and imbedded all their ties beforehand." That last wasn't true, but he went on anyway: "I never saw so much needless waste in building railroads." Then he admitted that the UP's Construction Department "has been inefficient." More specifically, he claimed, "There is no excuse for [the UP's] not being fifty miles west of Promontory Summit." That was sour grapes. But Dodge closed with a comment that summed up the triumphs and troubles he had seen, one that put his, the UP's, and the CP's achievement in reaching Promontory Summit into perspective. He noted that "everything connected with the construction department is being closed up," and then concluded, "Closing the accounts is like the close of the Rebellion."[29]

Chapter Seventeen

DONE

May 8–10, 1869

*T*HE celebration came with the completion of the transcontinental railroad. When the Golden Spike went into the last tie to connect the last rail, it brought together the lines from east and west. Lee's surrender four years earlier had signified the bonding of the Union, North and South. The Golden Spike meant the Union was held together, East and West.

The nation had known many celebrations, beginning with the Declaration of Independence. Victory in the Revolutionary War, the adoption of the Constitution, the election of George Washington, the peaceful passing on of power, the Louisiana Purchase, the Lewis and Clark Expedition had involved virtually all citizens in celebration. But the annexation of Texas, victory in the Mexican War, the acquisition of California had been marred by the controversy over slavery. And of course most white Southerners could not celebrate Lee's surrender. But present at the pounding of the Golden Spike were former Confederates alongside former Yankees. The ceremony brought together all Americans.

Hyperbole was common in the nineteenth century. In part that was because people had had so little with which to compare inventions, advances, or changes, in part because they just talked that way. Words like "the greatest achievement ever" came naturally to them. Thus the transcontinental railroad was called the Eighth Wonder of the World. The building of the road was compared to the voyage of Columbus or the landing of the Pilgrims. It was said that the road was "annihilating distance and almost outrunning time." The preacher at the Golden Spike ceremony, Dr. John Todd, called it "the greatest work ever attempted."[1] In 1883, General Sherman, in his last annual report as head of the army, called the building of the road "the most important event of modern times."[2]

They may have exaggerated, but for the people of 1869, especially those over forty years old, there was nothing to compare to it. A man whose birthday was in 1829 or earlier had been born into a world in which President Andrew Jackson traveled no faster than Julius Caesar, a world in which no thought or information could be transmitted any faster than in Alexander the Great's time. In 1869, with the railroad and the telegraph that was beside it, a man could move at sixty miles per hour and transmit an idea or a statistic from coast to coast almost instantly. Senator Daniel Webster got it exactly in 1847, when he proclaimed that the railroad "towers above all other inventions of this or the preceding age."[3]

*I*N the twenty-first century, everything seems to be in a constant flux, and change is so constant as to be taken for granted. This leads to a popular question, What generation lived through the greatest change? The ones who lived through the coming of the automobile and the airplane and the beginning of modern medicine? Or those who were around for the invention and first use of the atomic bomb and the jet airplane? Or the computer? Or the Internet and E-mail? For me, it is the Americans who lived through the second half of the nineteenth century. They saw slavery abolished and electricity put to use, the development of the telephone and the completion of the telegraph, and most of all the railroad. The locomotive was the first great triumph over time and space. After it came and after it crossed the continent of North America, nothing could ever again be the same. It brought about the greatest change in the shortest period of time.

Only in America was there enough space to utilize the locomotive fully, and only here did the government own enough unused land or possess enough credit to induce capitalists to build a transcontinental railroad. Only in America was there enough labor or enough energy and imagination. "We are the youngest of the peoples," proclaimed the *New*

York Herald, "but we are teaching the world how to march forward."[4]

America had the Civil War behind it and the Industrial Revolution ahead. It was an empire of liberty, stretching from the Great Lakes to the Gulf of Mexico, from the Atlantic to the Pacific Coast. The railroad was the longest ribbon of iron ever built by man. It was a stupendous achievement. It had spanned a continent, opened new lands for settlement, opened the mountains with their minerals. It had crossed a frontier of immense possibilities. It had inaugurated a new age, begun what would be called the American Century (which lasted beyond a hundred years).

One year before the rails were joined at Promontory, Walt Whitman began to celebrate this new force when he wrote in his "Passage to India":

> I see over my own continent the Pacific railroad surmounting every
>   barrier,
> I see continual trains of cars winding along the Platte carrying freight and
>   passengers,
> I hear the locomotives rushing and roaring, and the shrill steam-whistle,
> I hear the echoes reverberate through the grandest scenery in the world,
> I cross the Laramie plains, I note the rock in grotesque shapes, the buttes,
> I see the plentiful larkspur and wild onions, the barren, colorless,
>   sage-deserts . . .
> Tying the Eastern to the Western sea, The road between Europe and
>   Asia. . . .

PARTS of the Union Pacific and the Central Pacific ran through some of the grandest scenery in the world, but the spot where the two were joined together was improbable and undistinguished. No one had ever lived there, and shortly after the ceremony no one would ever again. The summit was just over five thousand feet above sea level. To the south the terrain rose sharply, covered with cedar. Its out-thrust offered a magnificent view of the great inland sea, a thousand feet below. To the north the bench again rose to form a parallel parapet. The summit itself was a flat, circular valley, bare except for sagebrush and a few scrub cedars, perhaps three miles in diameter. The only "buildings" were a half-dozen wall tents and a few rough-board shacks, set up by merchants selling whiskey. They ran along a single miserable street.

On May 6, Durant and UP director John Duff were riding a UP train headed west on their way to the ceremonies. Their train was about to pull in to Piedmont, just east of the Wyoming-Utah state line, when, like a bolt of lightning on a clear summer's day, rifle bullets zinged past their car as the locomotive was stopped by ties piled on the track. A mob of some three hundred men, all of them tie cutters and graders for the UP, loomed outside the windows of Durant's car. Just as quick as that, the mob uncoupled the official car, removed the ties from the rails, and waved to the engineer to go ahead. When Durant came to the door of his car to demand what the hell was going on, he was surrounded.

A spokesman for the mob said they wanted their back pay, overdue for months. They intended to hold Durant and Duff until it was paid. Something over $200,000 was due.

Durant said he didn't have such a sum on him, but assured the mob that he was in full sympathy with their demand. Taken to the telegraph station, he sent a message to Oliver Ames in Boston to send the money. But Oliver sent his own telegram later to Dodge, in Echo City, to call for a company of infantry from nearby Fort Bridger to free Durant. Dodge did, and the company was apparently sent, but for unknown reasons the troop train was waved right through at Piedmont.

The affair is shrouded in mist. No authoritative account exists. At some point the kidnappers wired Dodge to put up the money within twenty-four hours, or else. What the "or else" signified is not clear. In some accounts, it was that the mob would hang or shoot Durant if he called for troops rather than money.

Director Sidney Dillon was with Dodge in Echo City. He had been sending a series of telegrams to Boston begging for more money, to satisfy at least some of the demands in Utah. The Ames brothers had scraped up several hundred thousand dollars, but it had all been dispersed (which might have been the cause of the kidnapping: the word may have flashed through Utah that some railroad workers were being paid; word of Durant and Duff's kidnapping had spread). Now Dillon wired that he must have half a million more at once.

Dodge seconded Dillon's plea. On May 7, he sent a second message to Oliver: "You must furnish funds." He added a warning: "If you wait until [all the UP's] trains are stopped it will be too late to release them until we are forced to pay in fact every thing due on line." A half-million dollars, he felt, "will relieve necessities and enable us to keep moving." The money was dug up somewhere and furnished and distributed to the men, and Durant and Duff were released in time for the ceremony.[5] A reporter for the *San Francisco Bulletin* said Durant had turned over to the men some $253,000 in cash.[6]

Perhaps, but, as usual with Durant, there is more to the story. Both Dodge and Oliver Ames thought the whole thing a put-up job—put up by none other than Durant, who had a deal with one of the contractors, James W. Davis and Co., and wanted the money to pay what Davis was due. In his autobiography, Dodge wrote that without doubt Durant had staged the whole thing "for the purpose of forcing the [UP] to pay." Ames was the first to suggest that such was the case. He wrote to Dodge on May 12, "Davis & Associate men were the parties stopping the train. Could it be one of Durant's plans to have these men get their pay out of the Road and we suffer for his benefit." He closed with a generalization to which everyone who had ever dealt with Doc could subscribe: "Durant is so strange a man that I am prepared to believe any sort of rascality that may be charged against him."[7]

*T*HE ceremony was scheduled for May 8. The Central Pacific's regular passenger train left Sacramento at 6 A.M. on May 6, with a number of excursionists. Leland Stanford's special train followed. It was made in the early Pullman style, with a kitchen, dining room, and sleeping accommodations for ten. Aboard were Stanford, the chief justice of California, the governor of Arizona, and other guests. Also on board were the last spike, made of gold; the last tie, made of laurel; and a silver-headed hammer.

The spike was a gift from David Hewes of San Francisco. Hewes had been a resident of Sacramento and was a friend of the Big Four. He was somewhat embarrassed that he had not had enough money in 1863 or 1864 to participate in the financing of the CP. After moving to San Francisco and becoming a real-estate developer, he did have some money. He decided to make a gesture to thank his friends for building the road, and picked the spike as appropriate. It was six inches long, had a rough gold nugget attached to its point (later used to make rings for President Grant, Secretary of State William Seward, Oakes Ames, Stanford, and some others), and weighed eighteen ounces. It was valued at $350.[8]

The Stanford special moved along briskly, with excited and expectant passengers. But up ahead, just over the summit, some Chinese were cutting timber above the entrance to Tunnel No. 14. After seeing the regular train pass, with no knowledge that another train was coming right behind, they felled a log onto the track. The log was big, fifty feet long and three and a half feet in circumference. It landed in a cut, with one end against the bank and the other on a rail. As Stanford's train rounded the curve, the engineer had barely enough time to apply brakes. A guest, riding the cowcatcher, jumped off just before the collision. The engine struck the log and was damaged. A telegraph was sent ahead to Wadsworth to hold the passenger train until Stanford's coach could be attached.

This was done. The locomotive pulling the passenger train was named *Jupiter*. It was the CP's Engine No. 60, built in Schenectady, now headed toward a permanent place in railroad history.[9]

On Friday afternoon, May 7, the train arrived in Promontory. The telegraph operators for each line were present and set up to send and receive wires, but there was no official from the UP. Stanford sent a message to the UP's Ogden office, demanding to know where the hell the UP delegation was. Casement replied that very heavy rains had sent gushers through Weber Canyon. Devil's Gate Bridge had been damaged. The UP wouldn't get its trains to the summit before Monday, May 10.

Stanford and party were stuck in one of the least scenic spots, with the fewest and least agreeable residents, on a train that had made no provision for entertaining its passengers on a two-day layover. The UP did have a train in Ogden, beyond Weber Canyon, and on Saturday morning, Superintendent Reed sent it to the summit to invite Stanford and party for an excursion to Ogden and the mouth of Weber Canyon. That evening, on returning to the summit, Stanford had the train pull back to a more pleasant location at the Monument Point siding, thirty miles west of the summit, where at least there was a view of the lake. There he and party spent a quiet Sunday. For most of the day, it rained.[10]

SACRAMENTO and San Francisco had been told that the joining of the rails would take place on May 8, and that was the date they intended to celebrate. When telegrams arrived informing the city fathers of the postponement, they decided to go ahead anyway. At 5 A.M. on Saturday, a CP train pulled into Sacramento carrying celebrants from Nevada, including firemen and a brass band. They got the festivities going by starting their parade. A brass cannon, the very one that had saluted the first shovelful of earth Leland Stanford had turned over for the beginning of the CP's construction six years earlier, boomed once again.

The parade was mammoth. At its height, about 11 A.M. in Sacramento, the time the organizers had been told the joining of the rails would take place, twenty-three of the CP's locomotives, led by its first, the *Governor Stanford*, let loose a shriek of whistles that lasted for fifteen minutes.

In San Francisco, the parade was the biggest held to date. At 11 A.M., a fifteen-inch Parrott rifled cannon at Fort Point, guarding the south shore of the Golden Gate, fired a salute. One hundred guns followed. Then fire bells, church bells, clock towers, machine shops, streamers, foundries, the U.S. Mint let go at full blast. The din lasted for an hour.

In both cities, the celebration went on through Saturday, Sunday, and Monday.[11]

*T*HE *Alta California* correspondent spent Sunday poking around the summit looking for a story. He got it. As he was watching, the Wells Fargo Overland Stage No. 2 came into Promontory Summit with its last load of mail from the West Coast. "The four old nags were worn and jaded," he wrote, "and the coach showed evidence of long service. The mail matter was delivered to the Central Pacific Co., and with that dusty, dilapidated coach and team, the old order of things passed away forever."[12]

There is a famous, often reproduced Hart photograph in which the *Jupiter* is just pulling into Promontory Summit while a wagon train is headed west, just to the north of the train. The various captions usually read something like "The old gives way to the new" and identify the wagon train as the last immigrants headed for California. But the wagons, apparently, are bringing on supplies. They might have been returning to Monument Point after bringing up equipment for Strobridge's men. In any case, no immigrants would cross Nebraska, Wyoming, and a part of Utah on wagons when the UP would carry them.

The thought had occurred to both Dodge and Crocker that, if their railroad built a siding at Promontory Summit, it could claim terminal rights there. Crocker got all geared up. He had a train loaded with the rails, ties, spikes, bolts, and fishplates ready to go, along with a Chinese crew to build the siding and Strobridge to boss them. His plan, meticulous as always, was to run up to the summit during the early hours of Monday morning, May 10, and go to work at first light. That way he would have the siding in place well before any ceremonies began.

Dodge beat him. He talked to Jack Casement and had him start his gangs to work during Sunday night and through the wee hours of Monday morning. Under the light of lanterns and the moon, the UP men had a complete siding and Y-track in place before first light. Just as they finished, the CP construction train and the Chinese crews arrived. Casement's men greeted them with a hoot, a holler, and a laugh.[13]

The dawn on May 10 was cold, near freezing, but the rising sun heralded a bright, clear day, with temperatures rising into the seventies. Spring in Utah, as glorious as it can be. A group of UP and CP workers began to gather, but there were not many of them left, and the best estimates put the crowd at five or six hundred people, far fewer than the predictions (some of which went as high as thirty thousand). During the morning, two trains from the CP and two from the UP arrived at the site, bearing officials, their guests, and some spectators.

Among those representing the CP were Stanford, Strobridge, and some minor officials, plus George Booth, engineer of the *Jupiter*; R. A. Murphy, fireman; and Eli Dennison, the conductor. The UP contingent included Dodge, Durant, Duff, Dillon, Reed, Hoxie, Jack and Dan Casement, and Seymour. Sam Bradford was the engineer on No. 119, opposite number to the *Jupiter*, with Benjamin Mallory as conductor. Cyrus Sweet was the fireman.*

A battalion of soldiers, from the Twenty-first Infantry Regiment, under Major Milton Cogswell, were there. The soldiers had come on by train and were headed to the Presidio of San Francisco, which surely must make the Twenty-first the first army unit to cross the continent by rail. The military band from Fort Douglas, Wyoming, was also there, along with the Tenth Ward Band from Salt Lake City.

• • •

---

* Sweet was twenty years old. He lived through World War II and died on May 30, 1948.

*I*N the twenty-first century, public-relations officials from the two companies would have long since taken over the ceremony, but as things were, almost nothing had been planned. Mainly this was because it was the nineteenth century, with no radio, much less television, but it was also because only a month before the event no one had known where the meeting of the rails would take place.

To show how little preparation went into it, consider who was not there. Huntington was in New York. Crocker and Hopkins were in California. Lewis Clement was absent. The Ames brothers were in Boston. One of the most notable among the missing was Brigham Young, who was in southern Utah. He sent Bishop John Sharp to represent him. Given that the ceremony marked the completion of a dream that went back to before the Mexican War, and that it was of the type that modern politicians would kill to attend, the absence of politicians was striking. There were only a couple of territorial governors present. President Grant had expressed a wish to be there but could not because of other business.

There were reporters present from the Associated Press, *Frank Leslie's Illustrated Newspaper*, the *Chicago Tribune*, many from the various newspapers in San Francisco, Sacramento, and throughout California, Boston, Springfield, Massachusetts, the Salt Lake City newspapers, and a number from New York. Except for the *Chicago Tribune*, none of the reporters wrote that there were few women and children, something that their successors would immediately notice. Mrs. Strobridge was there, of course, along with the wife of Stanford's private secretary, and Mrs. S. B. Reed, Reed's wife, and the wives of two or three of the reporters and some of the army officers. Only a few children, including Mrs. Strobridge's adopted daughter Julia, age ten, and son Samuel, age seven, were there.[14]

Some decisions on what to do had been made earlier, including the two most important. One was to have a telegraph wire attached to the Golden Spike, with another to the sledgehammer. When the Golden Spike was tapped in, the telegraph lines would send the message all around the country. (The spike would be placed in a hole already drilled, so that it only had to be tapped down and could then be easily extracted.*)

If everything worked, this would be a wholly new event in the world.

* The spike today is at Stanford University.

364

People from New York, Philadelphia, Boston, Charleston, and all across the East Coast, people in Chicago, St. Louis, Milwaukee, New Orleans, and all across the midsection of the country, people in San Francisco, Sacramento, Seattle, Los Angeles, and all across the West Coast, even people in Montreal, Halifax, Nova Scotia, and London, England, would participate, by listening, in the same event. What people of the radio and later the television age came to take for granted was here taking place for the first time. At the moment it happened it would be known, simultaneously, everywhere in the United States, Canada, and England.

The second decision was to have Hart, Russell, and Colonel Savage of Salt Lake City free to roam, take whatever pictures they liked, ordering men to get into this or that pose and to stand still, and doing all the other things that modern men are accustomed to doing for photographers. Thanks to that arrangement, some of the most famous photographs in American history were taken.

Many of the decisions had to be improvised. Dodge, Durant, and Stanford argued for nearly an hour before the scheduled time to begin, which was at noon, over who should have the honor of placing in the Golden Spike. The CP officials declared that, since Leland Stanford had tossed the first shovelful of earth in the construction of the road, and since the CP had been incorporated earlier than the UP, Stanford was the man to drive the last spike. Dodge said Durant should do it, because the UP was the longer railroad. "At one time the Union Pacific positively refused connection," the *San Francisco News Leader* reported, "and told the Central people they might do as they liked, and there should be no joint celebration."[15]

Just a few minutes before noon, Stanford and Durant settled the controversy.

Strobridge and Reed came forward, from the CP train, bearing the laurel tie. Alongside them was a squad of Chinese, wearing clean blue frocks and carrying one rail, and an Irish squad with the other rail. The *Jupiter* and the No. 119 were facing each other, a couple of rail lengths apart. The engineers, Booth and Bradford, pulled on their whistles to send up a shriek. Cheers broke out. One veteran said, "We all yelled like to bust."

The crowd pressed forward. On the telegraph, W. N. Shilling, a telegrapher from Western Union's Ogden office, beat a tattoo of messages to impatient inquiries from various offices: "TO EVERYBODY. KEEP QUIET. WHEN THE LAST SPIKE IS DRIVEN AT PROMONTORY POINT, WE WILL SAY

'DONE!' DON'T BREAK THE CIRCUIT, BUT WATCH FOR THE SIGNALS OF THE BLOWS OF THE HAMMER."

The preacher was introduced, and he offered a prayer. Shilling clicked again: "ALMOST READY. HATS OFF; PRAYER IS BEING OFFERED."

The spikes were brought forward. Shilling clicked, "WE HAVE GOT DONE PRAYING. THE SPIKE IS ABOUT TO BE PRESENTED." Stanford gave a brief, uninspired speech. Dodge spoke up for the UP. He mentioned Senator Thomas Hart Benton and Christopher Columbus. Shilling again: "ALL READY NOW; THE SPIKE WILL SOON BE DRIVEN. THE SIGNAL WILL BE THREE DOTS FOR THE COMMENCEMENT OF THE BLOWS."

Strobridge and Reed put the last tie, the laurel tie, in place. Durant drove in his spike—or, rather, tapped it in, for it was partially seated in the predrilled hole already. Then Stanford. When he tapped the Golden Spike in, he would signal the waiting country. Reporters compared what was coming to the first shot fired at Lexington. One said the blow would be heard "the fartherest of any by mortal man."

Stanford swung and missed, striking only the rail. It made no difference. The telegraph operator closed the circuit and the wire went out, "DONE!"[16]

Across the nation, bells pealed. Even the venerable Liberty Bell in Philadelphia was rung. Then came the boom of cannons, 220 of them in San Francisco at Fort Point, a hundred in Washington D.C., countless fired off elsewhere. It was said that more cannons were fired in celebration than ever took part in the Battle of Gettysburg. Everywhere there was the shriek of fire whistles, firecrackers and fireworks, singing and prayers in churches. The Tabernacle in Salt Lake City was packed to capacity, with an astonishing seven thousand people. In New Orleans, Richmond, Atlanta, and throughout the old Confederacy, there were celebrations. Chicago had a parade that was its biggest of the century—seven miles long, with tens of thousands of people participating, cheering, watching.

A correspondent in Chicago caught exactly the spirit that had brought the whole country together. The festivity, he wrote in the *Tribune*, "was free from the atmosphere of warlike energy and the suggestions of suffering, danger, and death which threw their oppressive shadow over the celebrations of our victories during the war for the Union."[17]

In Promontory, the *Jupiter* and the UP's No. 119 were unhooked from their trains. Then they moved forward ever so slowly, until their pilots touched. Russell urged the crews to form a wedge radiating out from the point of contact. Men clinging to each engine held bottles of champagne aloft. On the track, Dodge and Montague clasped hands, framing the last tie beneath them. Russell captured the moment for posterity. When he told his subjects they were free to move, the whistles shrieked and a roar exploded from the crowd. Champagne bottles were smashed against each engine.

Jupiter and No. 119 backed up and hooked onto their trains. *Jupiter* backed up a bit more, and No. 119 then came forward until it had crossed the junction of the tracks, halted for an instant, then majestically backed away. *Jupiter* came forward, crossed the junction, and backed up. The transcontinental railroad was a reality.

The Golden Spike was snatched up and safely deposited in Stanford's car. Souvenir hunters quickly whittled the last tie to splinters. In all, six ties were cut to pieces before the end of the day.

Stanford invited the UP officials to his car for a celebratory lunch, with plenty of California fruit and wine to mark the occasion. There were speeches, including an awful one by Stanford, who argued that the government subsidy had been more a detriment than a boost to the companies, because of all the conditions attached to the bonds. People were stunned—that is, everyone except Dan Casement, who had been imbibing the champagne in heroic quantities. He hoisted himself up on Jack's shoulders and brayed, "Mr. President of the Central Pacific: If this subsidy has been such a detriment to the building of these roads, I move you say that it be returned to the United States Government with our compliments." There were cheers and laughter, except from Stanford, who glowered.[18]

Telegrams went out and came in. To President Grant: "Sir: We have the honor to report that the last rail is laid, the last spike is driven, the Pacific Railroad is finished." Signed by Stanford and Durant. Another from Dodge to Grant. One to Vice-President Schuyler Colfax, signed by Dodge, Duff, Dillon, and Durant, but not by Stanford, who had named a town after Colfax. One from Dodge to Secretary of War Rawlins, with a nice touch: "The great work, commenced during the Administration of Lincoln, in the middle of a great rebellion, is completed under that of Grant, who conquered the peace." And another from Dodge to Sherman, saying in part, "Your continuous active aid, with that of the Army, has made you a part of us and enabled us to complete our work in so short a time."

Sherman's reply: "In common with millions I sat and heard the mystic taps of the telegraphic battery and heard the nailing of the last spike in the great Pacific road. Indeed, am I its friend? Yes . . . As early as 1854 I was vice president of the effort begun in San Francisco." He promised Dodge he would ride the rails from the East to the West Coast as soon as possible, and make the passage in a much shorter time than his journey by water before the Mexican War. "All honor to you, to Durant, to Jack and Dan Casement, to Reed, and thousands of brave fellows who have fought this glorious national problem in spite of deserts, storms, Indians, and the doubts of the incredulous."[19]

Sherman later told Dodge that the transcontinental railroad "advanced our country one hundred years."[20]

There was one telegram never sent. It was to a person none ever thought to invite to the ceremony: Anna Ferona Judah. She stayed alone in her home in Greenfield, Massachusetts. "I refused myself to everyone that day," she later wrote. "I could not talk of the common events of daily living." Naturally she thought of Theodore. She would have anyway, because by coincidence May 10 was their wedding anniversary.

"It seemed as though the spirit of my brave husband descended upon me," she wrote, "and together we were there unseen, unheard of men."[21]

I N Salt Lake City, where there were many speeches, there was one by a man named John Taylor that put the achievement in perspective. It was, he said, "so stupendous that we can scarcely find words to express our sentiments or give vent to our admiration." Then he did what he said he could scarcely do. He was a Mormon from England, and old enough that "I can very well remember the time when there was no such thing as a railroad in existence." Impressive enough, but what came next was almost beyond contemplation to the members of his audience in 1869: "I rode on the first train that was ever made, soon after its completion; that was between Manchester and Liverpool, England."

Mr. Taylor could recall other changes in his life, such as the time when there was no telegraph in operation, "when the idea of conveying thought from one city to another, and from one continent to another by the aid of electricity, instantly, would have been considered magic, superhuman, and beyond the reach of human intellect, enterprise and ingenuity." But nothing could match the experience of having ridden on the first train ever in operation, then being in Salt Lake City to celebrate the completion of the railroad that linked together the North American continent.[22]

EPILOGUE

OF all the things done by the first transcontinental railroad, nothing exceeded the cuts in time and cost it made for people traveling across the continent. Before the Mexican War, during the Gold Rush that started in 1848, through the 1850s, and until after the Civil War ended in 1865, it took a person months and might cost more than $1,000 to go from New York to San Francisco.

But less than a week after the pounding of the Golden Spike, a man or woman could go from New York to San Francisco in seven days. That included stops. So fast, they used to say, "that you don't even have time to take a bath." And the cost to go from New York to San Francisco, as listed in the summer of 1869, was $150 for first class, $70 for emigrant. By June 1870, that was down to $136 for first class, $110 for second class, and $65 for third, or emigrant, class. First class meant a Pullman sleeping car. Emigrants sat on a bench.

Freight rates by train were incredibly less than for ox- or horse-drawn wagons, or for sailboats or steamers. Mail that once cost dollars per ounce and took forever now cost pennies and got from Chicago to California in a few days. The telegraph, meanwhile, could move ideas, thoughts, statistics, any words or numbers that could be put on paper, from one place to another, from Europe or England or New York to San Francisco or anywhere else that had a telegraph station, all but instantly.

The Pullman Company published a weekly newspaper called the *Trans-*

Continental for the passengers. On May 30, 1870, the paper had this item: "It was a cheering incident in our smoking car last evening when one of our party who had telegraphed to Boston to learn if his wife was well, received, after we had run forty-seven miles farther west, the answer: 'All well at home,' which fact was announced, and loud applause followed from all in the car."[1]

Together, the transcontinental railroad and the telegraph made modern America possible. Things that could not be imagined before the Civil War now became common. A nationwide stock market, for example. A continent-wide economy in which people, agricultural products, coal, and minerals moved wherever someone wanted to send them, and did so cheaply and quickly. A continent-wide culture in which mail and popular magazines and books that used to cost dollars per ounce and had taken forever to get from the East to the West Coast, now cost pennies and got there in a few days. Entertainers could move from one city to another in a matter of hours.

DODGE had concluded his short speech on May 10 with the words "This is the way to India." Whitman had called his poem "Passage to India." Throughout the building of the road, its proponents had predicted that the China-Japan-India trade with the East Coast of America and with Europe would pass through San Francisco and then over the transcontinental railroad to points east, or to be shipped to Europe via New York. The first through-car on the transcontinental line carried a shipment of India tea, forerunner of the future.

But the trade with Asia didn't happen, certainly not to the extent people had hoped. This was primarily because, in the same year the rails were connected, 1869, the Suez Canal opened, providing the shortest eastward sea route from Europe. But what did happen was beyond imagination when the 1862 Pacific Railroad Bill was passed. Sidney Dillon, a director of the UP, in an 1892 article in *Scribner's Magazine* called "Historic Moments: Driving the Last Spike of the Union Pacific," spoke to the point.

The relatively few people who saw the ceremony at Promontory Point, he wrote, "were strongly impressed with the conviction that the event was of historic importance; but, as I remember it now, we connected it rather with the notion of transcontinental communication and trade with China and Japan than with internal development, or what railroad men call local traffic." Dillon added that no one was disappointed "in the stupendous results attained," but admitted that "they are different from those we looked for, and of vastly greater consequence for the country." Expectations of trade with Asia "have fallen far short of fulfilment." But "the enormous development of local business has surpassed anything we could have ever dreamed of." The Asian trade yielded only 5 percent of the UP's business in 1891, while 95 percent was local.[2]

Putnam's Magazine, in its October 1868 issue, pointed out why the American people, "standing in the fore-front of the civilized world, have reaped the most signal advantages from this new servant," the locomotive. In the year 1868, there were forty thousand miles of track in the United States, "or four-tenths of all the railroads in the world." Without the railroads, Putnam's asserted, the Mississippi Valley would have fewer than four million inhabitants instead of the twelve million already there, with more coming. In the past fifteen years, Putnam's said, the population of the United States had increased 90 percent, while production had jumped 230 percent.

The conclusion in Putnam's was that the railroads, especially the transcontinental railroad, had "lightened human toil, made men richer in blessings and in leisure, increased their activity, shielded them from tempest and famine, enlarged the area available for man's residence and subsistence, enabled him to do more in the same period of time and spread knowledge and virtue over all this earth."[3]

*M*ISTAKES were made all along the line, caused both by errors of judgment and a certain cynicism, encouraged by Congress, and cheered on by the populace at large. There was an emphasis on speed rather than quality, on laying as much track and making as much grade as possible rather than doing it right.

One glaring reminder of the waste was the two grades running east and west from Promontory Summit, parallel to each other. Eventually, under dictate from Congress, in November 1869, the UP sold its line from near Ogden to the summit to the CP for $2,852,970 ($58,824 per mile). But just as the CP had to abandon grade it had made from the summit to Ogden (but it did use the Big Fill, ignored by the UP), so did the UP have to abandon everything west of Ogden, all the way to Humboldt Wells, 222 miles from Ogden. That cost the UP over $200,000. The CP abandoned parallel grades that cost it $752,000. Congress had watched as more than two hundred miles of the overlapping grade-work was being done. Not until April 10, 1869, did it step in to halt this.[4]

PROMONTORY Summit remained the terminus point for the railroads until the CP had paid for the tracks from there to Ogden. For a few months it was the last Hell on Wheels. Boxcars on a siding provided living quarters for railroad employees. A row of tents faced the railroad across a single dirt street. The tents served as hotels, lunch counters, saloons, gambling dens, a few shops, and as nests for the "soiled doves." There was plenty of whiskey, but precious little water. The railroads had to haul it on their cars, in barrels, from springs thirty to fifty miles distant.

A number of "hard cases" arrived in Promontory. A reporter for the *Sacramento Bee* wrote of "Behind-the-Rock Johnny, hero of at least five murders and unnumbered robberies." In the gambling tents the games included three-card monte, ten-die, strap game, chuck-a-luck, faro, and keno. A gang of gamblers and confidence men called the "Promontory Boys" set up headquarters there and were "thicker than hypocrites at a camp meeting of frogs after a shower." J. H. Beadle wrote that Promontory Summit "certainly was, for its size, morally nearest to the infernal regions of any town on the road." In January 1870, when the terminus was transferred to Ogden, Hell on Wheels moved out of Promontory.[5]

THE rails were joined but the UP's financial problems continued to grow. Aside from resources Durant had siphoned off, contractors had stolen much material that the UP had paid for, or at least signed for. And among many other creditors, there was Brigham Young, who bombarded the company headquarters in Boston with demands for payment in full. The UP had no money, but it did have equipment left over and Young was desperate to have a branch line, to be owned and controlled by the Mormons, running from Ogden to Salt Lake City. Finally, in September 1869, a deal was struck. The UP gave the Mormons four thousand tons of iron rail ($480,000), 144 tons of spikes ($20,000), thirty-two tons of bolts ($5,600), four first-class passenger cars ($5,000 each), second-class cars, mail cars, flatcars, and boxcars. The total value that Young signed for was $599,460. The Mormons got started on their railroad immediately and had it in service in a few months.[6]

WHILE building the road, the UP had relied on steamboats and ferries or, in the colder winters, on temporary tracks laid across the frozen Missouri River, to bring into Omaha supplies of all kinds from the east. What was needed was a permanent bridge, which was started in 1870 and opened in March 1872. It had eleven spans, each 250 feet in length and sixty feet above the water. It cost about $2.9 million to build.

With the completion of that bridge, there was a continuous line of track from New York to Sacramento. In Sacramento, the Big Four were putting their first pioneering line into the San Francisco Bay Area and through the broad, fertile, and largely unpopulated San Joaquin Valley. They were taking control of other railroads and had even bigger plans.

ON September 4, 1872, the *New York Sun* had a bold headline:

THE KING OF FRAUDS
How the Credit Mobilier Bought
Its Way Through Congress
COLOSSAL BRIBERY
Congressmen who Have Robbed the
People, and who now Support
The National Robber
HOW SOME MEN GET FORTUNES[7]

The newspaper had launched what became the biggest scandal of the nineteenth century. That scandal would scar the UP through the remainder of that century, and indeed to the end of the twentieth century. The House of Representatives had a series of hearings to inquire into the workings of the Crédit Mobilier, the UP, and the CP. Every official from the companies was required to testify. In virtually every case the testimony was twisted and given the worst possible interpretation. The hearings went on for a full six months, featuring for the most part acrimony and sensationalism, although most charges were true and would be proven.

A chief but by no means only target was Oakes Ames ("Hoax Ames," one newspaper called him), because as a congressman he had distributed Crédit Mobilier stock to some of his colleagues. Representative James G. Blaine was one of them. Representative James Garfield was another, Representative James Brooks another, and the list included Vice-President Schuyler Colfax. Ames had written (in a letter published by an inquiring reporter) that he wanted to place the stock "where it would do the most good."

The UP and the CP were the biggest corporations of their time, and the first to have extensive dealings with the federal, state, county, and township governments. They could not have been built without the government aid in the form of gifts—especially the land grants, plus state and county purchases of their stock and the loans in the form of national government bonds. At the CP, the Big Four became extraordinarily rich thanks to the railroad and the way it was financed. They spent their fortunes lavishly, to the point that they became the very model of conspicuous consumption. The men who held stock in the Crédit Mobilier also got rich from it. In large part this was done by defrauding the government and the public, by paying the lowest possible wages to the men who built the lines, and by delaying or actually ignoring payments of bills to the subcontractors and the workmen. In many ways they used their power to guarantee profits for themselves. Most Americans found it difficult, even impossible to believe that they had actually earned those profits.

The original congressional investigation into the machinations of the Crédit Mobilier provided sensational material for the investigative reporters, the politicians, and the public. There were cries of outrage. The general sentiment was, We have been bilked.

People were ashamed of their congressmen who had been complicit. When Oakes Ames said he could see no reason why a member of Congress should not hold Crédit Mobilier stock, most Americans were outraged. They were also furious at the revelations by the investigative reporters and politicians of the amount of corruption that had characterized the building of the UP, and by the amount of lying or dissembling by those who testified.

After a half-year of hearings, the Congress established that Oakes Ames had distributed and used as payoffs quite a lot of Crédit Mobilier stock, that he had lied to Congress about why he had passed out that stock, that the Crédit Mobilier had paid out astonishing sums as dividends, that the Union Pacific was so broke it could only just barely keep functioning, that the Union Pacific directors had a hard time explaining what happened to all the money the UP took in from its own and government bonds.

The case was a smash hit. People couldn't get enough of it. Papers everywhere ran summaries of the testimonies. Reporters listened for every word. As in so much else, the UP was once again leading the way as the central character in the action. As well it should have been, since what was being argued about was nothing less than the relationship between government and business. Practical matters were involved, such as when government intervention or regulation is justified. The headlines the case produced were nevertheless gripping.

Given the attention paid to the hearings, the House had to do something. After much talk, it passed two meek resolutions of censure, one against Ames, the other against Brooks. (Durant, lucky for him, was gone. Two weeks after the joining of the rails, President Grant made it clear to all concerned that Durant had to be forced off the board of directors. In late May 1869, he was.) For Oakes Ames, however, the shame of the resolution killed him. Or at least that shame was given as the major reason for his death on May 8, 1873. Brooks had died a week earlier.[8]

The CP, or more particularly the Contract and Finance Company, was also investigated by Congress, but all its books had been burned—whether deliberately or by accident was and is in dispute—so nothing was pinned on the Big Four, even though they were as vulnerable as the UP.

*T*HE Congress felt it had the right, the responsibility, and the power to go after the UP and the CP, because the companies would not exist had the Congress not loaned them government bonds and given them land grants. These two matters have caused enormous controversy ever since. Both companies have been accused of stretching out the lines in order to get more land grants, a notion that is completely wrong. Despite 130 years of working to reduce the length of the lines, only a few miles have been shaved off, and that mainly caused by the fall of the level of the Great Salt Lake, which allowed the railroad to make a shortcut below Promontory Summit by erecting a causeway through the water.

The land grants are much misunderstood, especially by professors teaching the American history survey course. They are denounced, lambasted, derided. In one of the most influential textbooks ever published, *Growth of the American Republic* by Samuel Eliot Morison and Henry Steele Commager, the authors, who were the most distinguished historians of their day, if not for the whole of the twentieth century, wrote: "The lands granted to both the Union Pacific and the Central Pacific yielded enough to have covered all legitimate costs of building these roads." A colleague of theirs, also distinguished, Fred Shannon, wrote, "The half billion dollars in land alone to the land grant railroads was worth more than the railroads were when they were built."[9]

Other historians—for example, Robert Henry—have been more tolerant. Henry writes that the land grants did "what had never been done before—provided transportation ahead of settlement."[10] True enough, but it is also true that what the Ames brothers, the Big Four, and others thought should have been regarded as a splendid achievement was widely viewed as full of serious abuse. For example, the corruption that was rife in the building of the railroads was widespread. Further, the railroads enjoyed a monopoly that allowed them to charge what most users came to regard as inflated rates for freight and passenger traffic. There was a great deal of shoddy construction that had to be replaced. Collis Huntington had lied and probably used bribes and certainly had drawn a fictitious map to get revisions highly favorable to the CP in the Pacific Railroad Act. He and his partners and their opposite numbers at the UP also lied to the various government commissions set up to examine the track. In these and other matters, they justified the concern and attention of the investigative reporters and the politicians. That was, after all, the people's money they had stolen.

It was the land grants and the bonds the government passed out that caused the greatest outrage, at the time and later. Still, although many of the owners of the railroads' stocks and bonds were guilty of most of the charges made against them, there is another side.

The land grants never brought in enough money to pay the bills of building either railroad, or even to come close. In California from Sacramento to the Sierra Nevada, and in Nebraska, the railroads were able to sell the alternate strips of land at a good price, $2.50 per acre or more. But in most of Wyoming, Utah, and Nevada, the companies never could sell the land. Unless it had minerals on it, it was virtually worthless, even to cattlemen, who needed far more acres for a workable ranch. So too the vast amount of land the government still owns in the West.

The total value of the lands distributed to the railroads was estimated by the Interior Department's auditor as of November 1, 1880, at $391,804,610. The total investment in railroads in the United States in that year was $4,653,609,000.[11] In addition, the government got to sell the alternate sections it had held on to in California and Nebraska for big sums. Those lands would have been worth nearly nothing, or in many cases absolutely nothing, if not for the building of the railroads.

With regard to the government bonds, generations of American students have been offered a black-and-white view. The bonds went not only to the CP and the UP but to six companies chartered to build the second, third, and so on Pacific railroads. In the textbooks, as in the lectures, the government was handing out a gift. Now, for those of us who were in college in the 1950s, the classes were taught by professors who had taken their own graduate training in the 1930s and had thus been brought up to blame big business for everything that went wrong, especially the Great Depression. Those professors who were not New Deal Democrats were socialists. They all knew that it helps the anti–big business case if you can call those bonds a gift.

But they were not a gift. They were loans, to be paid back in thirty years or less. The requirement was met. In the final settlement with the railroads, in 1898 and 1899, the government collected $63,023,512 of principal plus $104,722,978 in interest, making a total repayment of $167,746,490 on an initial loan of $64,623,512. Professor Hugo Meyer of Harvard looked at those figures and quite rightly said, "For the government the whole outcome has been financially not less than brilliant."[12]

An automatic reaction that big business is always on the wrong side, corrupt and untrustworthy, is too easy, and the error is compounded if we fail to distinguish between incentives, for example, and fraud.

*B*OTH roads went through major changes in the century and a third after they were built. And major expansion. The UP built Dodge's longtime dream, the Oregon Short Line. The CP expanded throughout California and became a major part of the Southern Pacific Company. The SP built and acquired another transcontinental line, the one Jefferson Davis had first favored, from southern California through Arizona, New Mexico, Texas, and Louisiana. By 1900, the SP had trains operating from Portland, Oregon, and Ogden, Utah, to New Orleans. By 1950, the track stretched fourteen thousand miles across twelve states, from the Pacific Ocean to the Gulf of Mexico, and through the states bordering the Mississippi River up to East St. Louis, Illinois.

The UP went into receivership, had Charles Francis Adams—of all people!—and later Jay Gould as its president, then E. H. Harriman, then others. But as the country turned into the twenty-first century, it remained one of the oldest and richest corporations in the world. In 1993, it acquired the Southern Pacific and named all the roads it controlled the Union Pacific.

*T*HE men who built the CP were mainly Chinese. For the most part, as individuals they are lost to history. Many of them stayed with railroad work and performed handsomely on the Northern Pacific, the Great Northern, the Oregon Short Line, and others. Dodge hired them whenever he could, saying, "The Irish labor with its strikes, its dead fall whiskey shops and reckless disregard of all our interests, must be gotten out of the way."[13] In nearly every Western railroad town, there used to be a Chinatown. Mostly they are gone now, victims of discrimination and modern times.

The Irishmen working for the UP also found jobs on other railroads, or they got work at the various mines in the West. They too were discriminated against—"no dogs or Irishmen allowed"—but not so thoroughly as the Chinamen. They and their sons and daughters and their grandchildren and great-grandchildren went on to participate fully and actively and with success in American life.

Firemen, brakemen, engineers, conductors, mechanics, welders, carpenters, repair-shop men, the clerical force (male and female), the foremen, directors, supervisors, and everyone else who worked for either the UP or the CP stayed with railroads. For their careers, and so too for their children, followed by the third generation and beyond. These are the people who make up the force that made the modern railroad. They repair it, improve it, take care of it, make sure the damn things run. More than in almost all other professions, railroading is something a family is proud of and wants to remain a part of.

Railroad people are special. Like all the rest, they lose jobs, have to move, are underpaid, and otherwise have a lot to bitch about. But on the job, they love being next to and able to run and being responsible for all that fabulous machinery. They love being around trains. More than the rest of us, they hold the locomotive in awe.

THE Big Four were also railroad men, in their own way, and they managed to remain working for the railroad—small wonder considering how rich they got from building and running the CP. Charles Crocker kept to construction, serving as the boss for the Southern Pacific Railroad of California. In 1884, he brought about the consolidation of the Central and Southern Pacific roads and was then involved in the construction of the California and Oregon road from San Francisco north to Portland. He built a mansion in San Francisco said to have cost $1.5 million. It was a showplace of the city, but it was destroyed in the 1906 fire. Crocker died in 1888, with a fortune estimated at $40 million.

Collis Huntington remained a railroad king, playing his role in the CP as it gathered unto itself what seemed to be every California railroad, and then expanded nationally as it formed the SP. He tried to sell the CP to financier Darius O. Mills in 1873 for a total price of $20 million, but he was rebuffed. He was therefore stuck with running the system and remained at the head through many problems and decades. The more power Huntington got, the more outspoken his views on the proper relationship between capital and labor became, and thus the more people hated him. He embodied the dark side of unbridled capitalism. He spent much time and money lobbying congressmen to vote the way the CP and then the SP wanted—that is, against any government regulation. He ran the CP and then the SP like a medieval king.

But there was a bright side, the things he did, the work he put in, the bounce he kept in his step. His largest investment, outside the SP, was in the Chesapeake & Ohio. He had acquired it in 1869. Among other things, Huntington founded the town of Newport News, Virginia, as the deep-sea terminus for the Chesapeake & Ohio. He built a mansion on Nob Hill in San Francisco and bought another on Fifth Avenue in New York. He died on August 13, 1900.

Stanford stayed in the railroad business. With his great wealth, he did other things too, including building extensive vineyards in Tehama County, California. He also had a large ranch called Palo Alto, where he bred and ran fine racehorses. He is credited with raising the grade of California horses, and his original methods of training have been widely adopted.

In 1884, Stanford was the one who suggested organizing the Southern Pacific company under the laws of Kentucky, and, the next year, bringing the CP under its umbrella. In 1885, he was elected by the California legislature to the U.S. Senate. This came about at the expense of A. A. Sargent, Huntington's personal friend. The two men feuded. In 1890, Huntington accused Senator Stanford of using the SP's influence to gain his election, and that year Huntington became president of the SP, a position Stanford had held since 1885. Stanford remained in the Senate (where he did nothing of distinction) until his death on June 21, 1893.

Of the Big Four, Hopkins's name is known for the hotel in San Francisco. Crocker is pretty generally unknown today. Huntington is remembered primarily because of the town and beach named for him. But "Stanford" is a name known to everybody, because he had the good sense to found a university and name it after his son, who died in 1884, just two months shy of his sixteenth birthday. The next year, Stanford founded Leland Stanford Junior University. From then until its opening in 1891, he was active in setting the curriculum and picking the faculty and administration for what became one of America's and the world's finest institutions. Because of it, not because of the CP or the SP or the governorship or the long period in the Senate, Stanford's name is remembered today.

*T*HE Ames brothers have also faded from general recognition. They thought they would make money and get great credit from their association with the Union Pacific. And the railroad did commission a famous architect, H. H. Richardson, to design a monument to the two men, sixty-five feet high. It stands at Sherman Summit, right beside the grade that used to carry the tracks of the road. But at the beginning of the twentieth century, the road was relocated southward (which also cut out the Dale Creek Bridge). The monument stands today, isolated and alone even though it is but a mile or so from Interstate 80 coming out of Cheyenne and headed toward Ogden, and has its own exit on the highway. With a sign. But only a handful of hard-core railroad buffs go there, and most of them once only. In Maury Klein's words, the Ames brothers "risked their fortunes and their reputations on the grandest enterprise yet undertaken by Americans. In return they received not praise but censure as participants in the major scandal of an age busy with scandals."[14]

Doc Durant got involved in the UP not so much to become famous as to make money. More than anyone else on the line, he is associated with getting it built fast. He insisted on speed in everything. He worked hard at it constantly from 1864 to 1869 and once said he did not remove his clothes for a week. He was the one who had the honor of tapping in the Golden Spike. But he was forced off the board in May 1869. His health broke. He lost almost everything he owned in the Panic of 1873, and his grandiose scheme to develop the iron and timber resources of the Adirondacks, including a railroad from Saratoga across the St. Lawrence into Canada, failed. He lived his later years in the Adirondacks and died there on October 5, 1885, neither rich nor famous. He had made a lot of mistakes, done lots of things wrong, but this must be said of Doc: without him, don't ask me how they would have built the Union Pacific in so short a time.

Grenville Dodge rightly gets most of the credit for building the UP. It was a stupendous project and his great ambition. In January 1870, he resigned as chief engineer of the UP and soon became chief engineer of the Texas and Pacific Railway (it collapsed in the Panic of 1873) and then joined with Jay Gould in developing railroads in the Southwest. During the next ten years, he was associated with building nearly nine thousand miles of road. After the war with Spain, he was a partner in the Cuba Railroad Company and helped build the line from Santa Clara to Santiago.

The Cuba Railroad was his last. By that time, his surveys alone totaled over sixty thousand miles. Not many men, in his lifetime or later, spent so many nights sleeping on the ground. But he was also active as a railroad lobbyist and as a projector, builder, financier, and director of railroads. His record places him high among the railroad builders of the world.

In his retirement, Dodge was active in the Society of the Army of the Tennessee and other patriotic organizations. He was the richest man in Iowa, but with nothing like the fortunes of the Big Four. He lived in a grand Victorian house in Council Bluffs, Iowa. Though it was modest by San Francisco or New York standards, it was entirely fitting for Dodge, who had from his office window something that no one on either the West or the East Coast had—a view of his beloved Missouri River. He died on January 3, 1916.

EPILOGUE

• • •

*T*HE dreamers, led by Judah; the politicians, led by Lincoln; the financiers, led by the congressmen and the Ames brothers, Durant, and Huntington; the surveyors, led by Dodge and Dey and Judah; the generals, led by Grant and Sherman; the engineers, led by Clement, Montague, Reed, and others; the construction bosses, led by Strobridge and the Casement brothers; the railroad men; the foremen; the Chinese, the Irish, and all the others who picked up a shovel or a sledgehammer or a rail; and the American people who insisted that it had to be done and who paid for it, built the transcontinental railroad.

None of this might have happened if different choices had been made, by any one of the foregoing groups and individuals. But a choice made is made, it cannot be changed. Things happened as they happened. It is possible to imagine all kinds of different routes across the continent, or a better way for the government to help private industry, or maybe to have the government build and own it. But those things didn't happen, and what did take place is grand. So we admire those who did it—even if they were far from perfect—for what they were and what they accomplished and how much each of us owes them.

Notes

CHAPTER ONE: PICKING THE ROUTE

1. J. R. Perkins, *Trails, Rails and War: The Life of General G. M. Dodge* (Indianapolis: Bobbs-Merrill, 1929), pp. 51–52. Wallace D. Farnham, "Grenville Dodge and the Union Pacific: A Study of Historical Legends," *Journal of American History*, vol. 51 (June 1964–March 1965), pp. 632–50, calls this story "false," as he does nearly everything else in Dodge's autobiography and in Perkins's biography. It strikes me as true, even down to the details.
2. Jeanne Minn Bracken, ed., *Iron Horses Across America* (Carlisle, Mass.: Discovery Enterprises, 1995), p. 5.
3. Thomas Curtis Clarke et al., *The American Railway: Its Construction, Development, Management and Appliances* (New York: Scribner, 1889), p. 1.
4. Sarah Gordon, *Passage to Union: How the Railroads Transformed American Life, 1829–1929* (Chicago: Ivan Dee, 1996), p. 136.
5. Quoted in Alfred D. Chandler, Jr., "Henry Varnum Poor," in *The Golden Spike: A Centennial Remembrance* (New York: American Geographical Society, 1969), p. 4.
6. Roy B. Basler, ed., *The Collected Works of Abraham Lincoln*, 9 vols. (New Brunswick, N.J.: Rutgers University Press, 1953–55), vol. 1, pp. 5–6.
7. Ibid., vol. 2, p. 62.
8. The census shows that Illinois grew from 157,000 in 1830 to 1.7 million in 1860; Iowa from 43,000 in 1840 to 675,000 in 1860.
9. John Hoyt Williams, *A Great and Shining Road: The Epic Story of the Transcontinental Railroad* (New York: Times Books, 1988), p. 14.
10. William Beard, "I Have Labored Hard to Find the Law," *Illinois Historical Journal*, Winter 1992, pp. 209–20; Charles Leroy Brown, "Abraham Lincoln and the Illinois Central Railroad," *Journal of the Illinois State Historical Society*, vol. 36 (1943), p. 128.

11. David Herbert Donald, *Lincoln* (New York: Simon & Schuster, 1995), p. 155.
12. Ibid., pp. 155–56.
13. Beard, "I Have Labored," p. 210.
14. Brown, "Lincoln and the IC," pp. 122–25, 133.
15. Donald, *Lincoln*, p. 157.
16. Grenville M. Dodge, *How We Built the Union Pacific Railway* (Council Bluffs, Iowa: Monarch Printing Co., 1997 reprint), p. 5.
17. William Goetzmann, *Army Exploration in the American West, 1803–1863* (New Haven, Conn.: Yale University Press, 1959), p. 295.
18. Perkins, *Trails, Rails and War*, p. 7.
19. Ibid., pp. 16–67.
20. Ibid., p. 19.
21. Dodge, *How We Built*, p. 6.
22. Perkins, *Trails, Rails and War*, p. 23.
23. Dodge, *How We Built*, p. 7.
24. Perkins, *Trails, Rails and War*, p. 31.
25. Williams, *Great and Shining Road*, p. 13.
26. *Chicago Tribune*, Jan. 14, 1864.
27. Perkins, *Trails, Rails and War*, pp. 54–55.
28. Dodge, *How We Built*, p. 9.
29. Donald, *Lincoln*, p. 206.
30. Dodge, *How We Built*, p. 5; Perkins, *Trails, Rails and War*, p. 33.
31. Perkins, *Trails, Rails and War*, p. 34.
32. Ibid., p. 35.
33. *Council Bluffs Bugle*, July 1859.
34. Perkins, *Trails, Rails and War*, p. 37.
35. *Council Bluffs Nonpareil*, Aug. 12, 1859.
36. Perkins, *Trails, Rails and War*, p. 53.
37. Quoted in George Kraus, *High Road to Promontory: Building the Central Pacific Across the High Sierra* (Palo Alto, Calif.: American West Publishing, 1969), p. 21.
38. Perkins, *Trails, Rails and War*, p. 55.
39. Ibid., p. 62.
40. Ibid., p. 63
41. Ibid.
42. Ibid., p. 66.

CHAPTER TWO: GETTING TO CALIFORNIA
1. Oscar Lewis, *The Big Four: The Story of Huntington, Stanford, Hopkins, and Crocker* (New York: Alfred A. Knopf, 1938), p. 49.
2. Charles Crocker Memoir, Bancroft Library, U.C. Berkeley.
3. C.B.V. DeLamater Memoir, Bancroft Library, U.C. Berkeley.
4. Lewis, *Big Four*, p. 55.

5. Crocker Memoir, Bancroft Library.
6. Robert Louis Stevenson, *Travels and Essays of Robert Louis Stevenson*, vol. 15 (New York: Scribner, 1895), pp. 124–25.
7. DeLamater Memoir, Bancroft Library.
8. Crocker Memoir, Bancroft Library.
9. DeLamater Memoir, Bancroft Library.
10. Ibid.
11. Ibid.
12. Collis Huntington Memoir, Bancroft Library, U.C. Berkeley.
13. David Lavender, *The Great Persuader* (Garden City, N.Y.: Doubleday, 1970), pp. 1–7.
14. Lewis, *Big Four*, p. 222.
15. Ibid., pp. 223–24.
16. Lavender, *Great Persuader*, pp. 12–16.
17. Huntington Memoir, Bancroft Library.
18. William T. Sherman, *Memoirs*, 2 vols. printed in 1 (New York: Library of America, 1990 edition, first published 1875), vol. 1, pp. 35–43.
19. Ibid., p. 58.
20. John Debo Galloway, *The First Transcontinental Railroad: Central Pacific, Union Pacific* (New York: Simmon-Boardman, 1950), p. 80.
21. Lavender, *Great Persuader*, pp. 48–50.
22. Sherman, *Memoirs*, vol. 1, p. 87.
23. Ibid., p. 95.
24. Ibid., p. 101.
25. "Mrs. Judah's Letter [to Bancroft], 12/14/89," as it is usually cited, is in Anna Judah Papers, Bancroft Library, U.C. Berkeley.
26. Ibid.
27. Carl Wheat, "A Sketch of the Life of Theodore D. Judah," *California Historical Society Quarterly*, vol. 4 (Sept. 1925), pp. 219–22; Lewis, *Big Four*, pp. 3–5.
28. *American Railroad Journal*, April 5, 1851.
29. Wheat, "Life of Judah," p. 222.
30. *Sacramento Union*, June 20, 1854.
31. Wheat, "Life of Judah," p. 223.
32. "Mrs. Judah's Letter," Bancroft Library.
33. Wheat, "Life of Judah," p. 229.
34. Lewis, *Big Four*, p. 11.
35. Ibid., pp. 229–33.
36. *Sacramento Union*, Jan. 29, 1859.
37. Lewis, *Big Four*, pp. 236–37.
38. *San Francisco Daily Alta California*, Oct. 20, 1859.

CHAPTER THREE: THE BIRTH OF THE CENTRAL PACIFIC

1. Quoted in Wesley S. Griswold, *A Work of Giants: Building the First*

Transcontinental Railroad (New York: McGraw-Hill, 1962), p. 15.

2. Oliver Jensen, *The American Heritage History of Railroads in America* (New York: American Heritage Publishing Co., 1975), p. 84.

3. Oscar Lewis, *The Big Four*, p. 17; see also Robert West Howard, *The Great Iron Trail: The Story of the First Transcontinental Railroad* (New York: Bonanza Books, 1962), p. 107.

4. Carl Wheat, "A Sketch of the Life of Theodore D. Judah," p. 238.

5. Lewis, *Big Four*, p. 17.

6. Howard, *Great Iron Trail*, p. 107.

7. Theodore Judah, *Report to the Pacific Railroad Convention*, published by *Sacramento Daily Union*, July 25, 1860, in Bancroft Library, U.C. Berkeley, p. 62.

8. Grenville M. Dodge, *How We Built the Union Pacific Railway and Other Railway Papers and Addresses*. (Council Bluffs, Iowa: Monarch Printing Co., n.d.), p. 10.

9. Wheat, "Life of Judah," p. 238.

10. Lewis, *Big Four*, p. 18.

11. "Mrs. Judah's Letter [to Bancroft], 12/14/89," Bancroft Library.

12. Judah, *Report to the Convention*.

13. "Mrs. Judah's Letter," Bancroft Library.

14. Ibid.

15. David Lavender, *The Great Persuader*, p. 87.

16. "Mrs. Judah's Letter," Bancroft Library.

17. Wheat, "Life of Judah," p. 242.

18. Ibid., pp. 243–44.

19. Ibid., p. 245.

20. "Mrs. Judah's Letter," Bancroft Library.

21. Charles Crocker Memoir, Bancroft Library.

22. "Mrs. Judah's Letter," Bancroft Library.

23. Lewis, *Big Four*, p. 25.

24. "Mrs. Judah's Letter," Bancroft Library.

25. Wheat, "Life of Judah," pp. 245–46.

26. Crocker Memoir, Bancroft Library.

27. Wheat, "Life of Judah," p. 247.

28. Quoted in George Kraus, *High Road to Promontory*, p. 33.

29. Quoted in ibid., p. 33.

30. *Sacramento Union*, Aug. 7, 1861.

31. Kraus, *High Road to Promontory*, p. 38.

32. *Report of the Chief Engineer of Central Pacific Railroad Company*, Oct. 1, 1861, Bancroft Library, U.C. Berkeley.

33. Wheat, "Life of Judah," p. 251.

34. Ibid.; John Debo Galloway, *The First Transcontinental Railroad*, p. 61.

35. Robert Russell, *Improvement of Communication with the Pacific Coast as an Issue in American Politics* (Cedar Rapids, Iowa: Torch Press, 1948), p. 294.

36. Wheat, "Life of Judah," p. 251.
37. Ibid., p. 252.
38. Griswold, *Work of Giants*, p. 14.
39. Kraus, *High Road to Promontory*, p. 38.
40. Lavender, *Great Persuader*, p. 105.
41. Ibid.
42. Wheat, "Life of Judah," p. 254.
43. Quoted in Russell, *Improvement of Communication*, p. 296.
44. Dodge, *How We Built*, p. 10.
45. Lavender, *Great Persuader*, p. 108.
46. Russell, *Improvement of Communication*, p. 296.
47. *Sacramento Union*, June 18, 1862.
48. Kraus, *High Road to Promontory*, pp. 47–48.
49. Wheat, "Life of Judah," p. 256.
50. Henry V. Poor, "The Pacific Railroad," *North American Review*, vol. 128 (June 1879), p. 665.

CHAPTER FOUR: THE BIRTH OF THE UNION PACIFIC

1. John Hoyt Williams, *A Great and Shining Road*, p. 50.
2. J. R. Perkins, *Trails, Rails and War*, p. 86.
3. Ibid., p. 123.
4. Ulysses S. Grant, *Personal Memoirs*, 2 vols. (New York: Charles L. Webster, 1885–86), vol. 2, chap. 2, p. 31.
5. Quoted in ibid., p. 89.
6. Perkins, *Trails, Rails and War*, p. 92.
7. Ibid., p. 91.
8. Ibid., pp. 95–96.
9. Ibid.
10. Ibid., pp. 100, 104.
11. Grenville M. Dodge, *How We Built the Union Pacific Railway*, pp. 10–12; John W. Starr, *Lincoln and the Railroads* (New York: Arno Press, 1981, reprint of 1927 ed.), pp. 201–5. Wallace Farnham, "Grenville Dodge and the Union Pacific: A Study of Historical Legends," *Journal of American History*, vol. 51 (June 1964), p. 636, calls this story "absurd." It doesn't seem so to me, or to Alan Nevins, or to other historians.
12. Perkins, *Trails, Rails and War*, p. 133.
13. Maury Klein, *Union Pacific*, vol. 1, *Birth of a Railroad, 1862–1893* (Garden City, N.Y.: Doubleday, 1987), p. 24.
14. Ibid., p. 23.
15. Ibid., p. 24.
16. Ibid., p. 25.
17. Williams, *Great and Shining Road*, pp. 72–73.
18. Ibid., p. 74.
19. Ibid., p. 70.

20. Starr, *Lincoln and the Railroads*, p. 204.
21. Ibid., pp. 26–27.
22. Williams, *Great and Shining Road*, p. 76.
23. Klein, *Birth of a Railroad*, p. 29.
24. Williams, *Great and Shining Road*, p. 80.
25. Ibid., p. 84.
26. Thomas C. Cochran, *Railroad Leaders 1845–1890: The Business Mind in Action*, (New York: Russell and Russell, 1965), p. 99.
27. Quoted in Robert G. Athearn, *Union Pacific Country* (Lincoln, Neb.: University of Nebraska Press, 1971), p. 345.
28. Starr, *Lincoln and the Railroads*, p. 208.
29. Perkins, *Trails, Rails and War*, p. 132.
30. Klein, *Birth of a Railroad*, p. 29.
31. Ibid., p. 30.
32. Ibid., p. 31.
33. Ibid., p. 32.
34. Ibid., p. 33.
35. Perkins, *Trails, Rails and War*, pp. 91–92.
36. Ibid., p. 151.
37. Ibid., p. 152.
38. Ibid.
39. Ibid., pp. 153–54.
40. Ibid., p. 142.
41. Starr, *Lincoln and the Railroads*, p. 214.
42. Klein, *Birth of a Railroad*, p. 39.
43. Alfred D. Chandler, *Strategy and Structure: Chapters in History of the Industrial Enterprise*. (Cambridge, Mass.: MIT Press, 1962), pp. 21–22.
44. Ibid., p. 23.

CHAPTER FIVE: JUDAH AND THE ELEPHANT

1. George Kraus, *High Road to Promontory*, p. 52.
2. *Sacramento Union*, July 12, 1862.
3. John Hoyt Williams, *A Great and Shining Road*, p. 56. Judah's report, dated Sept. 1, 1862, is in Bancroft Library, U.C. Berkeley.
4. David Lavender, *The Great Persuader*, p. 129.
5. Ibid., pp. 130–31; Williams, *Great and Shining Road*, pp. 58–59.
6. Williams, *Great and Shining Road*, p. 60.
7. *Sacramento Union*, Aug. 22, 1864.
8. Judah's report of Oct. 22, 1862, is in the Bancroft Library, U.C. Berkeley.
9. Charles Crocker interview, Bancroft Library, Berkeley.
10. Robert Utley and Francis Ketterson, Jr., *Golden Spike* (Washington, D.C.: National Park Service, 1969), p. 15. Southern Pacific historian Lynn Farrar in an Aug. 22, 1999, letter to S. E. Ambrose, comments, "Riegel is dreaming. No books of Crocker & Co. were ever produced for anyone to

disentangle. Mark Hopkins saw to that. They disappeared."

11. Williams, *Great and Shining Road*, p. 61.

12. Crocker interview, Bancroft Library, U.C. Berkeley.

13. *Sacramento Union*, Jan. 9, 1863, in Bancroft Library, U.C. Berkeley.

14. Crocker interview, Bancroft Library.

15. Wesley S. Griswold, *A Work of Giants*, pp. 22–23.

16. John W. Starr, *Lincoln and the Railroads*, pp. 214–15. Starr is the only one who points out that Sargent was no longer in Congress; all the other authorities on the CP list him as either a representative or a senator at this time.

17. Carl Wheat, "A Sketch of the Life of Theodore D. Judah," p. 262.

18. "Mrs. Judah's Letter [to Bancroft], 12/14/89," Bancroft Library.

19. *Sacramento Union*, April 29, 1863.

20. Williams, *Great and Shining Road*, p. 65; Bruce Clement Cooper, *Lewis Metzler Clement: A Pioneer of the Central Pacific Railroad* (privately printed, 1991), p. 5.

21. Quoted in Lavender, *Great Persuader*, p. 137.

22. Judah's 1862 report is in the Bancroft Library, U.C. Berkeley; see also Wheat, "Life of Judah," p. 259.

23. Wheat, "Life of Judah," p. 35.

24. Kraus, *High Road to Promontory*, p. 55.

25. Huntington to E. B. Crocker, May 13, 1868, Huntington Papers, Library of Congress.

26. Ibid.

27. Lavender, *Great Persuader*, p. 139.

28. Williams, *Great and Shining Road*, p. 67.

29. Lavender, *Great Persuader*, p. 140; Williams, *Great and Shining Road*, p. 67.

30. Lavender, *Great Persuader*, p. 141.

31. "Mrs. Judah's Letter," Bancroft Library.

32. Wheat, "Life of Judah," p. 262.

33. Ibid.; Williams, *Great and Shining Road*, p. 68.

34. Griswold, *Work of Giants*, p. 39.

35. *Sacramento Union*, Oct. 27, 1863.

36. This was the eleventh locomotive to arrive in California. It had been shipped on the *Herald of the Morning* in May 1863 and arrived on Sept. 20. (Wendell Huffman, "Railroads Shipped by Sea," *Railroad History*, Spring 1999, p. 27.)

37. *Sacramento Union*, Nov. 11, 1863.

38. Griswold, *Work of Giants*, p. 41.

39. Williams, *Great and Shining Road*, p. 90.

40. Lynn Farrar to Stephen Ambrose, Aug. 22, 1999.

41. *Sacramento Union*, Feb. 18, 1864.

42. Williams, *Great and Shining Road*, p. 91.

43. Crocker interview, Bancroft Library.

44. Griswold, *Work of Giants*, p. 92.
45. Crocker interview, Bancroft Library.
46. Williams, *Great and Shining Road*, p. 88.
47. Griswold, *Work of Giants*, p. 83.
48. Kraus, *High Road to Promontory*, p. 82.
49. Ibid., p. 87.
50. Williams, *Great and Shining Road*, p. 87.
51. Ibid., p. 92.
52. Crocker interview, Bancroft Library.
53. Griswold, *Work of Giants*, p. 93.
54. "Mrs. Judah's Letter," Bancroft Library.

CHAPTER SIX: LAYING OUT THE UNION PACIFIC LINE

1. Young to Durant, Oct. 23, 1863, and Jan. 26, 1864, Brigham Young Papers, Archives, Church of Latter-Day Saints Library, Salt Lake City.
2. Dey to Reed, April 25, 1864, Samuel Reed Papers, UP Archives, Omaha.
3. Maury Klein, *Birth of a Railroad*, pp. 52–53.
4. Ibid., p. 54.
5. Ibid., p. 55.
6. John Hoyt Williams, *A Great and Shining Road*, p. 103.
7. Quoted in ibid., p. 104.
8. Henry Morton Stanley, *Autobiography* (Boston, 1909), p. 226.
9. J. R. Perkins, *Trails, Rails and War*, pp. 172–72.
10. Williams, *Great and Shining Road*, p. 106.
11. Ibid., p. 174.
12. William T. Sherman, *Memoirs*, vol. 2, pp. 411–12; see also Robert Athearn, "General Sherman and the Western Railroads," *Pacific Historical Review*, vol. 5, page 39.
13. Perkins, *Trails, Rails and War*, p. 176.
14. Wesley S. Griswold, *A Work of Giants*, p. 130.
15. Robert G. Athearn, *Union Pacific Country*, p. 36.
16. *Chicago Tribune*, Aug. 14, 1865.
17. Klein, *Birth of a Railroad*, p. 63.
18. *Harper's Weekly*, July 22, 1865, p. 450.
19. The original of the Arthur Ferguson Journal is in the Utah State Historical Society, Salt Lake City; I worked from a typewritten copy.
20. Grenville M. Dodge, *How We Built the Union Pacific Railway*, pp. 20–21. Professor Wallace Farnham, in his article "Grenville Dodge" in the *Journal of American History*, pp. 638–40, calls this story "fanciful" and implies that Dodge not only saw no Indians but was never at the pass. For my part, the story rings true; besides, there were plenty of other eyewitnesses.
21. Klein, *Birth of a Railroad*, p. 67.
22. *Omaha Weekly Herald*, Oct. 27, 1865.
23. Oscar O. Winther, *The Transportation Frontier: Trans-Mississippi West*

1865–1890 (New York: Holt, Rinehart and Winston, 1964), p. 8.

24. Klein, *Birth of a Railroad*, p. 66.
25. Ibid., p. 67.
26. Ibid., pp. 69–70.
27. Ibid., p. 71.
28. James Maxwell Memoir, University of Delaware Library, Newark, Del.; H. K. Nichols Diary, March 11, 1867.
29. Arthur Ferguson Journal, Utah State Historical Society.
30. Reed to Durant, Nov. 1, 1865, Samuel Reed Papers, with thanks to Don Snoddy.
31. *Denver Rocky Mountain News*, May 25, 1866.
32. Quoted in Williams, *Great and Shining Road*, p. 110.

CHAPTER SEVEN: THE CENTRAL PACIFIC ATTACKS THE SIERRA NEVADA

1. John Logan Allen, *North American Exploration: A Continent Comprehended*, 3 vols. (Lincoln: University of Nebraska Press, 1997), vol. 3, pp. 488–92. King began his survey in 1867, just as the Central Pacific was making its way through the mountains.
2. Clarence King, *Mountaineering in the Sierra Nevada* (Lincoln: University of Nebraska Press, 1970 reprint), pp. 6–8. King went on to describe the desert that lay east of the mountains, a passage that will be excerpted when I describe how the Central Pacific graders and track layers came to it.
3. Charles Crocker interview, Bancroft Library.
4. *Sacramento Union*, Jan. 7, 1865.
5. John R. Signor, *Donner Pass: Southern Pacific's Sierra Crossing* (San Marino, Calif.: Golden West Books, 1985), p. 19.
6. Quoted in John J. Stewart, *The Iron Trail to the Golden Spike* (New York: Meadow Lark Press, 1994), p. 121.
7. Bancroft Library, U.C. Berkeley.
8. Hopkins to Huntington, Collis Huntington Papers, ser. 1, Incoming Correspondence, reel 1.
9. Thomas W. Chinn, ed., *A History of the Chinese in California: A Syllabus* (San Francisco: Chinese Historical Society of America, 1969), intro.
10. Quoted in John Hoyt Williams, *A Great and Shining Road*, p. 96.
11. Elliott West, "Unheard Voices: Digging Deeper into Western History," paper read before the Western History Conference, Denver, Colo., 1997.
12. Ibid.
13. Ibid.
14. Judge Samuel Yee oral history, April 19, 1975, by Antoria Chu and Heng Kok Lee; Rudy Kim interview by Jeffery Paul Chan, both in Bancroft Library, U.C. Berkeley.
15. "The Chinese in California," *Lippincott's Magazine*, March 1868, pp. 36–40.
16. Quoted in Williams, *Great and Shining Road*, p. 97.

17. Ibid., pp. 97–98.
18. Lee Chew, "A Chinese Immigrant Makes His Home in America," *Independent* magazine, reprinted on www.historymatters.gmu.edu/text/1650a-chew .html.
19. George Kraus, "Chinese Laborers and the Construction of the Central Pacific," *Utah Historical Quarterly*, vol. 37, no. 1 (Winter 1969), p. 51.
20. Hopkins to Huntington, May 31, 1865, Huntington Papers, ser. 1, reel 1.
21. Quoted in George Kraus, *High Road to Promontory*, p. 110.
22. Wesley S. Griswold, *A Work of Giants*, p. 117.
23. Quoted in *Sacramento Union*, June 16, 1865.
24. Williams, *Great and Shining Road*, p. 100.
25. Quoted in Bruce Clement Cooper, *Lewis Metzler Clement*, p. 7.
26. Robert West Howard, *The Great Iron Trail*, pp. 229–30; Griswold, *Work of Giants*, p. 123; Stewart, *Iron Trail*, p. 129.
27. Williams, *Great and Shining Road*, p. 113.
28. Griswold, *Work of Giants*, p. 211.
29. Williams, *Great and Shining Road*, p. 115.
30. Griswold, *Work of Giants*, p. 145.
31. *Sacramento Union*, Aug. 3, 1865; Griswold, *Work of Giants*, p. 121; Williams, *Great and Shining Road*, p. 102.
32. Quoted in Griswold, *Work of Giants*, p. 123.
33. Ibid., p. 124.
34. Williams, *Great and Shining Road*, pp. 116–17.
35. Stewart, *Iron Trail*, p. 130.
36. *Railroad Record*, Nov. 23, 1865.
37. Williams, *Great and Shining Road*, p. 98.
38. Griswold, *Work of Giants*, p. 120.
39. A. W. Loomis, "How Our Chinamen Are Employed," *Overland Monthly*, March 1869, quoted in Griswold, p. 121.
40. Quoted in Williams, *Great and Shining Road*, p. 98.
41. Quoted in Kraus, *High Road to Promontory*, pp. 116, 120.
42. Lewis Clement, "Statement Concerning Charles Crocker," Bancroft Library, U.C. Berkeley.
43. J. O. Wilder, "The Way Pioneer Builders Met Difficulties," *Southern Pacific Bulletin*, vol. 9, no. 11 (Nov. 1920), p. 23.
44. Griswold, *Work of Giants*, p. 144.
45. *Southern Pacific Bulletin*, vol. 5, no. 21 (Nov. 1917).
46. Griswold, *Work of Giants*, p. 151.
47. Ibid., p. 125.

CHAPTER EIGHT: THE UNION PACIFIC ACROSS NEBRASKA

1. Robert Athearn, *Union Pacific Country*, p. 39.
2. Samuel Bowles, *Across the Continent: A Summer's Journey to the Rocky Mountains* (Springfield, Mass.: S. Bowles, 1866), p. 19.

3. Quoted in Athearn, *Union Pacific Country*, pp. 42–43.
4. Quoted in Union Pacific Railroad, *The Union Pacific Railroad Across the Continent West from Omaha, Nebraska* (pamphlet published by the company, 1868), p. 15.
5. *Omaha Weekly Herald*, Jan. 12 and 19, 1865.
6. Ibid., March 23, 1865.
7. Magee Diary, quoted in the study done for C. B. DeMille for his movie *Union Pacific* and given to me by Don Snoddy.
8. Quoted in Maury Klein, *Birth of a Railroad*, p. 72.
9. Ibid.; Grenville M. Dodge, *How We Built the Union Pacific Railway*, p. 13.
10. Quoted in Klein, *Birth of a Railroad*, p. 73.
11. Grenville Dodge, *A Paper on the Trans-Continental Railways* (Omaha, Neb.: Union Pacific Railroad, 1891), p. 21.
12. Quoted in John Hoyt Williams, *A Great and Shining Road*, p. 105.
13. Ibid., pp. 73–74.
14. Quoted in Robert Athearn, "General Sherman and the Western Railroads," p. 41.
15. Quoted in UP, *Union Pacific Railroad*, pp. 15–17.
16. All these and many other Reed-to-Durant telegrams are in the UP Archives; I used typed copies prepared by Don Snoddy.
17. Klein, *Birth of a Railroad*, p. 74.
18. *New York Times*, Aug. 22, 1866.
19. DeMille collection, p. 16.
20. Quoted in Williams, *Great and Shining Road*, p. 125.
21. Ibid.
22. Quotations on the workers' daily routine in Williams, p. 125.
23. UP, *Union Pacific Railroad*; *Cincinnati Gazette*, June 1867, various articles; DeMille collection, passim.
24. John J. Stewart, *The Iron Trail to the Golden Spike*, pp. 152–53.
25. Henry M. Stanley, *My Early Travels and Adventures in America and Asia* (New York: Scribner, 1895), vol. 1, pp. 195–96.
26. *Cincinnati Gazette*, June 14, 1887.
27. Quoted in Oscar O. Winther, *The Transportation Frontier*, p. 111.
28. *Omaha Weekly Herald*, May 11, 1866.
29. Ibid., Aug. 2, 1866.
30. Reed telegrams in UP Archives, Omaha, courtesy of Don Snoddy.
31. *Omaha Weekly Herald*, Sept. 7, 1866.
32. Ibid., Sept. 21, 1866.
33. *Denver Rocky Mountain News*, June 18, 1866.
34. Athearn, "Sherman and the Western Railroads," p. 43.
35. *Omaha Weekly Herald*, Feb. 22, 1866.
36. The material in the preceding paragraphs is taken from Union Pacific Railroad, *Excursion to the Hundredth Meridian: From New York to Platte City* (1867 pamphlet). There is a copy in the UP Archives, Omaha.

37. Klein, *Birth of a Railroad*, p. 76.
38. Athearn, *Union Pacific Country*, p. 51.
39. Ibid., p. 62.
40. Ibid., pp. 78–79; Grenville Dodge, *Report of the Chief Engineer for 1866* (Washington, D.C.: Philip & Solomons, 1868), p. 11.
41. Dodge, *Report of 1866*, pp. 27–30.
42. Ibid., pp. 13–16.
43. Ibid., pp. 70–72.
44. The Reed telegrams to Durant are in the UP Archives.
45. Klein, *Birth of a Railroad*, pp. 82–83.
46. Ibid., pp. 18–20.

CHAPTER NINE: THE CENTRAL PACIFIC ASSAULTS THE SIERRA

1. Thomas C. Cochran, *Railroad Leaders 1845–1890*, p. 1.
2. Hubert Howe Bancroft, *History of California*, vol. 7, pp. 551–52.
3. George Kraus, *High Road to Promontory*, p. 125.
4. *Sacramento Union*, Jan. 13, 1866.
5. *Omaha Weekly Herald*, Nov. 2, 1866.
6. The Hopkins-Huntington letters are in Collis Huntington Papers, Library of Congress. The Cohen quote is from Kraus, *High Road to Promontory*, p. 88.
7. *Sacramento Union*, Nov. 25, 1865.
8. Quoted in Kraus, *High Road to Promontory*, p. 123.
9. John Hoyt Williams, *A Great and Shining Road*, p. 130.
10. Charles Crocker interview, Bancroft Library.
11. Williams, *Great and Shining Road*, p. 130.
12. Charles Crocker Memoir, Bancroft Library.
13. Williams, *Great and Shining Road*, p. 131.
14. Quoted in Wesley S. Griswold, *A Work of Giants*, p. 156.
15. *Dutch Flat Enquirer*, April 27 and June 2, 1866.
16. Quoted in *Southern Pacific Bulletin*, June 1927; Williams, *Great and Shining Road*, p. 133.
17. Quoted in Kraus, *High Road to Promontory*, p. 136.
18. Clement to Stanford, July 21, 1887, U.S. Pacific Railway Commission, exhibit no. 8, p. 2576.
19. Quoted in Williams, *Great and Shining Road*, p. 134.
20. Quoted in Griswold, *Work of Giants*, p. 149.
21. Ibid.
22. Quoted in *Sacramento Union*, Oct. 23, 1866.
23. *Dutch Flat Enquirer*, Oct. 30, 1866.
24. *Sacramento Union*, Nov. 27, 1866.
25. Williams, *Great and Shining Road*, p. 142.
26. Alexander Saxton, "The Army of Canton in the High Sierra," *Pacific Historical Review*, vol. 35 (June 1966), p. 147.

27. Ibid., p. 143; Thomas W. Chinn, ed., A History of the Chinese in California, p. 45.
28. John J. Stewart, The Iron Trail to the Golden Spike, p. 133; Chinn, ed., Chinese in California, p. 45.
29. Dutch Flat Enquirer, Dec. 25, 1866.
30. Kraus, High Road to Promontory, p. 136; Southern Pacific Bulletin, July 1924.
31. Sacramento Union, Dec. 27, 1866.
32. Ibid.
33. E. B. Crocker to Huntington, Dec. 22, 1866, Huntington Papers.
34. George Kraus, "Chinese Laborers and the Construction of the Central Pacific," Utah Historical Quarterly, vol. 37, no. 1 (Winter 1969), p. 49.
35. Kraus, High Road to Promontory, pp. 142–43.

CHAPTER TEN: THE UNION PACIFIC TO THE ROCKY MOUNTAINS

1. Wesley S. Griswold, A Work of Giants, p. 210.
2. The Reed telegrams are in Samuel Reed Papers, transcribed by Don Snoddy.
3. John Hoyt Williams, A Great and Shining Road, pp. 146–47.
4. The Reed diaries and letters are in Reed Papers; thanks to Don Snoddy for transcribing them for me.
5. E. C. Lockwood, "With the Casement Brothers While Building the Union Pacific," Union Pacific Magazine, Feb. 1931, p. 3.
6. Omaha Weekly Herald, April 12, 1867.
7. Robert G. Athearn, "General Sherman and the Western Railroads," p. 422.
8. Griswold, Work of Giants, p. 208.
9. Grenville M. Dodge, How We Built the Union Pacific Railway, p. 14.
10. Williams, Great and Shining Road, p. 147.
11. Reed to Mrs. Reed, April 27, 1867, Reed Papers.
12. Grenville Dodge, Romantic Realities: The Story of the Building of the Pacific Roads. (Omaha, Neb.: Union Pacific Railroad, 1891), p. 17.
13. Reed to Mrs. Reed, May 6, 1867, Reed Papers.
14. Chicago Tribune, Aug. 20, 1867.
15. Ibid., June 18, 1867.
16. Ferguson diary, UP Archives, Omaha.
17. Maury Klein, Birth of a Railroad, p. 136.
18. Ferguson Journal, Utah State Historical Society.
19. Williams, Great and Shining Road, p. 150.
20. Dodge, How We Built, pp. 15–16.
21. Ferguson Journal, Utah State Historical Society.
22. Dodge, How We Built, p. 20; Klein, Birth of a Railroad, p. 103.
23. Dodge, How We Built, p. 117.
24. Ibid., p. 105; Andrew Rosewater, "Finding a Path Across the Rocky Mountain Range," Union Pacific Magazine, Jan. 1923, pp. 6–7.

25. Robert Miller Galbraith, "Life on the Railroad," interview, in Carbon County Museum, Rawlins, Wyo.
26. My thanks to Richard Snow, editor of *American Heritage*, for sending me a copy of Benét's story.
27. Henry Morton Stanley, *My Early Travels and Adventures in America and Asia*, vol. 1, pp. 154–57.
28. Reed to Mrs. Reed, Aug. 15, 1867, Reed Papers.
29. Stanley, *My Early Travels*, vol. 1, pp. 163–67.
30. Samuel Bowles, *Our New West: Records of Travel: A Full Description of the Pacific Railroad* (Hartford, Conn.: Hartford Publishing, 1869), pp. 56–57.
31. *Chicago Tribune*, June 18, 1867.
32. Dodge, *How We Built*, pp. 118–19.
33. Klein, *Birth of a Railroad*, p. 104.
34. Ibid., pp. 106–7.
35. *New York Tribune*, Jan. 18, 1867.
36. *Harper's Weekly*, Nov. 16, 1867.
37. Ibid., Aug. 24, 1867.
38. Ferguson diary, UP Archives.
39. *New York Tribune*, Aug. 8, 1867.
40. *Chicago Tribune*, Aug. 20, 1867.
41. Quoted in Griswold, *Work of Giants*, p. 216.
42. Klein, *Birth of a Railroad*, p. 116. After serving as the chief assistant to President Ulysses S. Grant, beginning in 1869, Rawlins died in 1870.
43. Thomas Hubbard Diary, UP Archives, Omaha.
44. Ibid.
45. Dodge, *How We Built*, p. 22.
46. Athearn, "General Sherman and the Western Railroads," p. 43.
47. Griswold, *Work of Giants*, p. 229.
48. Charles Edgar Ames, *Pioneering the Union Pacific: A Reappraisal of the Builders of the Railroad* (New York: Appleton-Century-Crofts, 1969), pp. 173–77.
49. Williams, *Great and Shining Road*, p. 159.
50. Ames, *Pioneering the Union Pacific*, pp. 196–202.
51. *New York Times*, Dec. 4, 1867.
52. *Chicago Tribune*, Nov. 16, 1867.
53. Dodge, *How We Built*, p. 116.
54. Quoted in John Debo Galloway, *The First Transcontinental Railroad*, p. 285.
55. G. M. Dodge, *Report of the Chief Engineer for the Year 1867* (Washington, D.C.: Government Printing Office, 1868), pp. 26–27.
56. *Chicago Tribune*, Nov. 16, 1867.

CHAPTER ELEVEN: THE CENTRAL PACIFIC PENETRATES THE SUMMIT

1. Henry Poor, "Railroad to the Pacific," in *The Golden Spike: A Centennial Remembrance* (New York: American Geographical Society, 1969), p. 19.

2. Quoted in Bruce Clement Cooper, *Lewis Metzler Clement*, p. 7.
3. The details are taken from John R. Gilliss's speech before the American Society of Civil Engineers in 1870, reprinted in George Kraus, *High Road to Promontory*, pp. 144–152.
4. Ibid., p. 146.
5. Ibid.
6. Wesley S. Griswold, *A Work of Giants*, pp. 190–91.
7. *Sacramento Union*, March 9, 1867.
8. Clement to Stanford, July 21, 1887, in *U.S. Pacific Railway Commission Report No. 2576*, pamphlet provided by Cooper-Clement Associates, Ardmore, Pa. 19003.
9. Gilliss's speech, in Kraus, *High Road to Promontory*, p. 145.
10. Ibid., pp. 147–48.
11. Griswold, *Work of Giants*, p. 193.
12. Ibid.
13. Kraus, *High Road to Promontory*, p. 159.
14. J. D. Brennan, "The Romance of the Sacramento Division," *Southern Pacific Bulletin*, Aug. 1920, p. 4.
15. Charles Crocker to Huntington, Jan. 7, 1867, Collis Huntington Papers. Unless otherwise noted, all correspondence between Huntington and the other members of the board of directors comes out of the Huntington Papers.
16. Griswold, *Work of Giants*, p. 194.
17. Hopkins to Huntington, May 2, 1867.
18. E. B. Crocker to Huntington, May 8, 1867.
19. Charles Crocker to Huntington, Jan. 14, 1867.
20. E. B. Crocker to Hopkins, April 15, 1867; Stanford to Hopkins, April 16, 1867.
21. Kraus, *High Road to Promontory*, p. 182.
22. Ibid., p. 183.
23. E. B. Crocker to Huntington, Jan. 14, 1867.
24. Same to same, April 23, 1867.
25. Stanford to Huntington, Jan. 7, 1867.
26. On March 8, 1867, and March 9, 1867, in letters to Huntington, E. B. Crocker discusses this matter.
27. E. B. Crocker to Huntington, April 16, 1867.
28. Maury Klein, *Birth of a Railroad*, p. 148.
29. E. B. Crocker to Huntington, April 23, 1867.
30. Charles Crocker comments on the Bancroft biography, Bancroft Library, U.C. Berkeley.
31. Griswold, *Work of Giants*, p. 195.
32. Ibid., p. 196.
33. E. B. Crocker to Huntington, May 22 and 27, 1867.
34. Same to same, May 27, 1867.

35. *Sacramento Union*, July 12, 1867.
36. Griswold, *Work of Giants*, p. 197.
37. E. B. Crocker to Huntington, June 26, 1867.
38. Same to same, June 28, 1867.
39. Griswold, *Work of Giants*, p. 197.
40. E. B. Crocker to Huntington, July 2 and 6, 1867.
41. Huntington to E. B. Crocker, Dec. 28, 1867.
42. E. B. Crocker to Huntington, Sept. 12, 1867.
43. Same to same, July 10, 1867.
44. Same to same, Dec. 20, 1867.
45. Same to same, July 10 and Sept. 12, 1867.
46. Huntington to Charles Crocker, quoted in William Deverell, *Railroad Crossing: Californians and the Railroad, 1850–1910* (Berkeley: University of California Press, 1994), p. 14.
47. E. B. Crocker to Huntington, Aug. 28, 1867.
48. *Sacramento Union*, Aug. 30, 1867.
49. Huntington to E. B. Crocker, Oct. 3, 1867.
50. *Sacramento Union*, Dec. 9, 1867; Crocker to Huntington, Oct. 30, 1867.
51. Huntington to Stanford, Oct. 26, 1867.
52. Hubert Howe Bancroft, *History of California*, vol. 7, pp. 572–73.
53. Charles Crocker comments on his Bancroft biography, Bancroft Library.
54. E. B. Crocker to Huntington, Nov. 7, 1867.
55. Huntington's comments on the Bancroft history, Bancroft Library.
56. See Kraus, *High Road to Promontory*, chap. 11.
57. Ibid., p. 163.
58. See Harry Carman and Charles Mueller, "The Contract and Finance Company and the Central Pacific Railroad," *Mississippi Valley Historical Review*, vol. 14, no. 3 (Dec. 1927).
59. See Hopkins to Huntington, March 16, 1868.
60. Hopkins to Huntington, Dec. 1, 1867.
61. Samuel Bowles, *Our New West*, p. 67.
62. Bancroft, *History of California*, vol. 7, p. 570.

CHAPTER TWELVE: THE UNION PACIFIC ACROSS WYOMING
1. E. B. Crocker to Huntington, April 23, 1868, Collis Huntington Papers, Bancroft Library.
2. From the Virginia City [Nevada] *Territorial Enterprise*, quoted in the *Salt Lake Daily Reporter*, July 30, 1868.
3. *Chicago Leader*, July 20, 1868.
4. *New York Tribune*, Aug. 4, 1867.
5. Ibid., June 30, 1868.
6. Quoted in Robert G. Athearn, *Union Pacific Country*, pp. 114–15.
7. *Salt Lake Daily Reporter*, June 20, 1868.
8. *New York Tribune*, Sept. 18, 1868.

9. Grenville Dodge, *Romantic Realities*, p. 21.
10. Grenville M. Dodge, *How We Built the Union Pacific Railway*, p. 23.
11. Ibid., p. 22.
12. Wesley S. Griswold, *A Work of Giants*, p. 262.
13. Huntington to Stanford, May 22, 1868; E. B. Crocker to Huntington, Oct. 14, 1867; see also Maury Klein, *Birth of a Railroad*, p. 150.
14. All these telegrams and hundreds of others are in the UP Archives, Omaha; heartfelt thanks to UP Historian Don Snoddy for typing them all up.
15. Ibid.
16. John Debo Galloway, *The First Transcontinental Railroad*, p. 159.
17. Ibid.
18. Klein, *Birth of a Railroad*, p. 150.
19. Griswold, *Work of Giants*, p. 263.
20. David Dary, *Seeking Pleasure in the Old West* (New York: Alfred Knopf, 1995), p. 118.
21. Reed to Crane, Feb. 28, 1868, Reed Papers.
22. *Frontier Index*, Dec. 24, 1867.
23. *Cheyenne Daily Leader*, April 6, 1868.
24. Charles Edgar Ames, *Pioneering the Union Pacific*, p. 272. When Edward Harriman redid the entire line at the end of the nineteenth century, he went south of the Dale Creek crossing, and the bridge is no longer there. It is possible to walk through the cuts.
25. Reed's various telegrams are in Reed Papers.
26. Quoted in Griswold, *Work of Giants*, p. 263.
27. Dodge's April 16, 1868, telegram to Browning is in UP Archives, Omaha.
28. Klein, *Birth of a Railroad*, p. 151.
29. Griswold, *Work of Giants*, p. 264.
30. Klein, *Birth of a Railroad*, p. 272.
31. James Ehernberger and Francis Gschwind, *Sherman Hill* (Callaway, Neb.: E.G. Publications, 1978), pp. 14–17.
32. Ferguson Journal, Utah State Historical Society.
33. Ibid.
34. Ibid.
35. David Lemon, "An Experience on the Road," *Union Pacific Magazine*, May 1924, pp. 5–6.
36. Klein, *Birth of a Railroad*, p. 151.
37. Henry Morton Stanley, *My Early Travels and Adventures in America and Asia*, vol. 1, p. 211.
38. Ferguson Journal, Aug. 17, 1868, Utah State Historical Society.
39. Ibid., July 21, 1868.
40. Athearn, *Union Pacific Country*, p. 291.
41. Morris Mills, "With the Union Pacific Railroad in the Early Days," *Annals of Wyoming*, vol. 3, no. 4 (April 1926), p. 200.

42. *Chicago Tribune*, July 16 and Aug. 18, 1868.
43. Mills, "With the Union Pacific," p. 201.
44. Maury Klein, "The Coming of the Railroad and the End of the Great West," *Invention and Technology*, vol. 10, no. 3 (Winter 1995), p. 14.
45. Ferguson Journal, June 23, 1868, Utah State Historical Society.
46. Quoted in Klein, "Coming of the Railroad," pp. 14–15.
47. Charles Edgar Ames, *Pioneering the Union Pacific*, p. 247; Klein, *Birth of a Railroad*, p. 156.
48. Ames, *Pioneering the Union Pacific*, p. 275.
49. Griswold, *Work of Giants*, pp. 270–71.
50. Ames, *Pioneering the Union Pacific*, p. 283.
51. Quoted in ibid., pp. 283–84.
52. Quoted in ibid., p. 287.
53. Quoted in Klein, *Birth of a Railroad*, p. 165.
54. *Salt Lake Daily Reporter*, Aug. 21, 1868.
55. Quoted in Athearn, *Union Pacific Country*, p. 114.
56. Klein, *Birth of a Railroad*, pp. 168–69.
57. Ibid., p. 175.
58. *Western Railroad Gazette*, Sept. 5, 1868.
59. *Salt Lake Daily Reporter*, Dec. 15, 1868.
60. Klein, *Birth of a Railroad*, p. 176.
61. *Western Railroad Gazette*, Nov. 30, 1868.
62. Huntington to Mark Hopkins, May 30, 1868.
63. Klein, *Birth of a Railroad*, pp. 178–79.
64. Ames, *Pioneering the Union Pacific*, p. 287.
65. *Salt Lake Daily Reporter*, Sept. 30, 1868.

CHAPTER THIRTEEN: BRIGHAM YOUNG AND THE MORMONS
MAKE THE GRADE

1. Wesley S. Griswold, *A Work of Giants*, p. 274.
2. John Debo Galloway, *The First Transcontinental Railroad*, pp. 241, 244.
3. Robert G. Athearn, *Union Pacific Country*, pp. 69–71.
4. Young to Reed, Aug. 10, 1866, and to Dodge, Nov. 5, 1866, Brigham Young Papers.
5. Athearn, *Union Pacific Country*, pp. 69–71.
6. Ibid., pp. 75–78.
7. *Salt Lake Deseret News*, May 9, 1868.
8. Athearn, *Union Pacific Country*, pp. 89–90.
9. Durant to Young, May 6, 1868, Young Papers.
10. Young to Durant, May 6, 1868, Young Papers.
11. Young to Seymour and Reed, May 19, 1868, Young Papers.
12. Athearn, *Union Pacific Country*, pp. 90–91.
13. Lewis Barney Papers, Archives, Church of Latter-Day Saints Library, Salt Lake City.
14. Young to Reed, May 29, 1868, Young Papers.

15. Reed to Durant, May 31, 1868, Samuel Reed Papers.
16. Athearn, *Union Pacific Country*, p. 83.
17. *Cheyenne Daily Leader*, June 15, 1868, quoted in Athearn, *Union Pacific Country*, p. 95.
18. Athearn, *Union Pacific Country*, p. 90.
19. Ibid., pp. 93–94.
20. *Cheyenne Daily Leader*, June 16, 1868.
21. Dodge, *How We Built the Union Pacific Railway*, p. 34.
22. *Salt Lake Deseret News*, Sept. 11, 1868.
23. Ibid., June 5, 1868.
24. Griswold, *Work of Giants*, p. 270.
25. Clarence A. Reeder, "A History of Utah's Railroads," Ph.D. dissertation, University of Utah, 1959.
26. Samuel Schill Papers, Archives, Church of Latter-Day Saints Library, Salt Lake City.
27. Hubert Howe Bancroft, *History of Utah* (San Francisco: History Company, 1890), p. 754.
28. Galloway, *First Transcontinental Railroad*, pp. 277–79.
29. Ibid., p. 240.
30. Stanford to Hopkins, June 9, 1868, Huntington-Hopkins correspondence, Bancroft Library, U.C. Berkeley.
31. Young to Stanford, June 23, 1868, Huntington-Hopkins correspondence.
32. Stanford to Young, July 28, 1868, and Young to Stanford, July 29, 1868, Young Papers.
33. Young to Stanford, Aug. 10, 1868, Young Papers.
34. Young to bishops, Sept. 5, 1868, Young Papers.
35. Griswold, *Work of Giants*, p. 254.
36. Stanford to Hopkins, Nov. 9, 1868, Huntington-Hopkins correspondence.
37. Robert Utley and Francis Ketterson, Jr., *Golden Spike*, pp. 32–33.
38. Stanford to Hopkins, Dec. 10, 1868, Huntington-Hopkins correspondence.
39. Griswold, *Work of Giants*, p. 343.
40. Milando Pratt Memoir, Utah State Historical Library, Salt Lake City.
41. James Maxwell Memoir, University of Delaware Library, Newark, Delaware.
42. These telegrams and many others are in the Young Papers.
43. *Cheyenne Daily Leader*, June 15, 1868.
44. Young memo, Oct. 8, 1868, and Young to Durant, Jan. 9, 1869, Young Papers.
45. Young to Durant, Jan. 9, 1869, Young Papers.
46. Athearn, *Union Pacific Country*, p. 97.
47. W.C.A. Smoot, "Tales from Old-Timers," *Union Pacific Magazine*, Dec. 1923, p. 12.

CHAPTER FOURTEEN: THE CENTRAL PACIFIC GOES THROUGH NEVADA
1. Huntington to E. B. Crocker, Jan. 1 and 21, 1868, and E. B. Crocker to Huntington, Jan. 22, 1868, Huntington Papers.

2. Above letters and telegrams all in Huntington Papers.

3. Wesley S. Griswold, *A Work of Giants*, p. 234.

4. Clement to Stanford, July 21, 1887, U.S. Pacific Railway Commission, exhibit no. 8.

5. Ibid.

6. George Kraus, *High Road to Promontory*, p. 159; Griswold, *Work of Giants*, p. 193. Quote from Griswold.

7. Hopkins to Huntington, July 16, 1868, Huntington Papers.

8. Brown's account is reprinted in Kraus, *High Road to Promontory*, pp. 190–91.

9. *Southern Pacific Bulletin*, Aug. 1920.

10. Ibid., Sept. 1920.

11. Quoted in Bruce Clement Cooper, *Lewis Metzler Clement*, p. 7.

12. Ibid., p. 194.

13. Griswold, *Work of Giants*, pp. 227–29.

14. Huntington to Hopkins, April 14, 1868, Huntington Papers.

15. Huntington to Charles Crocker, April 15, 1868, Huntington Papers.

16. Stanford to Hopkins, June 9, 1868, Huntington Papers.

17. Charles Crocker to Huntington, June 16, 1868, Huntington Papers.

18. Kraus, *High Road to Promontory*, pp. 196–98.

19. Charles Crocker's remarks on his Bancroft biography, Bancroft Library.

20. *Reno Crescent*, July 14, 1868, quoted in Griswold, *Work of Giants*, p. 244.

21. Huntington to Charles Crocker, July 1, 1868, Huntington Papers.

22. Griswold, *Work of Giants*, pp. 245–46.

23. Clement to Stanford, July 21, 1887, U.S. Pacific Railway Commission, exhibit no. 8.

24. Charles Crocker to Huntington, July 15, 1868, Huntington Papers.

25. Kraus, *High Road to Promontory*, p. 203.

26. Crocker interview on his biography, Bancroft Library.

27. *San Francisco Chronicle*, Sept. 7, 1868, quoted in Kraus, *High Road to Promontory*, pp. 204–11.

28. Quoted in ibid., p. 211.

29. Griswold, *Work of Giants*, pp. 247–48.

30. Huntington to Charles Crocker, Oct. 21, 1868, Huntington Papers.

31. *Humboldt Register*, Aug. 1, Oct. 3, and Dec. 26, 1868.

32. Kraus, *High Road to Promontory*, p. 212.

33. Griswold, *Work of Giants*, p. 253.

34. Kraus, *High Road to Promontory*, pp. 216–21.

35. Huntington to Stanford, Nov. 13, 1868, Huntington Papers.

36. Stanford to Huntington, Nov. 21, 1868, Huntington Papers.

37. Stanford to E. B. Crocker, Dec. 1, 4, and 8, 1868, Huntington Papers. All these letters are reprinted in Kraus, *High Road to Promontory*.

38. Huntington to Hopkins, Dec. 15, 1868, in Kraus, *High Road to Promontory*, p. 227.

CHAPTER FIFTEEN: THE RAILROADS RACE INTO UTAH

1. Charles Edgar Ames, *Pioneering the Union Pacific*, pp. 558–59.
2. Young to Durant, Jan. 15, 1869, Brigham Young Papers.
3. Young to Dillon, May 19, 1869; to Durant, same date; to Duff, Aug. 12, 1869; to Bushnell, Aug. 12, 1869; to Oliver Ames, Aug. 12, 1869; to Durant, Aug. 14, 1869; to Hammond, Nov. 12, 1869, plus others, all in Young Papers.
4. Charles Francis Adams, Jr., "The Pacific Railroad Ring," *North American Review*, Jan. 1869, pp. 116–50 passim.
5. Ames, *Pioneering the Union Pacific*, pp. 244–45, 300.
6. Adams, "Pacific Railroad Ring," p. 118.
7. *Salt Lake Daily Reporter*, Feb. 16, 1869.
8. Crocker to Huntington, and Hopkins to Huntington, Jan. 20, 1869, Huntington Papers; also quoted in Griswold, *Work of Giants*, p. 297.
9. Crocker Memoir, Bancroft Library.
10. Ibid.
11. *Sacramento Union*, April 15, 1869, quoted in Griswold, *Work of Giants*, p. 296.
12. Griswold, *Work of Giants*, pp. 298–99.
13. Ibid., pp. 299–300.
14. Ibid, pp. 300–301.
15. Ibid., p. 305.
16. Ames, *Pioneering the Union Pacific*, p. 329.
17. Maury Klein, *Birth of a Railroad*, pp. 200–201.
18. *Sacramento Union*, March 6, 1869.
19. *New York Tribune*, March 6, 1869.
20. Quoted in Griswold, *Work of Giants*, pp. 292–93.
21. Ibid., p. 298.
22. *Omaha Weekly Herald*, Dec. 30, 1868.
23. Klein, *Birth of a Railroad*, p. 191.
24. George Kraus, *High Road to Promontory*, pp. 228–29.
25. Griswold, *Work of Giants*, p. 303.
26. *Sacramento Union*, Jan. 19, 1869.
27. Klein, *Birth of a Railroad*, p. 210.
28. Crocker Memoir, Bancroft Library.
29. Ames, *Pioneering the Union Pacific*, p. 328.
30. Ibid., pp. 329–32.
31. Kraus, *High Road to Promontory*, pp. 198–200.
32. Ibid., p. 197.
33. Ibid., pp. 229–31; Klein, *Birth of a Railroad*, p. 195.
34. Klein, *Birth of a Railroad*, pp. 196–97.
35. Quoted in Kraus, *High Road to Promontory*, p. 231.
36. *Salt Lake Daily Reporter*, Feb. 16, 1869.
37. *Reno Crescent*, March 20, 1869.
38. Robert Utley and Francis Ketterson, Jr., *Golden Spike*, pp. 34–35.

39. Grenville M. Dodge, *How We Built the Union Pacific Railway*, p. 118.
40. Collis Huntington Memoir, Bancroft Library, U.C. Berkeley. The affair is discussed in Griswold, *Work of Giants*, pp. 285–87.
41. Ames, *Pioneering the Union Pacific*, p. 312.
42. Kraus, *High Road to Promontory*, p. 237.
43. Young to Durant, April 2, 1869, Young Papers.
44. Ames, *Pioneering the Union Pacific*, p. 333.
45. Ibid., p. 314.
46. Klein, *Birth of a Railroad*, pp. 202–3.
47. Griswold, *Work of Giants*, p. 306.
48. Ibid., p. 305.
49. *Salt Lake Deseret News*, April 1, 1869. See also Kraus, *High Road to Promontory*, pp. 237–41.
50. Utley and Ketterson, Jr., *Golden Spike*, p. 35.
51. Ibid.
52. Klein, *Birth of a Railroad*, p. 210.
53. Griswold, *Work of Giants*, pp. 291–92.
54. Kraus, *High Road to Promontory*, p. 244.
55. Crocker Memoir, Bancroft Library.
56. Klein, *Birth of a Railroad*, p. 211.
57. Griswold, *Work of Giants*, p. 295.

CHAPTER SIXTEEN: TO THE SUMMIT
1. Maury Klein, *Birth of a Railroad*, p. 210.
2. Ibid., p. 212.
3. Ibid., p. 213.
4. Ibid., pp. 214–15.
5. Ibid., p. 217.
6. *San Francisco Daily Alta California*, April 23, 1869.
7. Ibid., April 26, 1869.
8. Robert Utley and Francis Ketterson, Jr., *Golden Spike*, p. 39.
9. *San Francisco Daily Alta California*, April 27, 1869.
10. Crocker Memoir, Bancroft Library.
11. Ibid.; Wesley S. Griswold, *A Work of Giants*, pp. 309–20.
12. *San Francisco Bulletin*, April 29, 1869.
13. Klein, *Birth of a Railroad*, p. 219.
14. *San Francisco Bulletin*, April 30, 1869.
15. Crocker Memoir, Bancroft Library.
16. Ibid.
17. Griswold, *Work of Giants*, pp. 311–13.
18. Huntington to Charles Crocker, May 10, 1869, Huntington Papers.
19. *San Francisco Daily Alta California*, April 30, 1869.
20. Ibid., May 2, 1869.
21. *San Francisco Bulletin*, May 1, 1869.

22. Grenville M. Dodge, *How We Built the Union Pacific Railway*, p. 54.
23. *San Francisco Daily Alta California*, April 28, 1869.
24. George Kraus, *High Road to Promontory*, p. 258.
25. Dodge, *How We Built*, p. 68.
26. *San Francisco Daily Alta California*, May 5, 1869.
27. *Salt Lake Deseret News*, May 6, 1869.
28. Quoted in Kraus, *High Road to Promontory*, p. 258.
29. Griswold, *Work of Giants*, p. 312.

CHAPTER SEVENTEEN: DONE
1. Wesley S. Griswold, *A Work of Giants*, p. 328.
2. Robert Athearn, "General Sherman and the Western Railroads," p. 48.
3. Maury Klein, *Birth of a Railroad*, p. 220.
4. *New York Herald*, May 10, 1869, quoted in ibid., p. 222.
5. Charles Edgar Ames, *Pioneering the Union Pacific*, pp. 321–23; Klein, *Birth of a Railroad*, pp. 219–20.
6. *San Francisco Bulletin*, May 11, 1869.
7. Ames, *Pioneering the Union Pacific*, pp. 322–23.
8. J. N. Bowman, "Driving the Last Spike," *California Historical Society Quarterly*, vol. 36 (1957), pp. 98–99.
9. George Kraus, *High Road to Promontory*, p. 264; Griswold, *Work of Giants*, p. 317.
10. Kraus, *High Road to Promontory*, p. 267.
11. See all the various newspapers from Salt Lake, Sacramento, San Francisco, and elsewhere for accounts of the festivities, as well as all the books on the UP and CP.
12. *San Francisco Daily Alta Californian*, May 10, 1869. It is not often that, when quoting someone else's writing, I say to myself, "I wish I had written that," but in this case I do wish that the last eight words were mine.
13. Klein, *Birth of a Railroad*, p. 220.
14. Hugh O'Neil, "List of Persons Present, Promontory, Utah, May 10, 1869," *Utah Historical Quarterly*, vol. 24 (1956), pp. 157–63.
15. Griswold, *Work of Giants*, p. 325.
16. Kraus, *High Road to Promontory*, pp. 278–81; Klein, *Birth of a Railroad*, p. 225.
17. *Chicago Tribune*, May 11, 1869.
18. Klein, *Birth of a Railroad*, p. 226.
19. *New York Tribune*, *Chicago Tribune*, *Salt Lake Deseret News*, *San Francisco Daily Alta California*, *San Francisco Bulletin*, and other newspapers for May 11 and 12, 1869, carry these and other telegrams.
20. Dodge, *How We Built the Union Pacific Railway*, p. 66.
21. Anna Judah Papers, Bancroft Library, U.C. Berkeley.
22. *Salt Lake Deseret News*, May 11, 1869.

Epilogue

1. *Trans-Continental*, May 30, 1870.
2. Sidney Dillon, "Historic Moments: Driving the Last Spike of the Union Pacific," *Scribner's Magazine*, Aug. 1892, p. 254.
3. "Pacific Railroad Grants," *Putnam's Magazine*, Oct. 1868, pp. 488–89.
4. Charles Edgar Ames, *Pioneering the Union Pacific*, pp. 371–73.
5. Robert Utley and Francis Ketterson, Jr., *Golden Spike*, pp. 83–84.
6. Oliver Ames to C. G. Hammond, Sept. 2, 1869, Brigham Young Papers.
7. *New York Sun*, Sept. 4, 1872.
8. Ames, *Pioneering the Union Pacific*, p. 492.
9. Both quoted in Lloyd Mercer, *Railroads and Land Grant Policy* (New York: Academic Press, 1982), p. 13.
10. Ibid., p. 9.
11. Robert Henry, "The RR Land Grant Legend in American History Texts," *Mississippi Valley Historical Review*, vol. 32 (1945–46), p. 186.
12. Ibid., p. 182.
13. Klein, *Birth of a Railroad*, p. 238.
14. Ibid., p. 4.

Bibliography

BOOKS

Allen, John Logan. *North American Exploration: A Continent Comprehended.* 3 volumes. Lincoln: University of Nebraska Press, 1997.

Ames, Charles Edgar. *Pioneering the Union Pacific: A Reappraisal of the Builders of the Railroad.* New York: Appleton-Century-Crofts, 1969.

Athearn, Robert G. *Union Pacific Country.* Lincoln: University of Nebraska Press, 1971.

Bancroft, Hubert Howe. *History of California,* vol. 7 (1860–1890). San Francisco: History Company, 1890.

——— *History of Utah.* San Francisco: History Company, 1890.

Basler, Roy P., ed. *The Collected Works of Abraham Lincoln.* 9 volumes. New Brunswick, N.J.: Rutgers University Press, 1953–55.

Bowles, Samuel. *Across the Continent: A Summer's Journey to the Rocky Mountains.* Springfield, Mass.: S. Bowles, 1866.

———. *Our New West: Records of Travel: A Full Description of the Pacific Railroad.* Hartford, Conn.: Hartford Publishing, 1869.

Bracken, Jeanne Minn, ed. *Iron Horses Across America.* Carlisle, Mass.: Discovery Enterprises, 1995.

Chandler, Alfred D. *Strategy and Structure: Chapters in History of the Industrial Enterprise.* Cambridge, Mass.: MIT Press, 1962.

Chinn, Thomas W., ed. *A History of the Chinese in California: A Syllabus.* San Francisco: Chinese Historical Society of America, 1969.

Clarke, Thomas Curtis, et al. *The American Railway: Its Construction, Development, Management and Appliances.* New York: Scribner, 1889.

Cochran, Thomas C. *Railroad Leaders 1845–1890: The Business Mind in Action.* New York: Russell and Russell, 1965.

Cooper, Bruce Clement. *Lewis Metzler Clement: A Pioneer of the Central Pacific Railroad*. Privately printed, 1991.

Dary, David. *Seeking Pleasure in the Old West*. New York: Alfred A. Knopf, 1995.

Deverell, William. *Railroad Crossing: Californians and the Railroad, 1850–1910*. Berkeley: University of California Press, 1994.

Dodge, Grenville M. *How We Built the Union Pacific Railway*. Council Bluffs, Iowa: Monarch Printing, 1997 reprint.

———. *A Paper on the Trans-Continental Railways*. Omaha, Nebraska, Union Pacific Railroad, 1891.

———. *Report of the Chief Engineer for 1866*. Washington, D.C.: Philip & Solomons, 1868.

———. *Report of the Chief Engineer for the Year 1867*. Washington, D.C.: Government Printing Office, 1868.

———. *Romantic Realities: The Story of the Building of the Pacific Roads*. Omaha: Union Pacific, 1891. [Paper read before Army of the Tennessee at its 21st reunion, 1888, then published.]

Donald, David Herbert. *Lincoln*. New York: Simon & Schuster, 1995.

Ehernberger, James, and Francis Gschwind. *Sherman Hill*. Callaway, Neb.: E. G. Publications, 1973.

Galloway, John Debo. *The First Transcontinental Railroad: Central Pacific, Union Pacific*. New York: Simmon-Boardman, 1950.

Goetzmann, William. *Army Exploration in the American West, 1803–1863*. New Haven, Conn.: Yale University Press, 1959.

Gordon, Sarah. *Passage to Union: How the Railroads Transformed American Life, 1829–1929*. Chicago: Ivan Dee, 1996.

Grant, Ulysses S. *Personal Memoirs*. 2 volumes. New York: Charles L. Webster, 1885–86.

Griswold, Wesley S. *A Work of Giants: Building the First Transcontinental Railroad*. New York: McGraw-Hill, 1962.

Howard, Robert West. *The Great Iron Trail: The Story of the First Transcontinental Railroad*. New York: Bonanza Books, 1962.

Jensen, Oliver. *The American Heritage History of Railroads in America*. New York: American Heritage Publishing, 1975.

King, Clarence. *Mountaineering in the Sierra Nevada*. Lincoln: University of Nebraska Press, 1970 reprint.

Klein, Maury. *Union Pacific*. Vol. 1, *Birth of a Railroad, 1862–1893*. Garden City, N.Y.: Doubleday, 1987.

Kraus, George. *High Road to Promontory: Building the Central Pacific Across the High Sierra*. Palo Alto, Calif.: American West Publishing, 1969.

Lavender, David. *The Great Persuader*. Garden City, N.Y.: Doubleday, 1970.

Lewis, Oscar. *The Big Four: The Story of Huntington, Stanford, Hopkins, and Crocker*. New York: Alfred A. Knopf, 1938.

Mercer, Lloyd. *Railroads and Land Grant Policy*. New York: Academic Press, 1982.

Perkins, J. R. *Trails, Rails and War: The Life of General G. M. Dodge*. Indianapolis: Bobbs-Merrill, 1929.

Russell, Robert. *Improvement of Communication with the Pacific Coast as an Issue in American Politics*. Cedar Rapids, Iowa: Torch Press, 1948.

Sherman, William T. *Memoirs*. Two volumes printed in one. New York: Library of America, 1990 reprint. [First published in 1875.]

Signor, John R. *Donner Pass: Southern Pacific's Sierra Crossing*. San Marino, Calif.: Golden West Books, 1985.

Stanley, Henry Morton. *Autobiography*. Boston: Houghton Mifflin, 1909.

———. *My Early Travels and Adventures in America and Asia*. New York: Scribner, 1895.

Starr, John W. *Lincoln and the Railroads*. New York: Arno Press, 1981 reprint of 1927 edition.

Stevenson, Robert Lewis. *Travels and Essays of Robert Lewis Stevenson*. New York: Scribner, 1895.

Stewart, John J. *The Iron Trail to the Golden Spike*. New York: Meadow Lark Press, 1994.

Union Pacific Railroad. *The Union Pacific Railroad Across the Continent West from Omaha, Nebraska*. Pamphlet published by the company, Omaha, 1868.

Utley, Robert, and Francis Ketterson, Jr. *Golden Spike*. Washington, D.C.: National Park Service, 1969.

Williams, John Hoyt. *A Great and Shining Road: The Epic Story of the Transcontinental Railroad*. New York: Times Books, 1988.

Winther, Oscar O. *The Transportation Frontier: Trans-Mississippi West 1865–1890*. New York: Holt, Rinehart and Winston, 1964.

ARTICLES

Adams, Charles Francis, Jr. "The Pacific Railroad Ring." *North American Review*, January 1869.

Athearn, Robert. "General Sherman and the Western Railroads." *Pacific Historical Review*, vol. 5.

Beard, William. "I Have Labored Hard to Find the Law." *Illinois Historical Journal*, Winter 1992.

Bowman, J. N. "Driving the Last Spike." *California Historical Society Quarterly*, vol. 36 (1957).

Brennan, J. D. "The Romance of the Sacramento Division." *Southern Pacific Bulletin*, August 1920.

Brown, Charles Leroy. "Abraham Lincoln and the Illinois Central Railroad." *Journal of the Illinois State Historical Society*, vol. 36 (1943).

Carman, Harry, and Charles Mueller. "The Contract and Finance Company and the Central Pacific Railroad." *Mississippi Valley Historical Review*, vol. 14 (December 1927).

Chandler, Alfred D., Jr. "Henry Varnum Poor." In *The Golden Spike: A Centennial Remembrance*. New York: American Geographical Society, 1969.

Chew, Lee. "A Chinese Immigrant Makes His Home in America." *Independent,* reprinted on www.historymatters.gmu.edu/text/1650a-chew.html.

"The Chinese in California." *Lippincott's Magazine*, March 1868.

Dillon, Sidney. "Historic Moments: Driving the Last Spike of the Union Pacific." *Scribner's Magazine*, August 1892.

Farnham, Wallace D. "Grenville Dodge and the Union Pacific: A Study of Historical Legends." *Journal of American History*, vol. 51 (June 1964).

Henry, Robert. "The RR Land Grant Legend in American History Texts." *Mississippi Valley Historical Review*, vol. 32 (1945–46).

Huffman, Wendell. "Railroads Shipped by Sea." *Railroad History*, Spring 1999.

Klein, Maury. "The Coming of the Railroad and the End of the Great West." *Invention and Technology*, vol. 10, no. 3 (Winter 1995).

Kraus, George. "Chinese Laborers and the Construction of the Central Pacific." *Utah Historical Quarterly*, vol. 37, no. 1 (Winter 1969).

Lemon, David. "An Experience on the Road." *Union Pacific Magazine*, May 1924.

Lockwood, E. C. "With the Casement Brothers While Building the Union Pacific." *Union Pacific Magazine*, February 1931.

Loomis, A. W. "How Our Chinamen Are Employed." *Overland Monthly*, March 1869.

Mills, Morris. "With the Union Pacific Railroad in the Early Days." *Annals of Wyoming*, vol. 3, no. 4 (April 1926).

O'Neil, Hugh. "List of Persons Present, Promontory, Utah, May 10, 1869." *Utah Historical Quarterly*, vol. 24 (1956).

Poor, Henry V. "The Pacific Railroad." *North American Review*, vol. 128 (June 1879).

———. "Railroad to the Pacific." In *The Golden Spike: A Centennial Remembrance*. New York: American Geographical Society, 1969.

Reeder, Clarence A. "A History of Utah's Railroads." Ph.D. dissertation, University of Utah, 1959.

Rosewater, Andrew. "Finding a Path Across the Rocky Mountain Range." *Union Pacific Magazine*, January 1923.

Saxton, Alexander. "The Army of Canton in the High Sierra." *Pacific Historical Review*, vol. 35 (June 1966).

Smoot, W.C.A. "Tales from Old-Timers." *Union Pacific Magazine*, December 1923.

Wheat, Carl. "A Sketch of the Life of Theodore D. Judah." *California Historical Society Quarterly*, vol. 4 (September 1925).

Wilder, J. O. "The Way Pioneer Builders Met Difficulties." *Southern Pacific Bulletin*, vol. 9, no. 11 (November 1920).

MEMOIRS, DIARIES, JOURNALS

Barney, Lewis. Papers. Archives, Church of Latter-Day Saints Library, Salt Lake City.

Clement, Samuel. Papers. Bancroft Library, University of California, Berkeley.

Crocker, Charles. Memoir. Bancroft Library, University of California, Berkeley.
DeLamater, C.B.V. Memoir. Bancroft Library, University of California, Berkeley.
Dodge, Grenville M. Papers. Union Pacific Archives, Omaha.
Ferguson, Arthur. Journal. Utah State Historical Society, Salt Lake City.
Hubbard, Thomas. Diary. Union Pacific Archives, Omaha.
Huntington, Collis. Memoir. Bancroft Library, University of California, Berkeley.
———. Papers. Library of Congress, Washington, D.C.
Judah, Anna. Papers. Bancroft Library, University of California, Berkeley.
Kim, Rudy. Interview. Bancroft Collection, University of California, Berkeley.
Maxwell, James. Memoir. University of Delaware Library, Newark, Del.
Nichols, H. K. Diary. Bancroft Library, University of California, Berkeley.
Pratt, Milando. Memoir. Utah State Historical Library, Salt Lake City.
Reed, Samuel. Papers. Union Pacific Archives, Omaha.
Schill, Samuel. Papers. Church of Latter-Day Saints Library, Salt Lake City.
Yee, Samuel. Oral History. Bancroft Collection, University of California, Berkeley.
Young, Brigham. Papers. Archives, Church of Latter-Day Saints Library, Salt Lake City.

NEWSPAPERS AND MAGAZINES

Cheyenne Daily Leader (Wyoming)
Cheyenne Frontier Index
Chicago Leader
Chicago Tribune
Cincinnati Gazette
Council Bluffs Bugle (Iowa)
Council Bluffs Nonpareil
Denver Rocky Mountain News
Dutch Flat Enquirer (California)
Harper's Weekly
Humboldt Register (Nevada)
New York Sun
New York Times
New York Tribune
Omaha Weekly Herald
Reno Crescent (Nevada)
Sacramento Union
Salt Lake Daily Reporter
Salt Lake Deseret News
San Francisco Bulletin
San Francisco Chronicle
San Francisco Daily Alta California
Van Nostrand's Engineering Magazine
Virginia City Territorial Enterprise (Nevada)
Western Railroad Gazette

Index

Page numbers in *italics* refer to maps.

About the Author

STEPHEN E. AMBROSE is the author of numerous books of history, including *Citizen Soldiers*, *Undaunted Courage*, and *D-Day*, as well as biographies of Dwight D. Eisenhower and Richard Nixon. He lives in Bay St. Louis, Mississippi, and Helena, Montana.